Anyone Can Intubate

A Step-By-Step Guide to Intubation and Airway Management

Anyone Can Intubate

A Step-By-Step Guide to Intubation
and
Airway Management
5th Edition

Written and Illustrated by
Christine E. Whitten, MD
Diplomat, American Board of Anesthesiology

Mooncat Publications
San Diego, California 92196

Copyright © 1989, 1990, 1994, 1997, 2003, 2010, 2012
by Christine E. Whitten, M.D.

Illustrations & Video © 1989, 1990, 1994, 1997, 2003, 2010, 2012
Christine E. Whitten, M.D.

All rights reserved. No part of this book shall be reproduced, stored in a retrieval system, or transmitted by any means, electronic, mechanical, photocopying, recording, or otherwise, without written permission from the publisher. This book is intended for the use of practicing medical professionals or students of those professions studying under the supervision of a trained medical instructor. It is not intended for use by lay people outside the profession.

Design by Christine Whitten M.D. and Drew Granston Ph.D.

ISBN 10: 1-4944-2517-3
ISBN 13: 978-1-4944-2517-3

Publication History:
　1st ed. published January 1989,
　2nd ed. January 1990,
　3rd ed. April 1994,
　4th ed. January 1997; revised January 2003,
　5th ed. September 2012

Printed in the United States of America

To my parents,
Ward and Bettye Whitten
&
to my sister, Pamela Niemi
— for all the years of
encouragement and belief

To my husband Drew Granston
— for promising me the universe
and then delivering

Correspondence to the author
Please address correspondence to:
Dr. Christine Whitten c/o
Mooncat Publications
11875 River Rim Rd, San Diego, CA
92126-1150
or e-mail at
anyonecanintubate@yahoo.com

Table of Contents

INTRODUCTION 7
    Acknowledgements 9

1 ANATOMY & PHYSIOLOGY 10
    Anatomy of the Larynx 10
    Anatomy of the Lungs 18
    Physiology of Breathing 23
    Some Key Points 53
    URL for Chapter 1 video.... http://bit.ly/12cAQki

2 ASSESSMENT 55
    Evaluating Your Patient 55
    Early Management 63
    What Are The Criteria For Intubation? 65
    URL for Chapter 2 video.... http://bit.ly/11b8zLU

3 ESTABLISHING AN AIRWAY 68
    Opening the Airway 68
    Use of the Nasal Airway 72
    Use of the Oral Airway 74
    Ventilating with a Bag and a Mask 78
    URL for Chapter 3 video.... http://bit.ly/12cVIYL

4 DIRECT LARYNGOSCOPY EQUIPMENT 88
    Checking Your Laryngoscope 88
    Checking Your Endotracheal Tube 91
    Placing Your Stylet 92
    Suction is Not Optional Equipment 94
    Always Have Equipment To Ventilate 94
    When You Don't Have Optimal Equipment 94
    URL for Chapter 4 video.... http://bit.ly/WDXPOg

5 ORAL INTUBATION OF THE ADULT PATIENT 95
    The Dummy vs. the Real Thing 95
    Intubating the Adult 96
    Straight vs. Curved Blades 107
    The Use of Cricoid Pressure to Improve the View 111
    Pulling the Cheek Can Help 114
    Securing the Tube 115
    URL for Chapter 5 video.... http://bit.ly/XMjIu8

6 COMMON ERRORS & HOW TO AVOID THEM 118
    Describing The View You See 118
    Errors 119
    URL for Chapter 6 video.... http://bit.ly/W30hzE

7 VERIFYING PLACEMENT 128
    Seven Steps for Correct Tube Placement 128
    URL for Chapter 7 video.... http://bit.ly/14AtjLQ

8	**VENTILATING AND INTUBATING THE CHILD** **134**
	Anatomy: Children Are Not Small Adults 134
	Pediatric Physiology 138
	Opening the Airway 140
	Ventilating With Bag-Valve-Mask 145
	Pediatric Intubation 147
	Pediatric Airway Emergencies 154
	URL for Chapter 8 video.... http://bit.ly/WB5mAG

9	**PREINTUBATION EVALUATION** **158**
	Medical and Surgical History 158
	Physical Signs 159
	Quickly Evaluating The Emergency Patient 166

10	**TRICKS OF THE TRADE** **168**
	Cardiac Arrest 168
	Obesity 171
	Receding Chin 173
	Overbites 173
	Poor Neck Mobility 174
	Fixed Airway Obstruction 175
	Blood in the Oropharynx 176
	Pregnancy 176
	The Use of Cricoid Pressure 177
	Pulling on the Cheek Helps 178
	Use a Bougie 179
	A Difficult Intubation Algorithm 181
	URL for Chapter 10 video.... http://bit.ly/WDE2RZ

11	**NASAL INTUBATION** **184**
	Indications 184
	Contraindications 184
	Anatomy 185
	Blind Nasal Intubation, Spontaneous Ventilation 186
	Managing Difficult Passage 191
	Adjunctive Techniques to Nasal Intubation 195
	Use of a Nasal Airway to Assist Ventilation 199
	Complications 199
	URL for Chapter 11 video.... http://bit.ly/Vy6vLe

12	**SPECIALIZED VENTILATION TECHNIQUES** **201**
	Needle Cricothyroidotomy and Jet Ventilation 211
	Surgical Cricothyroidotomy 212
	Esophageal Obturator Airway 213
	Emergency Airway Cart 215
	URL for Chapter 12 video.... http://bit.ly/11kZOhk

13	**AIRWAY MANAGEMENT OF TRAUMA** **216**
	Airway and Respiratory Assessment 217
	Airway Management 220
	Problems in the Field 227
	Caregiver Safety 234
	Stress and the Caregiver 235

14	**RAPID SEQUENCE INDUCTION**	**236**
	Cautions	236
	Preparing Equipment and Personnel	237
	Preparing the Patient	237
	Cricoid Pressure for RSI	238
	Sedative Agents	238
	Paralysis: Muscle Relaxants	242
	Reversal of Muscle Relaxation	245
15	**AWAKE INTUBATION**	**247**
	Awake or Not Awake? — That is the Question	247
	Contraindications to Awake Intubation?	248
	Awake Patient Preparation	248
	Factors Influencing Drug Effect	257
	URL for Chapter 15 video.... http://bit.ly/XoVRCu	
16	**EXTUBATION & EXCHANGING ENDOTRACHEAL TUBES**	**261**
	Extubation	261
	Exchanging an Endotracheal Tube	265
	URL for Chapter 16 video.... http://bit.ly/WB65BS	
17	**SPECIALIZED INTUBATING TECHNIQUES**	**268**
	Safeguarding Patient Safety	268
	Light Wands	268
	Video Assisted Intubation	270
	Use of Laryngeal Mask Airway Devices to Intubate	275
	Safety First	281
	URL for Chapter 17 video.... http://bit.ly/WVoIhZ	
18	**FIBEROPTIC INTUBATION**	**283**
	Preparing The Fiberoptic Bronchoscope	283
	Patient Preparation	285
	Insertion Technique	285
	URL for Chapter 18 video.... http://bit.ly/14tRnPt	
19	**COMPLICATION18**	**294**
	Complications Occurring During the Intubation	294
	Complications Occurring While Intubated	296
	Complications Following Extubation	299
	Creating a Safe Culture of Care	301
20	**BOREDOM, INTERRUPTED**	**302**
	Case 1. The Baby with Severe Bronchospasm	302
	Case 2. The Girl with Epiglottitis	303
	Case 3. Out of Sight Déjà Vu: Endotracheal Tube Obstruction	304
	Case 4. Can't Intubate, Can't Ventilate, What Can You Do?	305
	Case 5. Ventilate, Intubate and Communicate	306
	Case 6. The Popping Polyp	307
	Case 7. Anaphylaxis Analysis	309
	Case 8. Accidental Extubation in Ludwig's Angina	310
	Case 9. A Flood of Blood in the Airway	311
	Case 10. Tomorrow's Diseases Today: Post-Obstructive Pulmonary Edema	311
	URL for Chapter 20 video.... http://bit.ly/UGZRQd	

ON-LINE VIDEO URL LIST	**313**
NOTES	**315**
ABOUT THE AUTHOR	**329**
ALSO FROM MOONCAT PUBLICATIONS	**330**

INTRODUCTION

People need to breathe. Without oxygen, the human brain can suffer permanent damage in as little time as 3 minutes.

You have chosen to help people live by helping them breathe. This requires skill and knowledge. This book is designed to teach you both. You will learn what you need to know to handle respiratory distress, which may or may not require intubation. Other skills, such as manually assisted ventilation, and new technologies, are also taught.

Helping another person breathe is a great responsibility. You will never forget the first time you intubate a patent. My first intubation was one of the first times I literally held someone's life in my hands. I was nervous. The anesthesiologist teaching me tried to not look too anxious as I awkwardly grabbed my laryngoscope blade, fumbled while opening the patient's mouth, and cautiously maneuvered the endotracheal tube into the trachea. It felt like time stopped until the tube was in place, after which the three of us (me, my teacher and my patient) all took a deep breath. Since then, I've intubated thousands of people in the U.S. and, in Operation: Smile, seven countries.

I've also personally taught hundreds of people how to intubate. All my students started as I did: nervous, not knowing where to position their fingers or hold the blade, what to look for through the scope, and what resistance to expect during the procedure. All knew that you hold someone's life in your hands when you intubate. All nevertheless learned to intubate.

Good teachers never stop learning. One thing I learned as a teacher was that the printed materials available to teach intubation were limited. Medical textbooks lack detailed information about intubation because, traditionally, intubation has been a skill passed from mentor to student. Today, intubation is taught not only to medical students, who have the advantage of 1-on-1 mentoring, but also to civilian and military emergency medical responders, who often do not. Accordingly, a different textbook was required; this book fills that need, as it is designed to teach anyone how to intubate.

Intubation, however, is not always the right choice, as there are other ways to treat respiratory distress. The 5th edition has been expanded to include more information about techniques for managing the airway including, but not limited to, intubation.

Video clips are an important addition to this 5th edition. There are 58 video clips, all freely available on-line at anyonecanintubate.com and at the specific URL addresses listed in the book. In the electronic publication (EPUB) version on a device such as an ipad, the video clips are embedded within the text. If you are not using a format into which videos can be embedded, such as the print version or some "mobi" device such as the Kindle, you can find those same video clips free on-line.

These 58 free video clips provide almost an hour of footage of actual patients undergoing real surgical procedures, plus animations to allow you to visualize yourself intubating and ventilating in real situations. Most of the clips include narration.

The on-line video clips are organized as chapters. The URLs for the web links are provided at the end of each chapter, as well as in one unified list at the end of the book. You can choose between going to each isolated chapter file, or going to our Anyone Can Intubate portfolio page where all the chapter links can be viewed together. These video clips can be viewed on-line or downloaded in your choice of formats. You may also find the links to those clips at anyonecanintubate.com.

The 5th edition has been extensively rewritten and expanded. We start with a review of airway anatomy and respiratory physiology, with an emphasis on how this information is needed for patient assessment. Mastering the art of ventilation is just as important as learning to intubate - accordingly, we'll learn about techniques for ventilating the patient with a bag and mask apparatus, and for treating airway obstruction. Pediatric intubation is something we'll learn a lot about - there are many anatomical and physiological changes as the child grows and matures, and these changes require that you modify your techniques. A new chapter of case histories has been added – you will see how the information in this book applies to real-life difficult and dangerous intubations.

The goal of Anyone Can Intubate is to give you a visual picture of intubation and airway management. As you proceed through the book, use the video clips to picture yourself performing the steps. Understand why moving the patient's head in a certain way, or changing the angle of your laryngoscope blade alters your view.

I hope my efforts help make your first intubation a less nervous experience than mine. However, if you start to doubt yourself, just remember. Anyone can intubate.

Video clips are an important addition to this 5th edition.
The Keyframe (KF) sequences are taken from video clips
that are available on-line.

All video chapter files appear on Anyone Can Intubate Portfolio at:

http://bit.ly/U7EV7f

http://vimeopro.com/user15487933/anyone-can-intubate-5th-edition-chapter-video-clips
or
anyonecanintubate.com

In addition, the links for each chapter's videos are also found at the end of each chapter containing video.

Acknowledgements

Many friends and colleagues have edited and contributed to the evolution of Anyone Can Intubate over the years. I am indebted to all of them: Walter Carranza CST, Henry Chao MD, James Crawford MD, Susan Dickerson MD, Michael Dickerson MD, Sass M. Elisha CRNA/Ed.D, Clyde Jones MD, Suzanne Quenneville MD, Diane Rand MD, Alex Showah MD, Linda Jo Rice MD, and Anne Wong MD for their reviews and support.

I am especially grateful to the patients who consented to allow me to videotape their treatments and procedures. I also thank my colleagues who graciously permitted me to videotape them in action. There are too many to name individually, but I especially wish to thank Gail Dawson MD, Marcia Moudree MD, Cindy Owen MD, Joanne Zupan MD, Cheryl Cota CRNA, Sharon Hirako CRNA, Maureen Link CRNA, Debbie Mulvey CRNA, and Debbie Umlauf CRNA, all of whom kept a sense of humor whenever I approached them with camcorder in hand.

Last but never least, thanks to my husband Drew Granston for his invaluable assistance in editing the text, designing the new cover and many of the keyframes, and especially for helping with the production and publication of the print version. His effort and support made this possible

Any errors, in the end, are mine. Please let me know of any mistakes or omissions, whether they are big or small, by e-mailing me at anyonecanintubate@yahoo.com.

1
ANATOMY & PHYSIOLOGY

Anatomy is the study of body form and structure. Physiology is the study of the function of body parts — what they do and how they do it. Form dictates how each part moves in relationship to each other as well as how the body functions during normal activities or during stress and injury. Understanding anatomy and physiology is key to learning not just how, but why and when to ventilate and intubate.

Anatomy of the Larynx

The upper airway consists of our nose, mouth, and the pharynx, the membrane-lined cavity behind the nose and mouth connecting them to the esophagus. The lower airway consists of the windpipe (trachea), and air conduits (bronchi and bronchioles) that lead to the air exchange surface of the lungs (alveoli). The larynx is nothing more than a sophisticated valve connecting the two. We breathe through our larynx. It protects from aspiration, the inhalation of foreign material. Its regulation of lung pressures generates the force needed to cough. The larynx vibrates the air column to alter pitch and loudness when we speak.

When you ventilate a patient, you move the head, jaw, tongue, and ultimately parts of the larynx to open a clear passage to allow air to enter the lungs. When you intubate you manipulate the structures of the head, neck, and larynx in order to place an endotracheal tube between the vocal cords.

To feel your own larynx, place your hand on the front of your neck, with thumb and forefinger on either side of the firm, roughly cylindrical shape in the midline. Your Adam's apple is part of your larynx (Fig. 1-1, 1-2).

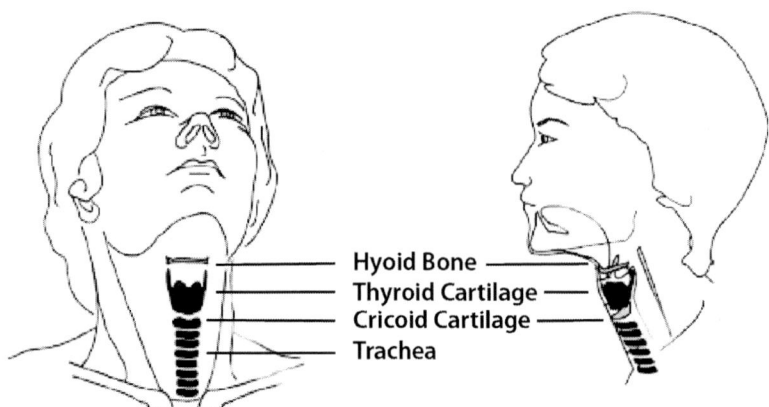

Fig. 1-1. Location of the larynx from the front

Fig. 1-2. Location of the larynx from the side

Anatomy and Physiology 11

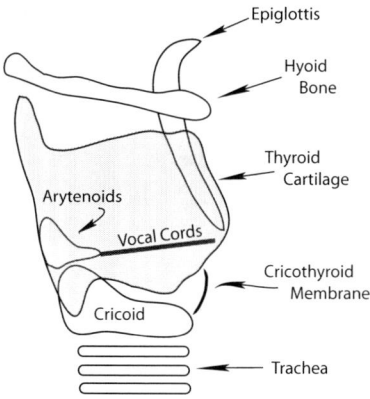 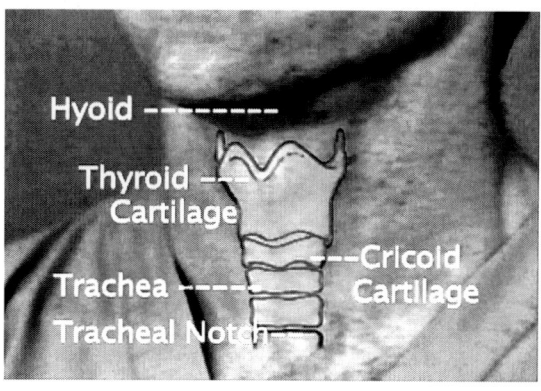

Fig. 1-3. Anatomy of the larynx (side view). The prominence of the thyroid cartilage is your Adam's Apple.

Keyframe 1-1. The single cartilages of the larynx provide its basic structure and serve as major external landmarks.

The adult larynx sits on top of the trachea opposite the fourth, fifth, and sixth cervical vertebrae. It is a boxlike structure composed of nine cartilages connected by ligaments and moved by nine muscles (Fig. 1-3, 1-4). The larynx is dynamic. The cartilages pivot and swing in relationship to each other, using true joints with a built-in range of motion. Movement of the surrounding tissues shifts the cartilages as well.

Single Cartilages

The larynx consists of 3 single and 3 paired cartilages. The single cartilages form its basic structure and serve as major external landmarks (Mov. 1-1, KF. 1-1.).

The cricoid cartilage is ring shaped, with the posterior aspect of the ring broader than the front. It sits on top of the first tracheal ring. To feel this cartilage, place your fingers on the trachea in the sternal notch and slide them upward. It's a firm, incompressible, ring shape about three to four fingers breadth above the notch. This non distensible ring is the smallest diameter in the child's airway.

Two cricothyroid joints connect the ring anteriorly to the thyroid cartilage, allowing the two to move both independently and as a unit. The prominence of the thyroid cartilage, also known as the Adam's Apple, consists of two quadrangular plates fused anteriorly in the midline. Feel this cartilage as a firm projection in the midline of the neck just superior to the cricoid ring. There is a notch on its top edge.

The epiglottis is a curved, leaf shaped cartilage whose upper, rounded edge projects into the pharynx. The stalk of the leaf connects anteriorly to the inside of the thyroid cartilage plate at its midpoint. It also connects to the hyoid bone and to the base of the tongue. The epiglottis can swing up and down over the laryngeal opening like a trapdoor. It's a major visual landmark during intubation.

Paired Cartilages

There are three sets of paired cartilages. The paired arytenoid cartilages are irregular, pyramid shapes mounted on top of the back of the cricoid cartilage, with the broad shaped flange on the ring separating them from each other. The sharp anterior vocal process of each arytenoid is the anchor for the vocal cords, which project forward to attach to the inside of the thyroid cartilage. Therefore structurally, the posterior 1/3 of each cord is cartilaginous. This rigid strut allows the arytenoids to tense, relax and swing the vocal cords from side to side as the arytenoids pivot in all planes. These actions let us phonate, breath, cough, and swallow without aspirating.

The cone shaped corniculate cartilages attach to the apex of the arytenoids and the elongated cuneiform cartilages attach to the posterior arytenoids. They add bulk and shape to the arytenoid outline, an important landmark during intubation.

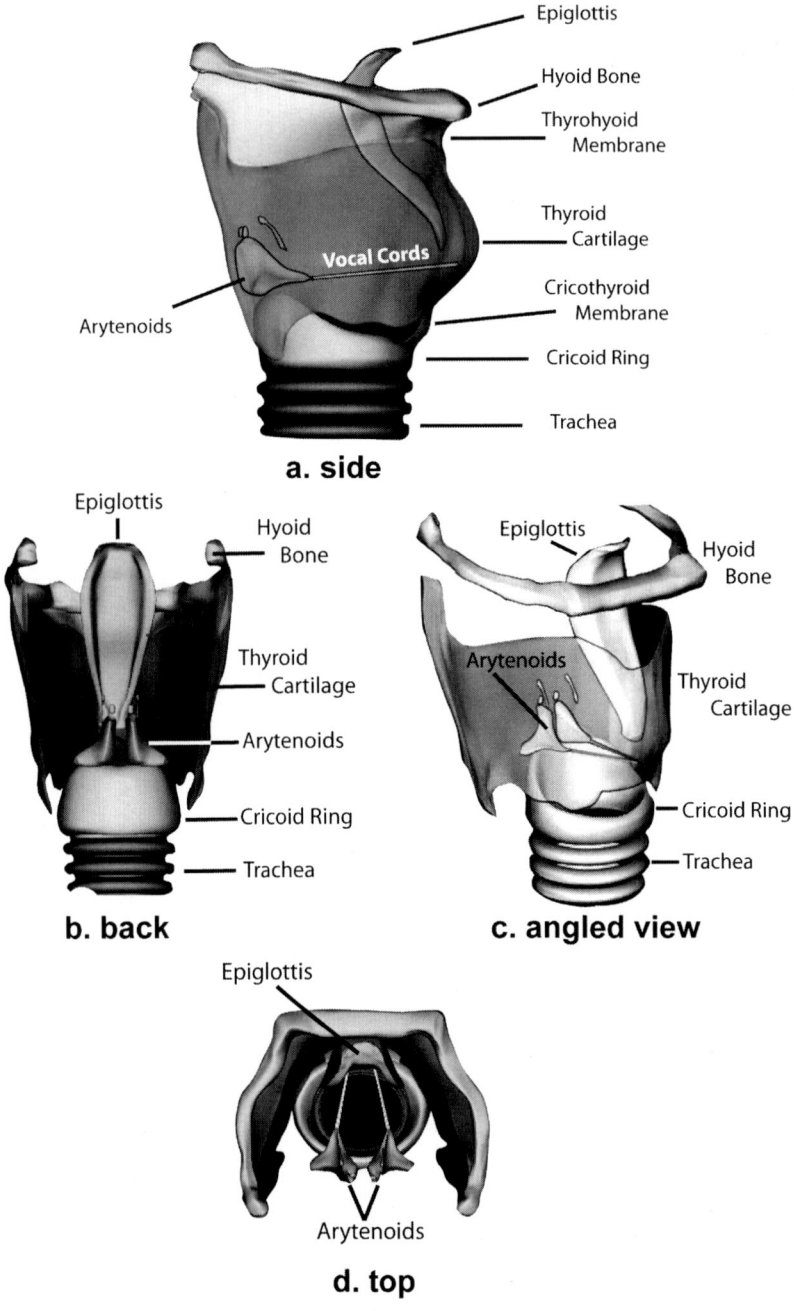

Fig. 1-4a-d. Laryngeal anatomy detail, multiple views

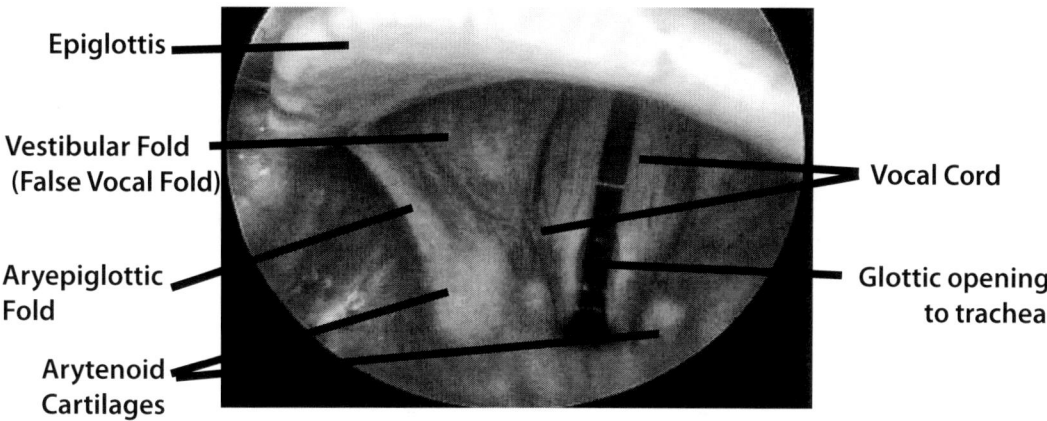

Fig. 1-5. Close up photo of the the larynx.

Laryngeal Movement

Several ligaments and two membranes connect the laryngeal cartilages. The vocal cords are formed by the upper free edge of the cricoid membrane, which runs from the arytenoids to the thyroid cartilage.(Fig. 1-5). Normally, the vocal cords are pale and pearly white. Because of the cord's direct and indirect attachments to the cartilages, pushing downward on the thyroid and/or cricoid cartilages during laryngoscopy can bring the vocal cords into view when they are hidden.

The false cords, formed by the aryepiglottic folds which run anteriorly from the lateral border of the arytenoids, lie above the true vocal cords. The false cords help close the glottis and are comprised of skeletal muscle.

Laryngeal muscles are classified as extrinsic (connecting the larynx to other structures within the neck, Fig. 1-6) or intrinsic (contained solely within the larynx, Fig. 1-7 a,b).

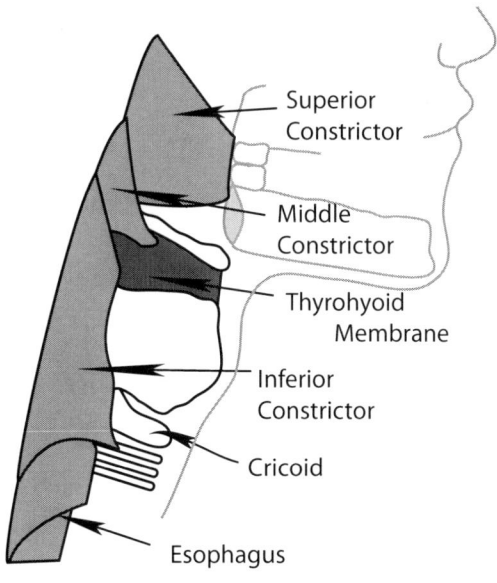

Fig. 1-6. Extrinsic muscles of the larynx provide a great deal of control, lifting and lowering the larynx during respiration, swallowing, and airway protection.

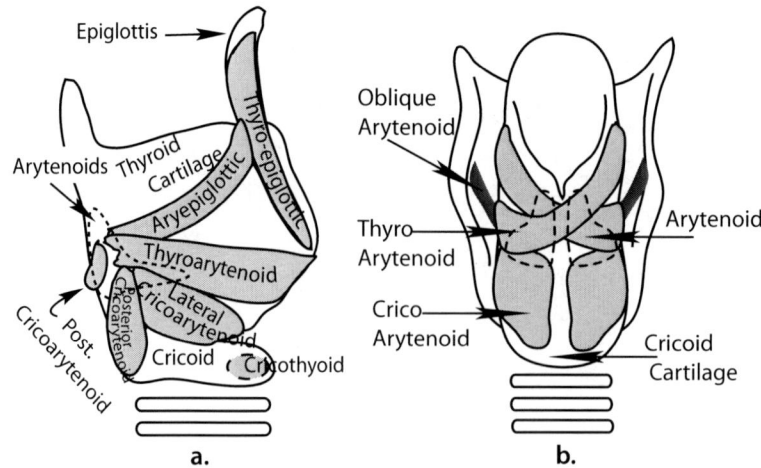

Fig. 1-7a,b. The intrinsic muscles of the larynx. A. shows the larynx from the side. B. shows the larynx from the back. Laryngeal function depends on precise motor control.

The recurrent laryngeal branch of the vagus nerve is the nerve supply to all of the laryngeal muscles, except for the cricothyroid muscle which is supplied by the external laryngeal branch of the vagus. This extremely important nerve is particularly vulnerable to injury because of its long and complicated journey. It travels down the neck and enters the chest. The left branch loops around the aortic arch and the right branch loops around the right subclavian artery before both rise again between trachea and esophagus to reach the larynx. Both branches travel through the rigid cricoid ring before reaching their destinations. Because the nerve is so long, injury can occur far from the larynx from many causes.

Unilateral injury to a recurrent laryngeal nerve causes temporary or permanent hoarseness due to one sided vocal cord paralysis. Bilateral injury leads to difficulty breathing as well as aphonia (difficulty or inability to speak) — serious injuries to be avoided.

There are 3 major types of movement.
1. Movement affecting tension of the vocal cords
2. Movement swinging the vocal cords open and closed
3. Movement that close off and protect the larynx

1. **Movement affecting the tension of the vocal cords**, e.g. pitch of the voice, occurs by pivoting the thyroid cartilage backward and forward on the cricoid cartilage at the cricothyroid joint. (Fig. 1-8.)

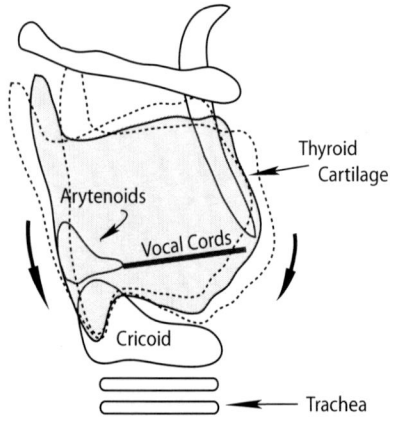

Fig. 1-8. Movements affecting tension of the vocal cords

2. **Movements that swing open (*ab*duct) or close (*ad*duct) the opening between the vocal cords** occur by pivoting the arytenoid cartilages on the back of the cricoid ring. (Fig. 1-9, Mov. 1-2, KF. 1-2ab)

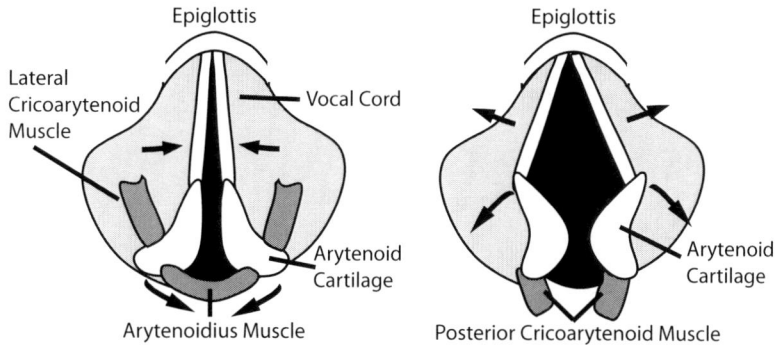

Fig. 1-9. Movements that swing the vocal cords open and closed

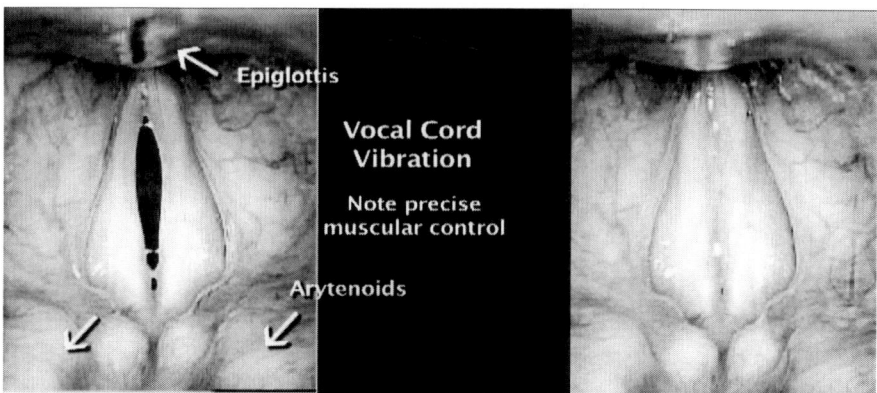

Keyframes 1-2a,b. The vocal cords are under precise motor control.

3. **Movements that close off the larynx**, for example to protect it during swallowing or from aspiration. (Fig. 1-10, 1-11.) The left picture is a larynx with the vocal cords relaxed. On the right is the same larynx in laryngospasm (Mov. 1-3).

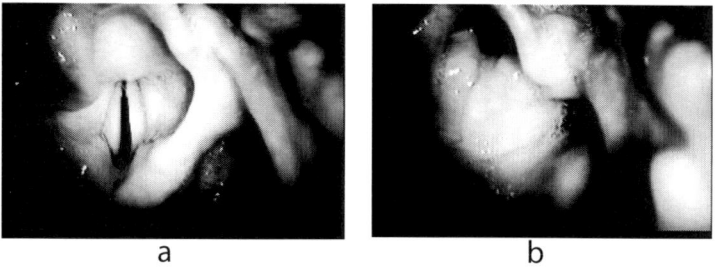

Fig. 1-10a,b. Laryngospasm: involuntary reflex closure of the larynx. Larynx relaxed in (a) and in spasm in (b). Active laryngospasm includes closure of vocal cords and false cords, mounding of paraglottic tissues, and folding of the epiglottis over the glottis.

Closure of the larynx occurs by four mechanisms (Fig. 1-10a,b):
- closure of the vocal cords
- closure of the false cords
- mounding of the paraglottic tissues (lower epiglottis, paraglottic fat, base of tongue) by elevation of the larynx.
- folding of epiglottis over glottic opening (1-11)

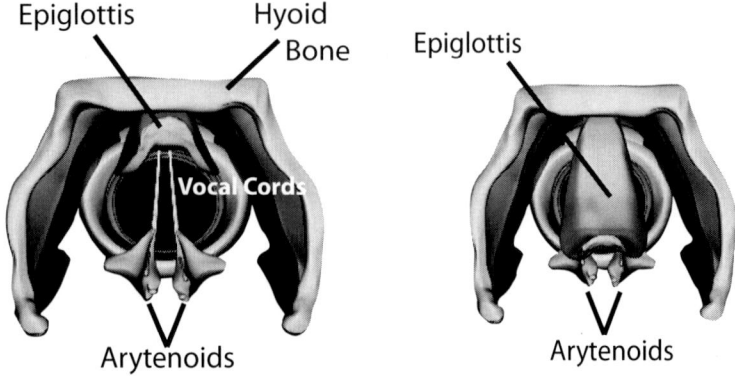

Fig. 1-11. Closing the larynx. The epiglottis swings up and down over the laryngeal opening like a trapdoor.

Form and Function in the Larynx

Table 1-1 shows the intrinsic muscles of the larynx and their related actions. The larynx depends so strongly on muscle control that loss of muscle tone can cause airway obstruction.

The entire larynx falls on inspiration and rises on expiration. It also rises on coughing, straining, and swallowing. Functionally, a lower larynx opens the airway while a higher one places the epiglottis and the tongue in better position to close it. Place your hand on your larynx and you can feel the movements. The larynx depends so strongly on muscle control that loss of muscle tone can cause airway obstruction.

By contrast, excessive secretions, or aspiration stimulate the airway and activate defense reflexes. Forceful cord closure and elevation of the larynx seal the airway. Laryngospasm, or spasmodic closure of the vocal cords, is the most severe form of airway closure (Fig. 1-10b, Mov. 1-2, KF. 1-3). It can physically prevent the passage of an endotracheal tube. You have experienced laryngospasm when you accidentally aspirated water. Carried to extreme, laryngospasm prevents air exchange.

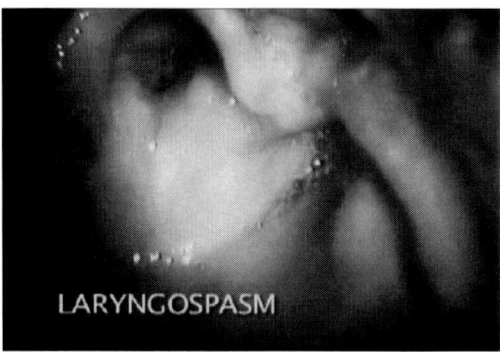

Keyframe 1-3. Closure of the vocal cords and false cords, the mounding of the paraglottic tissues, and the folding of the epiglottis over the glottis protects the larynx.

Table 1-1

INTRINSIC MUSCLES OF LARYNX	ACTION
Cricothyroid	lengthens and stretches vocal cords
Posterior cricoarytenoid	abducts and externally rotates the arytenoid cartilages, separating (abducting) vocal cords
Lateral cricoarytenoid	adducts and internally rotates the arytenoid cartilages, which closes the cords
Transverse arytenoid	adducts the arytenoid cartilages, resulting in adducted vocal cords
Oblique arytenoid	narrows glottic opening by constricting distance between the arytenoid cartilages and epiglottis
Vocalis	adjusts tension in vocal folds/cords
Thyroarytenoid	narrows the glottic opening

When at rest, the vocal cords lie partially separated, or *ab*ducted. During forceful inspiration or hyperventilation, the cords open widely, producing an oval shaped opening. This minimizes resistance to breathing.

To produce a high pitched voice, or in response to tracheobronchial irritation, the arytenoidius muscles pinch the cords together, or *ad*duct them.

Injury to the recurrent laryngeal nerve produces vocal cord paralysis on the affected side. A paralyzed cord often lies halfway between fully closed and fully open, the cadaveric position. Airway obstruction can occur if the vocal cord dysfunction occurs on both sides because the undamaged approximating fibers pull the cords together.

Laryngeal Variation

Let's turn to the actual appearance of the larynx. Although covered by mucous membrane, you can still see the basic, underlying cartilage shapes (Fig. 1-12). There is a lot of individual variation in how each larynx appears. The appearance also changes with age (Fig. 1-13).

Look for this view each time you intubate. Picture how the underlying skeleton will move when you pull or push on the membrane draped over the top. Knowing the anatomic and spatial relationships will let you intubate even if you only see an incomplete view of some of the landmarks. Understanding the anatomy puts you in control.

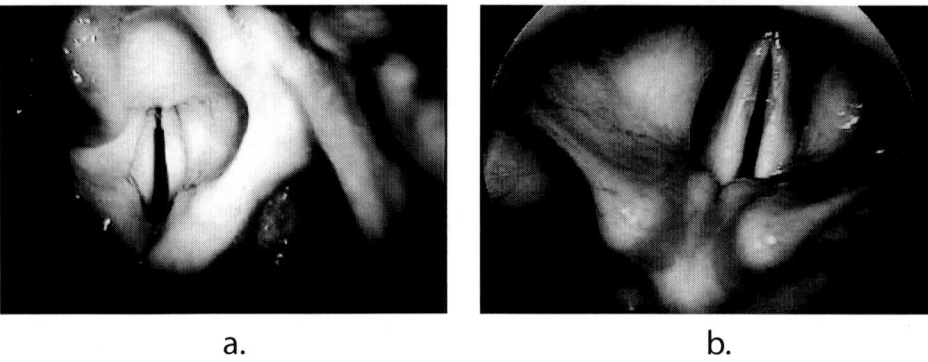

Fig. 1-12 a,b. Notice how different these two larynxes appear. You must identify the landmarks despite variations between individual patients.

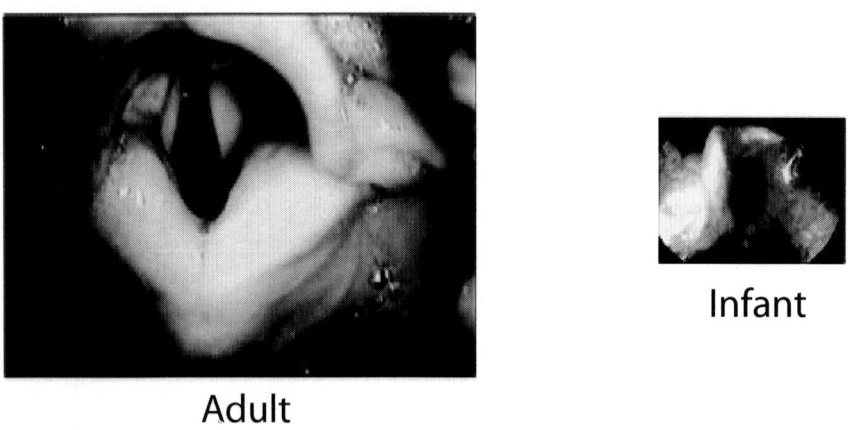

Fig. 1-13. Adult and infant larynxes shown enlarged, but in relative size. In addition to differences in size, note difference in shape of the structures. Pediatric anatomy will be discussed in greater detail in Chapter 9.

Anatomy of the Lungs

Knowledge of the trachea and lungs, and the dynamics of breathing are important when assessing a patient's respiration and/or when manually ventilating him.

Trachea and Lung

The average adult trachea is about 10-12 cm long. It extends from the cricoid cartilage down to the 6th cervical vertebrae where it splits into a right and left mainstem bronchus. Mean adult tracheal diameters are about 22 mm for males and 19 mm for females. The full term infant trachea, in contrast, has a diameter of 3 mm and grows about 1 mm a year until the adult diameter is reached.

The tracheal shape varies from nearly circular to elliptical to "C" and "D" shaped. The anterior wall is cartilaginous and the posterior wall is muscular. The tone of the trachealis muscle making up this muscular wall varies with position, consciousness, coughing, inspiration, expiration and mechanical ventilation. This makes the trachea a much more dynamic, distensible organ than is commonly appreciated.

Anatomy and Physiology 19

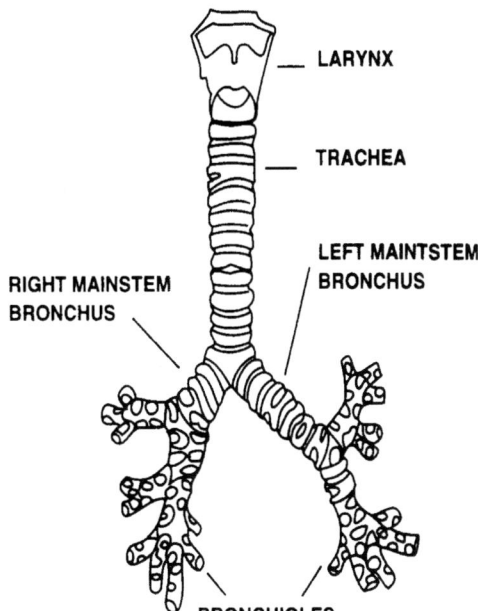

Fig. 1-14 Tracheal tree showing the mainstem bronchi and bronchioles.

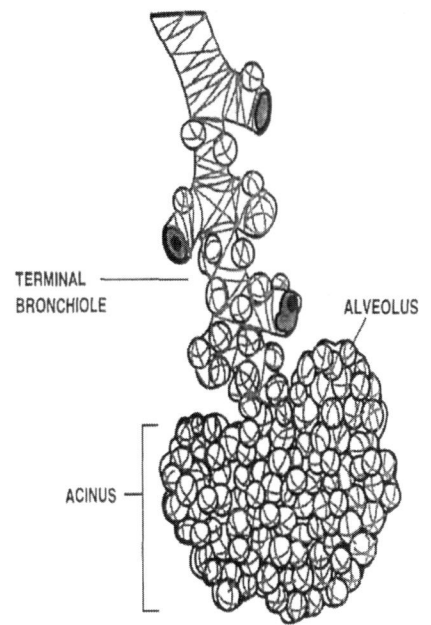

Fig. 1-15. Alveoli. The capillary network is shown in gray.

The trachea splits into 2 mainstem bronchi, which then branch into the smaller bronchi leading to the major lobes of the lung. The right lung has three major divisions: an upper, middle, and lower lobe. The left has two lobes. Each lobe in turn subdivides into smaller segments. This division is similar to the way the branches of a tree split from the main trunk. The bronchi branch into smaller and smaller airways called bronchioles.

The shorter right mainstem bronchus comes off the trachea at a more vertical angle. As a result, aspirated materials, or endotracheal tubes inserted too far, tend to go down the right rather than left side (Fig. 1-14).

Finally, the smaller terminal bronchioles branch into the alveolar ducts and the alveoli. Alveoli are the microscopic air sacs where all of the air exchange takes place. Each alveolus looks like a tiny balloon. Its 0.02 micron thick wall, which is the barrier to diffusion of oxygen and carbon dioxide, consists of the alveolar cell wall and its basement membrane separated from the capillary bed by loose connective tissue. Like a balloon, surface tension tries to pull the alveolus closed. Special cells inside the alveolus produce surfactant, a detergent-like substance that decreases surface tension and allows the alveoli to inflate more easily and with less pressure. Without surfactant, the alveoli would collapse.

Lung function is about functional surface area for gas exchange. In an adult human, a lung volume of four liters is exposed to an alveolar area of 40 to 100 square meters. There are 200-600 million alveoli in the normal lung, providing a total alveolar surface area of about 70 square meters (Fig. 1-15). For comparison, half a tennis court is 75 m^2. A cluster of alveoli on a terminal bronchiole along with their capillaries is called an acinus.

The alveoli give the lung a fairly spongy

texture. Once expanded from an inhalation, the lung passively and effortlessly returns to its resting state due to its elasticity. Expelling all of the air from the lungs in forced exhalation requires effort because the alveoli are "designed" to stay inflated.

Oxygen passively diffuses through the alveolar wall into the capillaries, where it is carried back via the pulmonary veins to the left side of the heart and distributed to the rest of the body. The capillary surface area is enormous. If all of the capillaries that surround the alveoli were unwound and laid end to end, they would extend for about 616 mi (992 kilometers). Carbon dioxide passively leaves the capillaries to enter the alveoli, where it is then exhaled from the body. This ongoing exchange is essential for life: too little oxygen or too much carbon dioxide can quickly lead to death.

Alveoli must have free access to the inspired gas. If blockage prevents oxygen from entering alveoli, absorption of trapped oxygen causes alveoli to collapse. Blockage prevents carbon dioxide from leaving. A person with too little O_2, or too much CO_2, is too close to death. Alveolar blockage can occur with mucous plugging or foreign body aspiration. It also occurs in pneumonia, where inflammation produced by infection or chemical exposure fills the alveoli with fluid, white cells, and debris.

The mucous membrane lining the airways consists of 2 types of specialized cells: one type produces mucous. The other type is covered with cilia, microscopic hair-like projections which sweep the mucous and any collected particulate matter up the trachea and into the oropharynx where they're swallowed. This process, plus coughing, removes debris from the lungs. The cilia are very sensitive to the effects of breathing cold, dry air and also to smoke. Smoke from one cigarette can paralyze cilia for 20-30 minutes.

Pulmonary Blood Supply

Like other tissues, bronchiolar arteries carry blood from the left heart to the lung tissues to keep them alive. Unlike other organs, the lungs have a second set of arteries — the right and left pulmonary arteries — which carry poorly oxygenated blood from the right heart to the alveolar capillaries to pick up oxygen for delivery to the rest of the body.

Normally blood flow moves from an area of high pressure (arterial pressure during systole when the ventricle contracts) to an area of lower pressure (venous pressure during diastole when the ventricle relaxes). Resistance to flow in the blood vessel itself also plays a role.

Things are different in the lungs. In addition to these factors, air pressure inside the alveoli also effects blood flow. When alveolar pressure is higher than the capillary blood pressure, the higher air pressure will restrict capillary flow by compressing the vessels from the outside. Gravity can also effect blood flow.

Chest Wall

The ribs form three functional groupings. The first rib attaches rigidly to the sternum and serves to anchor the rib cage. It hardly moves during respiration.

The 2nd through 7th ribs flexibly expand in two dimensions with each inhalation: mostly anterior-posteriorly with a little lateral motion. You can compare this movement to a pump handle, mostly up and down in the front of the chest, expanding the depth of the chest cavity (Fig. 1-16a).

The 8th through 12th ribs expand mostly laterally during inhalation, effectively

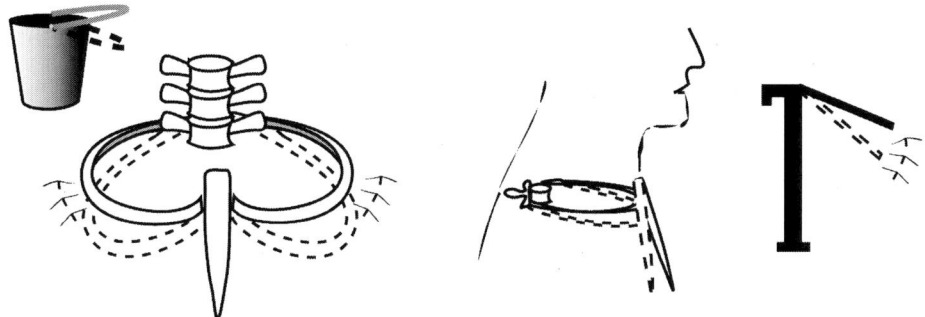

Fig. 1-16. a: Ribs 8-12 expand mostly laterally, like a bucket handle. **b:** Ribs 2-7 expand mostly anterior-posteriorly, like a pump handle.

increasing intra-abdominal space for organs pushed downward by the diaphragm. This motion is like a bucket handle, swinging up and down toward the side away from the center line and expanding the width of the chest cavity (Fig. 1-16b).

The angulation and rigidity of the ribs during the breathing cycle maximizes efficiency in the adult. Full contraction of the intercostals and the diaphragm allows for significant expansion of the chest cavity and produces a large breath.

In the infant or small child, the ribs are less angled and they are more compliant, so they can flex during the extremes of movement. To take a deep breath the infant's chest expands a little and the abdomen rises a lot as the diaphragm descends, pushing abdominal contents down and out of the way. Babies "belly breathe". Anything that interferes with descent of the diaphragm, such as a stomach distended with air, can seriously impair an infant's breathing.

The infant's chest wall is also more compliant. When the infant takes a breath against resistance, such as with airway obstruction or poor pulmonary compliance, the chest wall actually moves inward as the belly moves outward. The inward movement of the chest wall decreases the amount of air that enters. The baby must work harder to breathe and may tire if this effort goes on too long. Many aspects of pediatric anatomy and physiology place children at risk for respiratory insufficiency and failure. See Chapter 8 for more detail.

Diaphragm and Intercostal Muscles

The diaphragms are two large dome-shaped sheets of muscle separating the thoracic cavities from the abdominal cavity. They are controlled by the phrenic nerves, which originate in the neck at cervical nerve roots 3 through 5. The intercostal nerves supply the muscles between the ribs.

As the diaphragm contracts with each inhalation, it descends toward the abdomen and assumes a more flattened shape. The intercostal muscles contract, pulling the ribs outward. Both actions increase intrathoracic volume. The resulting drop in intrathoracic pressure draws air into the lungs, which expand.

During exhalation, the diaphragm and intercostals relax. The chest wall passively resumes its previous shape. The diaphragm returns to its resting dome shape and rises higher into the chest cavity. This decreases intrathoracic volume. Pressure inside the thorax rises and the patient passively exhales. Unless there is obstruction, exhalation is passive, requiring little energy (Fig. 1-17).

This system is very efficient during normal spontaneous respiration. Things change when

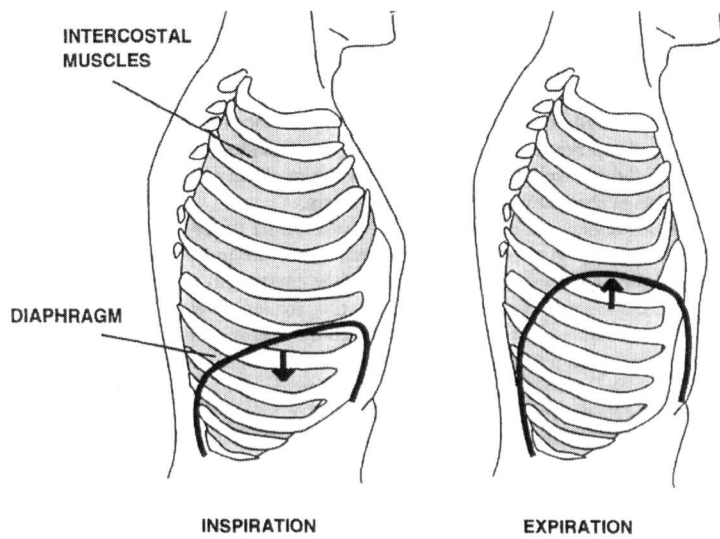

Fig. 1-17. Diaphragm. You can easily imagine how any obstruction to diaphragmatic movement such as abdominal fat, ascites, pregnancy, or gastric distention would interfere with lung expansion.

a patient must be manually ventilated. During manual ventilation, enough positive pressure must be applied to an open airway to expand the lungs by actively filling the alveoli. The chest wall must be lifted and the diaphragms pushed downward, displacing the abdominal contents to do so. If the airway is not held open, the gas will often take the path of least resistance and enter the stomach, producing distension and increasing the risk of vomiting. A distended stomach then pushes the diaphragm upward, impairing lung expansion. You can begin to see how form effects function.

Conditions that make ventilation more challenging include:
- increased intra-abdominal pressure which limits diaphragm descent, such as obesity or pregnancy;
- increased intrathoracic pressure, such as pneumothorax;
- poor pulmonary compliance, such as pneumonia where alveoli are filled with fluid or asthma where the bronchioles are in spasm;
- upper airway obstruction, such as foreign body, obstructive sleep apnea, or altered consciousness
- lower airway obstruction such as lung tumor
- spinal cord injury

The effects on breathing of a spinal cord injury will vary depending on where the injury occurs. With a spinal cord injury of C4 and higher, the intercostal muscles, the diaphragm and the abdominal muscles all of which control breathing will be paralyzed. The patient will need a ventilator to breathe.

Spinal injuries between C4 and T6 will leave some ability to breathe because the phrenic nerves can still move the diaphragm. Intercostal muscle function may be weakened but some chest wall expansion will still be present. The patient may or may not need assistance for adequate ventilation.

Injuries between T6 and T12 usually don't effect breathing, although the patient may not be able to cough forcefully enough to protect or clear their airways. Patients with injuries below T12 won't have problems breathing or coughing.

Physiology of Breathing

In order to work well, the body's cells and organs must be surrounded by a specific environment, consisting of an optimal range of blood acid-base balance (pH), arterial blood oxygen level (P_aO_2), arterial carbon dioxide level (P_aCO_2), and temperature, among other things. This optimal range can be disrupted by *external* factors such as ambient temperature and breathing contaminated air. The optimal range is more commonly disrupted by *internal* factors, such as infections like pneumonia, dehydration, starvation, traumatic damage, and progressive changes caused by such things as aging and smoking. In the face of such internal disorders, the concentration of oxygen that you breathe in, the *inspired* concentration, may need to be increased in order to maintain adequate tissue oxygen supply. The fraction of inspired oxygen in the gas we breathe is called the FiO_2. Room air contains an FiO_2 of 21% oxygen mixed with roughly 79% nitrogen.

When physiologic changes occur, the body compensates and tries to return the cellular environment closer to normal. If the changes are too great or too prolonged then the body can't compensate and organ systems can start to fail.

The following sections will define new terms as they appear. Table 1-2 shows some common abbreviations.

Table 1-2. Common Symbols and Abbreviations

SYMBOL/ABBREVIATION	DEFINITION
a (subscript)	arterial blood
v (subscript)	venous blood
A (subscript)	alveolar
O_2	oxygen
P_aO_2	arterial blood oxygen level
FiO_2	fraction of oxygen inspired
CO_2	carbon dioxide
P_aCO_2	arterial blood carbon dioxide level
pH	a measure of the acid-base balance (pH >7 is basic; pH < 7 is acidic. Physiologic pH ranges from 7.35-7.45

Why Do We Breathe?

Our bodies depend on breathing in order to absorb oxygen (O2), to eliminate carbon dioxide (CO_2), and to help maintain a normal blood acid-base balance. All three functions are essential to survival.

Our cells use oxygen to burn, or metabolize, fuel in the form of carbohydrates in order to release the energy the cells needs to function. No oxygen, no energy, and the cells become damaged and eventually die. This happens quickly. Brain cells usually suffer damage after 4-6 minutes without oxygen and brain cell death may occur within 10 minutes. Lack of oxygen can cause cardiac arrest.

CO_2 is a major waste product of cellular metabolism. If it starts to accumulate, the bloodstream and cells become increasingly acidic. Very high levels of CO_2 are toxic. The patient may hallucinate, lose consciousness or possibly die if he can't eliminate CO_2.

The symbol "pH" is a measure of relative acidity. It ranges from 0 (very acidic) to 14 (very basic). Neutral pH equals 7.0. When pH goes below 7, the solution is said to be acidic. When pH goes above 7, the solution is basic or alkaline. The pH scale is logarithmic so, for example, a pH of 8 is 10 times more basic than a pH of 7. Thus even the smallest changes in the pH value represent a big change in acid base balance and can have significant effects.

Normal blood pH is slightly basic, between 7.35 and 7.45. This pH must be maintained for optimal cellular enzyme function. If pH becomes too abnormal, cellular enzymes stop working, organ systems shut down and cause shock, and potentially death. Clearly, effective ventilation is critical.

Ventilation and oxygenation are different. Ventilation exchanges air between the lungs and the atmosphere so that oxygen can be absorbed and carbon dioxide can be eliminated. Oxygenation is simply the addition of oxygen to the body. If you hyperventilate with room air, you will lower my arterial carbon dioxide content (P_aCO_2) significantly, but my oxygen levels won't change much at all. On the other hand, if I breathe a high concentration of oxygen, but don't increase or decrease my respiratory rate, my arterial oxygen content (P_aO_2) will greatly increase, but my P_aCO_2 won't change.

Ventilation changes P_aCO_2. Oxygenation changes P_aO_2.

The Mechanics of How We Breathe

To inhale, the muscles between the ribs (intercostal muscles) and the diaphragm contract. Contraction of the intercostal muscles lifts the ribs upward and outward, increasing the volume of the chest cavity. As the diaphragm contracts, it moves downward, further expanding the chest cavity. When the volume of a container increases, the pressure inside goes down. A good analogy is using a syringe. When you pull the syringe plunger, the chamber inside becomes larger, the pressure inside goes down, and the fluid is drawn into the chamber. Like liquid, air is also a fluid. Chest expansion lowers the pressure inside the chest cavity, the intrathoracic pressure, below atmospheric pressure. If the airway is open, air flows into the lungs until the two pressures are again equal (Fig. 1-18a, Mov. 1-4, KF. 1-4).

When we exhale (Fig 1-18b), normal elastic recoil of our chest wall compresses the rib cage. The diaphragm relaxes. The chest cavity becomes smaller. When volume decreases, pressure increases. Think of pushing the plunger on our syringe inward. As intrathoracic pressure rises higher than atmospheric pressure it pushes the remaining air (minus some of its oxygen and now containing CO_2) out through the unobstructed airway.

Anatomy and Physiology 25

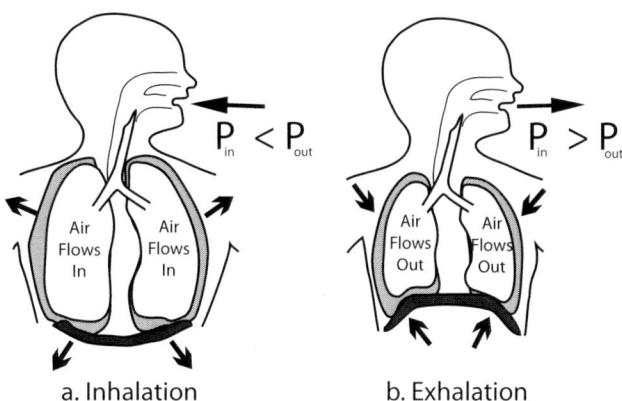

Fig. 1-18 a,b. While breathing, air pressure changes inside the thoracic cavity cause the lungs to expand (a) and contract (b).

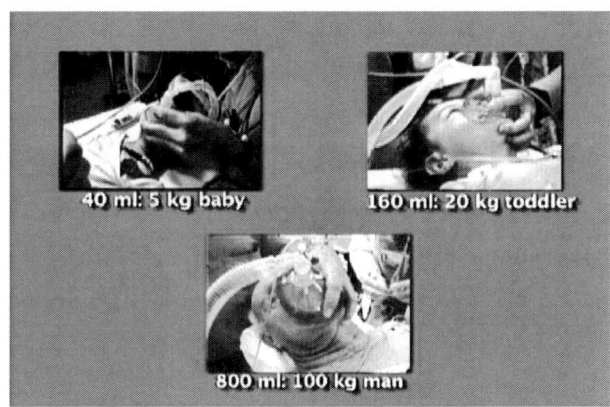

Keyframe 1-4a. The average tidal volume of 8 ml/kg means something very different depending on the size of your patient.

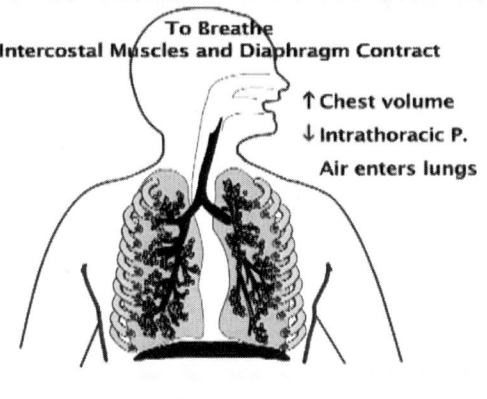

Keyframe 1-4b. Inhalation depends on contraction of intercostal muscles and diaphragm.

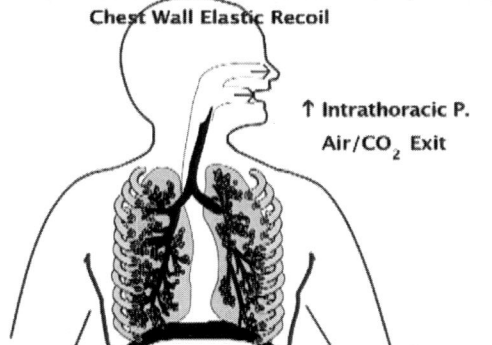

Keyframe 1-4c. Exhalation is passive, dependent on relaxation of muscles and elastic recoil.

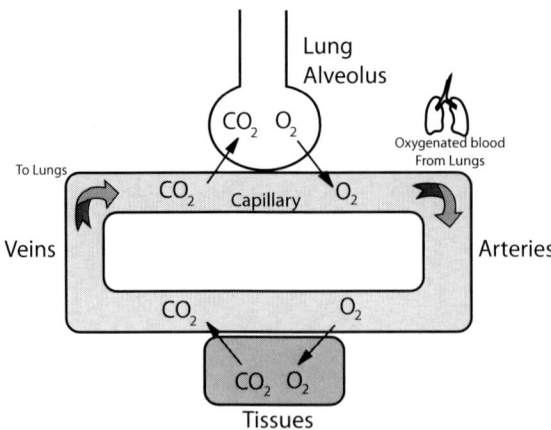

Fig. 1-19. The relationship between lung gas exchange and blood flow.

The lungs are elastic. As the chest wall expands, air flows into and inflates the lungs like a balloon — although in this case the balloon is composed of millions of tiny balloons like a sponge. These air sacs are called alveoli. The volume of an average breath, the tidal volume, thus generated is about 8 ml/kg and can be as high as 10-15 ml/kg with maximum expansion of the chest.

The Forced Vital Capacity (FVC) — the volume of air that a patient can exhale after a maximal inhalation — is about 70 ml/kg.

In the brief pause between inhaling and exhaling, O_2 leaves the inspired gas and passes through the capillary walls into the bloodstream, where blood circulation delivers it to the tissues. In the meantime, the CO_2 that the blood brought back to the lungs from the tissues passes from the capillaries into the alveoli (Fig 1-19).

Because of the interaction between lung function and circulation in oxygen delivery, we always need to look at both the respiratory rate and heart rate when assessing ventilation (Table 1-3). An infant, with a higher metabolic rate uses roughly double the oxygen consumption of an adult per body weight. This makes infants highly dependent on both rapid respiratory and heart rates and therefore more vulnerable to respiratory failure.

Table 1-3. Variation Of Normal Respiratory And Heart Rate With Age

AGE	RESPIRATORY RATE (Breathes per minute)	HEART RATE (Beats per minute)
Infant (birth to 1 yr)	30-60	110-160
Toddler (1-3 yrs)	24-40	90-150
Preschooler (3-6 yrs)	22-34	80-140
School age (6-12 yrs)	18-30	70-120
Adolescent to Adult	12-16	50-100

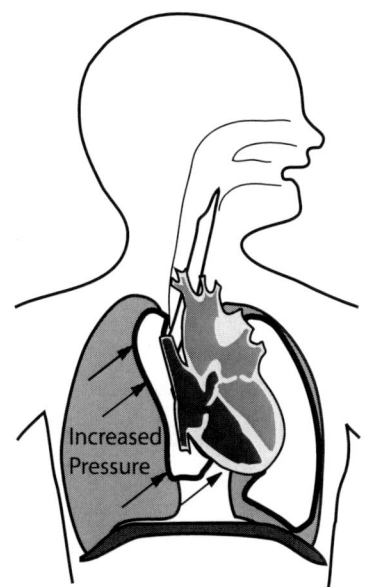

Fig. 1-20. Tension pneumothorax. Note how the right lung (pink) is compressed by the expanding air. The heart and opposite lung also pushed and compressed.

Holes in the lungs or chest wall can alter the mechanics. Open pneumothorax results when a penetrating chest wound enables air to rush in and collapse the lung. Closed pneumothorax results when air leaks from a lung (or a perforated esophagus) into an intact chest cavity.

With an open pneumothorax, expansion of the chest cavity can't effectively decrease intrathoracic pressure. The lung may only may or may not partially expand depending on severity.

When the chest wall expands in the presence of closed pneumothorax, air follows the path of least resistance and fills the thoracic space. The lung itself can't expand very well because the escaped air compresses it. If intrathoracic pressure gets high enough, it flattens the lung, shifts the remaining chest contents, such as the heart, to the other side, and prevents blood return. This life-threatening situation is called a tension pneumothorax (Fig 1-20).

In emphysema, lung damage breaks down alveolar walls, producing decreased numbers of enlarged alveoli. Poor oxygenation results from decreased surface area for oxygen exchange. Loss of alveoli also causes loss of lung elasticity, hampering passive exhalation and causing the lung to remain hyperinflated. The diaphragm is pushed downward, becoming more flattened. With this relative mechanical disadvantage, the patient works harder to breathe. Carbon dioxide diffuses so freely that its passage is rarely impaired due to lung damage.

If a diaphragm is paralyzed by phrenic nerve damage, then during spontaneous respiration that diaphragm will move in reverse: upward during inspiration and downward during expiration. Tidal volume decreases and work of breathing increases. The patient with marginal respiratory reserve may need assistance.

Oxygen Supply and Demand

When we run up the stairs, we breathe faster and take deeper breaths in order to increase oxygen supply and eliminate the additional CO_2. Our hearts pump faster and more forcefully, increasing cardiac output to circulate more oxygen.

Speed of air flows depends on differences in airway pressure and airflow resistance. A person takes deeper breaths by more forcefully contracting the chest wall muscles and diaphragm. Accessory muscles of respiration in the neck tense to lift the clavicles higher to more fully expand the chest. They're called accessory muscles because the body uses them when extra effort is needed to breathe.

Greater chest expansion during inhalation generates more negative intrathoracic pressure and pulls in a larger volume of air. Then we *forcefully* exhale, actively compressing our chest wall to expel air. The volume of air breathed in a minute — the minute volume — greatly increases.

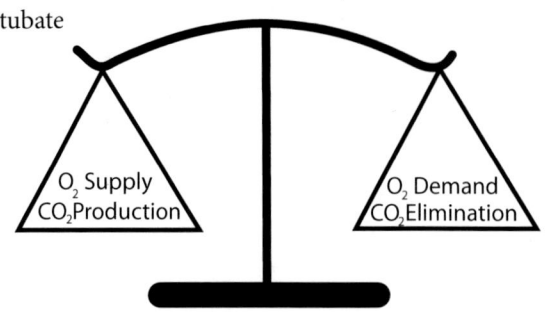

Fig. 1-21. The respiratory system must balance O_2 supply with O_2 demand as well as CO_2 production with CO_2 elimination to prevent respiratory failure.

Meanwhile, the heart circulates non-oxygenated blood rich in CO_2 back to the lungs to pick up more oxygen and expel CO_2. Oxygenated blood low in CO_2 returns to the body. With good cardiac output and lung function, O_2 delivery meets O_2 demand and CO_2 is eliminated from the body as it's produced (Fig 1-21).

Increasing cardiac output, respiratory rate and breath volume all increase the work of breathing — which uses up more oxygen. To compensate, blood vessels and bronchi dilate to decrease airflow resistance and increase blood flow in order to lessen workload and improve efficiency. We breathe through our open mouths and dilate our nostrils. Our larynx opens more fully. We tilt our heads back to straighten the air passages to decrease airway resistance.

If, during our dash up the stairs, our body can't keep up with the work of delivering O_2 and removing CO_2, we have to stop and catch our breath. If we're very out of breath, we often assume the tripod position (Fig 1-22). We lean forward, putting our outstretched hands on our knees and breathe deeply with our heads tilted back.

Fig. 1-22. The tripod position

Table 1-4. Causes of Respiratory Failure

PROBLEM	CAUSE
Upper Airway obstruction	Foreign body, edema, trauma, sleep apnea, tumor
Lower Airway Obstruction	Asthma, emphysema, chronic bronchitis, pneumonia, cystic fibrosis, tumor
Respiratory control center	Altered mental status due to trauma, drug intoxication, stroke, hemorrhage, infection, or tumor
Peripheral Nervous System	Spinal cord injury, stroke, polio, Guillain-Barre Syndrome
Muscle weakness	Myasthenia gravis, muscular dystrophy, drug effect
Abnormal lung tissue	Infection, tumors, radiation, burns, ARDS, collapsed lung
Abnormal chest wall	Trauma, Scoliosis, extreme obesity

The tripod position allows maximum descent of the diaphragm and allows us to take the deepest breaths with the least resistance.

Cardiac or respiratory failure will result if the body can't increase cardiac output or ventilation in response to increased demand. Respiratory failure occurs for many reasons. See Table 1-4.

Mechanics of Airway Obstruction

The ability to breathe effectively, and protect the airway from aspiration, depends on muscle coordination. The opening between the vocal cords, called the glottis, widens when we inhale due to dynamic contraction of the muscles — reducing resistance to breathing. These muscles can contract more forcefully if needed. The harder you try to breathe, the wider the larynx opens, up to a limit. The result is both faster inflow and outflow of air as effort demands. During exhalation, the glottis naturally narrows as the muscles relax.

The most common clinical symptoms of upper airway obstruction are:

- dyspnea — discomfort due to perceived work of breathing,
- exercise intolerance — due to inability to increase oxygen supply,
- respiratory noise — due to turbulence in the air stream.

Because of the structure of the larynx, conditions causing airway obstruction usually produce more symptoms with inhaling than with exhaling. Symptoms of airway obstruction at rest usually do not occur until 70-80% of the diameter is lost. At this point, respirations sound harsh and "creaking" due to turbulence, a noise called stridor. It's important to remember that airway obstruction can be asymptomatic during quiet breathing, but can become very symptomatic with exercise or stress.

During swallowing, the tongue and pharyngeal muscles direct food and liquid boluses backward into the esophagus (Fig 1-23a). As the bolus descends, the pharyngeal muscles contract, causing the whole larynx to rise in the neck (Fig 1-23b), and forcing the epiglottis to fold over the glottis. This closes and protects the larynx from aspiration. (Fig. 1-23c, Mov. 1-5, KF. 1-5a,b).

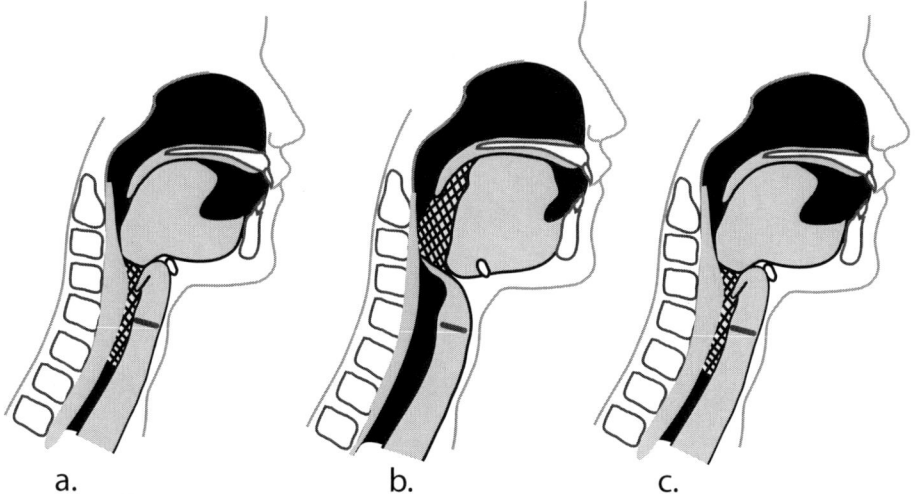

Fig. 1-23. Swallowing depends on coordinated muscle movement to send the bolus of food or liquid down the esophagus and not the trachea. Coordinated laryngeal movements help prevent aspiration.

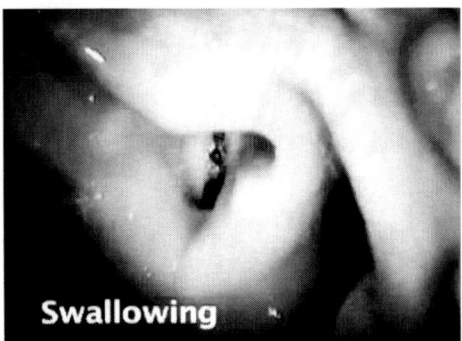 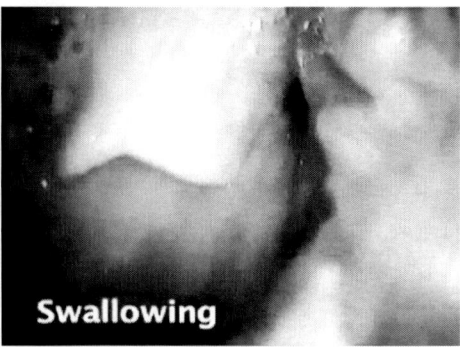

Keyframes 1-5a,b. To swallow, the pharyngeal muscles contract and force the larynx to rise in the neck, forcing the epiglottis down over the glottic opening.

Weakened or poorly coordinated muscles, or anything in the mouth that interferes with normal muscle movement, increases the risk of aspiration. This includes a laryngoscope blade, which interferes with normal muscle movement, and thus increases the risk of aspiration.

Upper airway obstruction occurs from loss of muscle tone, foreign body aspiration or oropharyngeal edema. Lower airways obstruction occurs with conditions such as bronchospasm. Observing the mechanics of breathing may reveal signs of airway obstruction.

Snoring and Airway Obstruction

Snoring, the most common sign of upper airway obstruction, appears with decreased levels of consciousness, including sleep. Snoring occurs when the soft tissue at the back of the throat collapses over the larynx, causing partial or total obstruction (Fig. 1-24, Mov. 1-6, KF 1-6). Typically the snorer is lying face up, with the chin sagging backward. You can hear, and see, the tissues vibrating with the turbulent airflow. As snoring worsens, the lower jaw and tongue get sucked further back into the airway and the snore gets louder.

The accessory muscles of respiration in the neck, the sternocleidomastoid and scalene muscles, contract to lift the clavicles and allow fuller expansion of the chest wall. These muscles become tense and rope-like.

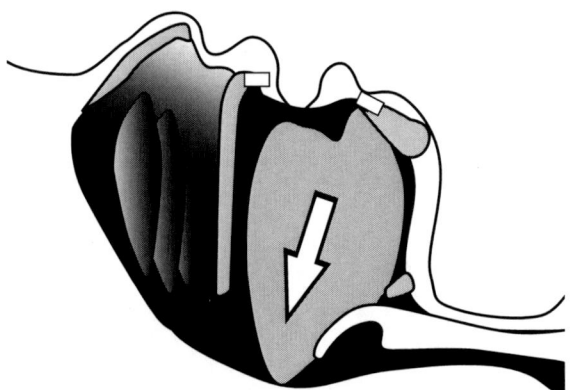

Fig. 1-24, KF 1-6. Snoring occurs when soft tissue obstructs the glottic opening during breathing.

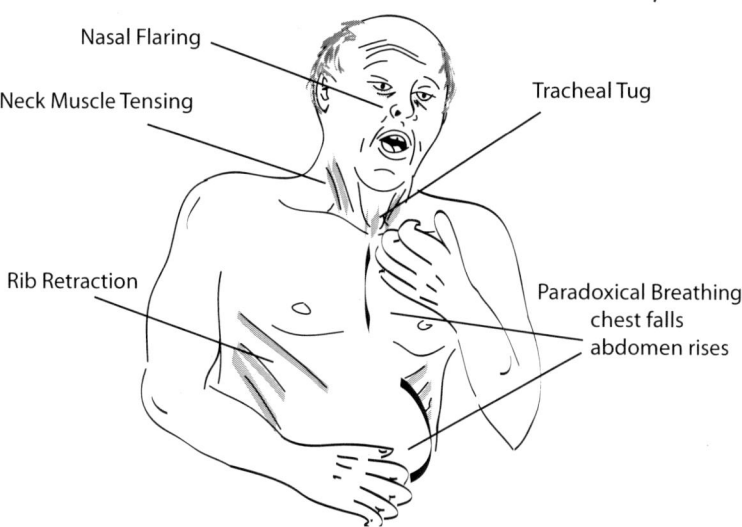

Fig. 1-25. Common signs of airway obstruction.

When the diaphragm descends maximally, it pushes the abdominal contents downward and outward, further decreasing intrathoracic pressure. The harder the patient tries to breathe against airway obstruction (either upper or lower) the more negative pressure is generated inside the chest. Think of what happens when you cover the end of a vacuum cleaner hose with your hand. You can feel the skin being sucked inward because airflow is blocked. This pressure differential sucks the soft tissue between ribs and at the sternal notch inward. These are respectively called rib retractions and a tracheal tug.

With mild to moderate obstruction you will see these common patterns of retractions (Fig. 1-25):

- abdomen below the breast bone (substernal)
- abdomen below the rib cage (subcostal)
- soft tissue between the ribs (intercostal muscles or rib retractions)

With severe obstruction you will see all of the above plus retractions of the:

- neck soft tissue above the collar bone (supraclavicular)
- soft tissue at the sternal notch (tracheal tug)
- sternum toward the spinal column (sternal)

Obstruction can produce a rocking chest motion, called paradoxical breathing. With inhalation, the diaphragm descends maximally, pushing the abdominal contents down and out and generating increased negative pressure. This negative pressure pulls the chest wall *inward*, resulting in the abdomen rising and the chest falling during inhalation — the opposite of normal breathing. During exhalation the chest rises and the abdomen falls. The more compliant or flexible the chest wall, such as in young children, the easier it is to see this. In Chapter 2 as we discuss assessment, Movie 2-1 let you see examples of these signs.

If obstruction becomes complete, the jaw and tongue are pulled backward the head starts to bob and the nostrils flare. There may be grunting but snoring usually stops. While the typical sleeper usually rouses, inhales deeply, and turns over, a patient with altered consciousness due to drugs or illness may not.

Other sounds accompanying airway obstruction include:

Stridor

Stridor is a high-pitched, harsh, creaking, inspiratory sound produced by turbulent air flow past a swelling or constriction of the laryngeal structures. Laryngospasm, croup, and epiglottis are examples of conditions causing stridor. Loudness of stridor does not correlate with degree of obstruction. It may be absent at rest and only appear with moderate exertion. In fact, stridor may be hard to hear with severe obstruction because there is too little air flow to create noise.

Grunting

A grunt is a short, low-pitched sound during exhalation produced by exhaling against a partially closed glottis. It's most often heard during labored respirations associated with lung tissue disease such as pneumonia or pulmonary edema. It's especially common in infants with respiratory distress. Grunting increases end expiratory pressure and helps to keep small airways open — improving oxygenation and ventilation in conditions with small airway closure.

Bronchospasm (Wheezing)

Wheezing, or bronchospasm, is a high or low pitched whistling sound heard most often during exhalation. It's produced by turbulent air flowing through bronchi in spasm. This lower airway obstruction, like upper airway obstruction, can present with signs of obstructed breathing.

Bronchospasm accompanies asthma, allergic reaction, chronic lung disease such as emphysema or chronic bronchitis, infection, trauma and chemical irritation. In addition to constriction of airway diameter, it's commonly associated with edema of the airway lining and increased mucous production. Sticky mucous plugs airways and further decreases airflow. It stimulates coughing, increases smooth muscle contraction, and worsens airway edema resulting in a vicious cycle. Work of breathing increases.

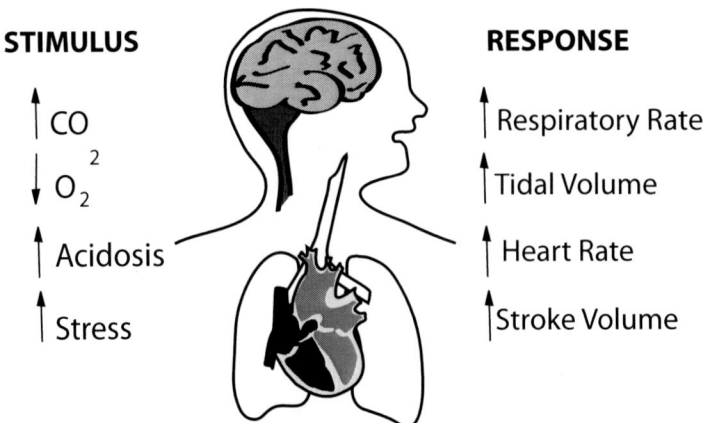

Fig. 1-26. Four major stimuli — rising CO_2, falling oxygenation, acidosis, and stress — can trigger improved oxygen delivery by raising respiratory rate, tidal volume, heart rate, and stroke volume.

What Factors Control Breathing?

Respiration varies throughout the course of the day depending on the body's needs and on the feedback signals received by the brain. Given the importance of maintaining normal oxygen, CO_2, and pH, it should not be surprising that the most important stimuli for respiration are the level of oxygen, the level of CO_2, and the acid/base balance in the blood (Fig 1-26).

Breathing is controlled by 4 main centers in the body: the chemoreceptors of the central respiratory center (inside the brain), the peripheral chemoreceptors (outside the brain), the brain itself, and the lungs. A chemoreceptor is a receptor that responds to change in the chemical composition of the blood or other fluid around it. The build-up of CO_2 (hypercapnia or hypercarbia) and decrease of O_2 in the circulation (hypoxia) are two of the strongest stimuli to increase respiratory rate.

The respiratory "center" is found in the midbrain, comprised of sections of both the medulla and pons. Central chemoreceptors are surrounded by brain extracellular fluid, or fluid outside the cells.

You would think that P_aO_2 level would be the major driving force to breathe, but it's not. Central chemoreceptors don't respond to changes in blood oxygen, they respond to changes in pH. As CO_2 diffuses out of the brain's capillaries, it changes the pH of this extracellular fluid (fluid outside the cells). As CO_2 accumulates, pH goes down, becoming more acidic. A pH more acidic (lower) than the normal pH of 7.35-7.45, stimulates ventilation. A higher (more basic) pH inhibits ventilation.

Because of its effect on the pH, the most powerful stimulus to breathe tends to be the level of carbon dioxide in the bloodstream (P_aCO_2). Under most conditions CO_2 is tightly controlled. Small changes in arterial CO_2 cause significant changes in pH and thus in respiratory drive.

The sensors detecting the oxygen tension in the arterial blood (P_aO_2) are peripheral chemoreceptors located in the carotid bodies at the bifurcation (first major branch point) of the carotid artery, and at the thoracic curve of the aorta. Information from the carotid and aortic bodies is believed to regulate breathing by the respiratory control center, breath by breath.

The conscious brain plays a minor role in respiratory control. We all can decide to consciously hyperventilate and then hold our breath for a while, but only for so long. Breathing is for the most part an automatic reflex. We can't really hold our breath until we "turn blue in the face". In fact, the reflex is so strong it's hard to consciously stop breathing for any length of time.

Finally, the lung contains receptors that trigger protective mechanisms. Inhaling an irritating substance causes coughing, breath holding, and sneezing. Other receptors located in the smooth muscle of the airways are sensitive to stretch. The Hering–Breuer reflex actively inhibits inspiration once a certain lung stretch occurs, allowing expiration to occur and preventing over inflation.

How Does CO_2 Help Maintain Acid/Base Balance?

Hypoventilation means not enough respiration is occurring to support oxygen demands and to eliminate CO_2. Usually hypoventilation causes falling oxygen levels and rising levels of CO_2, leading to increasing blood acidity.

Hyperventilation means an increased rate or depth of breathing over and above that needed to maintain the blood gas levels within the normal range. With hyperventilation, CO_2 level fall, and pH rises to become more basic or alkaline.

To start each normal respiration, signals travel from the brain down the phrenic nerves going to the diaphragms, and also down the intercostal nerves going to the muscles of the rib cage. Upon arrival, the signals stimulate the muscles to contract, the chest expands and the person inhales. Under normal circumstances, the respiratory rate and depth will automatically change to try to counteract any changes in the tension of oxygen, carbon dioxide, and acid in the blood stream.

The level of carbon dioxide in the arterial blood stream is called the P_aCO_2. The level of oxygen in the arterial blood is called the P_aO_2. The "P" refers to the partial pressure of the dissolved gas in the blood, measured in mmHg. The term mmHg refers to millimeters of mercury, the same units used for barometric pressure.

The normal blood concentration, or partial pressure, of arterial CO_2 is 35 - 45 mmHg. Changes in pH are brought about according to the chemical reaction:

$$CO_2 + H_2O \rightleftharpoons H_2CO_3 \rightleftharpoons H^+ + HCO_3^-$$

What this formula means is that carbon dioxide is highly reactive with water, and when combined with water will form the weak acid carbonic acid (H_2CO_3). Carbonic acid will then break up into positively and negatively charged ions in such a way as to keep the blood acid/base balance as neutral as possible. The bloodstream normally has a certain amount of the base bicarbonate (HCO_3^-) in solution that helps to buffer or neutralize any acids being produced.

The symbol $\rightleftharpoons$ means that this chemical reaction is in equilibrium. In other words it moves automatically from right to left or left to right depending on what's going on in the bloodstream. More CO_2 drives the reaction to the right. More H^+ and/or HCO_3^- drives the reaction to the left.

Blood acidity will rise and the pH will fall if the amount of H^+ rises, such as from lactic acid production during shock or low arterial oxygen. The blood will also become more acidic if the amount of HCO_3^- falls, resulting from diarrhea or certain types of kidney dysfunction. In either case, the extra H^+ combines with HCO_3^- and more CO_2 is formed as the above equation shifts to the left. Carbon dioxide levels rise above normal and the patient becomes hypercarbic.

In addition to acidity from CO_2, the body contains many other natural acids, such as stomach acids. Much of the food we eat contains both acids and bases that we absorb. Proteins break down to make acidic compounds. It's imperative to keep these acids and bases in proper balance to maintain a neutral pH. The kidneys serve the major role of long-term acid-base balance by excreting excess acids or bases. But it can take days for the kidneys to correct a major imbalance — time the body can't afford to lose if the cells are to continue to function.

Fortunately the body has a safety mechanism: hyperventilation. As we saw above, as blood acidity rises, this automatic chemical reaction shifts the extra H^+ into CO_2 production. Hyperventilation can quickly lower the level of CO_2 dissolved in the bloodstream. Removal of CO_2 allows the chemical reaction to continue as more H^+ and HCO_3^- combine. As extra

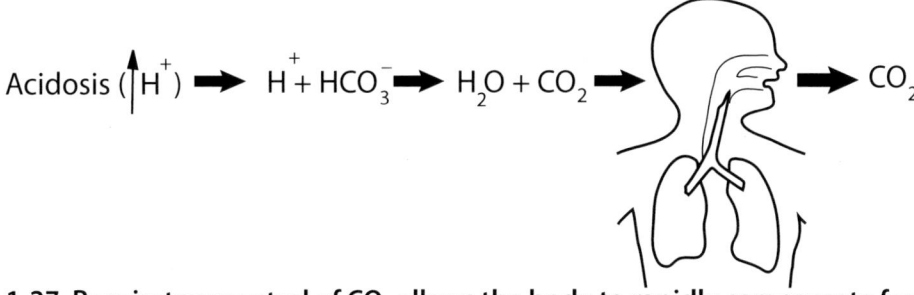

$$\text{Acidosis } (\uparrow H^+) \rightarrow H^+ + HCO_3^- \rightarrow H_2O + CO_2 \rightarrow \rightarrow CO_2$$

Fig. 1-27. Respiratory control of CO_2 allows the body to rapidly compensate for changes in pH.

CO_2 is produced it's eliminated by the lungs. In this way the blood becomes less acid.

This reaction can run both ways. Increasing or decreasing the rate and depth of respiration allows the body to acutely and rapidly compensate for acid base imbalance by quickly changing the amount of CO_2 dissolved in the blood. It's a short-term fix, but it's very effective (Fig 1-27) in keeping pH more normal while the kidneys perform the longer-term process to restore acid-base balance by excreting the excess ions.

However, this compensatory mechanism has its limits. Acidosis will continue if the amount of H^+ produced overwhelms the body's ability to eliminate the CO_2. However, this doesn't mean that the hyperventilation is not serving any purpose. In this case hyperventilation is *partially* compensating for the acidosis, in other words making it less severe. The result is a pH higher than it would if the patient were not hyperventilating at all. Not normal, but closer to normal.

It's crucial to understand this fact. When providers step in to take over the ventilation of a patient who can't breathe for himself, then it's essential for the provider to remember to take this compensatory mechanism into consideration. If the acidotic patient can't hyperventilate for himself, then the provider must hyperventilate for him in order to bring the pH back toward normal. If you don't, the patient can remain severely acidotic, a state which can cause organ damage and promote hypotension and cardiac arrythmias, even cardiac arrest.

A full explanation of acid-base balance can get very complex — and for the purposes of this discussion we don't need to fully explore it. The important point is that our body will alter its respiratory rate and depth of respirations to try to maintain our pH as normal as possible. Most commonly this means we hyperventilate in order to try to compensate for a low pH in the face of poor cardiac output, poor respiratory function, or shock of any sort.

When Hyperventilation Is a Problem

Too much hyperventilation, however, is not necessarily a good thing. Hyperventilation, as we've mentioned, is a condition in which the body exhales carbon dioxide at a rate faster than it's being produced. For example, when a patient with normal pH hyperventilates, perhaps in response to anxiety, fear, or pain, the P_aCO_2 drops and the blood pH rises. A level of P_aCO_2 less than baseline is called hypocarbia. Hypocarbia causes vasoconstriction and decreases blood flow to the major organs, including the brain. If the P_aCO_2 is much less than 20 mmHg, the brain may not have enough oxygen to function normally. Whenever an organ lacks enough oxygen it is said to be ischemic. Ischemia causes localized acidosis in the cerebral spinal fluid (CSF). This local acidosis can continue to promote over breathing because it tricks the body into thinking that it needs to correct it. A vicious cycle starts and the patient continues to hyperventilate to try to resolve the acidosis now present in the spinal fluid (Fig 1-28).

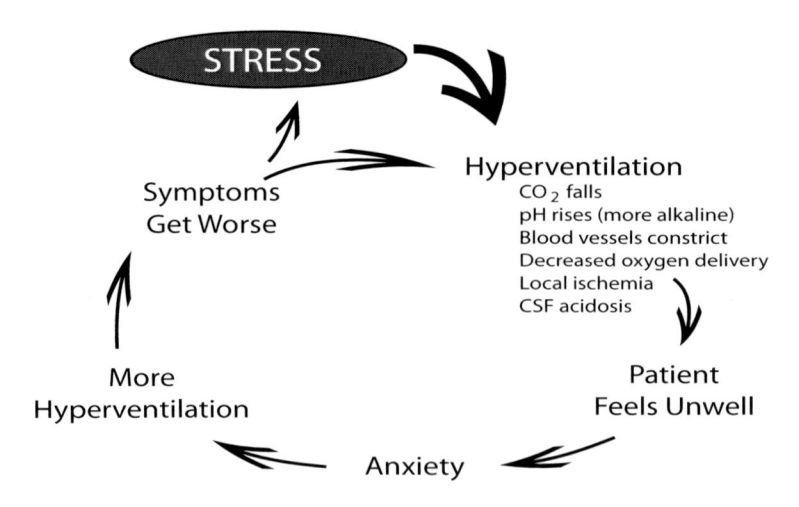

```
                    STRESS
                      ↘
    ↗           Hyperventilation
Symptoms          CO₂ falls
Get Worse         pH rises (more alkaline)
                  Blood vessels constrict
  ↑               Decreased oxygen delivery
                  Local ischemia
                  CSF acidosis
                              ↘
   More                    Patient
Hyperventilation         Feels Unwell
        ⇐      Anxiety      ⇐
```

Fig. 1-28. Hyperventilation can cause severe hypocarbia producing localized ischemia and C.S.F. acidosis, tricking the body into more hyperventilation.

This phenomenon is the main reason that we can treat patients hyperventilating from anxiety by having them rebreathe into a paper bag. Rebreathing exhaled CO_2, raises the patient's blood P_aCO_2 improves CSF acidosis, and breaks the cycle.

When performing manual ventilation, the normal tendency is to hyperventilate the patient. A standing joke in the medical profession is that the rate of manually ventilating a patient is directly proportional to the *provider's* own anxiety levels. It's not always possible to have blood gas results to guide ventilation. Because of the risk of uncorrected metabolic acidosis, it's better to err on the side of *moderate* hyperventilation if you aren't sure — but be aware of the tendency to over ventilate.

What Factors Can Affect The Sensitivity to CO_2?

Normally the respiratory center tries to maintain the P_aCO_2 within the "set-point" of 35-45 mmHg. Drugs and the status of the patient can affect the sensitivity of the respiratory center.

This phenomenon is similar to the way an infection can cause the temperature regulatory center to "reset" the body's normal temperature "set-point" of 98.6°F (37° C) to a fever of 102°F (39° C). When we have a fever, the body considers the elevated temperature the new "norm". It does everything it can, from shivering, to constricting blood vessels, to raising our metabolic rate in order to raise the core temperature to the new norm of 102°F. Aspirin and acetaminophen (Tylenol) work because they return the temperature "set-point" to a normal 98.6° F (37° C) and the body stops the over-heating process.

Narcotics are one of the most common types of drugs affecting the respiratory center. They effectively raise the respiratory "set point," causing the center to accept a higher level of P_aCO_2, for example 50, as the new norm. As a result, the patient will decrease the respiratory rate and depth in a dose dependent fashion until the higher P_aCO_2 of 50 is reached. If the dose of narcotic is high enough, the patient will stop breathing completely (become apneic) until that higher P_aCO_2 is reached. Unfortunately, the patient may become hypoxic during this period of time if ventilation is not supported, potentially leading to fatal respiratory arrest. Treating a narcotic overdose with naloxone (Narcan) will return the respiratory "set-point" to normal and the patient will increase the respiratory rate and depth to return the P_aCO_2 back to the normal range.

It's very common to see this phenomenon in anesthetized patients, or when trying to wean a patient from the ventilator in the ICU. In our example, if the patient's manually ventilated P_aCO_2 is, say, 30 mmHg, the patient simply will not breathe until their new "set-point" of 50 mmHg is reached. To get the patient to start breathing again during weaning from the ventilator, the provider gradually decreases the rate and depth of ventilation to allow the P_aCO_2 to slowly rise, while at the same time maintaining adequate oxygenation. As soon as the P_aCO_2 goes above the patient's "set-point," he will begin to breathe again.

Obviously if the patient's "set point" is too high to safely allow him to breathe on his own without causing excessive respiratory acidosis or hypoxemia, then you have to continue to assist ventilation or consider reversing any narcotic effect.

Sepsis, probably through the effect of endotoxin on the respiratory center, is a powerful stimulus to hyperventilation. Other conditions increasing ventilation are pulmonary embolus, shock, fear, fever, and pain. Anything that tends to turn on the sympathetic nervous system tends to increase respiratory rate.

Chronically high levels of CO_2 above 70 mmHg, for example in *some* patients with severe Chronic Obstructive Pulmonary Disease (COPD), will desensitize the respiratory center to CO_2. The primary driving force to breathe then becomes the level of oxygen or P_aO_2, which as we have seen is a weaker stimulus. When the P_aO_2 drops too low for normal body function, the patient is said to be hypoxic. A patient who depends on a low P_aO_2 to stimulate breathing is said to be dependent on hypoxic drive, and is diagnosed as a CO_2 retainer. Unlike the CO_2 sensors, the carotid bodies never get used to a low P_aO_2 and will continue to detect it even in patients with chronic hypoxia.

Administering a high concentration of oxygen to a CO_2 retainer may cause hypoventilation by taking away the hypoxic drive to breathe. We'll talk more in detail about the acute management of the CO_2 retainer later.

There is always a balance in each patient between the stimuli to increase and to decrease respiratory drive. An exhausted, hypoxemic patient with respiratory distress who is also afraid and in pain has powerful negative and positive drives to breathe. A small dose of narcotic and sedative to relieve anxiety or pain may be enough to tip the balance and produce apnea. Monitor such patients carefully.

How Does Hypoventilation Cause Hypoxemia?

Hypoventilation is a common cause of too little oxygen in the blood. When breathing room air, CO_2 takes up space in the alveoli, leaving less room for oxygen. Let's see how big an effect this is. The concentration of oxygen in the alveoli can be calculated using the Alveolar Gas Equation:

$$P_AO_2 = FiO_2 (PB - PH_2O) - P_ACO_2 / R$$

Where:
  P_AO_2 = partial pressure of oxygen in the alveoli
  FiO_2 = concentration of inspired oxygen
  PB = the barometric pressure where the patient is breathing
  PH_2O = the partial pressure of water in the air (usually 47 mmHg)
  P_ACO_2 = alveolar carbon dioxide tension
  R = respiratory quotient, a constant usually assumed to be 0.8

Let's say that our emergency room patient with a narcotic overdose, at sea level and breathing room air, has an alveolar P_ACO_2 of 80 mmHg, or twice normal. That CO_2 takes up space and leave less room for O_2. The P_AO_2 calculation is:

$$P_AO_2 = .21\ (760 - 47) - 80/0.8 = 49\ \text{mmHg}$$

Normal P_AO_2 is about 100 mmHg, so this is quite hypoxic, especially since the alveolar P_AO_2 is always a little higher than the arterial P_aO_2. If it weren't, oxygen would not flow out of the alveoli into the blood — it would stay in the alveoli.

Now let's treat this patient with 50% oxygen and see what happens:

$$P_AO_2 = 0.5\ (760 - 47) - 80/0.8 = 256\ \text{mmHg}$$

That's a five-fold increase. Putting the patient on oxygen will buy you time for treatment. If this is a quickly reversible process, such as a narcotic overdose, you may not need to intubate. However, if this is not quickly reversible, then oxygen protects brain and heart while you manually ventilate or intubate.

This is also a good time to point out that a patient can have a normal O_2 sat and even a normal P_aO_2 and still be in respiratory distress or failure because ventilation and CO_2 elimination is failing. In the above example our treated patient's O_2 sat would be 100%, but with a P_aCO_2 of 80 mmHg, the pH would be about 7, a dangerous and potentially life-threatening respiratory acidosis. Don't be lulled into missing a patient's tenuous status just because the oxygen looks good.

The Challenge of the CO_2 Retainer

Let's look at a CO_2 retaining emphysema patient relying on hypoxic drive — which by the way, is only a very small minority of patients with end stage pulmonary disease. This patient was in respiratory distress from pneumonia with a P_aO_2 of 65 mmHg upon arrival to the hospital. The nurse placed her on 50% oxygen. After oxygen therapy, her blood gas shows her P_aO_2 is now 256 (good) and her P_aCO_2 is now 80 (bad) and she's getting sleepy, probably from the high CO_2. The high oxygen levels have decreased this particular patient's drive to breathe. Seeing CO_2 retention, the nurse might be tempted to take all the oxygen off this patient in order to stimulate her breathing and get her CO_2 down — *but that would be the wrong thing to do.*

Why? As we saw in the calculation above, we'd expect the alveolar P_AO_2 to abruptly drop to 49 with this change. A better way to deal with this situation would be to wean the oxygen back slowly, maintaining a good oxygen level while allowing the respiratory drive to improve. Keep reminding the patient to take deep breaths. Intubation might be needed so watch the patient carefully.

Never let the fear of CO_2 retention stop you from treating a COPD patient with oxygen in an emergency. The vast majority of patients with COPD do *not* retain CO_2. And even if the patient you happen to be treating does retain CO_2, the worst-case scenario is that you relieve their hypoxia and protect their brain and heart (good) but might have to temporarily assist ventilation.

How Does Hypoxemia Differ From Hypoxia?

The inspired oxygen concentration, or FiO_2, for room air is 21%. Sick and injured patients often require more oxygen than this. Air exhaled from a person at rest typically contains 16

– 17% oxygen — meaning they've absorbed about 5-6% of it. One disadvantage of mouth-to-mouth ventilation is that unless the provider breathes enriched oxygen herself, the patient will receive no more than 17% oxygen, and probably less.

Normal room air P_aO_2 varies with age and can be estimated by the formula:

$$P_aO_2 = 102 - 0.33 \text{ (age in years) mmHg}$$

A 30 year old breathing room air would have a P_aO_2 of about 92 mmHg.

The normal P_aO_2 is roughly equal to 5 times the FiO_2. Thus an average patient breathing 40% FiO_2 will have a P_aO_2 of about 200 mmHg. A patient breathing room air, or 21% FiO_2, will have a P_aO_2 of 100 mmHg. Knowing this relationship alerts you to whether a patient is or isn't relatively hypoxemic relative to the FiO_2.

Hypoxemia refers to a subnormal concentration of oxygen in the blood relative to the concentration of oxygen being inhaled. *Hypoxia* refers to an insufficient amount of oxygen in the tissues. The distinction is important. A patient breathing an FiO_2 of 50% oxygen who has a P_aO_2 of 100 is relatively hypoxemic — his P_aO_2 should be about 250 with that FiO_2. But he's *not* hypoxic, since a P_aO_2 of 100 provides a normal amount of oxygen to his tissues. On the other hand, a patient with a P_aO_2 of 50 is both hypoxic *and* hypoxemic. His tissues need more oxygen.

The presence of hypoxemia is an early warning sign that a problem exists. Perhaps the patient is not ventilating well, has pneumonia, or is suffering from heart failure. But hypoxemia can progress to hypoxia if the patient's condition worsens.

Hypoxemia is not by itself an indication for intubation. It may not even be abnormal. For example, a healthy man living in Denver, the mile high city, will have an O_2 sat of about 93% and a P_aO_2 of about 77 mmHg. Although the FiO_2 is the same 21% in Denver, the atmospheric pressure is lower and therefore the absolute number of oxygen molecules in the air is less. Our man is hypoxemic, but normal. He compensates by having a higher red blood cell count and Hgb plus a tendency to hyperventilate a bit compared to sea level. His hemoglobin releases oxygen to the tissues more easily so delivery is increased. However, this also means that our patient in Denver has far less reserve than one at sea level, and if injured or ill may require more aggressive oxygen support.

What's The Difference Between Arterial O_2 Saturation And P_aO_2?

Another important distinction to master is the difference between P_aO_2 and oxygen saturation.

Oxygen saturation (often abbreviated O_2 sat) is the percent of Hemoglobin (Hgb) binding sites in the blood that are carrying oxygen. Hemoglobin is a chemical molecule in the red blood cell (RBC) that carries oxygen on specific binding sites. Each Hgb molecule, if fully saturated, can bind four oxygen molecules. Depending on conditions, Hgb releases some percentage of the O_2 molecules to the tissues when the RBC passes through the capillaries. We can measure how many of these binding sites are combined, or saturated, with oxygen. This number, given as a percentage, is called the oxygen saturation or simply O_2 Sat, commonly pronounced "Oh Two SAT". When all the Hgb binding sites are filled, Hgb is 100% saturated.

The P_aO_2 is the partial pressure of oxygen in the arterial blood in mmHg. People sometimes confuse the partial pressure of oxygen with oxygen saturation. Partial pressure refers to the pressure exerted on the container walls by a specific gas in a mixture of other

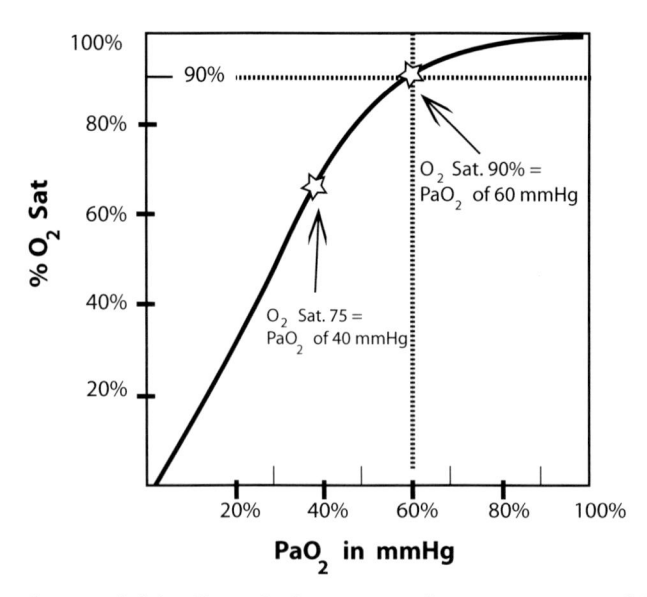

Fig. 1-29. Oxygen-hemoglobin dissociation curve shows % oxygen binding to Hgb per mmHg P_aO_2. An O_2 Sat of 90% corresponds to PaO_2 of 60 mmHg. Note how quickly Hgb loses oxygen below 90% sat.

gases. When dealing with gases dissolved in liquids like oxygen in blood, partial pressure is the pressure that the dissolved gas would have if the blood were allowed to equilibrate with a volume of gas in a container. In other words, if a gas like oxygen is present in an air space like the lungs and also dissolved in a liquid like blood, and the air space and liquid are in contact with each other, the two partial pressures will equalize.

To see why this is relevant, look at the oxygen-hemoglobin dissociation curve (Fig. 1-29, Mov. 1-7, KF. 1-7abc). As the partial pressure of oxygen rises, there are more and more oxygen molecules available to bind with Hgb. As each of the four binding sites on an Hgb molecule binds to an oxygen molecule, its attraction to the next oxygen molecule increases and continues to increase as successive molecules of oxygen bind. The more oxygen is bound, the easier it is for the next oxygen molecule to bind, so the speed of binding increases and the oxygen saturation percentage rises rapidly on the curve. As all of the binding sites fill up, very little additional binding occurs and the curve levels out as the hemoglobin becomes saturated with oxygen. This tendency makes it easy for Hgb to rapidly pick up oxygen in the lungs as it passes through.

As P_aO_2 falls, the Hgb saturation also falls as Hgb releases oxygen to the tissues in the areas of lower oxygen supply. Notice that around a saturation of 90%, that the dissociation curve drops off quickly. This is because Hgb binding sites become less attracted to oxygen as it is bound to fewer oxygen molecules. This property allows Hgb to rapidly release oxygen to the tissues.

Deoxygenated blood returns to the heart to be pumped to the lungs and the cycle repeats.

Since a normal P_aO_2 is between 90-100 mmHg, some people may think that an O_2 saturation of 90 is normal as well — after all 90 was a pretty good grade to get in school. However, this interpretation is very wrong.

An O_2 sat of 90% corresponds to a P_aO_2 of 60 mmHg. This is the minimum oxygen

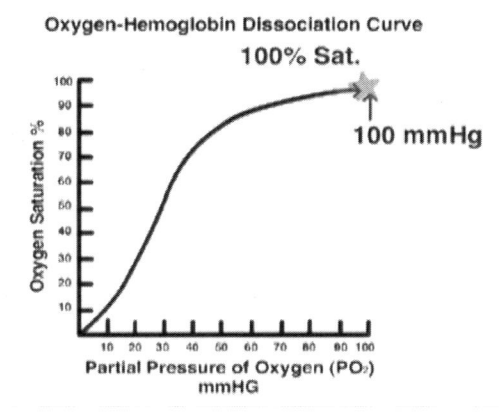

Keyframe 1-7a. Oxygen-hemoglobin dissociation curve shows % oxygen binding to Hgb per mmHg PaO_2.

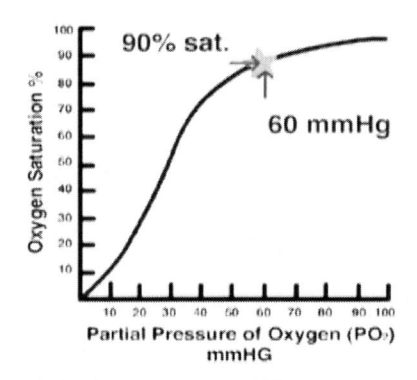

Keyframe 1-7b. An O_2 sat of 90% corresponds to PaO_2 of 60 mmHg.

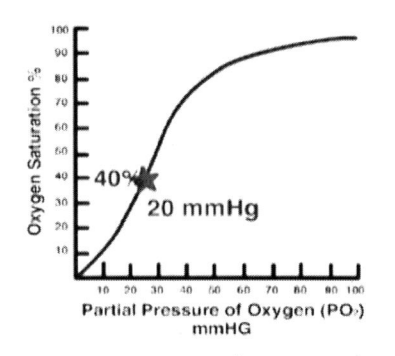

Keyframe 1-7c. Note how quickly Hgb loses O_2 below 90% sat.

concentration providing enough oxygen to prevent ischemia in tissues. Once the O_2 sat falls below 90%, the P_aO_2 drops quickly into the dangerously hypoxic range as fewer and fewer oxygen molecules are bound to Hgb. We want to try to keep O_2 saturation above 90%.

Is an O_2 sat of 100% always normal? No, it's not. Let's go back to our example of the patient breathing 50% FiO_2 who has a P_aO_2 of 100. We know that his P_aO_2 should be 250 and that therefore something is wrong. But if you look at the Oxygen-Hemoglobin Dissociation Curve, a P_aO_2 of 100 and 250 *both* have an O_2 sat of 100% because both provide enough oxygen molecules to fill all of the Hgb binding sites. So in this case O_2 saturation doesn't help us very much.

Another potential problem with O_2 sat involves carbon monoxide (CO) exposure. Carbon monoxide also binds to hemoglobin but the oxygen saturation monitor can't tell the difference between CO and O_2. The presence of CO fools the monitor into reading high. The patient with CO poisoning appears flushed and pink. However, CO can't provide oxygen to tissues and P_aO_2 may be very low.

If O_2 sat can miss potential problems of this magnitude, why use it instead of P_aO_2? Oxygen saturation has become a standard of care because it's measured using a noninvasive sensor placed on the skin. The monitor is small, portable for use in the field, operating rooms, and in patient hospital rooms to provide continuous, real time monitoring of the patient. It's a trending tool to ensure saturation stays above 90%.

Measurement of P_aO_2 requires drawing and testing an arterial blood sample —something that requires a trained provider, a lab, and time. While it's extremely useful in the hospital setting, you're not always going to have it in an emergency.

Breathing 80 - 100% oxygen for more than 24-48 hours is toxic to the lungs and can cause pulmonary congestion and edema. An FiO_2 less than 40 - 50% even for prolonged periods appears to be safe. When giving supplemental oxygen over a longer period of time, we try to keep the FiO_2 as low as possible while still providing an adequate O_2 sat. *However, the concern for oxygen toxicity should never interfere with the acute stabilization of the patient.*

How Does Severe Anemia Increase The Risk Of Tissue Ischemia?

Blood passing through the pulmonary capillaries picks up oxygen in 2 forms: oxygen bound to hemoglobin and oxygen dissolved in the serum. The vast majority is bound to hemoglobin (Hgb).

You can calculate the amount of oxygen content in the blood with the following formula.

O_2 *content (ml/100 ml blood) = O_2 bound to Hgb + O_2 dissolved*

O_2 *content = (Hgb x % sat x 1.39) + (P_aO_2 x 0.003)*

If the Hgb is 12 (a normal value corresponding to a Hct of about 36) and the O_2 sat is 100%, then the amount of oxygen bound to Hgb will be:

O_2 *bound to Hgb = 12 x 100/100 x 1.39 = 16.68 ml/100 ml blood*

By contrast, a patient with a normal P_aO_2 of 100 has only 0.3 ml of oxygen dissolved in 100 ml of serum.

O_2 *dissolved = 100 mmHg X 0.003 = 0.3 ml/100 ml blood*

The total oxygen content per 100 ml in our example is 16.68 + 0.3 = 16.98 ml. The concentration of Hgb is critical. If the Hgb in a trauma patient is only 5 (Hct of about 15), then the oxygen content will fall critically, even if the P_aO_2 stays 100:

O_2 *content = (5 x 100/100 x 1.39) + (100 x 0.003)*

O_2 *content = 7.25 ml/100 ml blood or a decrease of more than half.*

This is the same O_2 content as a patient with a Hgb of 12, but with an O_2 sat of 43%. As you can see, the development of severe anemia, from any cause, places the patient at risk for poor tissue oxygenation, even if lungs perform well and the Hgb is fully saturated. This is one reason why trauma patients need aggressive respiratory monitoring and oxygen support.

How Can The Body Improve Oxygen Delivery?

Increase Cardiac Output

In addition to the amount of oxygen bound to Hgb, the amount of oxygen delivered to tissues depends on cardiac output (CO). Normal ventilation and blood oxygen content won't help the patient if the heart can't deliver the oxygen.

$$O_2 \text{ Delivery} = CO \times (\text{blood } O_2 \text{ content})$$

An average adult with a Hgb of 15 has blood carrying about 20 ml of oxygen per 100 ml blood or 200 ml of oxygen per liter. With the normal adult cardiac output of 5 liters per minute, this means that 1,000 ml of oxygen is delivered per minute (5L/min blood X 200 ml oxygen/liter) or about 520-570 ml/min/m². At rest, the typical adult oxygen consumption is 250 ml to 300 ml/minute/m². The remaining unused oxygen is not wasted: it represents the oxygen reserves, waiting for when our adult must run for the bus or carry groceries up 4 flights of stairs to their apartment. It's also available for when the patient gets sick.

The body can augment oxygen delivery even more by increasing cardiac output, respiratory rate and tidal volume. For example, an elite athlete can increase cardiac output to 15 L/min., potentially tripling O_2 delivery.

This delivery comes at a cost, however, because the heart and muscles of respiration use more energy to supply it. An injured or ill athlete has a lot of cardiorespiratory reserve to improve oxygen transport. A patient with heart disease or severe end stage lung disease may not be able to maintain even a modest increase in heart rate or stoke volume for long without compromising oxygen flow to the heart — causing ischemia or heart failure.

When the heart rate drops lower than 60 beats per minute, or bradycardia, it also lowers cardiac output. A patient with low oxygen content for any reason might not tolerate bradycardia because the lowered cardiac output can worsen hypoxemia. The combination of low oxygen content and decreased cardiac output can be rapidly fatal. You must guard against it and treat it when it occurs.

Increase Hemoglobin Concentration

Increasing Hgb concentration is another compensatory mechanism to improve oxygen delivery. Patients living at high altitude or those with chronic respiratory failure often develop higher RBC counts. These patients depend on higher levels of Hgb and will develop organ ischemia more readily if their Hgb is allowed to drop significantly — *even if it drops to what would be a normal value at sea level.* Thus, the question of what represents an acceptable Hgb really depends on the patient's clinical status, athletic endurance, and geographic location. The decision of when to transfuse will thus vary from patient to patient and the clinical situation.

Cause Hemoglobin to Release Oxygen More Easily

Changes in body chemistry effect how easily the hemoglobin releases, or dissociates, from the oxygen molecules. Conditions that cause Hgb to release oxygen more easily are:

- increased production of the enzyme 2-3 DPG in blood cells. This occurs with chronic hypoxia, chronic anemia, and living at high altitude.
- elevated body temperature
- metabolic acidosis
- increased P_aCO_2 (respiratory acidosis)

These conditions are usually associated with increased oxygen requirements, so having Hgb release oxygen more easily is a benefit. When Hgb releases oxygen more easily, the oxygen-hemoglobin dissociation curve shifts to the right (Fig 1-30). If you read this graph for a P_aO_2 of 60 mmHg, the baseline curve shows about 90% of the Hgb binding sites are saturated with O_2. On the right shifted curve, however, Hgb is only 80% saturated at 60 mmHg, which means that the Hgb has released 15% more O_2 to the tissues at the same P_aO_2.

Low $PaCO_2$, and a higher pH (both of which can result from hyperventilation), as well as hypothermia cause the curve to shift to the left, meaning that Hgb holds on to oxygen more strongly. This is a potentially harmful disadvantage to an hypoxic patient. In Fig. 1-30, the Hgb is still 90% saturated at a PaO_2 60 mmHg.

Fetal hemoglobin also has a left shifted curve and binds more strongly to oxygen. This makes sense because the fetus must take its oxygen from the mother's circulation across the placenta and so must bind oxygen more efficiently than the mother. Newborns, who have a significant percentage of fetal hemoglobin during the first few months of life have less reserve if they become hypoxic because their fetal Hgb can't let go of oxygen as easily.

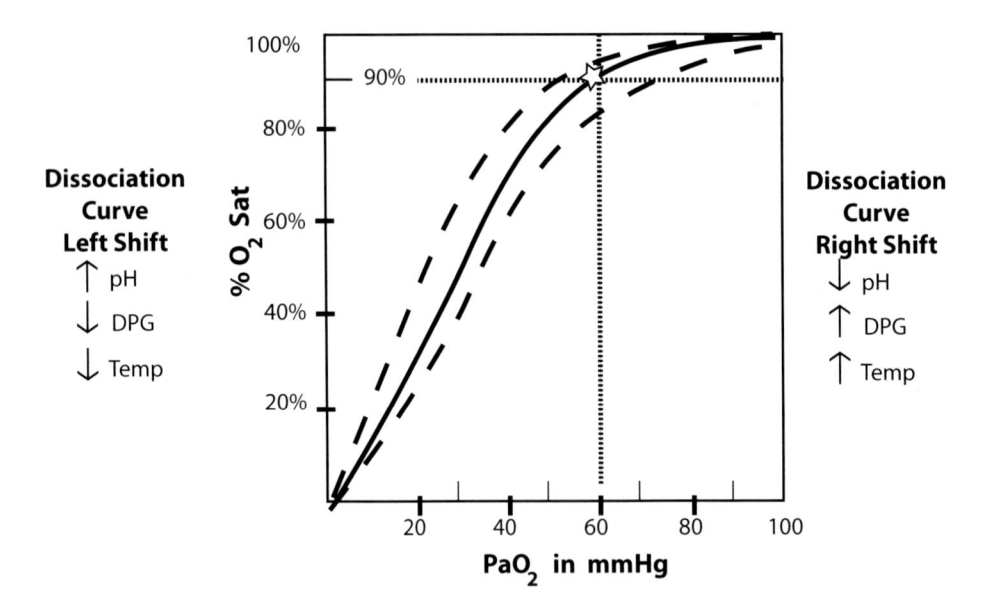

Fig. 1-30. The relationship between Hemoglobin's oxygen binding and P_aO_2 can change depending on conditions surrounding the RBC. Physiologic changes shift the curve right or left. A right shift makes oxygen release easier.

Anatomy and Physiology 45

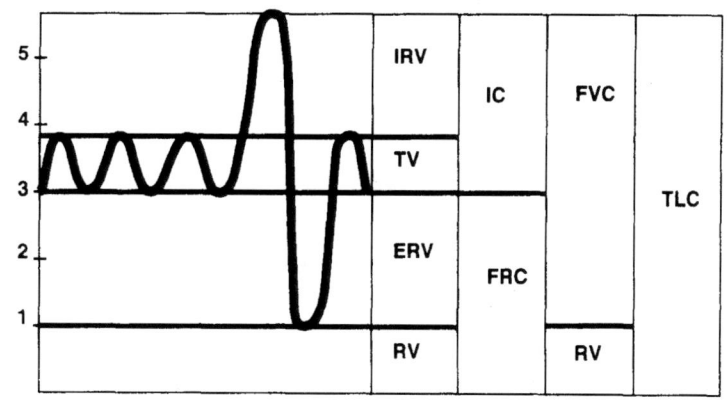

Fig. 1-31. Typical lung volumes and capacities in a 20 year old male.

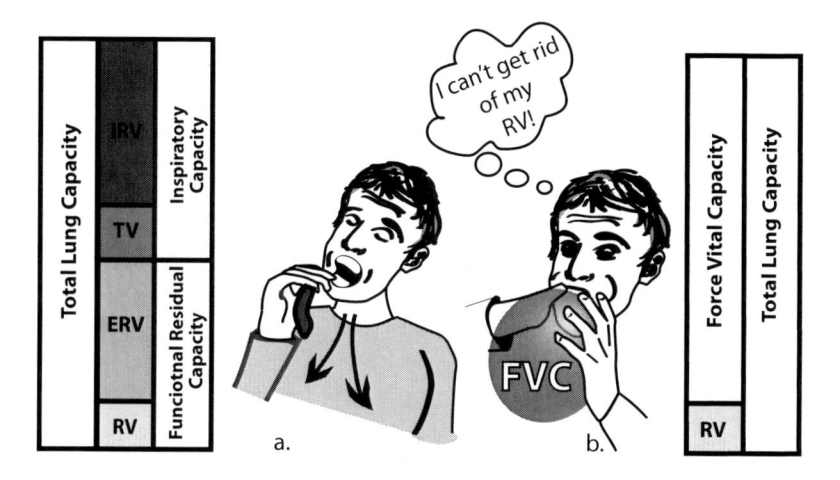

Fig. 1-32. a,b. An example of day to day use of lung volumes. (a) In preparation for blowing up the balloon, our young man takes a maximal breath, filling his Inspiratory Capacity (IC). His Total Lung Capacity (TLC) is now full. (b) The amount of air in the balloon after one maximal exhalation represents his Forced Vital Capacity (FVC). The air remaining in his lungs, no matter how hard he continues to blow, is his Reserve Volume (RV).

Lung Volumes

Measures used to determine lung function include volumes and capacities. Volumes and capacities are measured using pulmonary function tests, studies that are useful in the management of patients with acute and chronic pulmonary problems.

The important respiratory volumes are:

Tidal Volume (TV): the amount of air moved into and out of the lung during normal quiet breathing.

Inspiratory Reserve Volume (IRV): the maximum amount of air that can be inhaled after a normal inhalation.

Expiratory Reserve Volume (ERV): the maximum amount of air which can be exhaled after a normal exhalation.

Reserve Volume (RV): the amount of air remaining in the lungs after exhaling as much as possible. The lungs never completely deflate.

Lung capacities are combinations of volumes:

Total Lung Capacity (TLC): the total volume of the lungs when they are maximally inflated. TLC = IRV + TV + ERV + RV

Forced Vital Capacity (FVC): the volume of air that a patient can exhale after a maximal inhalation. FVC= IRV + ERV + TV

Functional Residual Capacity (FRC): the amount of air left in the lung after a normal exhalation. FRC = ERV + RV

Inspiratory Capacity (1C): the amount of air that can be inhaled after a normal exhalation. 1C = TV + IRV

Vital Capacity (VC): the total lung volume minus the residual volume, representing the patient's maximum breathing ability.

The relationships between these volumes and capacities are shown in Fig. 1-31 and 1-32.

A full discussion of pulmonary function testing is beyond the scope of this book. We'll concentrate on those volumes which will give you greater understanding of how to ventilate a patient.

Functional Residual Capacity

Functional Residual Capacity, or FRC, is an important concept. FRC represents the combined gas volumes providing most of the normal functional lung oxygen exchange. Think of it as the patient's oxygen tank. The larger the FRC, the bigger the "tank". A small child, who has a smaller FRC than an adult, can't hold his breath as long without getting hypoxic because he has a smaller "tank".

Position also changes FRC. An awake adult who lies supine loses about a liter of FRC as the abdominal contents push the diaphragms upward by about 4 cm. The diaphragms become more concave in the process. During spontaneous ventilation, this more concave shape allows the diaphragms to contract more forcefully, producing a larger tidal volume. The patient naturally takes a deeper breath as the result.

The patient with marginal respiratory reserve or morbid obesity may feel short of breath in the supine position because he can't compensate for the decreased FRC as well: too much weight pushing up from below the diaphragm.

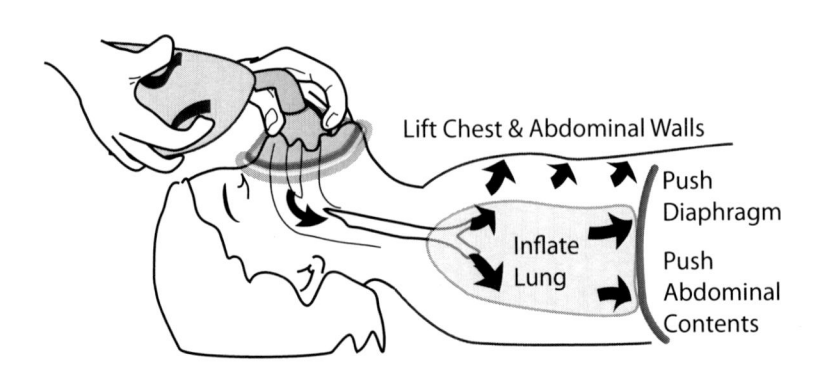

Fig. 1-33. Manual ventilation must compensate for a diaphragm resting higher in the chest, the weight of the chest wall and abdominal contents, and the compliance of the lungs.

Induction of anesthesia, and presumably unconsciousness, causes the diaphragm to move still higher, further decreasing FRC by approximately 0.4 liters. If the patient is spontaneously ventilating, hypoventilation can occur.

How Does Manual Ventilation Effect Ventilation?

First, you have to use pressure to inflate the lungs themselves. If the patient's lungs are stiffer, as often occurs in bronchospasm and pneumonia, overcoming this decreased lung compliance to provide an adequate tidal volume becomes more challenging.

In addition, when you squeeze the bag, the fact that the diaphragms in the supine patient are higher acts as a disadvantage. You must now use enough pressure to force the diaphragms, and the abdominal contents underneath them, down and out of the way. You also have to lift the chest wall (Fig 1-33). If the patient is obese the weight of the abdominal wall and contents further hinders ventilation.

If ventilation is difficult and vital signs allow, placing the patient 30-45 degrees head up will drop the abdominal contents away from the diaphragm and make lung inflation easier. This can be especially helpful in the morbidly obese patient.

Assisting a patient who is breathing spontaneously is easier because as the diaphragm continues to contract, it starts lung inflation and pushes the abdominal contents down. The intercostal muscles contract, expanding the chest wall. Your manual breath is simply making the patient's spontaneous breath bigger and deeper. During assisted ventilation, it's important to time your manual breath with the patient's inhalation to take advantage of this situation. Squeeze the bag just as the patient starts to inhale and the airway opens. After a few breaths you'll fall into the rhythm.

Squeezing the bag while the patient is exhaling means that your inflation pressure must not only overcome the diaphragm, but also reverse the passive outflow of air, the elastic recoil of the lungs, and the rebound of the chest wall combined. The vocal cords may be closed. Ventilating out of synch with the patient won't be as effective. The breath you deliver will take the path of least resistance to enter the stomach or escape from the mask. It often makes the patient cough.

Tidal Volume: Why Size Matters

Tidal volume (TV) is another important concept. The tidal volume is the volume of a normal breath of a person at rest. The average tidal volume is 7-8 ml/kg, for both children and adults. A deep breath usually equals 10 ml/kg and a maximal breath of 15 ml/kg.

It's important to know the appropriate size of a patient's tidal volume. An infant weighing 3 kg has a 21 ml tidal volume. A 70 kg adult has a 490 ml tidal volume. Giving an adult sized tidal volume to a small child can over pressurize the lungs, "pop" alveoli, and cause a collapsed lung, or pneumothorax.

The tidal volume numbers noted above are for *ideal body weight*. A 152 cm (5'0") obese woman who weighs 120 kg (260 lb.) probably won't tolerate a tidal volume of 1.2 liter (10ml/kg X 120 kg) without the risk of pneumothorax. This patient's expected *maximum* tidal volume of 15 ml/kg, for an ideal body weight of 45 kg (99 lb.), would normally be 675 ml. On the other hand, due to her obesity or clinical status, she may require more ventilation than an average adult. The way to compensate for this patient is to increase the respiratory rate, not to greatly increase the tidal volume. Pay attention to the amount of pressure you need to deliver the breath and use the least amount that can be effective.

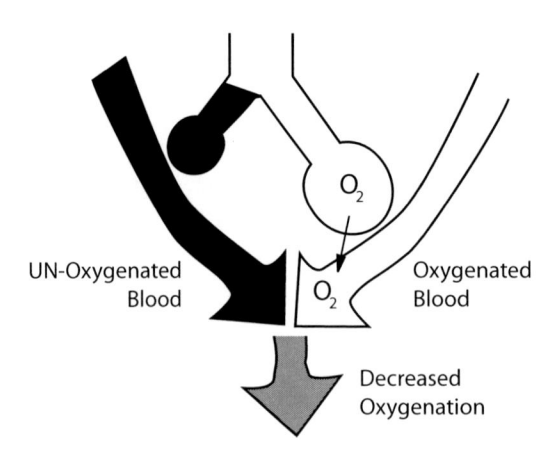

Fig. 1-34. In pulmonary shunt, the alveoli are perfused but not ventilated.

Too small a tidal volume places the patient at risk for hypoventilation. When a patient hypoventilates, many of the alveoli tend to remain collapsed, a condition called atelectasis. Atelectasis is a type of shunt, which is our next topic.

Ventilation and Perfusion

What Is Shunt?

Pulmonary shunt is a region of lung where blood flows past *un*ventilated alveoli, leaving the blood *un*-oxygenated. This un-oxygenated blood returns to the heart and mixes with oxygenated blood coming from other areas of the lungs that are ventilated. The mixture lowers the total oxygen content of the arterial blood, producing hypoxemia. The larger the shunt, the lower the oxygen content (Fig 1-34).

Giving a patient with an intrapulmonary shunt 100% oxygen to breathe won't increase the P_aO_2 much, if at all, depending on the size of the shunt because the alveoli that are being ventilated are already filled with oxygen and the non-ventilated alveoli won't pick up any more.

Common causes of shunt are pneumonia, pulmonary edema, tissue trauma, and atelectasis. Pneumonia and pulmonary edema cause shunting because some alveoli are at least partially filled with fluid. Lung tissue trauma allows fluid to leak into alveoli and promotes alveolar wall swelling, interfering with gas diffusion.

Atelectasis, the presence of collapsed alveoli, can occur either because the alveoli failed to expand or because the air was absorbed out of the alveoli without replacing it. To prevent atelectasis, the average person takes a deep breath, called a sigh, several times an hour, often without even being aware of it. Patients who take very shallow breaths without sighing often develop atelectasis.

Less common anatomic causes of pulmonary shunt include pulmonary arteriovenous fistulas and defects in the heart that allow mixing of oxygenated and un-oxygenated blood through the walls dividing the chambers.

When manually ventilating a patient, either with a ventilation bag or a ventilator, it's important to give appropriate tidal volumes and to provide several "sighs" an hour to periodically maximally expand all alveoli.

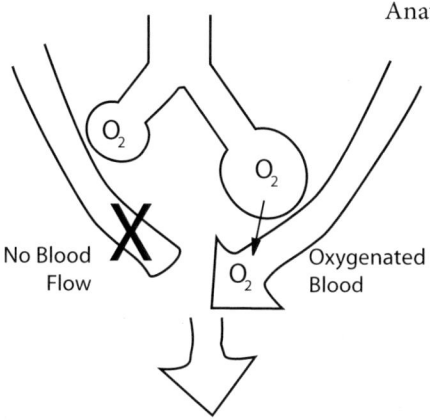

Fig. 1-35. Dead space is the portion of tidal volume that doesn't participate in gas exchange and is therefore wasted.

Factors that can cause atelectasis to develop are:
- painful breathing from surgery or trauma
- depressed levels of consciousness such as from drugs or injury
- the disease process itself
- breathing 100% oxygen

How can breathing 100% oxygen cause some of the alveoli to collapse? Normally, the presence of nitrogen in the alveoli helps to hold the alveoli open in the event that the alveolus is only ventilated now and then. With 100% oxygen, all of the oxygen may be easily absorbed, leaving an empty alveolus. A partially inflated alveolus is easier to inflate than a deflated alveolus – just as a partially inflated balloon is easier to inflate than a flat one. Once flat they tend to stay flat.

What Is Dead Space and Why Is It Important?

Dead space is the opposite of shunt. Dead space is the portion of the lung where tidal volume doesn't participate in gas exchange and is therefore essentially wasted (Fig 1-35). About a third of each normal breath we take is dead space. Why is this?

There are 2 types of dead space: anatomic and physiologic. Anatomic dead space consists of the conducting airways such as the trachea, bronchi, and bronchioles –structures that don't have alveoli. It's called anatomic because it's fixed by anatomy and doesn't change. It's roughly equal in milliliters to the patient's ideal body weight in pounds, or about twice the body weight in kg. Thus a patient weighing 81 kg (180 lb.) will have a dead space of about 180 ml. Give this 81 kg patient a tidal volume of 150 ml and you won't ventilate his alveoli very well at all. The patient will become hypercarbic and possibly hypoxic.

Physiologic dead space consists of alveoli which are ventilated but without capillary blood flow to pick up O_2 and drop off CO_2. In other words, they are not perfused. Many things can prevent this perfusion.

Physiologic dead space can increase or decrease depending upon the status and pathology of the patient. For example, when pulmonary emboli obstruct blood flow to certain sections of the lung, it increases physiologic dead space because the embolus acts as a plug and blocks blood flow. Tumor or mass effect increase dead space because the mass compresses blood vessels and impedes flow. Dead space also increases in patients with emphysema, where the number of available capillaries is decreased due to enlargement of the alveoli themselves.

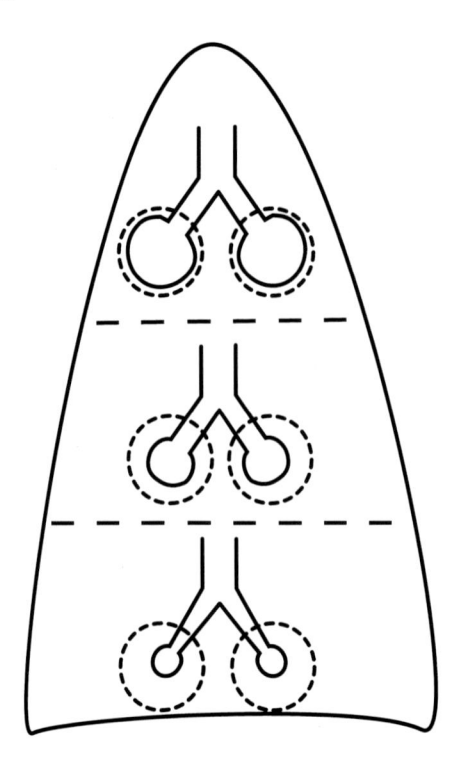

Fig. 1-36. Tissue compression due to gravity causes the dependent (lowest) alveoli to be smaller than the non-dependent (highest) alveoli. Red dashed circles show fully inflated alveoli. Although the force of gravity makes them smaller at the start, the alveoli at the base expand more during ventilation and participate in greater gas exchange.

Hypovolemia and shock also increase physiologic dead space. Decreased cardiac output throughout the lungs causes a redistribution of blood flow. Some of the capillary beds don't get perfused because the pressure in the alveoli becomes greater than the pressure in the arteries, pinching them shut. When we treat shock, we improve perfusion to these areas of the lung and decrease dead space, thereby improving oxygenation.

A patient with significantly increased dead space will either need a higher FiO_2, a larger tidal volume, and/or a faster respiratory rate to treat any hypoxemia, as well as optimized cardiac output.

V/Q Mismatch: Blood Flow, Gas Flow And Gravity

In the above discussions, we have seen that efficient oxygenation and elimination of CO_2 depends on adequate blood flow past ventilated alveoli. When the proper balance is lost, ventilation/perfusion mismatch is said to exist. The ventilation/perfusion ratio is often abbreviated V/Q.

Alveoli that are ventilated, but not perfused, contribute to dead space. Alveoli that are perfused, but not ventilated, contribute to shunt. Either can lead to hypoxemia and hypercarbia.

Ventilation and Gravity

Dependent means the lowest part, or the area where gravity has the most effect. It's important to remember that dependent is a relative term. If the patient is sitting or standing,

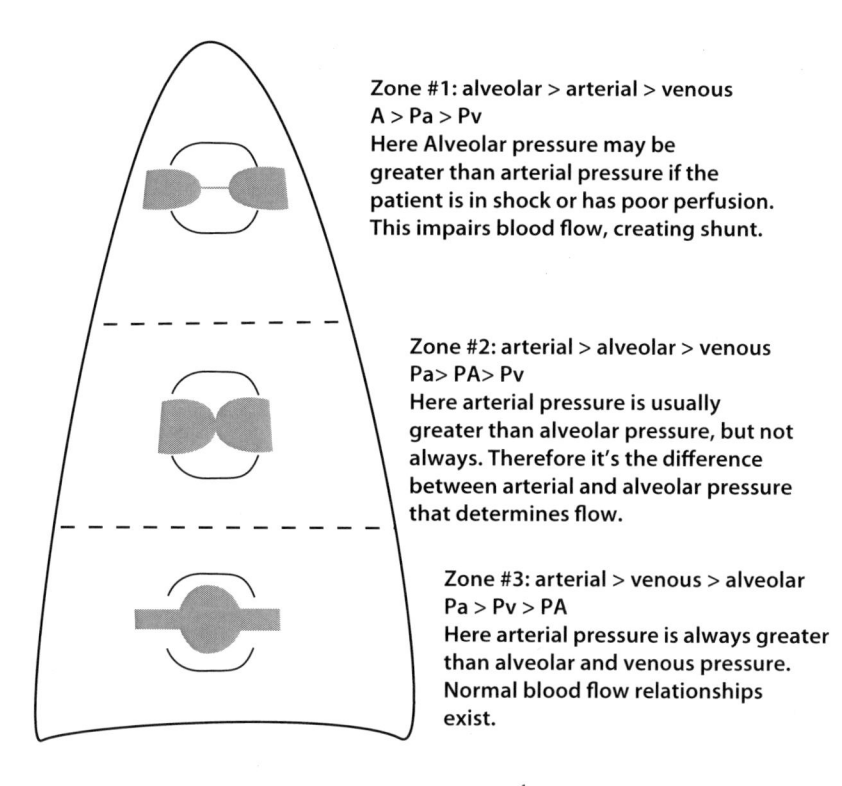

Zone #1: alveolar > arterial > venous
A > Pa > Pv
Here Alveolar pressure may be greater than arterial pressure if the patient is in shock or has poor perfusion. This impairs blood flow, creating shunt.

Zone #2: arterial > alveolar > venous
Pa > PA > Pv
Here arterial pressure is usually greater than alveolar pressure, but not always. Therefore it's the difference between arterial and alveolar pressure that determines flow.

Zone #3: arterial > venous > alveolar
Pa > Pv > PA
Here arterial pressure is always greater than alveolar and venous pressure. Normal blood flow relationships exist.

Fig. 1-37 Zones of the lung as described by West.[1] The ventilation/perfusion ratio is higher in Zone #1 (the apex of the lung when a person is sitting or standing) than it is in Zone #3 (the base of the lung). Note that if the patient is lying down, the distribution of Zones changes.
Pa = pulmonary artery pressure
PA = intra-alveolar pressure
Pv = pulmonary venous pressure

dependent means the base of the lungs. If the patient is on the side, dependent refers to the lung that is on the down side.

Because gravity causes the lung to sag toward the bottom of the chest cavity, the more dependent part of the lung is more dense than the upper. The alveoli there are smaller at rest. The alveoli at the upper parts of the lung are about four times more inflated. Picture each alveolus as a balloon. During inspiration, the smaller, dependent alveoli will be able to accept more air and grow bigger than the already nearly full upper alveoli. The dependent alveoli will have more air exchange and will therefore be better ventilated. The larger and already filled alveoli in the non-dependent areas, although more inflated, won't exchange air much at all and will not participate as much in respiration (Fig. 1-36).

Perfusion and Gravity

Distribution of blood flow in the lungs is controlled by 3 factors: pulmonary artery pressure (Pa) compared to intra-pulmonary air pressure (PA); and gravity. In the upright lung, as the right ventricle beats, it sends blood into the pulmonary arteries where it then flows into the pulmonary vascular bed. As it rises, gravity slows its ascent and kinetic energy is lost. Pulmonary arterial pressure (Pa) decreases about 1 cm H_2O per cm vertical lung distance it climbs. Ultimately Pa becomes zero (atmospheric) and then negative (sub-atmospheric) the higher one goes. On the other hand, the *pressure* inside the alveoli (PA) remains constant, independent of lung location and gravity. Three different lung zones exist because of these effects (Fig 1-37).

Zone 1 can be found in the uppermost regions of the lung. Here, the capillaries are poorly perfused. Because alveolar air pressure is often higher than pulmonary arterial pressure the capillaries can collapse. In normal lungs this rarely occurs. Zone 1 appears or increases in hypotension and shock, because pulmonary arterial pressure critically decreases compared to pulmonary alveolar gas pressure. Increased alveolar pressure, such as from positive pressure ventilation, also increases Zone 1. In fact, for the patient in shock, providing high pressure ventilation can worsen hypotension because alveolar filling pressure impairs capillary flow (by collapsing capillaries) and interferes with venous return from the lungs. If the patient in shock is on a ventilator, switching to manual ventilation will often decrease pulmonary filling pressure and will help raise blood pressure.

Zone 2 lies in the middle lung regions. Here Pa is above PA only some of the time. Perfusion is driven by the difference between arterial pressure and the alveolar pressure (Ppa - PA), instead of the usual difference between arterial and venous pressures.

In *Zone 3*, near the bottom of the lungs, perfusion is controlled by conventional arterial/venous pressure differences because arterial and venous pressures are always higher than intra-alveolar pressures. The lower in the lung one goes, the higher Pa becomes and the better the perfusion.

Near the top of the lung the alveoli are slightly over-ventilated and near the bottom of the lung the alveoli are slightly over-perfused. For the most part in the normal lung V/Q is fairly well matched.

For example, when an awake patient lies on her side, the abdominal contents push the lower, dependent diaphragm higher into the chest cavity than the upper diaphragm. The dependent diaphragm is more concave as the result, and the upper is flatter. In addition, the alveoli in the dependent lung are smaller, and therefore have more room to expand than the more fully inflated upper alveoli. Thus, when the dependent diaphragm contracts, the dependent lung expands more than the upper lung. Because of gravity, blood flow to the dependent lung is also greater. Ventilation/perfusion remain matched.

If the patient loses consciousness, her FRC decreases further. Her dependent alveoli lose volume and are harder to inflate. This is similar to a deflated balloon that requires significant opening pressure to start the inflation process.

What happens when this patient must be manually ventilated on her side? The more concave dependent diaphragm is a liability to push out of the way. In addition, the heart and mediastinum is resting on the dependent lung as a passive weight impeding inflation. Ventilation is more likely to go to the upper lung. Perfusion is still preferentially pulled by gravity to the dependent lung. V/Q mismatch appears. Depending on the patient's condition, this may or may not be clinically significant.

Avoiding the need for high pulmonary filling pressures when possible and maintaining adequate blood flow are essential to minimizing V/Q mismatch. If high filling pressures are needed, you may need to ensure higher blood pressures or cardiac output to compensate.

The body has one more mechanism to prevent V/Q mismatch: hypoxic pulmonary vasoconstriction. The typical physiologic response to hypoxia is to dilate arteries to improve oxygen delivery. Hypoxic pulmonary vasoconstriction paradoxically constricts pulmonary arteries in the presence of hypoxia, thereby redirecting blood flow to alveoli with higher oxygen content. This improves gas exchange and increases blood oxygen content.

However, several factors inhibit hypoxic pulmonary vasoconstriction including hypocarbia (low CO_2), acidosis, alkalosis, increased pulmonary pressures, hypothermia, inhaled anesthetics, nitrous oxide, calcium channel blockers, and vasodilator drugs.

Some Key Points:

Knowledge of anatomy and physiology gives you the power to influence oxygen delivery, ventilation, and perfusion in powerful ways.

1. Know the anatomy and movements of the larynx and lungs in detail. The larynx is particularly challenging to get to know, as it has a complex structure and carries out several complicated functions. Nevertheless, this is essential knowledge for anyone who wants to intubate.
2. Pathologic processes far from the larynx, such as damage to the recurrent laryngeal nerve in the chest, can lead to laryngeal dysfunction and airway obstruction.
3. Ventilation and oxygenation are different:
   - Ventilation is the exchange of air between the lungs and the environment. It mostly changes P_aCO_2 (the arterial carbon dioxide level).
   - Oxygenation only adds O_2, changing P_aO_2 (the arterial oxygen level).
4. The majority of oxygen is carried from the lungs on red blood cells attached to a protein called hemoglobin (Hgb), which has binding sites for O_2 molecules. Only a small amount of O_2 is dissolved in blood serum.
5. Oh two sat (O_2 sat) is the percentage of Hgb binding sites to which O_2 is bound. Normal levels range from 97% to 100%.
6. An O_2 sat of 90% sounds good, but is actually quite low and potentially dangerous. Because of the way Hgb binds O_2 molecules, an O_2 sat of 90% corresponds to a P_aO_2 that is roughly half normal levels.
7. CO_2 is dissolved in the bloodstream, and helps maintain a normal acid/base level (pH = 7.35–7.45).
8. Hyperventilation lowers P_aCO_2, and makes blood less acidic, but it has its limits. Even so, it's important to remember that hyperventilation may be at least partially compensating for a metabolic acidosis.
9. Too much hyperventilation can be a bad thing. When you don't have blood gas values, err on the side of moderate hyperventilation, because providers tend to over-hyperventilate
10. Respiration is described by volumes:
    - During normal breathing, tidal volume (TV), like the tide, comes in and goes out.
    - If you're inspired to blow up a balloon, you will breathe in the inspiratory reserve volume (IRV) in addition to your normal inhalation.
    - When you expire, you will breathe out the expiratory reserve volume (ERV) in addition to your normal expiration.
    - Even then, the lungs should always have some air in them; you can't get rid of your reserve volume (RV) .

11. Lung capacities are the sums of volumes.
    - TLC is everything you have; the total lung capacity (TLC) is the total volume of the lungs when they are maximally inflated.
    - TLC = TV + IRV + ERV + RV.
    - VC is everything you can use; the vital capacity (VC) is your maximum breathing capacity.
    - VC = TLC – RV
12. Estimate the tidal volume (TV) before manually ventilating. Normal tidal volume is 7-10 ml/kg. Too large a tidal volume can over pressurize the lungs, especially in children, and can lead to serious problems.

The Keyframe (KF) sequences in this chapter are taken from video clips that are available on-line, for free, from anyonecanintubate.com at:

For Chapter 1 video clips go to:
http://bit.ly/12cAQki

All video chapter files appear on Anyone Can Intubate Portfolio at:
http://bit.ly/U7EV7f

2
ASSESSMENT

When cardiorespiratory dysfunction occurs, rapid assessment is critical. Your treatment will vary based on the cause and severity of the dysfunction. Particularly in emergency situations, assessment is as important as having good technical skills. You need to have the ability to assess your patient's status and determine what steps are needed to optimize it.

Evaluating Your Patient

A patient is said to be in ***respiratory distress*** when they have to breathe faster and work harder than normal in order to maintain adequate oxygenation.

A patient who despite extra effort and increased respiratory rate still can't maintain acceptable oxygenation or CO_2 levels is in ***respiratory failure***.

The degree of respiratory compromise can be mild, moderate or severe. It can be acute, or chronic. It's often accompanied by increased heart rate, stroke volume, respiratory rate, and tidal volume to improve oxygen delivery as much as possible (Fig. 2-1). The progression from distress to failure is a continuum. The earlier we intervene, the less likely full failure is to occur.

Early recognition and treatment of respiratory compromise is essential. When breathing room air, apnea for more than about a minute can lead to a severe lack of circulating oxygen. Permanent brain damage can occur after as little as three minutes and death will inevitably ensue after a few more minutes unless ventilation is restored. Once respiratory arrest progresses to cardiac arrest, outcome is poor.

We can almost always sense when someone is "sick", and even gauge how seriously ill the person may be. Whether we are aware of it or not we are using all of our senses to look, listen, feel, and evaluate:

- state of consciousness
- air movement and breath sounds
- effort to breathe, including rate, depth, and the mechanics of breathing
- color of skin and mucus membranes: oxygen saturation
- circulatory response

This type of global assessment can be invaluable before you have more objective data such as vital signs, lab tests and radiologic studies — especially if your patient is too young or too ill to give you a complete history. As you assess your patient, be alert for life-threatening conditions that need immediate intervention, such as:

- unresponsiveness
- complete or severe airway obstruction
- apnea, slow respiratory rate (***bradypnea***)
- potentially unsustainable work of breathing
- poor perfusion, irregular, poor, or no pulses, hypotension, bradycardia

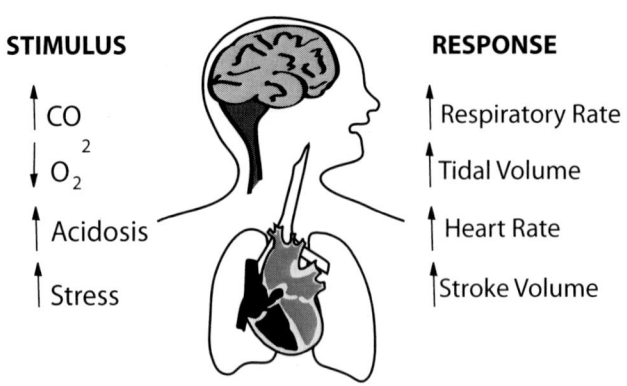

```
STIMULUS                    RESPONSE
↑ CO₂                       ↑ Respiratory Rate
↓ O₂                        ↑ Tidal Volume
↑ Acidosis                  ↑ Heart Rate
↑ Stress                    ↑ Stroke Volume
```

Fig. 2-1. The response to progressive respiratory compromise is to try to improve oxygen delivery and removal of CO_2.

Is Your Patient Conscious, Semi-conscious or Unconscious?

Many conditions effect level of consciousness. A quick scale to assess responsiveness is called the A.V.P.U. scale.

- A: Alert —fully awake but not necessarily oriented
- V: Voice — pt. responds when you talk to them, but may or may speak oriented speech. Any verbal response to you counts, even a moan
- P: Pain — patient responds to painful stimuli only. The response may or may not be purposeful, localizing the pain
- U: Unresponsive— unconscious, no response at all to any stimuli

Another tool is the Glascow Coma Scale (GCS) (Table 2-1), used in trauma assessment. Intubation is indicated for a head injury with GCS of 7 or *less*.

Patients who respond only to voice or pain, or not at all, are clearly at greater immediate risk than those who are still alert. Alert patients can tell you if they feel short of breath (*dyspneic*), any other symptoms they may be experiencing, and what happened to them.

Semi-conscious and unconscious patients can't provide this information. You are much more dependent on physical exam and other testing. These patients are at high risk of hypoventilation and therefore development of hypoxia, hypercarbia, aspiration, and further deterioration. When patients are poorly responsive, monitor carefully and reassess often. Administration of supplemental oxygen is wise, even if O_2 saturation appears normal.

Patients with altered consciousness may have a poor gag reflex and risk aspiration. Test the gag reflex by gently touching the back of the throat when suctioning.

In the conscious patient, respiratory distress often presents as air hunger. The patient appears anxious and breathes rapidly and deeply, often through an open mouth. Retractions may be present. He complains of dyspnea. He may panic as though drowning and struggle if you attempt to lay him flat.

As respiratory distress progresses to respiratory failure, however, non-specific signs of hypoxia and poor ventilation appear including restlessness, confusion, agitation, tachycardia, hypertension, or sweatiness. Eventually the patient will become lethargic and poorly responsive. It's easy to make the mistake of treating agitation and disorientation caused by hypoxia or hypercarbia with sedatives, an action which can unintentionally cause apnea. If you must sedate a patient with respiratory distress do so slowly and monitor carefully.

Table 2-1. Glasgow Coma Scale	
Eye Opening (E)	
• Spontaneous	4
• To speech	3
• To pain	2
• None	1
Best Motor Response (M)	
• Obeys	6
• Localizes	5
• Withdraws	4
• Abnormal flexion	3
• Abnormal extension	2
• None	1
Verbal (V)	
• Oriented	5
• Confused conversation	4
• Inappropriate words	3
• Incomprehensible words	2
• None	1
Coma Score = E + M + V (e.g. 3 to 15)	

Glasgow Coma Scale: Add the value for each category to obtain the total score. The higher the score, the better the status of the patient.

Is There Evidence of Airway Obstruction?

Airway obstruction can occur in conscious or unconscious patients from both upper and lower airway causes. You must be able to recognize the signs.

Does tidal volume seem adequate? Chest wall motion can be subtle, especially under clothing. You may need to expose the chest to assess movement.

How much air is moving in and out of the mouth? Watch for condensation inside the mask. Place your hand over nose or mouth. When wearing gloves, use the back of your hand or wrist to improve your ability to feel flow. If you don't feel air movement then tidal volume is inadequate. Open the airway, check again.

The signs of airway obstruction include (Mov. 2-1, KF. 2-1 a-d).

- poor movement of air in and out of the mouth and nose,
- noisy breathing, including snoring, stridor, and wheezing,
- rocking chest wall motion,
- use of accessory muscles of respiration ,
- exaggerated neck vein filling with respirations,
- rib and other retractions such as tracheal tug,
- nasal flaring,
- faint or absent breathe sounds,
- head bobbing or grunting,
- inability of the awake patient to make sounds.

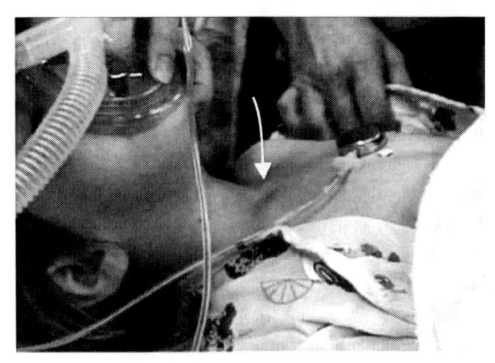

Keyframe 2-1a. Tracheal tug during airway obstruction.

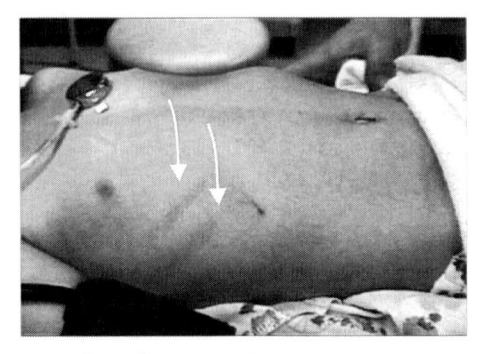

Keyframe 2-1b. Rib retractions are easier to see in thin patients.

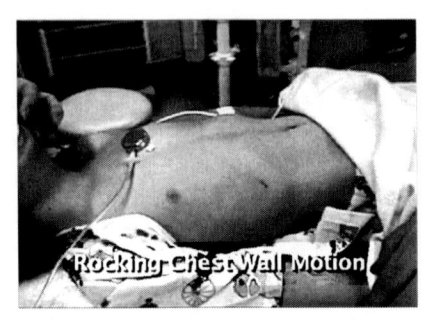

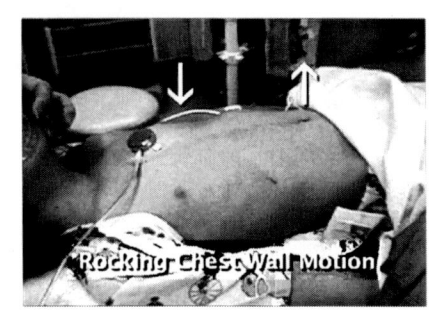

Keyframes 2-1c,d. With a rocking chest wall motion, the chest falls on inhlation and rises on exhalation, the opposite of normal breathing.

Is There Evidence of Pulmonary Dysfunction?

The sounds of breathing can often alert you to the pathologic processes. (Table 2-2). Normal breath sounds are quiet, like a gentle breeze. Noisy breathing, such as stridor, snoring, wheezing, grunting, gasping or gurgling should alert you to possible airway problems. However, when there is little air movement, you may not be able to hear any of these sounds — even if obstruction is severe. Be alert to the fact that more than one pathologic process may be present.

Table 2-2. Sounds And Breathing Mechanics Of Different Conditions

CONDITION	EXAMPLES	PATHOLOGY	SOUNDS	MECHANICS
Upper Airway Obstruction	• Foreign body aspiration • Croup • Epiglottis • Upper airway edema	• Edema of oropharyngeal and laryngeal structures either from inflammation/infection or from irritation of foreign object	• Stridor • Hoarseness • Altered voice • Inspiratory wheeze • Barking cough • Snoring	• Inspiratory retractions • Use of Accessory muscles • Nasal flaring • Mild to moderate increase RR • Flow more limited at very high rates
Lower Airway Obstruction	• Asthma • Emphysema/COPD • Bronchospasm • Mass effect	• Spasm of small airways • Edema of bronchial walls	• Expiratory wheeze • If severe, inspiratory	• Prolonged expiratory phase • Increase expiratory effort • Very rapid respiratory rate
Lung parenchymal disease	• Pneumonia • Bronchiolitis • Fluid aspiration • Chemical/physical burn • Pulmonary edema	• Alveolar collapse • Inflammatory debris in alveoli • Fluid filled alveoli	• Grunting • Rales • Crackles • Rhonchi	• Lungs stiffer and less compliant • Increased inspiratory effort • Retractions • Tachypnea • Use of accessory muscles
Neuromuscular dysfunction	Brain/brainstem injury Spinal cord injury Muscle relaxant Muscle disease such as Guillain Barre, Muscular Dystrophy	• Impaired nervous control, either peripheral or central • Impaired muscle control	Gasping breaths	Abnormal pattern: "breathing funny" Crescendo shallow to deep, gasping inspirations with a pause at full inspiration followed by a brief apnea. Hypoventilation despite deep breaths Tachypnea with shallow breaths due to muscle weakness

Listen to the chest bilaterally. Are breath sounds equal on both sides of the chest? Do both sides expand equally and symmetrically? Unequal chest breath sounds or wall motion occur in the presence of a collapsed lung (*pneumothorax*), collection of blood on one side of the chest (*hemothorax*), or an endotracheal tube inserted too deeply and ventilating only one lung (*mainstem intubation*). Pneumonia can cause unequal breath sounds. They can also occur if the patient has had part or all of a lung removed (partial or total *pneumonectomy*).

Are there rales or rhonchi? If so, where are they heard loudest? *Rales*, a crackling sound like crumpling cellophane, can occur with pneumonia or pulmonary edema. *Rhonchi* are coarse rattling sounds heard on listening to the chest, usually caused by secretion in a bronchial tube. However, don't be fooled. The absence of abnormal breath sounds may mean that little or no air exchange is occurring. Sometimes wheezing and rhonchi only become audible after airflow improves.

Mechanics: How Hard Is Your Patient Working To Breathe?

Normal quiet breathing is effortless. The rate is neither too fast nor too slow, however it varies greatly depending on age and metabolic rate (Table 2-3). The chest rises and falls easily and symmetrically.

Table 2-3. Variation Of Normal Respiratory And Heart Rate With Age

AGE	RESPIRATORY RATE (Breathes per minute)	HEART RATE (Beats per minute)
Infant (birth to 1 yr)	30-60	110-160
Toddler (1-3 yrs)	24-40	90-150
Preschooler (3-6 yrs)	22-34	80-140
School age (6-12 yrs)	18-30	70-120
Adolescent to Adult	12-16	50-100

Notice in Table 2-3 that "normal" is very different depending on the age. The youngest patients have the highest respiratory and heart rates.

Severe respiratory compromise often shares many of the same signs as airway obstruction. Assess the mechanics of breathing. When the patient is working hard to breathe, the accessory muscles of respiration — the sternocleidomastoid and scalene neck muscles — tense as though the patient is straining (Mov. 2-2, KF. 2-2a,b). These muscles lift the clavicles and allow fuller expansion of the chest.

When the patient works hard to take a breath, he generates a more negative pressure inside the chest cavity. The intercostal muscles more fully contract. Retractions, noisy breathing, and a rocking chest wall motion are common. Work of breathing increases. As respiratory failure progresses, the pattern of respiration becomes more inefficient and ineffective.

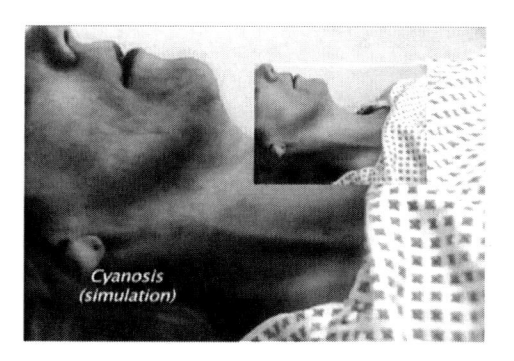

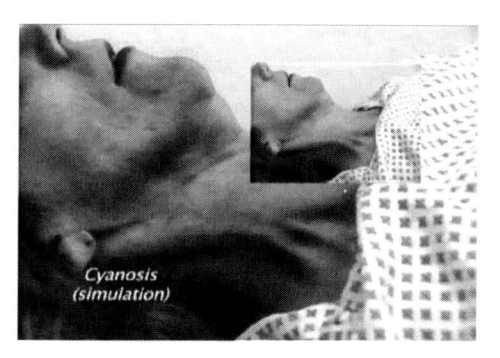

Keyframes 2-2ab. Tensing of sternocleidomastoid with simulation of cyanosis showing the contrast with normal skin color.

In the patient exhausted to the point of respiratory collapse, or in the patient with respiratory depression due to altered mental status, there may be little effort to breathe. Hypoventilation worsens hypoxia, hypercarbia, and respiratory acidosis — all of which increase sedation and further depress respiratory drive.

Allowed to progress to the extreme end point, the patient with respiratory depression can become apneic with little warning. When severe hypoxia develops you'll see slowed respirations, hypotension, cyanosis, and impaired consciousness. Bradycardia can develop. These signs often indicate that cardiac arrest is imminent. You must act immediately.

Evaluating the degree of airway obstruction or respiratory compromise is a judgment call. Mild or potential obstruction may have no signs or symptoms at all. In certain patients such as facial burn victims or patients having a severe allergic reaction, mild airway obstruction can convert to total obstruction quickly as edema forms. Constant reassessment is important so that you may intervene early if necessary — before the airway is lost.

Look At The Skin Color

While pale skin coloration can be natural, *paleness* is often a warning sign of anemia or the severe vasoconstriction that accompanies poor circulation. Patients often turn pale before they become cyanotic because circulating catecholamines cause peripheral vasoconstriction. *Skin mottling*, random patches of bluish or pale skin, may also be present if distal perfusion is poor.

Cyanosis is the bluish coloration of mucous membranes and skin due to deoxygenated hemoglobin in the blood vessels near the skin surface (Mov. 2-2, KF. 2-2a,b). Oxygenated blood is bright red. Desaturated blood (unbound to oxygen) is dark blue. Cyanosis occurs when there is at least 5g/dl of desaturated blood present. The bluish skin color associated with cyanosis is a late and sometimes unreliable sign of hypoxia. Ambient lighting and skin pigment can make it hard to see. An oxygen saturation monitor is much more reliable if you have one.

There must be at least 5g/dl of desaturated blood (unbound to oxygen) for most people to see cyanosis. You may not see it at all if the patient is severely anemic. With a normal Hgb of 18g/dl, cyanosis would be visible once saturation fell below about 72% (18g/dl − 5g/dl =13g/dl, 13/18=72%). With a Hgb of 7g/dl, then O_2 Sat would have to fall below 30% before cyanosis even appeared.

Normal oxygen saturation is 97-100% on room air, corresponding to an arterial P_aO_2

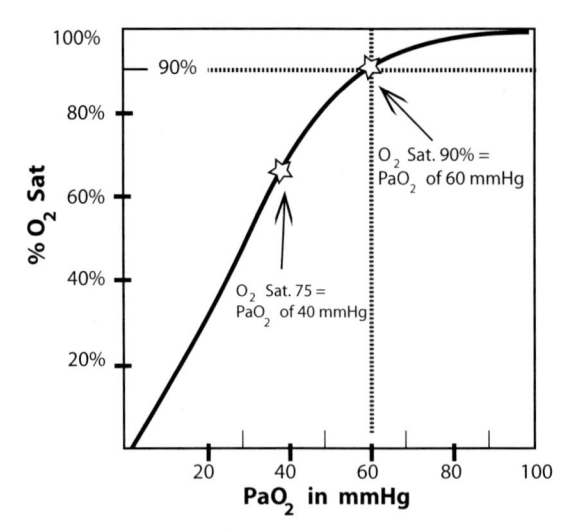

Fig 2-2. Oxygen-hemoglobin dissociation curve showing the % of oxygen binding to hemoglobin (Hgb) per each P_aO_2. Note how quickly hemoglobin loses oxygen below an O_2 saturation of 90%.

of about 100 mmHg. Be especially alert if your patient's oxygen saturation falls below 90%, corresponding to an arterial P_aO_2 of 60 mmHg. These values provide the minimum oxygen delivery to prevent metabolic acidosis. You may need to maintain a higher saturation if the patient is anemic.

It is worth noting that a patient in respiratory distress or failure can have normal oxygen saturation when receiving supplemental oxygen, but may have serious hypercarbia and respiratory acidosis from poor ventilation. Remain alert to potential hypoventilation, even when the O_2 sat is reassuring.

Warning: Carbon monoxide also binds to Hgb and causes the O_2 sat monitor to read too high. The patient will appear flushed and pink. However, carbon monoxide cannot provide oxygen to the tissues and the P_aO_2 may be quite low. For patients exposed to carbon monoxide (such as in a fire), a co-oximeter can be used to definitively assess the quantity of carbon monoxide in the blood.

Oxygen Saturation

An O_2 sat of 90% corresponds to a P_aO_2 of 60 mmHg, the minimum oxygen concentration providing enough oxygen to prevent ischemia in tissues. Once the O_2 sat falls below 90%, the P_aO_2 drops quickly into the dangerously hypoxic range. Try to keep O_2 saturation above 90%. (See Fig. 2-2) If your patient's O_2 sat is abnormally low or trending downward, evaluate why, and intervene.

Evaluate The Circulatory Response

As oxygenation falls or CO_2 rises, the body activates the sympathetic nervous system to increase cardiac output. Think of a conveyor belt carrying boxes. You can deliver the same number of boxes (our oxygen equivalent) by having lots of boxes on a slow conveyor belt or fewer boxes on a fast one.

As hypoxia progresses in adults and older children, sympathetic nervous system hyperactivity predominates and hypertension and tachycardia develop in an attempt to improve perfusion and oxygenation. Hypertension and tachycardia increase cardiac work, which for the patient with marginal cardiac reserve can increase the risk of heart attack, heart failure, and stroke. With severe oxygen deprivation, the heart muscle fails. Hypotension and bradycardia develop and cardiac arrest is likely unless hypoxia is relieved.

In infants and young children, unlike adults, bradycardia may be the first sign of hypoxia, not the last, because their sympathetic nervous system is immature. A slow heart delivers less oxygen, starting a vicious cycle. Cardiac arrest can occur within minutes. *Bradycardia in an infant or young child means hypoxia until proven otherwise — treat with oxygen and improved ventilation.*

Checking the time for capillary refill to occur after pressing on a finger nail is a quick bedside test for adequacy of perfusion, especially in children. Normal capillary refill is typically less than 2 seconds. Anything longer than 3 seconds is prolonged. Longer than 5 seconds is significantly prolonged.

Shock can precipitate hypoventilation and hypoxia and in turn can be made worse by hypoventilation and hypoxia. If the patient in shock is deteriorating, intubating the patient may help to stabilize the situation.

Early Management

There are many potential causes for respiratory failure, and they are not mutually exclusive; the patient can suffer from more than one at a time (Table 2-4). When faced with a patient in respiratory distress or failure, ask yourself:

- Will treatment rapidly improve oxygenation or ventilation?
- Can the condition causing the problem be quickly improved or reversed?
- Will respiratory insufficiency progress to failure?

Start treatment to improve ventilation while continuing to evaluate. Maneuvers to improve ventilation include stimulating the patient, opening the airway, stimulating the patient, and encouraging deep breaths. It may include intubation, but many patients treated for respiratory distress or even early failure *don't* need intubation.

Table 2-4. Causes of Respiratory Failure

PROBLEM	CAUSE
Upper Airway obstruction	Foreign body, edema, trauma, sleep apnea, tumor
Lower Airway Obstruction	Asthma, emphysema, chronic bronchitis, pneumonia, cystic fibrosis, tumor
Respiratory control center	Altered mental status due to trauma, drug intoxication, stroke, hemorrhage, infection, or tumor
Peripheral Nervous System	Spinal cord injury, stroke, polio, Guillain-Barre Syndrome
Muscle weakness	Myasthenia gravis, muscular dystrophy, drug effect
Abnormal lung tissue	Infection, tumors, radiation, burns, ARDS, collapsed lung
Abnormal chest wall	Trauma, scoliosis, extreme obesity

Table 2-5. Comparison Of Oxygen Delivery Systems

Delivery System	Oxygen %	Flow Rate (L.min)
Low Flow system		
Nasal canula	22-60%	0.25-4
Oxygen mask	35-60%	6-10
High Flow System		
Face tent	< 40%	10-15
Oxygen hood	80-90%	10-15
Oxygen tent	> 50%	>10
Partial rebreathing mask with reservoir	50-60	10-12
Non-rebreather mask with reservoir	95%	10-15
Venturi mask	25-60% mask specific	variable

Agents often used to improve respiratory status include O_2, bronchodilators for bronchospasm, diuretics for pulmonary edema, and antibiotics for infection. Naloxone can reverse narcotic induced respiratory depression. A chest tube can be curative in the presence of pneumothorax.

The supine adult loses about 1 liter of functional lung capacity, the obese or paralyzed patient even more. Just sitting a patient up, if he tolerates it, significantly improves ventilation by increasing FRC. Always give supplemental oxygen to the patient in distress. Table 2-5 shows how much oxygen you can provide using the various canulas and masks. Percent of oxygen delivered will vary depending on the size of the patient and the flow delivered. The smaller the patient and/or higher the flow, the less room air will be entrained and the higher the oxygen concentration.

Avoid agitating the patient. Provide reassurance. Panicked breathing worsens obstruction by increasing turbulence. Crying and agitation increase swelling and worsen airway obstruction. It may take time to diagnose and treat the problem. A calm patient will have a lower metabolic rate and lower oxygen needs than a patient in panic who is struggling. Leave the patient in a position of comfort during assessment if possible. You may need to leave a child in the parent's lap rather than risk potential deterioration by making the child cry and struggle.

A high respiratory rate and heart rate that decrease back toward normal may be a good sign if accompanied by improvement in oxygen saturation, level of consciousness and signs of decreased work of breathing.

However, to confuse matters, respiratory rate can also slow and effort can decline when a patient *de*compensates during respiratory failure. Tachycardia can change to bradycardia. The patient often relaxes. *Beware of the patient who appears to normalize breathing, pulse and blood pressure but whose mental and physical status, and oxygen saturation is worsening. Such a patient is in extreme peril.* Observe carefully and act quickly to prevent apnea and perhaps cardiac arrest.

What Are The Criteria For Intubation?

Intubation has advantages. The tube helps protect the airway from aspiration, permits positive pressure ventilation with 100% oxygen and allows tracheal suctioning. It avoids the gastric distention from use of bag and mask. And it maintains an open airway in the face of edema or other fixed obstruction.

The main criteria for intubation are:
- ventilatory support
- ventilation failure: e.g. cardiac arrest, stroke, paralysis
- oxygenation failure: e.g. pneumonia, pulmonary edema
- protection of the airway
- relief of airway obstruction: e.g. edema, trauma
- relief of excess work of breathing
- inability to closely monitor the patient at high risk for serious respiratory failure for further decompensation
- depressed Glasgow Coma Scale (less than 7 or 8 with head injury)
- lung isolation (prevention of bacterial contamination of clean lung: requires double lumen tube or other means of ventilating each lung separately)
- elective intubation for surgery

Need For Ventilatory Support

These criteria must be evaluated in context with the clinical situation.
- apnea
- respiratory rate significantly outside of the normal range (see Table 2-3).
- impaired alveolar ventilation (as assessed by $PaCO_2$ >55mmHg) *with*:
  - depressed mental status
  - increasing fatigue
  - reduced PaO_2 (e.g. < 60 mmHg) that:
    - cannot otherwise be improved with an FiO_2 less than 50%, *and*
    - is causing symptoms or seriously impairing function
    - severely abnormal pH that cannot otherwise be corrected
- severe head injury —hyperventilation can be used to decrease CO_2 as a way to decrease elevated intracranial pressure

The following objective criteria are often used as starting points:
- Tidal Volume <10 ml/kg
- Vital Capacity < 15 ml/kg
- O_2 sat (SpO_2) < 90% with FiO_2 >40%
- RR >35
- $PaCO_2$ > 55

Protection of the Airway

Altered consciousness may depress the gag reflex and impair the ability to protect the airway from aspiration. Trauma and shock patients are at high risk of vomiting due to gastrointestinal tract dysfunction. Securing the airway in these patients can be lifesaving.

Occasionally a patient won't be able to clear secretions from the tracheobronchial tree by coughing. For example, a patient with end-stage chronic obstructive pulmonary disease with pneumonia may need intubation to allow suctioning of the thickened secretions in order to allow the patient to recover.

Relief of Airway Obstruction

Patients suffering from facial trauma or burn injuries, or having a severe allergic reaction may have significant distortion of the airway with ongoing and worsening edema and airway obstruction. Early placement of an endotracheal tube can be lifesaving in these situations.

Excessive Work of Breathing

An exhausted patient who is laboring to breathe may develop respiratory failure. Early warning signs include:
- "tripod" positioning
- increased confusion or more difficulty in arousing the patient
- inability to maintain an open airway
- worsening pH, PO_2 or oxygen saturation.
- normalizing blood gases with *worsening* patient condition. Alert: As the patient with respiratory distress tires, he may be unable to continue to hyperventilate. Blood gases may return toward normal right before respiratory failure occurs.
- slow respiratory rate or shallow breathing in face of worsening pathology

Inability to Closely Monitor The High Risk Patient

Fortunately inability to monitor the patient closely doesn't happen very often in a high tech modern health care system, but consider these sample scenarios:
- Mass casualty situation where the number of providers skilled in advanced airway management are few.
- A COPD patient with progressive respiratory failure due to pneumonia in a small hospital where the attending MD is on call at night from home.
- A trauma victim with facial burns and early signs of airway edema who must be transported a significant distance to the hospital.

Intubation in these types of cases is a judgment call, and should be based on the patient's condition such as sign, symptoms; objective data such as blood gases and chest X-rays; and the presence of coexisting disease.

Elective Intubation For Surgery

Airway management methods for patients under *general* anesthesia include:
- spontaneous or assisted ventilation with a bag/valve/mask device

- laryngeal mask airway
- intubation

We tend to intubate a patient who is undergoing surgery who:

- requires muscle paralysis (patient can't breath on their own)
- impairs the respiratory system (airway, chest/lung or major abdominal)
- carries a high risk of blood loss or hemodynamic instability
- requires positioning during general anesthesia that would make later intubation difficult (e.g. prone or lateral)
- will undergo surgery of prolonged duration (with its increased risk of atelectasis)

In addition, we look at patient factors such as:
- high risk of aspiration (full stomach, history of reflux, pregnancy)
- abnormal airway anatomy (might make later intubation difficult)
- co-morbid conditions (severe heart or lung disease, instability)
- morbid obesity (potentially poor mechanics of spontaneous ventilation)

Managing respiratory distress or failure requires ongoing assessment of both the airway and the total patient status. Knowledge of physiology makes you better able to adapt your treatment plans in quickly changing clinical situations.

The Keyframe (KF) sequences in this chapter are taken from video clips that are available on-line, for free, from anyonecanintubate.com at:

For Chapter 2 video clips go to:
http://bit.ly/11b8zLU

All video chapter files appear on Anyone Can Intubate Portfolio at:
http://bit.ly/U7EV7f

3
ESTABLISHING AN AIRWAY

Opening an obstructed airway is a different skill from intubation, but the two are inseparable. The ability to ventilate a patient is often more important than the ability to intubate a patient and should be learned first. Intubation is merely one means of ventilating and protecting the airway. Rarely will intubation — by itself — save a life. Ventilation, on the other hand, frequently saves lives.

Let's quickly review the signs of airway obstruction:

• poor movement of air	• tracheal tug
• faint or absent breath sounds	• intercostal retractions
• use of accessory muscles of respiration	• rocking chest wall and abdominal motion
• stridor	• lack of chest rise
• cyanosis	• lack of end-tidal CO_2

Opening the Airway

Look, listen and feel for air movement. If the patient is apneic proceed immediately to ventilate with a bag and a mask. On the other hand, if the patient is breathing spontaneously, but is obstructed, try simple arousal. With the head in a relaxed and flexed position, the tongue and soft tissues tend to collapse over the larynx and cause obstruction. Stimulating the patient may improve muscle tone and respiratory effort.

If it doesn't, there are several ways to open the airway of a patient who is breathing spontaneously. The following maneuvers assume no cervical spine injuries. Most common is the head tilt/chin lift maneuver (3-1). Tilt the head backward. Place your fingertips under the rim of the mandible and lift upward, keeping pressure on the bones, not the soft tissue. Pressing on the soft tissue potentially obstructs the airway, especially in small children.

Fig. 3-1. Head tilt/chin lift maneuver. Pulling upward on the bony mandible lifts the chin and opens the airway.

Pulling the angles of the jaw upward puts tension on the base of the tongue and soft tissues and lifts the epiglottis off the trachea. Further thrust of the jaw opens the mouth and fully opens the airway. (Fig. 3-2a-d). We naturally assume this position when sniffing the air, which is why it's called the sniffing position.

a. Obstructed airway

b. Sniffing position

c. Tilt head back

d. Pull the angles of the jaw upward

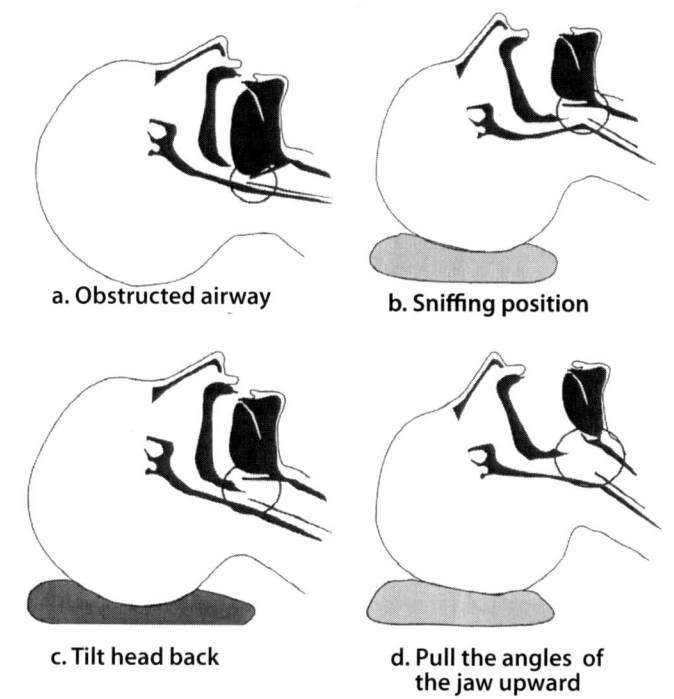

Fig. 3-2a-d. Relieving airway obstruction in cross section. Placing the head on a small pillow and pulling the jaw upward both tend to lift soft tissue away from the posterior pharyngeal wall, opening the airway. Tilting the head backward (c) and thrusting the jaw forward (d) pulls soft tissue off of the larynx, further relieving any obstruction.

To use the jaw thrust maneuver (Fig 3-3a,b), grip the angles of the mandible with both hands to pull the jaw forward. This motion frequently pulls the head into extension. If you're using cervical precautions because of potential cervical spine injury, pull upward only on the jaw, keep the head and neck stable. Pressing on the bone 1-2 cm above the angle of the jaw and below the ear is painful and may help rouse a sedated patient enough to breathe on their own.

The triple airway maneuver combines the previous techniques (Fig. 3-4, Mov. 3-1, KF 3-1abcd). Tilt the head into extension and lift the angles of the jaw. Use your thumbs to pull the mouth open.

While it's easy to pull the mandible upward by placing your thumb in the patient's mouth to grip the chin (Fig. 3-5), it's potentially dangerous because the patient may bite you.

Look, listen, and feel for evidence of good ventilation:
- The chest rises and falls appropriately with breathing
- You can hear breath sounds.
- There is good movement of air in and out of the mouth and nose.
- A clear oxygen mask fogs with each breath
- End-tidal CO_2 is present.

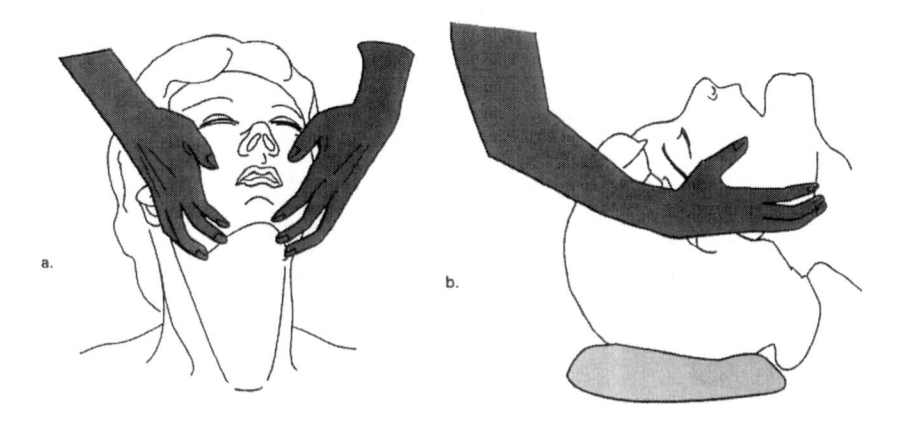

Fig. 3-3a,b. Jaw thrust with a patient. It's important to keep your fingers on the bony mandible and not the soft tissue under the chin. Pressing under the chin can sometimes worsen obstruction by pushing the tongue and soft tissue down over the larynx.

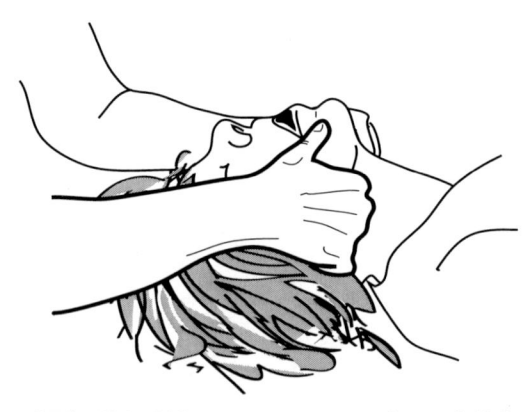

Fig. 3-4. The Head Tilt Chin Lift maneuver consists of tilting the head, jaw thrust, and opening the mouth using both hands. Look back at Fig. 3-2a-d to see how this maneuver can fully open the airway.

Fig. 3-5. It's tempting to pull the jaw open but be careful — patients can bite!

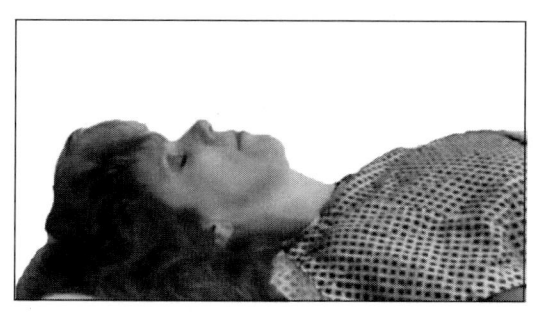

Keyframe 3-1a. Triple airway maneuver assumes you don't need to protect the cervical spine.

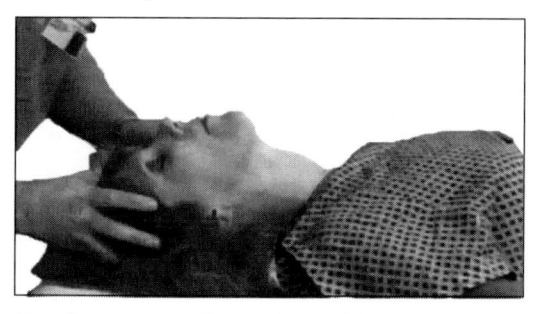

Keyframe 3-1b. Tilt head back.

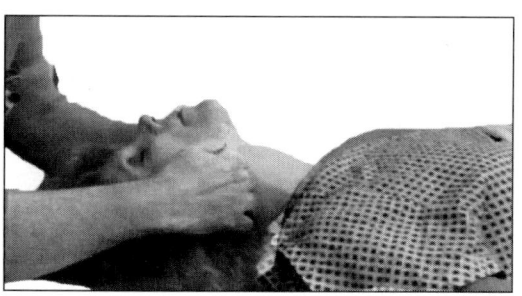

Keyframe 3-1c. Lift the jaw.

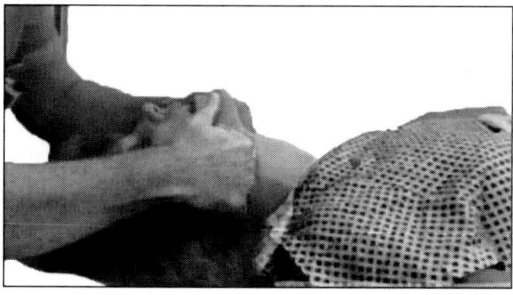

Keyframe 3-1d. Pull mouth open.

If you still have an obstructed airway, insert a nasal or an oral airway. Terminology can be confusing. Not only do we call the patient's passageway from mouth to trachea an airway, we also call the tools to establish an open breathing passage airways. Context usually makes the meaning clear.

Use of the Nasal Airway

Nasal airways, also called nasopharyngeal airways, nasal cannulas or nasal trumpets, are soft, flexible tubes which slide through one side of the nose. This position places the opening of the tube in the posterior pharynx, behind the tongue. The opening is often, though not always, in line with the trachea.

Awake patients often tolerate a nasal airway better than an oral airway because it stimulates the gag reflex less. Choose the correct size airway by measuring the device on the patient: the nasal airway should reach from the patient's nostril to the earlobe or the angle of the jaw and is usually 2-4 cm longer than the oral airway. Selecting nasal airway size based either on nostril opening or comparing it to the size of the little finger is not very accurate because the cartilage turbinates inside the nasal passages also play a role and cannot be easily seen.

Liberally coat your nasal airway with lubricating ointment or gel if available. You can also use water. Local anesthetic ointment has the advantage of numbing the nose and making the tube more easily tolerated. Slide the nasal airway into the nares and gently advance it along the floor of the nose (Fig. 3-6a,b, Mov. 3-2, KF 3-2a,b). The beginner will frequently try to thread the nasal airway up the nose toward the frontal sinus. Not only will the tube not pass in this direction, you risk a nosebleed.

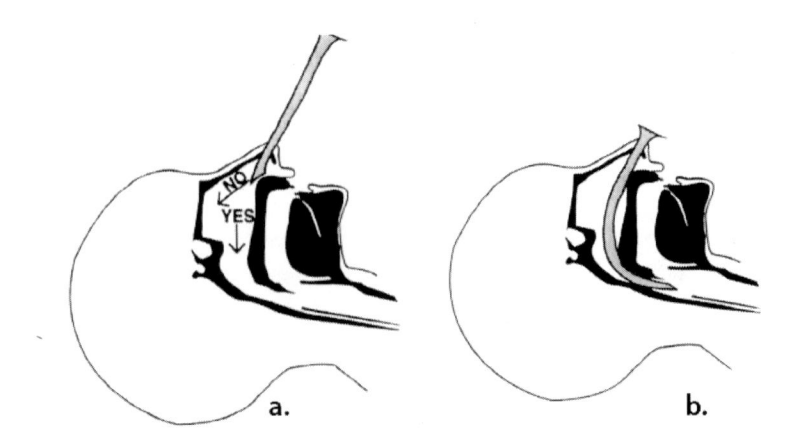

Fig. 3-6 a,b. Direct the nasal airway along the floor of the nose. Slide it forward to position it in the posterior pharynx.

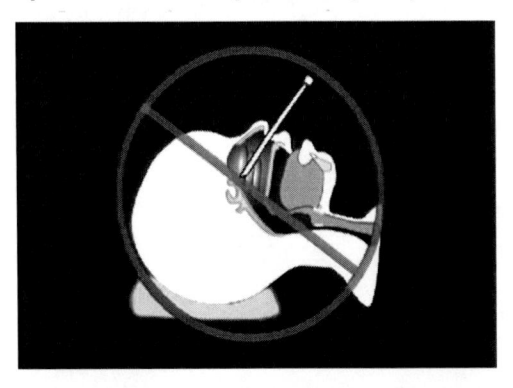

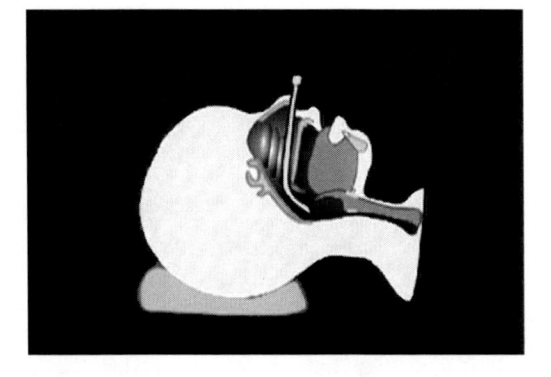

Keyframes 3-2a,b. When inserting a nasal airway, insert perpendicular to the plane of the face, NOT upward toward the frontal sinus.

If you meet an obstruction then carefully twist the tube while slowly pushing it forward Mov. 3-3, KF. 3-3 a,b,c). Don't force it. The turbinates can be fragile and easily fractured and the mucosa is easily torn. Check your angle of insertion and try again. If the nasal airway will not pass, try the other nostril or switch to a smaller tube.

The nasal passage sometimes pinches the tube as it turns the corner. The resultant narrowing may make passing a suction catheter down the nasal airway difficult.

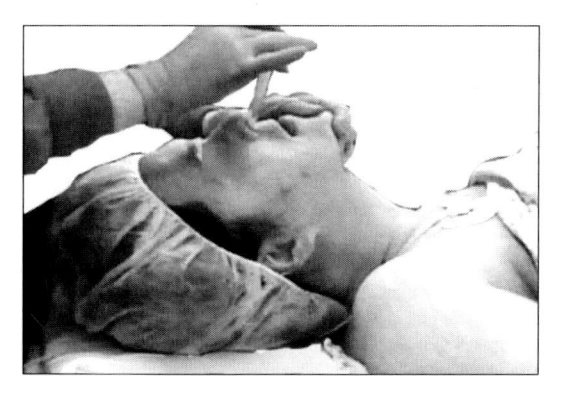

Keyframe 3-3a. Insert the nasal airway perpendicular to the plane of the face.

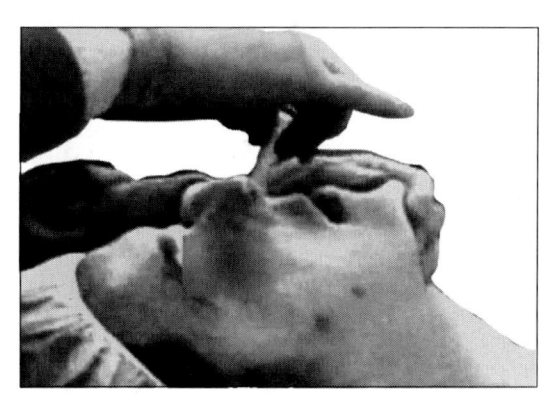

Keyframe 3-3b. Never force it, instead gently twist or rotate into position.

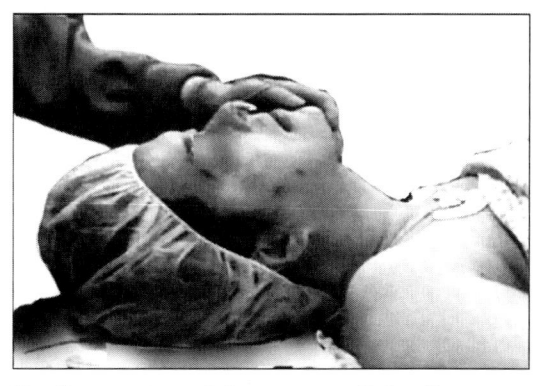

Keyframe 3-3c. Advance until the flange seats against the nostril.

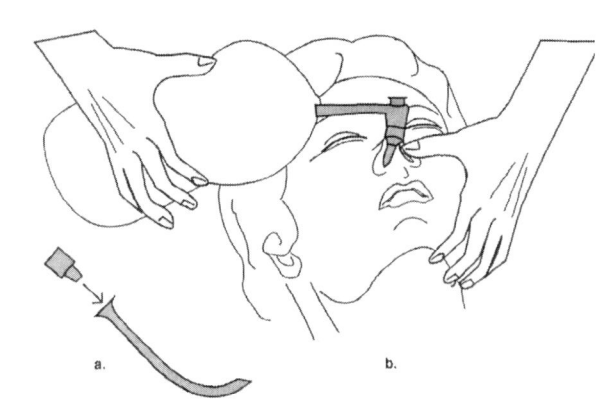

Fig. 3-7. An alternate means of ventilation — insert an endotracheal tube connector into a nasal airway as in *a*. Place the nasal airway, close the opposite nostril and mouth. Ventilate as in *b*.

Nasal airways are relatively contraindicated in facial trauma when there is risk of skull or midface fracture. There is a low risk of passing the nasal airway through a fractured frontal sinus and into the cranial vault.

Use of the Nasal Airway To Ventilate

You can use a nasal airway to ventilate any patient when ventilation with a bag and a mask is difficult. Simply insert an endotracheal tube connector into the nasal end of a nasal airway. Choose one that fits snugly. The nasal airway will now connect to your ventilation circuit. Hold the mouth and opposite nostril firmly closed. Squeezing the bag will now ventilate the patient (Fig. 3-7).

The use of a nasal airway to ventilate a patient is useful in anesthetic situations when a spontaneously ventilating intubation is desired, such as with pediatric patients. Typically young children cannot cooperate for an awake sedated intubation. When using this technique, once the child is anesthetized, connect the endotracheal tube adapter as described above to the anesthesia machine. Maintain depth of anesthesia through the nasal airway while nasal intubation is performed through the other nostril. The nasal airway must occasionally be withdrawn slightly if it's deflecting the nasal endotracheal tube in the posterior pharynx.

Use of the Oral Airway

An oral airway, also called an oropharyngeal airway, is a fairly firm, curved piece of plastic. It sits on top of the tongue and it is very effective at opening the airway because it pulls the tongue and associated structures forward, away from the larynx.

Oral airways have several disadvantages, however. First, the oral airway must be placed inside the mouth between the patient's teeth, sometimes a difficult and personally risky task in patients who can protect their airway. Second, firm, plastic oral airways can damage teeth — especially if the teeth are already loose or decayed. Third, an awake patient will commonly gag, and possibly vomit and aspirate. The patient can also develop laryngospasm.

Despite the disadvantages, oral airways relieve most types of obstruction very effectively. They are one of our most important tools. The correct size oral airway places the flange immediately outside the teeth or gums and positions the tip near the vallecula. To estimate the correct size, place the airway next to the patient's jaw parallel to the mouth and judge where it will lie. The tip should extend from the center of the patient's mouth to the angle of the lower jaw.

Too small an airway places the tip in the middle of the tongue, bunching the tissue and worsening obstruction. It can obstruct the lingual vein and cause tongue swelling. Too large an airway extends from the mouth and prevents sealing the mask over the face. It can fold the epiglottis down over the glottic opening.

There are several ways to insert an oral airway (Fig. 3-8, 3-9, 3-10, Mov. 3-4, KF 3-4 abc).

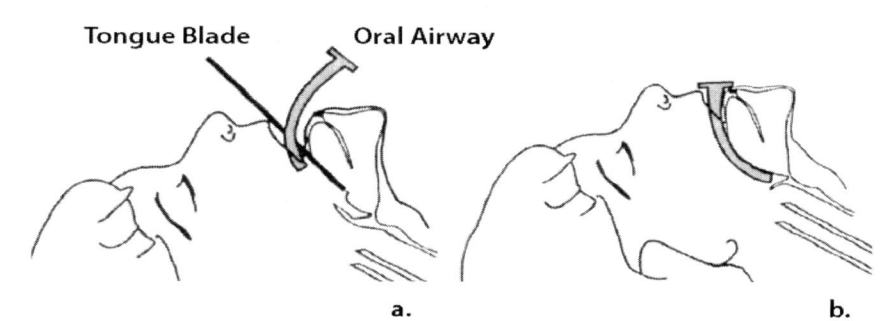

Fig 3-8a,b. Push tongue down with tongue blade (a). Slide oral airway into position.

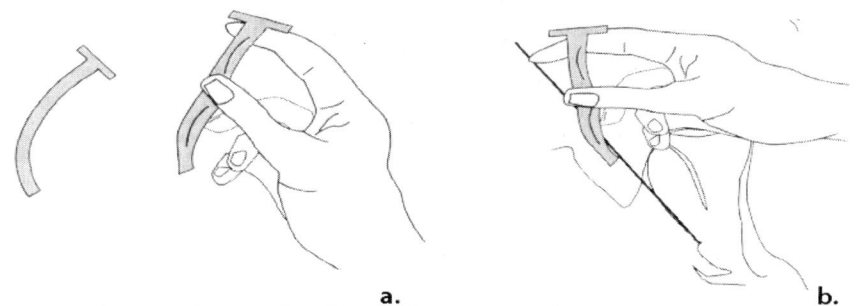

Fig. 3-9a,b. Straighten a flexible oral airway with your fingers (a), then slide it down the tongue blade until its tip is behind the tongue (b).

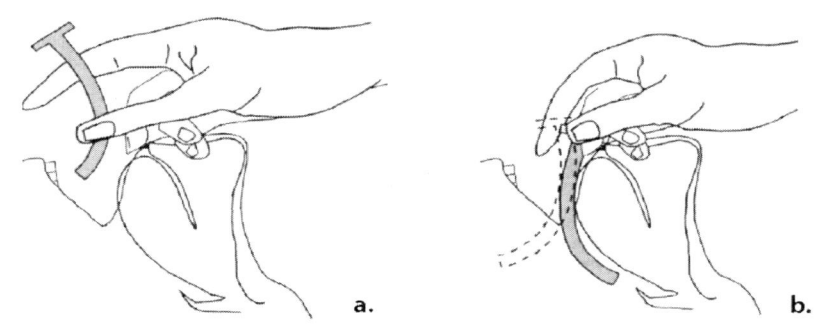

Fig. 3-10a,b. Alternatively, insert the oral airway upside down. Advance until the tip lies behind the tongue (a). Rotate (b). When flipping the airway, avoid pressure on the upper teeth. Don't scrape the roof of the mouth.

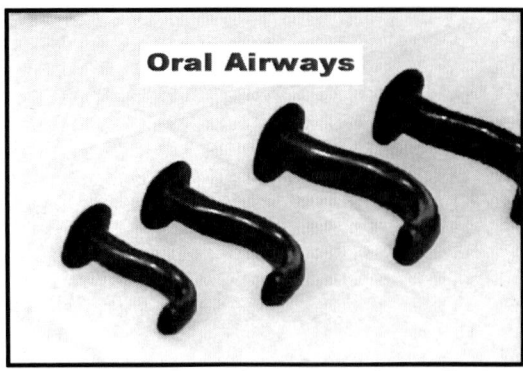

Keyframe 3-4a. Oral airways, also called oro-pharyngeal airways, open the airway by pulling the tongue and soft tissue forward.

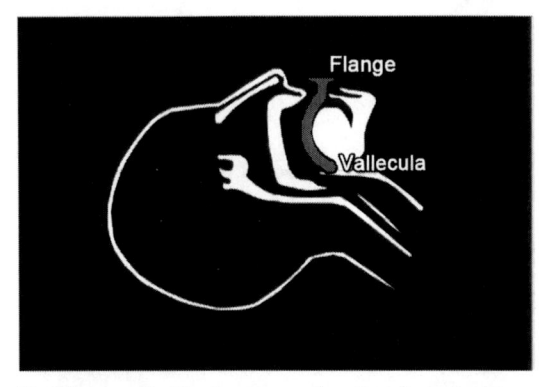

Keyframe 3-4b. A properly sized oral airway places the flange at the gums and the tip just into the vallecula.

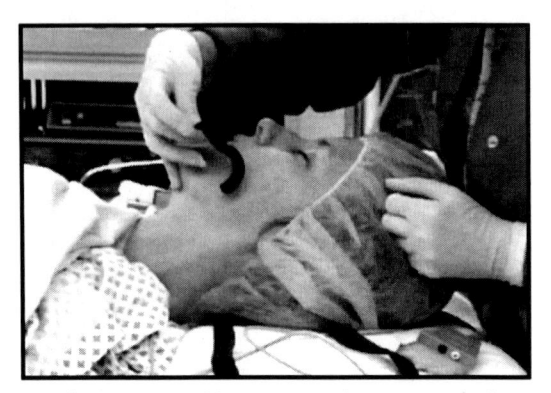

Keyframe 3-4c. You can estimate oral airway size by placing it against the outside of your patient's face.

Open the mouth widely, as you would to intubate the patient. Insert the oral airway with the curve either down toward the tongue, or up toward the roof of the mouth. With the curve down, advance the airway until the tip is behind the back of the tongue.

Properly placed, the airway pulls the tongue forward. Improperly placed it pushes the tongue into the back of the pharynx and further obstructs the airway. Wetting the airway with water will allow it to slide more easily.

Use of a tongue blade can help. Use your left hand to place the tongue blade to the rear of the tongue and pull it forward. Slide the oral airway in with your right hand, either by sliding it down the tongue blade or by rotating the oral airway into position (Mov. 3-5, KF. 3-5a,b).

If I am using a flexible oral airway and I still can't insert it, I grasp it firmly in my right hand and force it to straighten as much as possible (Mov. 3-6 KF 3-6). I then place the straightened airway on the tongue blade and slide it down the blade to the back of the mouth. Once in position I relax my grip. The oral airway springs back into its curve and pulls the tongue forward.

Providers sometimes insert an oral airway by turning its curve toward the roof of the mouth. They advance it until its tip lies behind the tongue and then flip it into position (Mov. 3-7, KF 3-7a,b). While effective, you must use caution. You can easily damage teeth and the roof of the mouth.

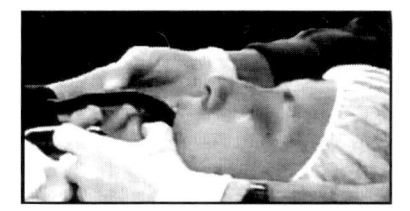

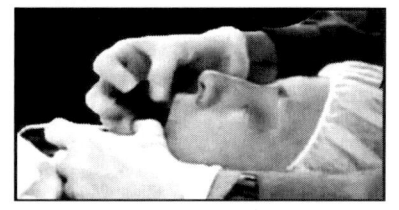

Keyframes 3-5ab. Insert the oral airway so that it rotates around the tongue until it seats. You can use a tongue blade to pull the tongue forward if needed.

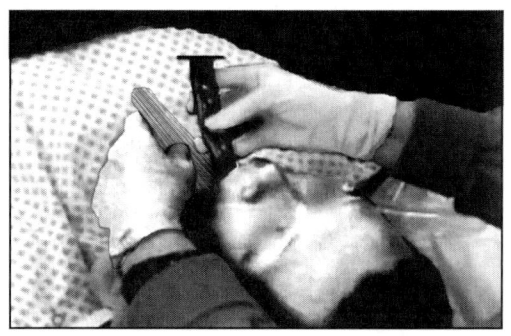

Keyframe 3-6. When placing a flexible oral airway, straighten it and slide it into position using a tongue blade.

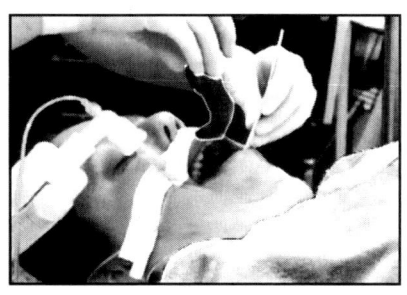

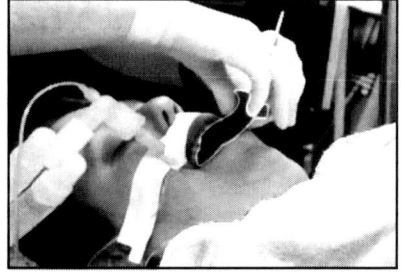

Keyframes 3-7ab. You can flip the oral airway upside down and then rotate it into position. Be careful of the teeth and roof of the mouth.

Ventilating with a Bag and a Mask

Once the airway is open, check ventilation. If the patient is breathing adequately, you can decide next steps with less haste. Apply oxygen while evaluating.

If the patient is not breathing well you must immediately assist or control his respiration. Both require some form of bag and mask apparatus. For the bag and mask to work you must have a good seal on the mask and an open airway.

First, choose the correct size mask for the patient. When you squeeze the bag, the gas will take the path of least resistance. A good mask fit makes an airtight seal against the contours of the patient's face and forces the gas into the patient's lungs, expanding the chest. The wrong size mask prevents a good seal, allowing gas to escape and making it difficult to inflate the lungs. Most women take a small to medium adult mask. Most men will use a medium. Tall or obese men may need a large. Large children need a size 3, toddlers a 2, infants a 1.

The proper size mask just covers the space between the bridge of the nose and the crease in the chin. The entire upper and lower lips fit inside the mask.

Pull the head into extension and open the airway (Fig. 3-11a). Hold it with your left hand. All masks are roughly triangular in shape. Place the apex of the triangle on the bridge of the nose and press firmly (Fig. 3-11b). Reach down with your free index and middle fingers and pull the loose cheek tissue forward to bunch on either side of the mouth.

Place your remaining fingers on the jawbone and pull upward. This action also holds the head in extension and holds the airway open while you position the mask. Lower the mask over the cheeks and allow the edges to grab the bunched cheek tissue (Fig. 3-11c, d). Make sure the lower lip is inside the mask.

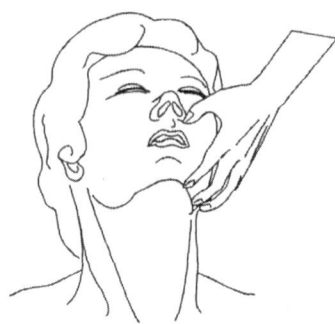

a. Extend the head to open the airway.

b. Masks have a triangular shape. Place the apex triangle over the nose bridge.

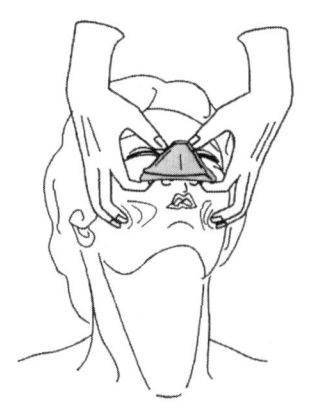

c. Hold mask top against bridge of nose. Spread sides with hands. Push cheek tissue under mask edges.

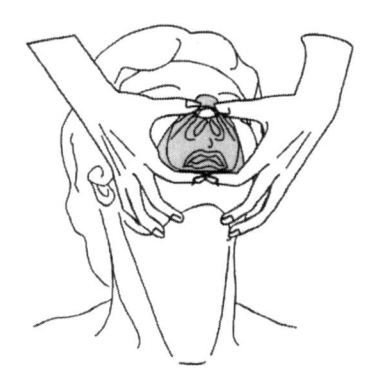

d. Lower mask over cheeks. Let edges grab bunched tissue. Seat over chin. Make sure lower lip is inside mask.

Fig. 3-11a-d. Getting a good mask seal.

Take your right hand off the mask while you maintain your seal and jaw lift with the left hand (Fig. 3-12, Mov. 3-8, KF 3-8a,b). Your right hand will squeeze the bag.

Note the final finger position (Fig 3-13, Mov. 3-8). Thumb and forefinger press the mask against the face and form a "C" shape. The remaining fingers grip the boney mandible and pull upward, forming an "E". The mask seal is created by the opposing force of thumb and index fingers pushing down, against the force of the last three fingers pulling the mandible up.

You are basically sandwiching the patient's face between the mask and your fingers pulling up on the jawbone (Fig. 3-14, Mov. 3-8, KF 3-8ab). Pressing on the soft tissue under

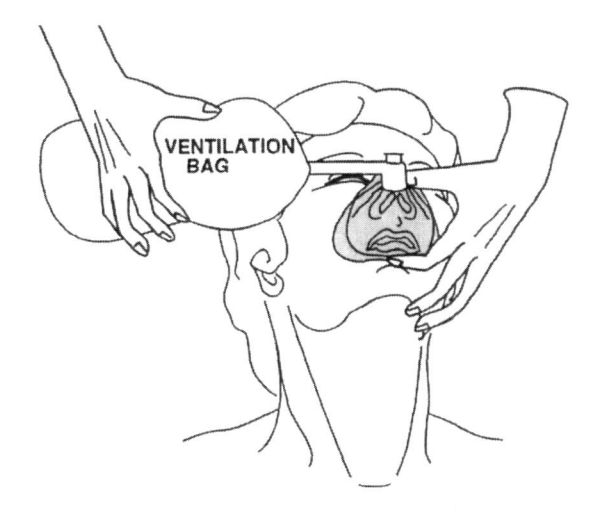

Fig. 3-12.
Holding the mask while squeezing the bag. Most bags have an adjustable pop-off valve that allows you to increase or decrease the force of the breath. This allows you to optimally inflate while preventing over pressurization.

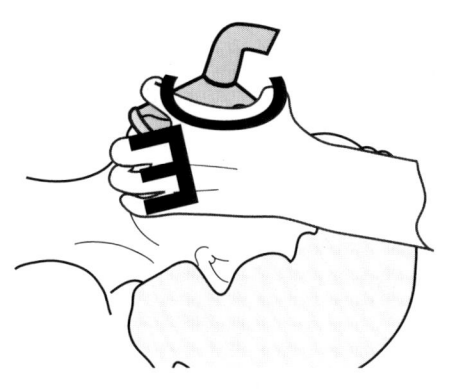

Fig. 3-13. Note finger positions.

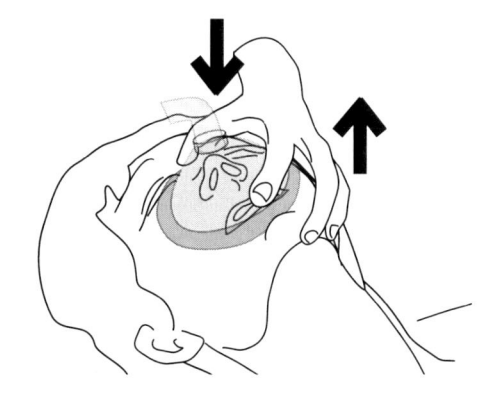

Fig. 3-14. Don't just push the mask down, pull the patient's face *into* the mask to seal.

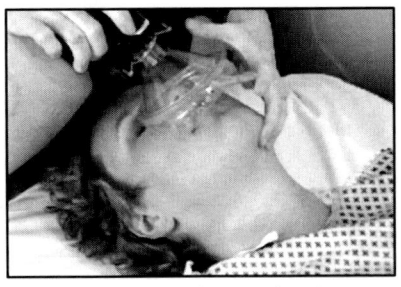

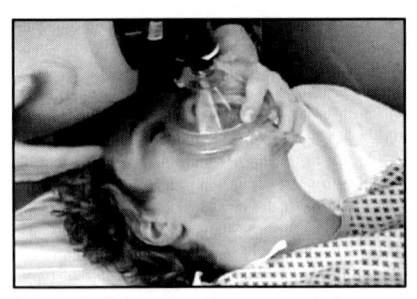

Keyframes 3-8ab. To obtain a good mask fit, seat the top of the mask against the bridge of the nose and pull the face into the mask.

the chin can increase airway obstruction by pushing soft tissue and the epiglottis back over the larynx.

Most people are taught to maintain the mask seal with the left hand and to squeeze the bag with the right. This delegation of tasks allows the strength of the usually dominant right hand to do the more physical part of squeezing the bag. Sometimes the situation or patient position requires you to reverse your hands. Using the ventilation bag with the left hand can easily be done, but requires a little practice since motor skills are not as developed and it's a bit intimidating to do it "backwards" at first.

Protect the eyes. It's easy for the mask to push open the eyelids, exposing the eyes to corneal abrasion. Consider taping them closed if the patient is unconscious. Don't tape the eyes of a conscious patient.

To ventilate, squeeze the bag (Mov. 3-9, KF. 3-9a,b). The chest should rise with each breath. Pay attention to the resistance you feel as the lungs inflate. Obstruction makes squeezing the bag difficult. A leak in the ventilation system makes squeezing the bag very easy. In both these cases however the chest won't rise. When in doubt, have a helper listen to both sides of the chest for breath sounds. The absence of breath sounds means inadequate ventilation until proven otherwise. You should see evidence of exhaled CO_2 if an end-tidal CO_2 device monitors the patient.

Always use the least force required to effectively inflate the lungs. Slow, steady inflation is more effective than rapid, jerky puffs because the gas is more likely to expand the chest and less likely to distend the stomach. Stomach distention pushes the diaphragm up into the chest cavity, impairing lung inflation and increasing the risk of vomiting and aspiration.

Remember, allow the patient to exhale between breaths.

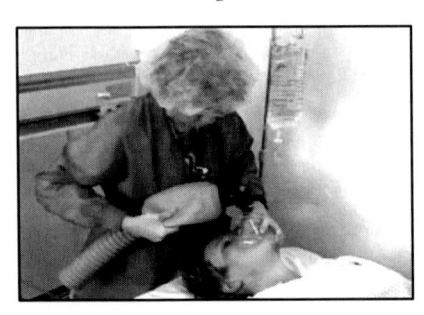

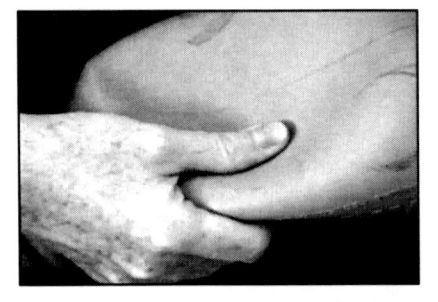

Keyframes 3-9ab. Pay attention to resistance as you squeeze the bag. Obstruction will make it harder. A poor mask seal will make it too easy. In both cases the chest will rise poorly and you won't see condensation inside the mask.

Your left hand holding the mask will tend to tire quickly if you keep it constantly tensed. Fatigue then interferes with your ability to ventilate. Learn to maintain the mask seal using the least amount of tension in your hands as possible. Don't allow your hand to assume a "claw" shape as it goes into tetany. Instead, rest the palm of your hand against the cheek. Use your shoulder and arm strength to help maintain the seal, not just your finger grip. Relax the left hand slightly as the bag refills to allow yourself stamina to ventilate for prolonged periods of time (Mov. 3-10, KF. 3-10abc).

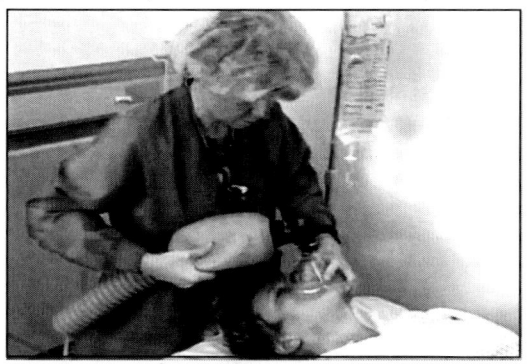

Keyframe 3-10a. When ventilating, seal the mask well. Squeeze the bag paying attention to compliance. Watch the chest rise.

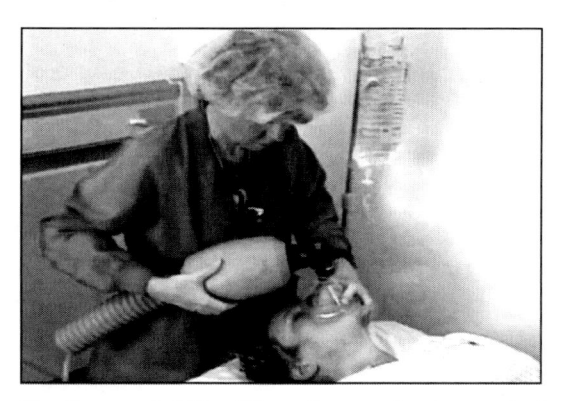

Keyframe 3-10b. Allow the patient to exhale completely.

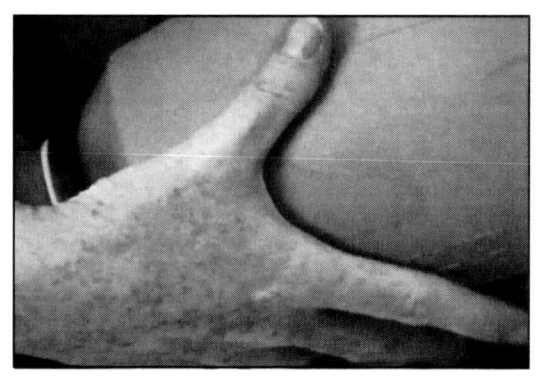

Keyframe 3-10c. Let your hand relax between breaths.

The bulk of the bunched cheek tissue fills in the gaps between the mask and the patient and helps seal it. If you have a good mask seal, little or no air will escape around the mask. You can tolerate some leakage as long as you can ventilate.

In certain patients, especially edentulous ones, the mask may not seal easily. Typically the leak will be on the side with the bag, opposite the hand holding the mask. You can rotate the ventilation bag attachment to change the point of maximum pressure and improve your seal. Reposition your hands if necessary. You can also ask a helper to push the cheek up against the outside of the mask at the leak sites. This seals very effectively. (Fig. 3-15, Mov. 3-11, KF. 3-11abc)

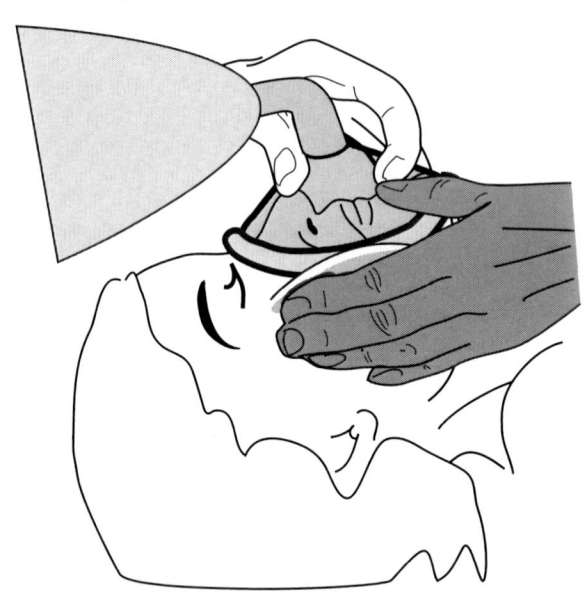

Fig. 3-15. A helping hand can often help seal a leak if adjusting the weight of the mask fails.

Educating your hand to the correct "feel" of ventilation is valuable. If you can tell how well you ventilate the patient without looking at the chest, you free your attention for other matters. Don't forget that difficulty in ventilation may be due to your patient's illness and not your technique. Congestive heart failure, bronchospasm, and pneumothorax can also make airway resistance worse, breath sounds fainter, and ventilation difficult. You must prove, however, that the fault is not your own before blaming poor ventilation on the patient.

Placing oral or nasal airways at this point may improve ventilation if obstruction is due to soft tissue. Suction the secretions, if any, to prevent aspiration.

You may sometimes need to reposition the head to optimally open the airway for ventilation. Start by placing the external ear canals level with the chest. Placing a folded sheet or towel under the head of a patient older than 2 years aligns the pharyngeal and laryngeal axes. A child younger than 2 years has a relatively large occiput. Placing the towel under the shoulders in this age group is often more effective (Fig. 3-16a,b).

Establishing An Airway 83

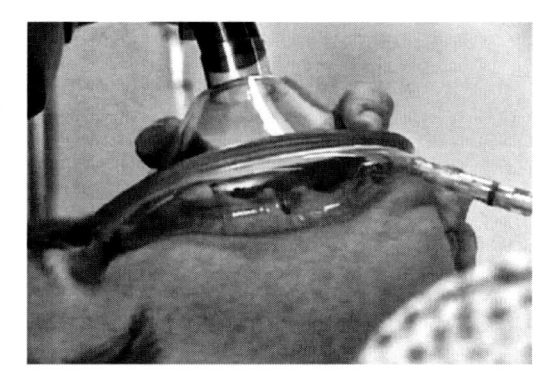

Keyframe 3-11a. Sometimes there is a leak. This is more common on the side opposite the hand holding the mask.

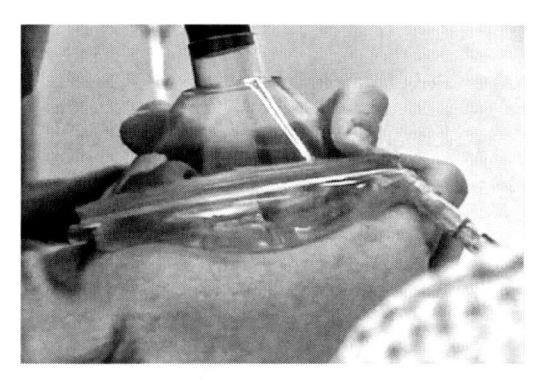

Keyframe 3-11b. Here the mask has been tilted toward the side with the leak. Positioning the weight of the bag over the leak can help.

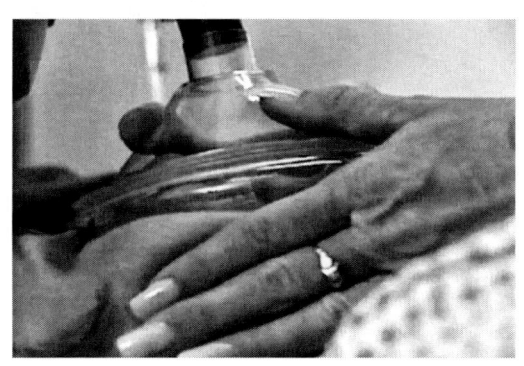

Keyframe 3-11c. Your assistant can help seal the mask against the face.

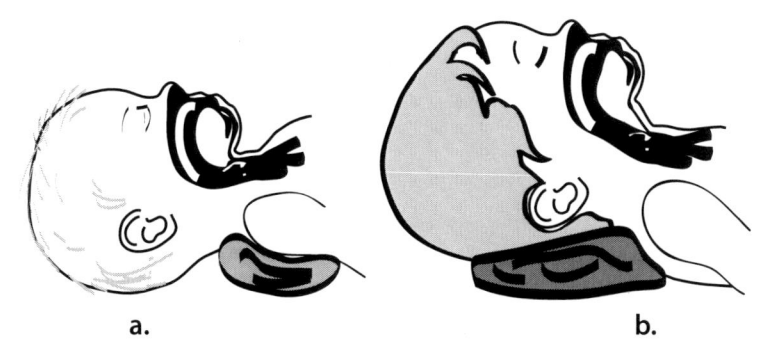

Fig. 3-16. Changing head position can sometimes make ventilation easier. (a) In children less than 2 yrs, use a small roll under the shoulders. (b) In adults or children older than 2 yrs, a towel under the head aligns the airway.

Self-Inflating vs Plenum Flow Ventilation Bags

Self-filling bags, which refill themselves during use, are more common because they're easier for the novice to use. Plenum, or inflow dependent bags, while more challenging to use are common on anesthesia machines as well as in neonatal ICUs because they allow finer control of tidal volume.

The use of a self-inflating bag without supplemental oxygen will deliver an oxygen concentration of 21%. Most sick or injured patients need more. When the bag is attached to oxygen at a rate of 10-12 liters per minute you will deliver O_2 levels of 40-60%. Adding a reservoir bag and running O_2 at 12-15 liters per minute raises the concentration to 100%, but only if the reservoir is allowed to fill.

When using a self-inflating bag it's important to squeeze the bag in a manner designed to maximize oxygen concentration. When you abruptly allow the bag to refill after squeezing, it will tend to refill with room air rather than with oxygen, whose inflow is time limited. It is better to allow the bag to refill over 3-4 seconds by releasing the pressure of your hand gradually over that time period.

Plenum refers to the fresh gas flow of oxygen free flowing into the bag to refill it. The mask seal against the face allows it to inflate and provide positive pressure. A good seal allows ventilation just like a self-filling bag. A poor seal, however, causes the plenum flow bag to deflate like a big balloon. You will know immediately when you have lost the seal because the bag will go flat, unlike a self-filling bag that may lure you into a false sense of security because it's always full, even if the lungs are not filling well.

Because the plenum bag is soft, you can easily feel lung compliance and changes in resistance as you ventilate the patient. When ventilating a neonate with a 500 ml bag, extremely fine control of tidal volume is possible, even while giving tidal volumes less than 50 ml. If the patient is breathing spontaneously, you can actually see and feel the plenum bag deflate with each inhalation before it reinflates with the gas flow. The amount of deflation gives a good indication of the patient's tidal volume.

On the negative side, plenum flow bags won't refill if the oxygen source is empty. In addition, you absolutely must maintain a good seal or you can't ventilate. If you're having trouble don't hesitate to ask one of your assistants to help you create the seal by holding the mask tight against the patient's face at the leak points.

Assisting Ventilation

You may wish to assist the ventilation of a patient who is breathing spontaneously, to improve their tidal volume. Gently squeeze the bag just after the patient starts to inhale. The airway is most open at that point and the resistance least. The breath you deliver should continue to expand the patient's chest for the few seconds after he stops inhaling. Always allow the patient to exhale.

If you squeeze the bag during exhalation or coughing, the gas will simply take the path of least resistance to enter the stomach or exit around the mask. Coordinate your efforts with the patient's own breathing rhythm and time your squeeze for the start of the next inhalation.

Conditions Making Ventilation Difficult

Poor Compliance

Compliance is a term used to describe how easy it is to inflate the patient's lungs. Poor compliance can be caused by many conditions including:
- compression of the lungs, such as pneumothorax or hemothorax;
- change in lung tissue consistency, such as pulmonary edema;
- change in airway resistance, such as bronchospasm;
- increased intra-abdominal pressure, e.g. pregnancy, obesity, ascites;
- chest wall rigidity, from certain drugs or from muscle spasm.

Regardless of the cause, manual ventilation may be difficult. Obtain a good mask seal and an open airway. If the airway is not open the air will tend to take the path of least resistance and enter the stomach, predisposing to vomiting and perhaps worsening compliance. You may need to decompress the stomach with a nasogastric tube when the situation permits.

If the inflation pressures are very high you may need both of your hands on the mask to effectively seal it. Your assistant will probably need both hands on the bag to deliver an adequate tidal volume. Squeeze the bag more slowly, allowing the gas time to enter. When ventilation is this difficult, consider intubation.

Obese Patients

Excess soft tissue collapsing over the laryngeal structures may make manual ventilation difficult in the obese patient. Try placing an oral or nasal airway.

If difficulty persists, use both your hands to seal the mask. Have a helper squeeze the bag for you. Place thumbs on top of the mask, index fingers on the bottom, bunching the soft tissue of the cheeks under the mask. Pull the jaw upward with your remaining fingers by spreading them along the jaw line, underneath the angle of the mandible. Pull up forcefully, squeezing the patient's face between the mask and your hands. Hold just the bone. Pushing on the soft tissue under the jaw can force it into the airway and worsen obstruction.

Use of both hands makes it easier to shift the mandible forward and pull the obstructing tissue up and off the larynx. Move your fingers as needed to perfect your seal. You may still sometimes need a helper to stop leaks (Fig. 3-17, Mov. 3-12, KF. 3-12abc).

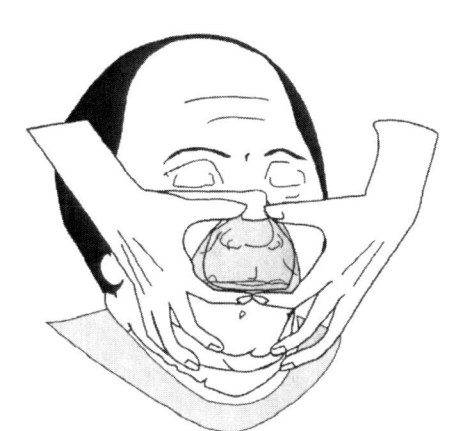

Fig. 3-17. How to place the hands for two handed ventilation with an assistant.

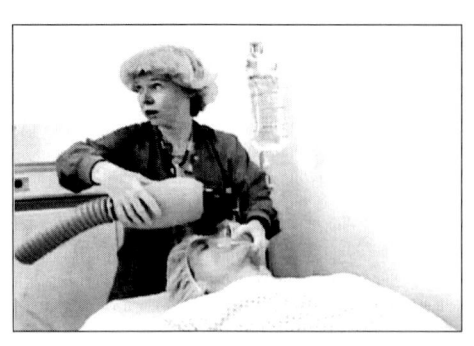

Keyframe 3-12a. If you have trouble ventilating, ask for help.

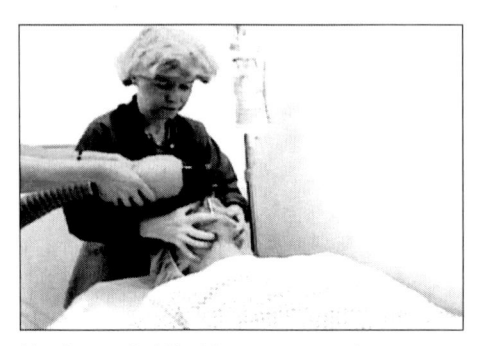

Keyframe 3-12b. Have your assistant squeeze the bag while you open the airway and seal the mask.

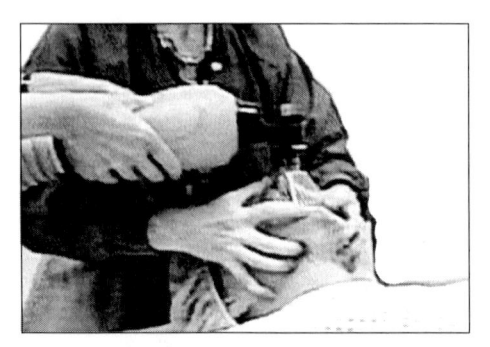

Keyframe 3-12c. You and your helper must communicate to ensure that your ventilation is effective.

When someone else is squeezing the bag, it's especially important to verify adequate ventilation — since you can no longer feel the compliance of the bag yourself. Watch the chest rise, see the air condense on the mask (if mask is clear plastic), and have someone listen for breath sounds. Make sure your helper communicates any signs of obstruction or lack of seal immediately. This technique is a team effort.

Manual ventilation can be very difficult in the morbidly obese patient or the patient with increased intra-abdominal pressure because it limits the ability to deliver an adequate tidal volume. When possible, placing this type of patient in reverse trendelenburg (tilted so the head is higher than the feet) allows the abdominal contents to drop away from the diaphragm and lowers the inflation pressure needed.

Fig. 3-18. One technique to obtain a good seal with leak over nose.

Patient on His Side

With the patient on his side, pressing the mask against the face will push the head back, making it hard to maintain a seal. Have your assistant stabilize the head as you seal the mask against the face. You may need to reposition the bag or switch hands.

Edentulous Patients

Teeth give support and form to the mouth and their absence can make manual ventilation challenging. You might consider leaving dentures in place.

Improve mask seal by turning the ventilation bag on its connector in order to center the weight of the bag over any leak. An assistant can also help push cheek tissue up over the mask edge at the site of the leak. You can also try a variation on the two handed technique (Mov. 3-12, KF 3-12abc). Place your thumbs on the top of the mask, your index fingers on the bottom. Use your middle and ring fingers to bunch the cheek tissue up to seal the mask on either side. This leaves your fifth fingers free to hook under the mandible and lift.

You can use the weight of your own chin over the bridge of the mask to stop leaks here (Fig. 3-18). While the position is awkward, it does allow you to ventilate a patient on a raised surface fairly well when you don't have a helper.

When Is It Safe To Stop Ventilation

It is safe to stop ventilating when the patient has an adequate tidal volume and respiratory rate and is able to maintain good oxygenation and ventilation. The oral or nasal airway should be left in until he is able to hold his own airway open. Be alert. The patient may recover enough to breathe on his own before he is awake and aware enough to protect himself from aspiration.

The Keyframe (KF) sequences in this chapter are taken from video clips that are available on-line, for free:

For Chapter 3 video clips go to:
http://bit.ly/12cVIYL

All video chapter files appear on Anyone Can Intubate Portfolio at:
http://bit.ly/U7EV7f

4
DIRECT LARYNGOSCOPY EQUIPMENT

This chapter discusses the equipment needed for basic direct laryngoscopy, the most common method for intubation. Later chapters will discuss the equipment required for more advanced techniques, such as use of the GlideScope, fiberoptic bronchoscope, and the LMA Fastrach.

Direct laryngoscopy uses an instrument called a laryngoscope to expose and illuminate the larynx so that an endotracheal tube can be passed through the patient's vocal cords. The laryngoscope comes in two pieces, a handle with a power source, and a blade with a light source.

Placement of an endotracheal tube through the larynx interferes with its natural protective functions of breathing and protection from aspiration. Intubation can cause hypertension and tachycardia, with their potential complications. Finally, the physical act of intubating can potentially inflict trauma on the airway.

You must be prepared to perform the intubation as quickly as possible, while safeguarding your patient from possible harm. Check to ensure that all of your equipment is present and functioning prior to use in order to avoid delay or equipment failure at a critical moment.

There are many different types of laryngoscope blades, however, the curved Macintosh blade and the straight Miller blade are commonly used. Some patients may be more easy to intubate using one type of blade vs. the other. We'll talk more about the differences in these two blades later when we discuss technique.

Equipment for direct laryngoscopy and ventilation afterward includes:
- laryngoscope handle with functioning batteries
- laryngoscope blade with functioning light, both straight and curved
- proper sizes of endotracheal tubes
- suction apparatus, with yankauer and flexible catheters
- syringe for inflating endotracheal tube cuff
- stylet
- bag-valve-mask device, with masks of appropriate size for the patient
- oral and nasal airways
- oxygen source
- tape or other means of securing the tube
- stethoscope to verify placement

Checking Your Laryngoscope

First check your laryngoscope blade and handle. To attach the blade to the handle notice that the handle has a post on top, inside of a square depression. The blade has a matching hook shaped flange. Hold the handle in your left hand and the blade in your right so the flange hooks over the post and seats into the depression (Fig. 4-1a, Mov. 4-1, KF. 4-1abc). Push the blade forward until you feel it snap into place (Fig. 4-1b). The blade will be at an angle to the handle. The fit should be snug so the blade does not fall off the handle when in the off position.

To turn the laryngoscope on, pull the blade into a right angle with the handle (Fig. 4-1c). Again you should feel a snap as it locks. The light should turn on. If it doesn't, tighten any light bulb connection. Note that a fiberoptic blade won't have a light bulb. If the bulb still fails to light, change the batteries and/or the bulb and try again. Finally, remove the blade and check the contact points between the blade and the handle. Occasionally you must clean the contacts just as you clean the contacts on a battery. Use an alcohol swab, an eraser, or an Emory board. Periodically check the intubation equipment *before* you need it. Trouble shooting in the middle of an emergency is inappropriate. Always have a second blade and handle available.

If you haven't done so, look at the differences between a curved and a straight blade. There are many variations of straight and curved blades and the technique varies when using the different blade shapes. The most common types in use are the curved Macintosh blades and the straight Miller blades (Fig. 4-2a,b).

a. Align flange on the blade with post on handle.

b. Push flange onto post. Attachment is often snug and may require a little bit of force to mount.

c. Pull blade down until it snaps into position.

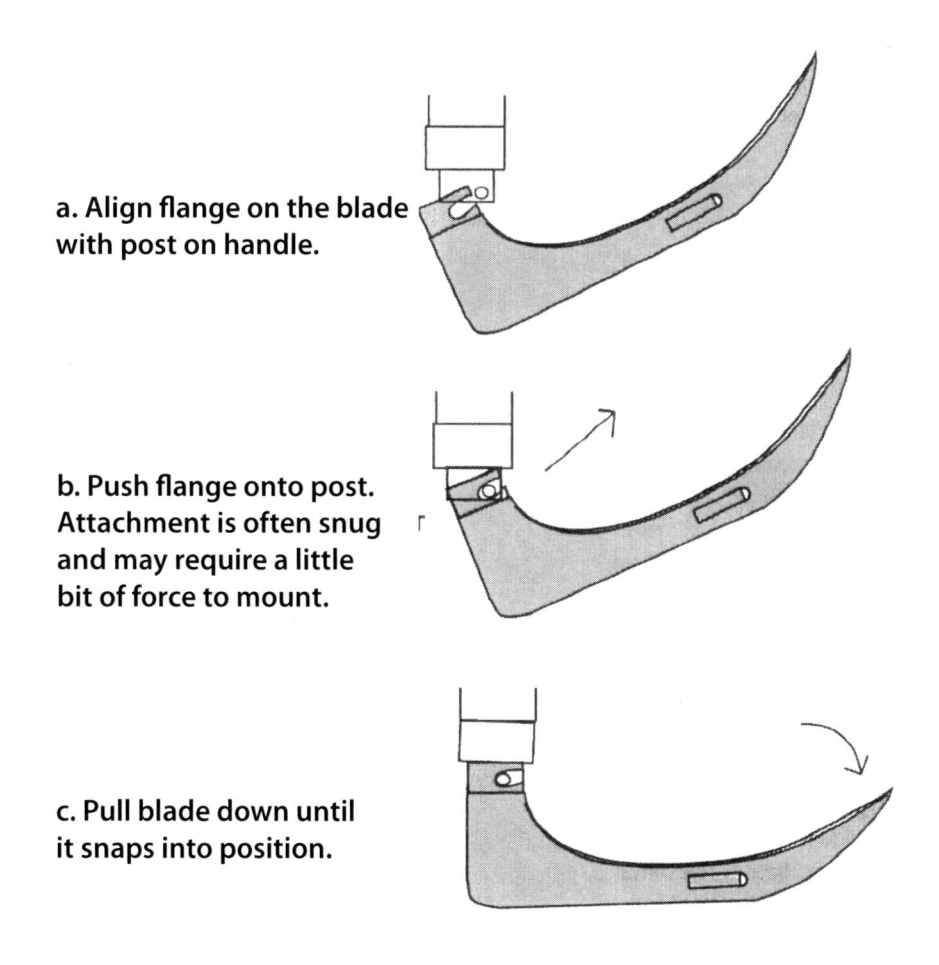

Fig. 4-1a,b,c. Placing the blade on your laryngoscope.

Keyframe 4-1a. Identify the flange on the blade.

Keyframe 4-1b. Hook flange over post on handle.

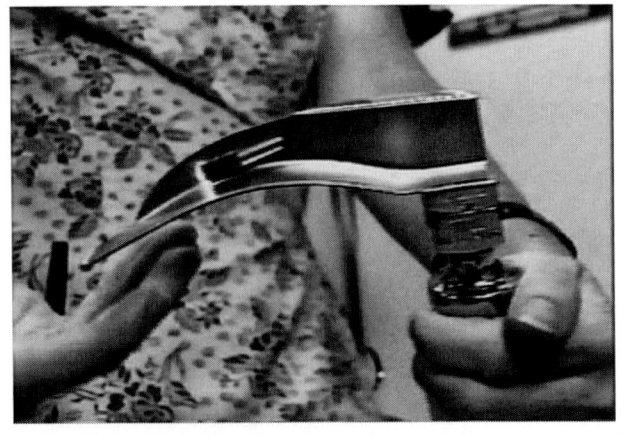

Keyframe 4-1c. To turn on, pull blade to right angles until it snaps into position.

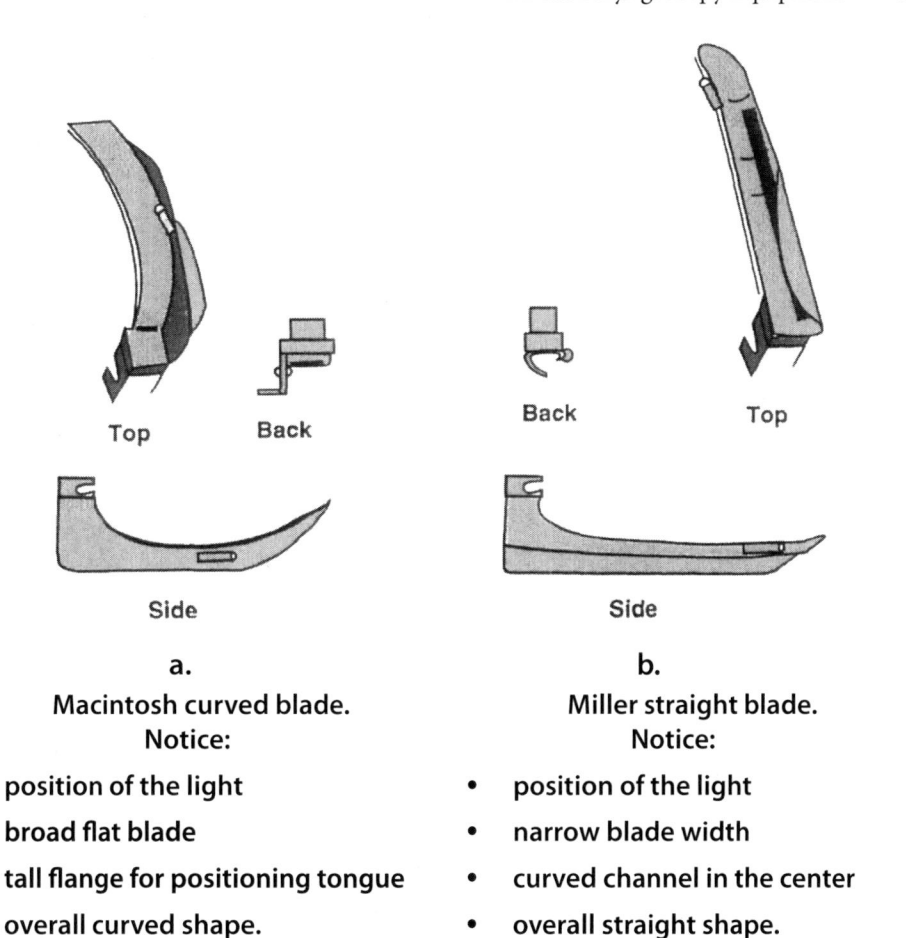

a.
Macintosh curved blade.
Notice:
- position of the light
- broad flat blade
- tall flange for positioning tongue
- overall curved shape.

b.
Miller straight blade.
Notice:
- position of the light
- narrow blade width
- curved channel in the center
- overall straight shape.

Fig. 4-2a,b. The difference between curved MacIntosh vs. straight Miller blades

Checking Your Endotracheal Tube

Next, check the endotracheal tube cuff (Fig. 4-3, Mov. 4-2). Although specialized endotracheal tubes exist, the high-volume, low pressure tube is the type you'll use most often. The larger the tube you insert, the less resistance to breathing and the easier it is to keep free of secretions. Have smaller sizes immediately available, especially in the presence of trauma or swelling.

The endotracheal tube has two openings on the patient end. The side opening, called a Murphy eye, prevents obstruction when the tip of the endotracheal tube is up against the tracheal wall. The beveled tip serves the same purpose when the tube tip is against the carina.

Positive pressure ventilation depends on providing enough pressure to inflate the lungs. If there is a break in the pressure seal — such as through a leak back out through the glottis around the endotracheal tube — then ventilation may be inadequate and the patient can potentially aspirate around the tube.

Although we use cuffed endotracheal tubes to provide this seal in adults, we can use uncuffed tubes in infants and small children, because their larynxes are anatomically different. In a child younger than about 8 years, the smallest diameter of the airway is the cricoid ring. A properly sized round endotracheal tube will seal this round cricoid opening.

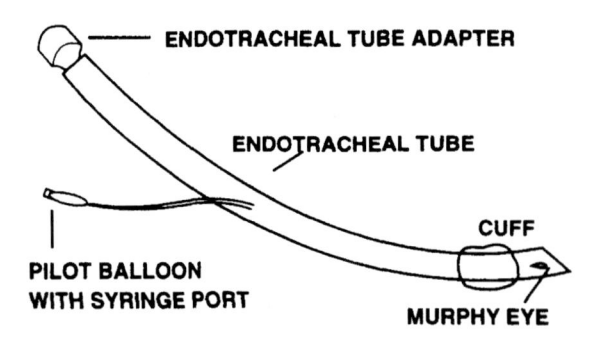

Fig 4-3. Parts of an endotracheal tube.

In an adult or child older than about 8 years old, the opening through the vocal cords is smaller than the cricoid. The vocal cord gap is triangular in shape and a round tube won't seal it. Therefore a cuff below the cords is now needed to provide the seal. Other differences in pediatric airway anatomy and intubation will be discussed in Chapter 8.

Always test the endotracheal tube cuff for leaks before use by filling it with air through the pilot balloon. By keeping the tube inside the sterile wrapper you can squeeze the cuff without contaminating it.

Attach your syringe, usually a ten ml syringe, to the pilot balloon and distend the cuff with air. Detach the syringe and check to see if the cuff leaks — as shown by the loss of air when you squeeze the cuff. Leaks can occur in either the cuff or in the balloon assembly. If you leave your syringe attached while testing you may miss a faulty pilot balloon. Discard any tube that leaks. Endotracheal tube cuffs may break during intubation if they snag on the teeth, etc. Hence tubes, which initially tested fine, may leak after the intubation.

Check the endotracheal tube adapter to make sure it's snugly inserted into the tube, not loose, to avoid disconnection.

Placing Your Stylet

Next, placing your stylet inside the tube (Fig. 4-4, Mov. 4-2, KF. 4-2abc). A stylet is a rod of flexible metal used to maintain the desired curve of a tube for ease of insertion.

You can intubate without a stylet and you should practice doing so. However, the stylet can be very useful during a challenging intubation. I always use one in emergency situations because failure to intubate rapidly in an emergency can lead to aspiration and lack of oxygen.

Lubricate the stylet before you insert it. You can use a lubricating gel, or plain water. Slide the stylet into the tube. Make sure that the stylet does not extend beyond the tip of the tube because the protruding stylet can gouge the trachea. Place a bend at the top of the stylet at the correct point to prevent it from sliding past the tip of the endotracheal tube.

Now bend the tip of the endotracheal tube slightly so the tube looks like a hockey stick. This curve helps you if the patient has an anterior larynx.

Make sure you can still pull the bent stylet out easily. Lubricating gel can dry out and get sticky. If the stylet has been in the tube a while make sure it's not stuck before you intubate. You don't want to be unable to take the stylet out of the tube after successfully intubating.

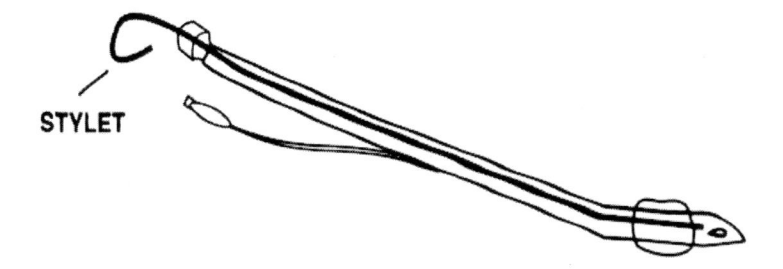

Fig. 4-4. Bending the stylet like a hockey stick is a useful shape for intubation. Giving the endotracheal tube a curved shape is also common. Note the tip of the stylet is completely inside the tube to avoid patient injury. The upper end of the stylet is bent over to lock it in place so it can't slide out the end of the tube.

Keyframe 4-2a. Murphy Eye helps avoid endotracheal tube obstruction

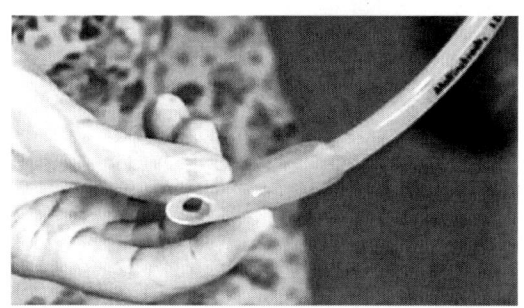

Keyframe 4-2b. Beveled edge common on standard tubes to avoid obstruction against carina.

Keyframe 4-2c. *Never* allow stylet to exit tube tip or Murphy Eye.

Suction is Not Optional Equipment

Always check that you have suction ready, with all of the connecting tubing, suction catheters, extension cords, and the power to go with it. Have both yankauer suction tips as well as flexible catheters. Yankauers allow you to remove a lot of secretions or emesis quickly. Flexible catheters allow you to suction down the endotracheal tube, and also inside the mouth if you have to pass the tip behind an endotracheal tube or an oral airway/endotracheal tube combination when space is tight.

Always Have Equipment To Ventilate

If you can't intubate you must be able to ventilate. Appropriately sized masks, oral and nasal airways, and oxygen should always be available. Magill forceps are often useful if you need to do a nasal intubation.

Sometimes you can predict that an intubation may be difficult. If you have advanced intubation equipment available — such as GlideScopes, Fiberoptic Bronchoscopes, or LMA Fastrachs — and you feel you might need it for a particular patient, then have it ready. You can always put it away if it turns out you didn't need it.

When You Don't Have Optimal Equipment

The reason I originally referred to the list of suggested equipment as optimal is simple. On occasion you may have to intubate a patient without all of the equipment available. Be flexible and let your knowledge of the anatomy and of what you need to accomplish be your guide.

People were intubated before the laryngoscope was invented. You can intubate a patient without a functioning laryngoscope in several ways. For example, you can intubate by feel. Place the fingers of your left hand inside the patient's mouth until your index and middle fingers straddle the larynx. Pass the endotracheal tube with your right hand, using your left hand to direct it between the vocal cords.

First, use your unlighted laryngoscope, or some other similarly shaped instrument such as a bent spoon or oral speculum, to lift the jaw. Have an assistant hold a flashlight up to the outside of the neck to transilluminate the larynx through the skin. The vocal cords light up. Once you can see them you can pass your tube. Its helpful if the room lights are slightly dim.

If you don't have a ventilation bag use mouth-to-mouth or mouth-to-tube ventilation.

Suction is critical. Improvise it if you don't have it. Quickly turn the patient on his or her side to clear the airway with gauze or other tissue. Use a syringe bulb or a syringe attached to some intravenous extension tubing.

Have someone place an ear to the chest and listen for breath sounds if you don't have a stethoscope.

Always open your mind to alternatives. Flexibility saves patient's lives.

The Keyframe (KF) sequences in this chapter are taken from video clips that are available on-line, for free, from anyonecanintubate.com at:

For Chapter 4 video clips go to:
http://bit.ly/WDXPOg

All video chapter files appear on Anyone Can Intubate Portfolio at:
http://bit.ly/U7EV7f

5
ORAL INTUBATION OF THE ADULT PATIENT

We've learned the anatomy and physiology of breathing, how to assess respiratory problems, how to establish an airway, and the equipment used to intubate. Now, we're ready to intubate.

The Dummy vs. the Real Thing

Many of you are familiar with basic intubation technique and have already intubated a mannequin. However, intubating the dummy differs from intubating a typical patient.

The dummy's plastic face is very stiff and noncompliant. The mouth already lies fully open and is difficult to open further. In contrast, you must open the patient's mouth, and do so without blocking your laryngoscope. Being soft and very compliant, the human cheek will hang limply, obstructing the view.

The dummy's head is so light that it takes little effort to lift the entire mannequin off the table. Often instructors have to hold the mannequin on the table to help the trainee out. In contrast, the average adult head weighs about 5 kg. The added weight makes balancing the head on the blade and lifting the head into the proper alignment technically more difficult. Holding the head in proper position, especially through a long and difficult intubation, is very tiring.

You can often see the dummy's larynx even without the laryngoscope lit because the pale plastic reflects light so well. In contrast, the mucous membranes in the human patient are darker. The larynx, deep in the hole, lies in shadow. Placing the laryngoscope light correctly and then interpreting the view is easier if you know what the real larynx looks like.

The dummy's tongue is fairly firm, difficult to shift from side to side and will remain out of the way of your blade. Your patient's tongue will be a soft, slippery mound of flesh. It will invariably block your view if you fail to control it.

Psychology is the final difference. You know that you can't hurt the dummy even if you fail. On the other hand, you worry about failure with a patient because you doubt your ability to succeed and are fearful of what will happen if you fail. It's normal for your first intubations to be frightening. But if you approach the patient with gentle, purposeful movements, and ventilate the patient between attempts, your likelihood of hurting the patient is low. Panic hurts patients: apprehension does not. Use your apprehension as a tool to heighten awareness and promote caution. If you believe you can intubate, you will (Mov. 5-1, KF. 5-1abc).

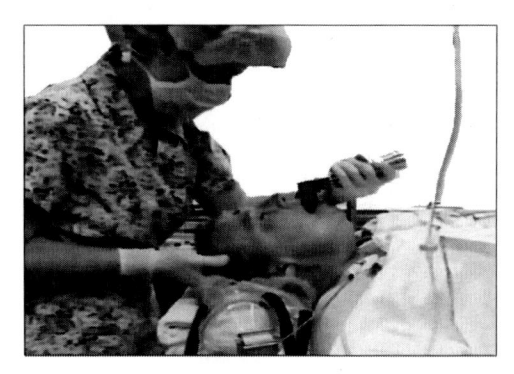

Keyframe 5-1a. Insert the curved blade and lift. Don't press on the teeth.

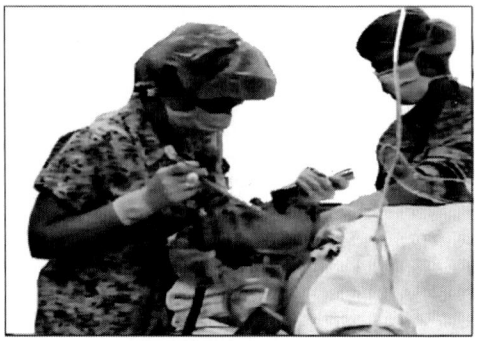

Keyframe 5-1b. Keep the head steady, keep your eye on the larynx, and insert the tube.

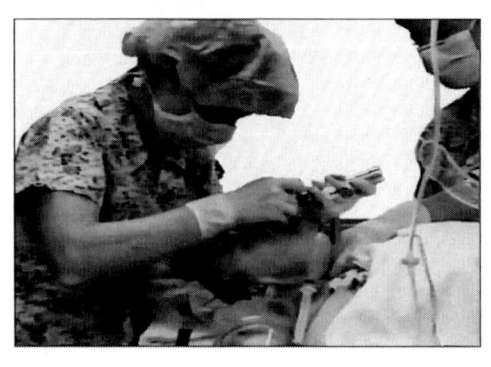

Keyframe 5-1c. Try to keep the larynx in sight as you insert the tube. Your helper may need to press on the larynx to improve your view.

Intubating the Adult

Here we discuss the basic intubation technique assuming optimal conditions.

Optimizing Head Position

To orally intubate you need to bring the path from the incisor teeth to the larynx into a straight line. This path has three axes (Fig. 5-1a,b,c):
1. axis of the cavity of the mouth (oral axis)
2. axis of the cavity of the pharynx (pharyngeal axis)
3. axis of the larynx and trachea (laryngeal axis)

The angle of the axis of the mouth to the larynx is 90°. That of the pharynx to the trachea is obtuse. Aligning them is merely a matter of applied mechanics. You make this alignment by moving the patient's head and neck and then using the laryngoscope blade to make the final adjustment. (Other techniques can be used if you shouldn't move the patient's head, such as in cervical trauma and some facial fractures. We'll discuss cervical spine precautions in Chapter 13.) You can intubate in any position, however, placing the patient's head at the level of the lower tip of the breastbone, or xiphoid process, gives the best mechanical advantage.

To get the average, non-obese patient's head into this position, raise the head about 10 cm (4 inches) off the bed by placing a folded sheet or other object under their head. Leave the shoulders on the bed (Fig. 5-1b). This positioning aligns the pharyngeal and laryngeal axes. The cervical spine is now straight and the patient is in the so-called "sniffing position." Picture how someone out of breath holds her head: forward and tilted slightly back. We automatically straighten the airway to minimize resistance when we want to move a lot of air easily. Another analogy is picturing the sword swallower. In order to pass the sword without injury down the esophagus, which is parallel to the trachea, everything has to be in as straight a line as possible. The sniffing position typically places the ear canal level with the anterior shoulder.

Once you head is optimally positioned, tilt the head into extension with your right hand to bring all the axes into alignment (Fig. 5-1c).

Different Ways to Position the Head

You can always use personal strength to lift the head into optimal position, and many times in the emergency situation, such as in the field, you may not have much choice.

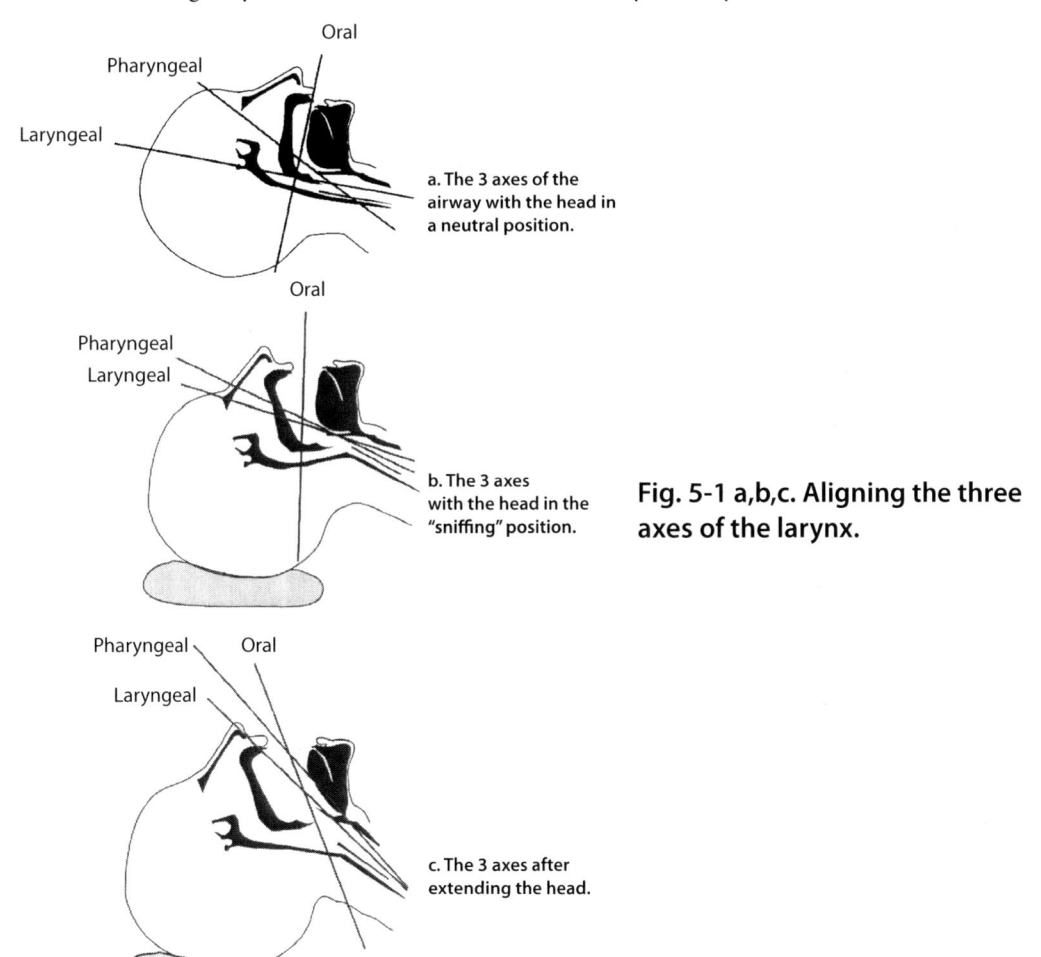

a. The 3 axes of the airway with the head in a neutral position.

b. The 3 axes with the head in the "sniffing" position.

c. The 3 axes after extending the head.

Fig. 5-1 a,b,c. Aligning the three axes of the larynx.

However, it can be very tiring, especially if intubation attempt is prolonged. It's easy to loose focus, pivot your wrist and damage teeth.

The most common things used to position the head are folded towels, folded sheets, rolled blankets, foam "donuts", foam headrests, and a helper's hand. Does it matter what you use? Actually the density and texture does affect technique.

Folded towel:
- Pros: 1-2 folded towels usually optimal. Soft and easily malleable, allowing quick alteration in shape (mounding or flattening) as needed. Easy to tilt the patient head backward even if the stack of towels is too high because they slide and mold to the shape you need quickly.
- Cons: May shed some minimal lint (possible Operating Room issue).

Folded sheets:
- Pros: Easily available in most settings. Soft and somewhat malleable but not quite as much as towels. Can usually tilt head backward even if too high by shoving the top sheet inward toward the patients shoulders. No lint.
- Cons: Not quite as malleable as towels but pretty good.

Folded blankets
- Pros: Don't need as may to lift the head because they are thicker.
- Cons: Very dense. Hard to change shape if the head position is not optimal. If too high may prevent tilting the head back and impede opening mouth.

Foam donut and foam headrest (e.g. Shea type headrest)
- Pros: designed to hold the head steady for procedures so head won't "roll".
- Cons: Makes it harder to tilt the head back. It's also easy to be fooled into thinking head is optimally positioned when it isn't. The back of head is in the donut hole flat on the surface — but from the side it looks like the head is lifted into the sniffing position. (Fig 5-2).

Assistant's Hand
- Pros: You usually have one immediately available
- Cons: It's easy to accidentally move the head during intubation, which is dangerous for teeth. The most secure way is to have your assistant place her closed fist under the head and rest it on the surface (Fig 5-3). If your assistant is providing lift make sure you're both communicating. If the assistant shifts suddenly teeth can be broken.

The Ramp
If the patient is obese, the width of their chest wall and breast tissue can interfere with laryngoscopy and visualization. Building a shallow ramp by placing folded linen under the shoulders, with the goal of aligning the mastoid process with the chest, often improves your ability to open the mouth and see the larynx (Fig 5-4). We'll discuss intubating in obese patients in Chapter 10.

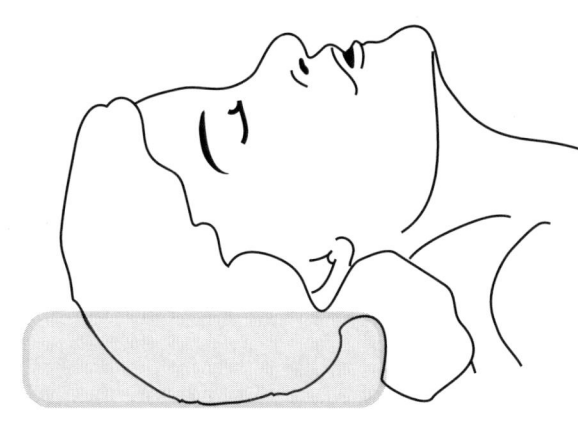

Fig 5-2. When using a foam "donut" or a Shea head rest, the head often sits low in the central hole.

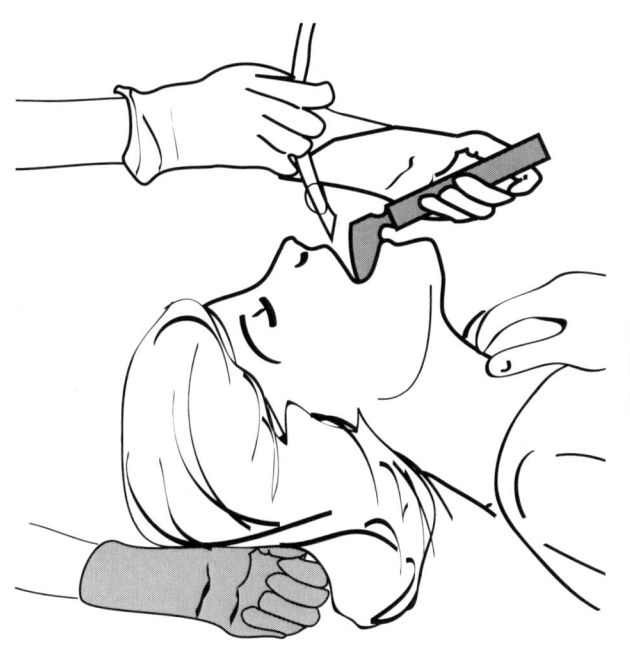

Fig 5-3. When having an assistant lift the head, the assistant must keep the head steady.

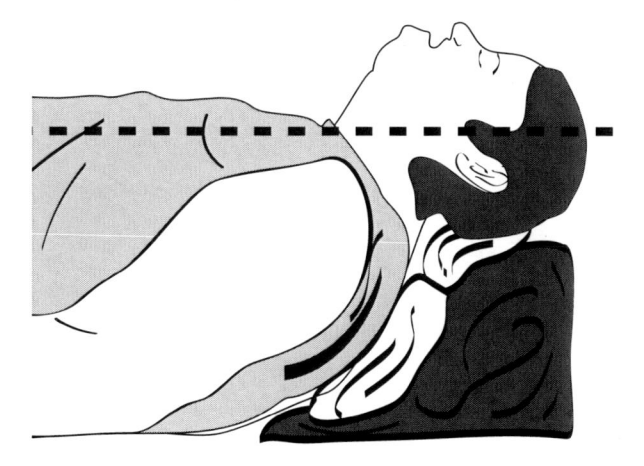

Fig. 5-4. Using a ramp to optimally position a morbidly obese patient.

Oral Intubation Technique

The act of intubation alternates hands. One hand positions the patient for the next action by the other hand. With practice, coordinating the alternating hand movements becomes natural. Once the head is optimally positioned, tilt the head into extension with your right hand to bring all the axes into alignment (Fig. 5-1a,b,c). Anchor it there momentarily using your left hand (Fig. 5-5 a,b).

Anchoring the head frees your right hand. Open the mouth with your right hand by placing your thumb on the lower jaw and your middle finger on the upper jaw (Fig. 5-6). The position is similar to snapping your fingers. By using a pushing rather than a spreading motion, you can open the mouth wider and more forcefully. Make sure that you place your fingers as far to the right side of the mouth as you can in order to keep your fingers out of the way of the blade. Your right hand now does double duty. It holds the mouth open as wide as possible. Pulling toward you also places the head in extension.

You can now step back from the head and use your left hand to pick up and insert the blade (Fig. 5-7a). Because my hands are small, I place my hand lower down on the handle. By positioning the heel of my hand on the junction between blade and handle, I can fine tune the angle of the blade. Notice how easily you can change the angle of the blade by tilting your wrist (Fig. 5-7b). You must control this motion carefully to avoid tooth damage.

Insertion of the blade should be delicate and deliberate. Hold the handle in your left hand, blade down, pointing away from you (Fig. 7b). Grasp it firmly but don't clench your fist because this decreases control and causes early fatigue.

With the mouth open, insert the blade, slightly to the right of the tongue (Fig. 5-8a). Don't hit the teeth as you insert. If necessary, you can tilt the top of the handle slightly to insert the blade into the mouth, then rotate the blade back, scooping it around the right side of the tongue as you do so.

Avoid catching the lips between the blade and the teeth. I use my right index finger to sweep the lips out of the way of the blade as I insert it. You may need to angle a curved blade slightly to pass the teeth and then return the blade to a more neutral position once it has entered the mouth.

Slowly advance the blade with your left hand until you see the tip of the epiglottis, your first important landmark. Simultaneously sweep the tongue to the left as you advance (Fig. 5-8b). Leave your blade toward the left side of the mouth with the tongue pushed out of the way.

For optimal mechanical advantage lift upward with the left arm held fairly rigid. Lift on a line connecting the patient's head with the intersection of the opposite ceiling and the wall (Fig. 5-9). It won't be perfectly straight, but keeping your arm fairly straight gives you the strength of your shoulders to lift the head. It prevents you from using the teeth as a fulcrum — dangerous for the teeth. And it allows you to use binocular vision for depth perception.

When you lift the jaw upward you have an unobstructed view of the larynx (Fig. 5-10). Pressure from the tip of a curved blade in the vallecula pulls the epiglottis forward. Placement of the blade is critical. If you place the blade in the center of the tongue, it will mound up blocking your view. You must sweep the tongue to the left or you will see nothing.

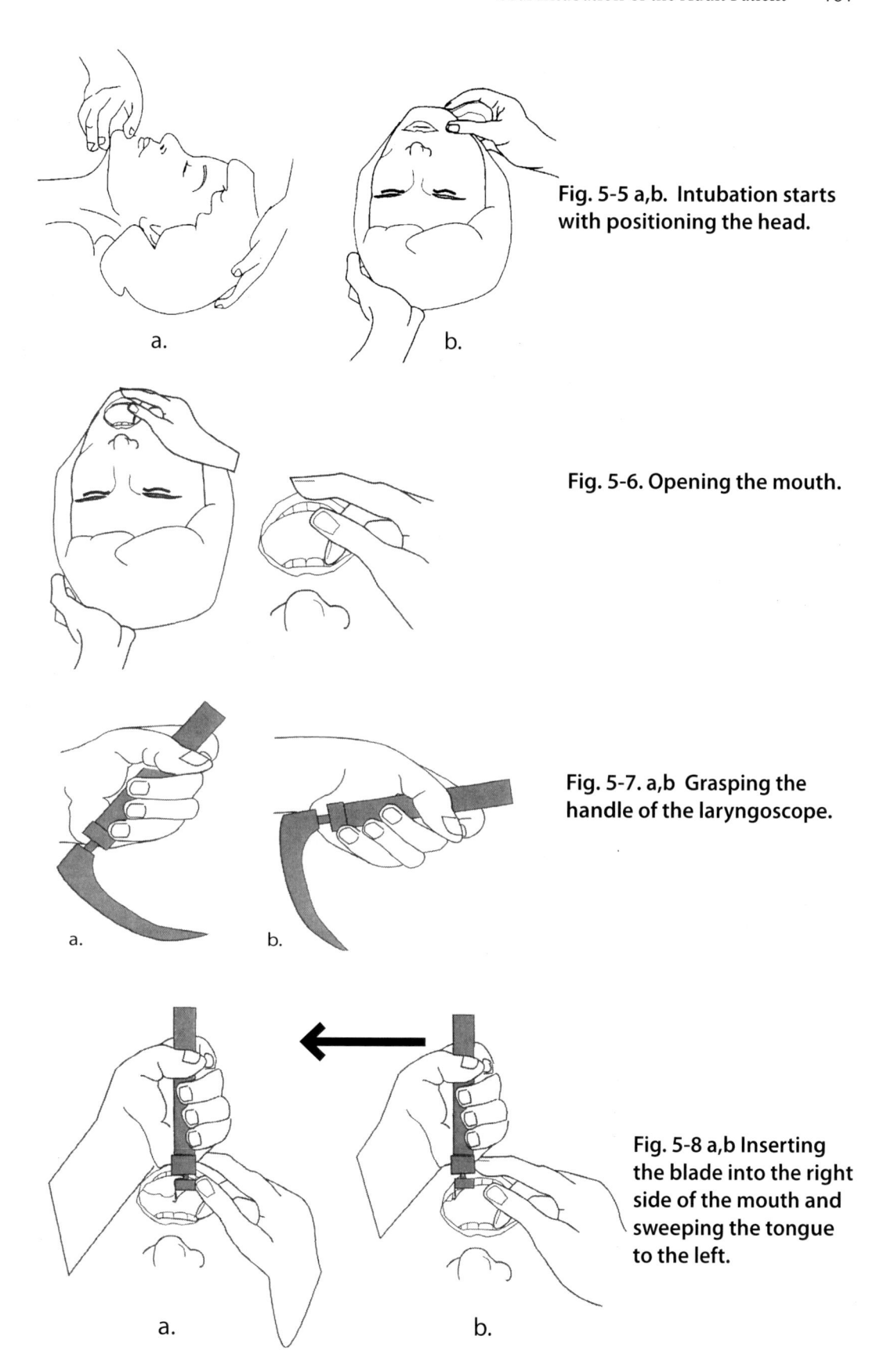

Oral Intubation of the Adult Patient 101

Fig. 5-5 a,b. Intubation starts with positioning the head.

a.   b.

Fig. 5-6. Opening the mouth.

Fig. 5-7. a,b Grasping the handle of the laryngoscope.

a.   b.

Fig. 5-8 a,b Inserting the blade into the right side of the mouth and sweeping the tongue to the left.

a.   b.

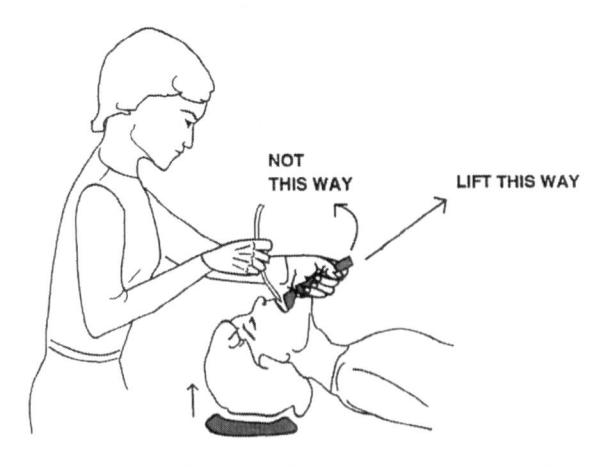

Fig. 5-9. Keep back and left arm fairly straight

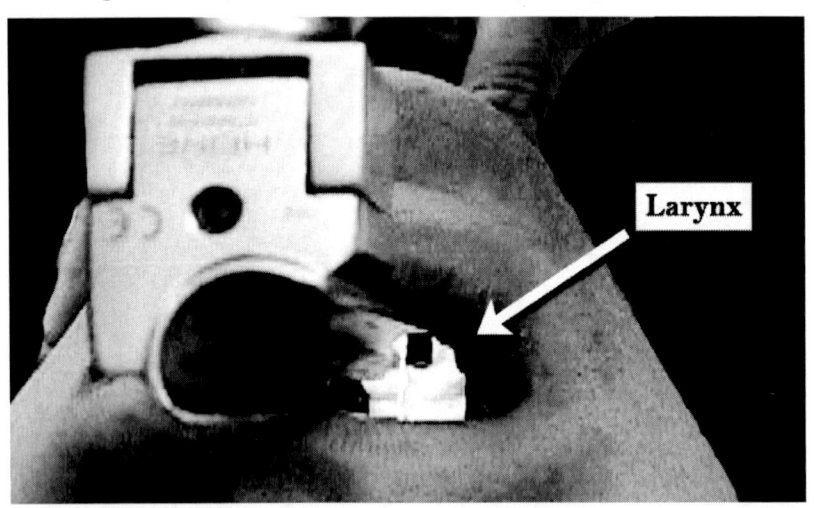

Fig. 5-10. Visualization of the vocal cords using the Miller straight blade. Beginners frequently try to pass the tube down the slot in the blade. Instead, you should pass the tube to the right of the blade.

The typical beginners (Fig. 5-11) mistakenly hunch close to the patient, bend the elbow completely, and place the right eye practically in the patient's mouth. They then can't understand why he or she has no leverage or control.

The head is now suspended from the blade held in your left hand, freeing your right hand to place the tube. Use a 6.5-8 for a woman and a 7.5-9.0 for a man. The larger the tube, the less resistance to breathing there will be. Hold the preselected tube in your right hand like a pencil, curve forward (Fig. 5-12).

Pass the tube into the larynx through the cords in one smooth motion (Fig. 5-13). If the patient is breathing, time the forward thrust for inspiration when the cords are fully open. During expiration, the tube may bounce off the closing cords into the esophagus.

Beginners frequently try to pass the tube down the slot in the blade. The slot is not big enough for this purpose. Instead, pass the tube to the right of the blade, past the right side of the tongue. You can understand why the blade should optimally be as far to the left side of the mouth as possible.

Oral Intubation of the Adult Patient 103

Fig. 5-11. Avoid stooping over the patient and bending your arm. You lose mechanical advantage, binocular vision, strength, and leverage when you stoop.

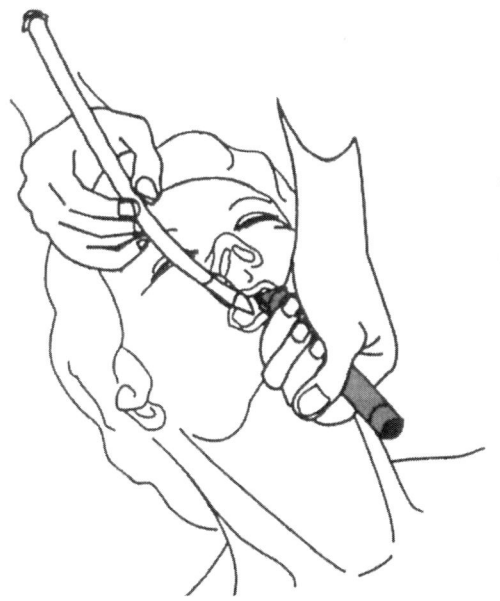

Fig. 5-12. As your left hand holds the handle and maintains your view of the larynx, your right hand picks up and holds the tube like a pencil, curve forward.

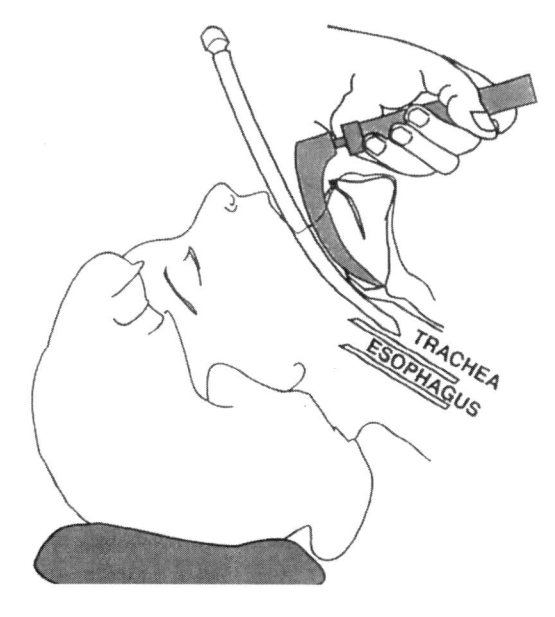

Fig. 5-13. Your right hand passes the endotracheal tube forward into the trachea under direct vision. While not always possible, try to watch the tube pass between the cords.

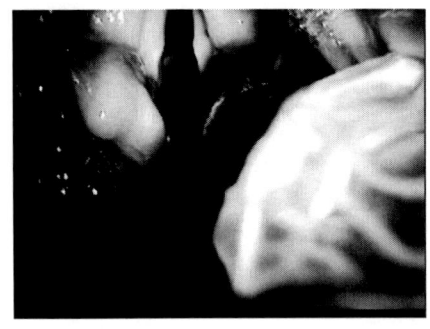

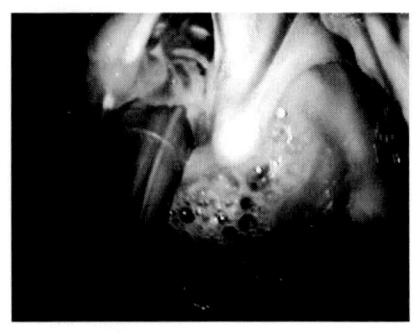

Fig. 5-14. Photos showing the intubation. In "a", the endotracheal tube is aimed at the laryngeal opening. In "b", the tube is passing between the vocal cords.

Try to watch the tube pass through the cords into the trachea (Fig. 5-14a,b, Mov. 5-2, KF 5-2abcd). Although there may be a blind spot impairing your view at the moment of intubation, you can often see the arytenoid cartilages behind the tube after proper placement. Don't relax and pull the blade out without trying to be sure of success with your own eyes. Get into the habit of seeing the tube between the cords and you will be less likely to intubate the esophagus. Stop advancing the tube when you see the cuff completely pass the cords, usually 21-22 cm at the front teeth in an adult. Carefully hold the tube where it exits the right side of the mouth and remove the blade with your left hand.

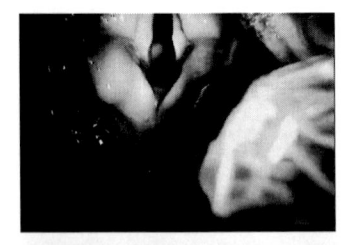

Keyframe 5-2a. Line the tube up with the glottic opening.

Keyframe 5-2b. Be gentle if you bump the arytenoids or other structures.

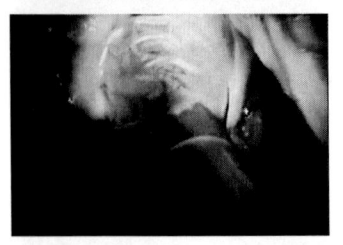

Keyframe 5-2c. Insert the tube between the vocal cords. You may need to rotate slightly.

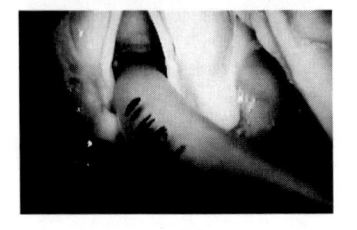

Keyframe 5-2d. Slide the tube down the trachea. Advance until the cuff is completely through the cords.

If you've used a stylet, remove it *before* you fully advance the tube down the trachea. Make sure you have a strong grip on the tube where it exits the mouth because the force needed to remove the stylet will sometimes threaten to pull the tube out with it.

To inflate the cuff, slowly inject air through the pilot tube until the pilot balloon just *starts* to get tense. Don't overfill. You don't want the pilot balloon to feel hard when you squeeze it or it may apply excessive pressure to the tracheal mucosa. Later, after verifying tracheal placement you can go back to check the minimal sealing pressure of the cuff. To check minimal seal, suction the airway free of secretions. Apply constant airway pressure of about 20 mmHg. Remove some air until you hear a leak and then refill the cuff until the tracheal leak just disappears. Excessive cuff inflation can damage mucosa by impairing its blood supply.

Before doing anything else, be sure that the tube is in the trachea. Listen for the presence and equality of breath sounds over both lung fields and for the absence of gurgling sounds over the stomach. Never assume that the tube is in the trachea until you have checked it yourself.

In the event you can't intubate easily, stop after 30 - 60 seconds. Ventilate the patient briefly before your next attempt in order to maintain oxygenation. As long as you can ventilate the patient you have time. Time to alter your technique, change the position of the head, or use a different type of laryngoscope blade. Keep your suction handy and use it. Don't be afraid to ask for help.

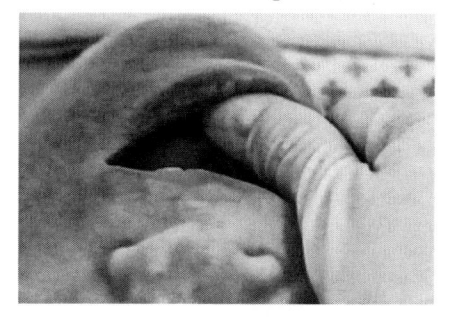

Keyframe 5-3a. Open the mouth

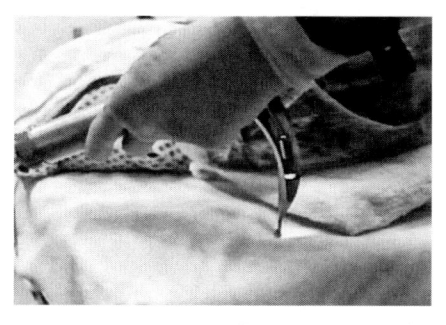

Keyframe 5-3b. Turn on the laryngoscope and grasp it in your right hand.

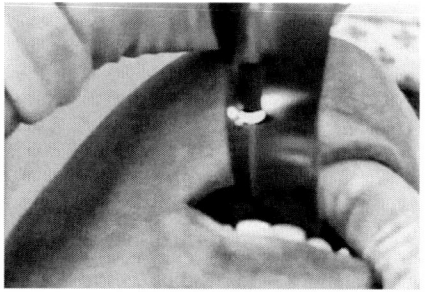

Keyframe 5-3c. To avoid the teeth while inserting the blade you may need to tilt it slightly.

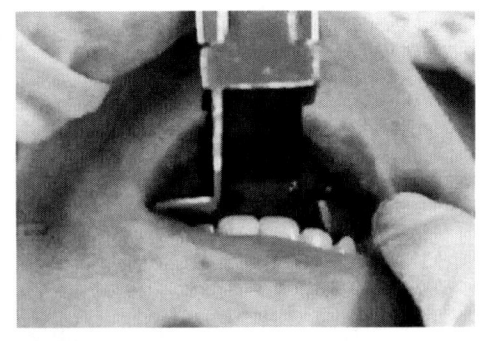

Keyframe 5-3d. Slide the tongue to the left.

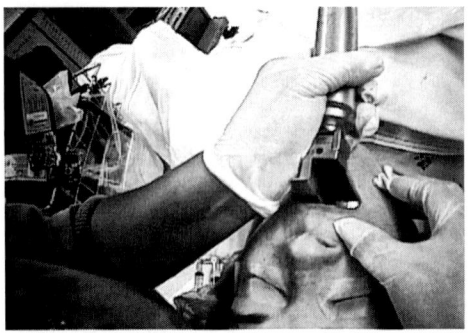

Keyframe 5-3e. Lift jaw upward during final positioning.

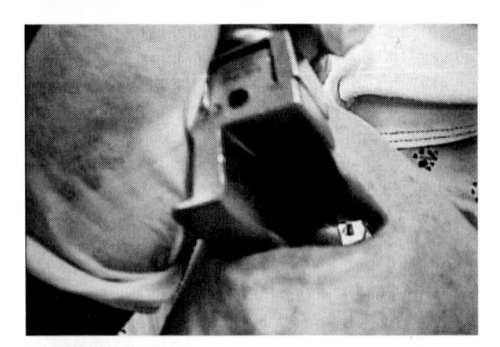

Keyframe 5-3f. Obtain the best view of the larynx.

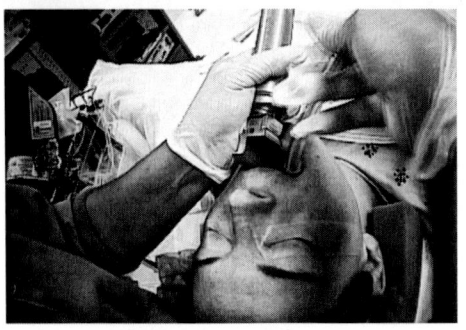

Keyframe 5-3g. Keep the head steady. Any movement can break teeth. Insert the tube and guide it into the larynx.

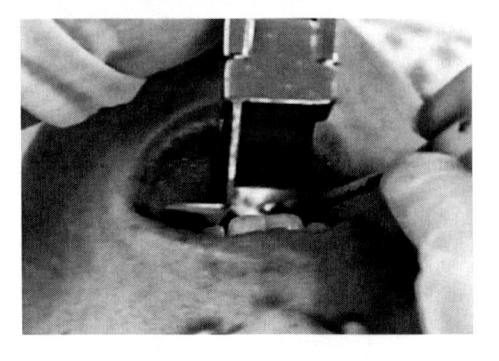

Keyframe 5-3h. Stabilize the tube as you remove the blade. Please note that you can just as easily break teeth taking the blade out as you can putting it in.

Movie 5-3 and Keyframes 5-3abc, 5-3def, 5-3gh show an entire intubation sequence using the Macintosh blade.

Straight vs. Curved Blades

A straight blade, such as the Miller, actually picks up the epiglottis during the intubation. The curved Macintosh (Mac) blade fits into the vallecula, the dip between the tongue and the epiglottis. The effect on the tissues differs between the blades. The curved blade lifts the epiglottis passively by pulling the tissue folds attached at its base. The straight blade flattens

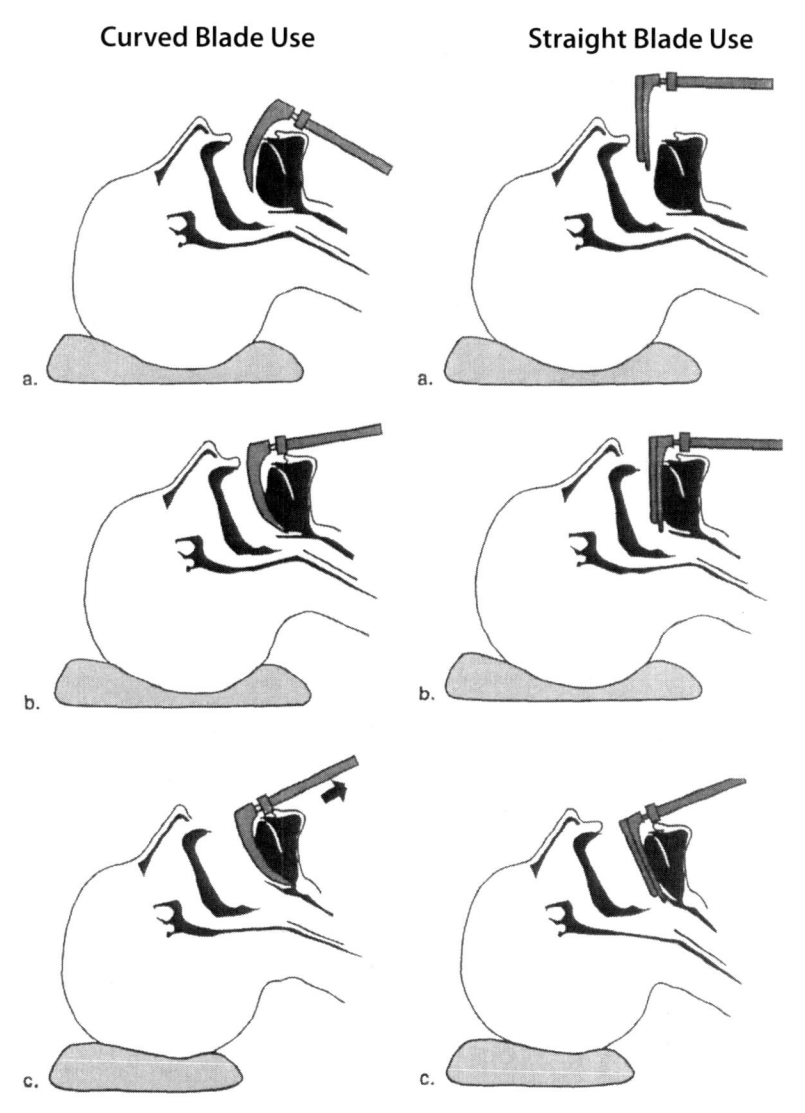

Fig. 5-15. Placement of the curved blade. Notice the position of the tip in the vallecula.

Fig. 5-16. Placement of the straight blade. Note that the blade flattens the tissue and lifts the epiglottis

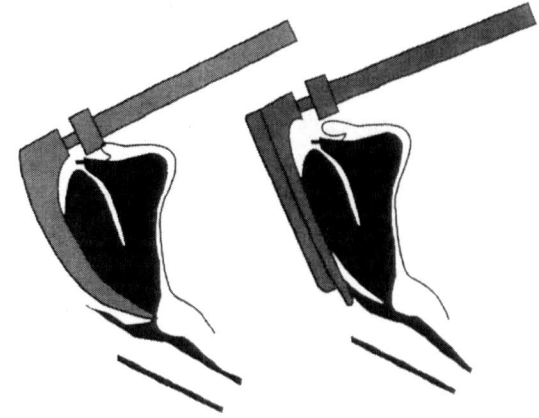

Fig. 5-17.

Curved Blade
- Note tip in vallecula
- Blade displaces tongue forward

Straight Blade
- Note tip lifting epiglottis
- Blade flattens tongue

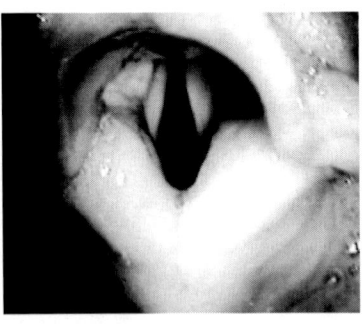

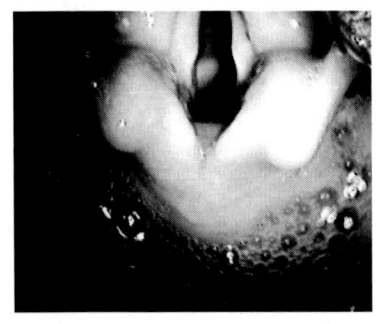

a.   b.

Fig. 5-18 Different views of the larynx with the curved (a) and the straight blades (b). Notice how you can see the epiglottis in the curved blade view on the left, but not the straight blade view on the right. The straight blade is physically lifting the epiglottis, hiding it.

the tongue and actively lifts the epiglottis. See Figures 5-15, 5-16, 5-17, 5-18 and Mov. 5-4 (KF 5-4ab), and Mov. 5-5 (KF. 5-5ab) for illustrations of these effects.

You can begin to see that a straight blade might be more helpful in situations where there is little room to displace the tongue and attached tissues forward. Patients with short necks, high larynxes, or obesity frequently need straight blades. Straight blades can also work better in patients with larynxes fixed from scar, trauma, or mass effect. Again, displacement is not as critical. Movie 5-6 shows a straight blade intubation.

In the average patient, it really doesn't matter which blade you use. Many beginners find the Mac curved blade easier. It's larger flange holds the tongue to the left and makes it easier to balance the head. It's more forgiving of placement errors. Straight blades often give a better view but are harder to use. Remember that you can reverse normal blade use and pick up the epiglottis with the Mac or use the Miller in the vallecula.

Oral Intubation of the Adult Patient 109

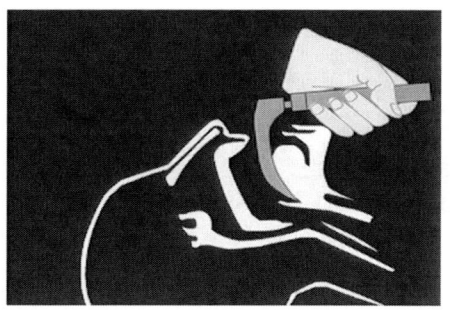

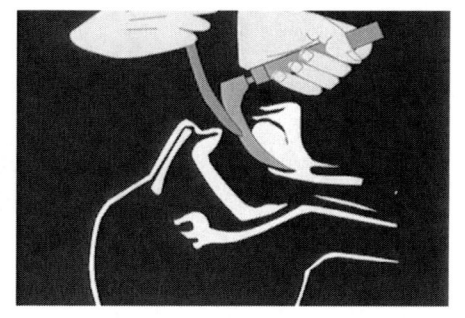

Keyframes. 5-4a,b. The curved blade pulls the soft tissue under the vallecula at the base of the tongue upward, lifting the epiglottis and opening the larynx.

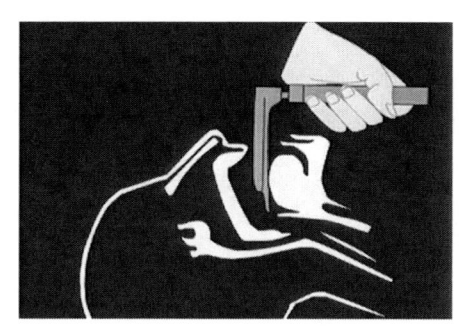

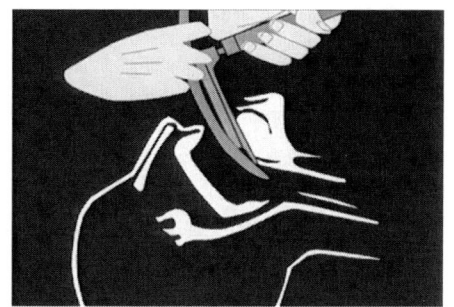

Keyframes. 5-5a,b. The straight blade lifts the epiglottis up directly, revealing the laryngeal opening.

Keyframe Sequence 5-6 a-i. Intubation using the Miller straight blade.

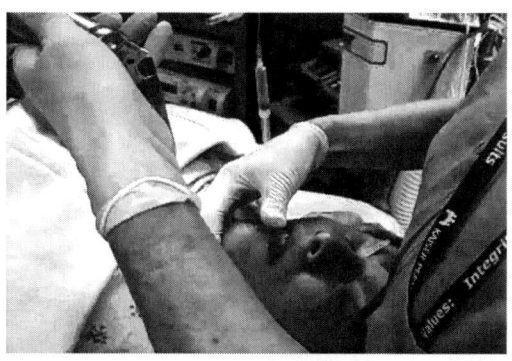

Keyframe 5-6a. Open the mouth.

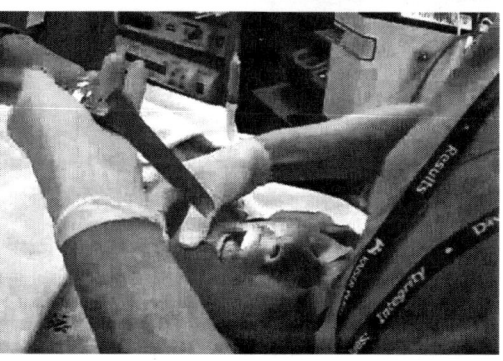

Keyframe 5-6b. Insert the blade. Careful with the teeth.

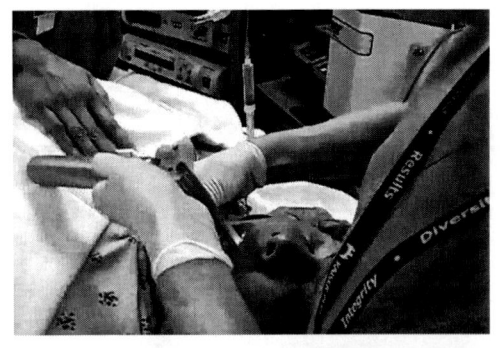

Keyframe 5-6c. Lift the tongue and lower jaw upward, while sweeping the tongue to the left.

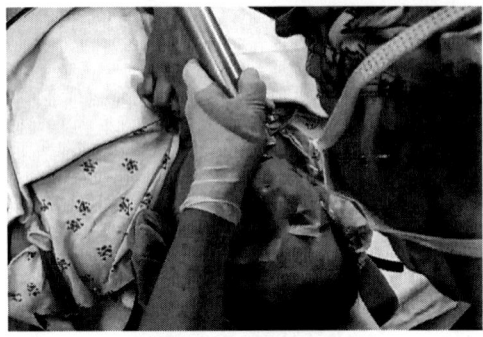

Keyframe 5-6d. Lift the jaw upward. Do NOT press on the teeth!

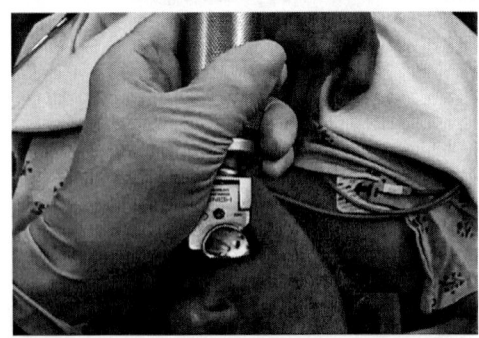

Keyframe 5-6e. Optimize your view of the larynx.

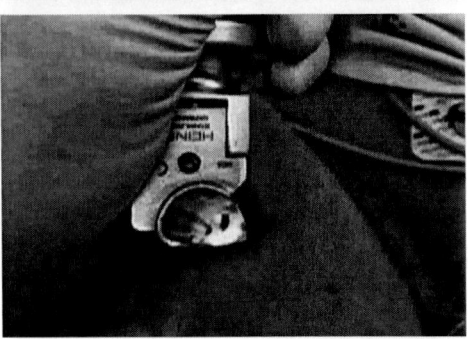

Keyframe 5-6f. Close-up of the larynx.

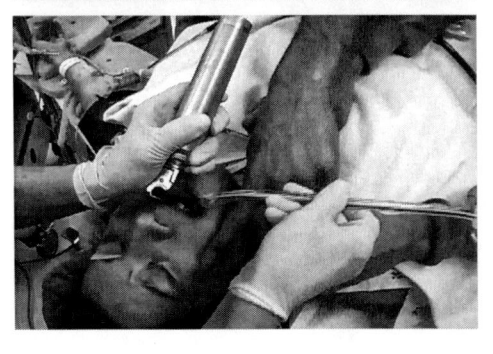

Keyframe 5-6g. Insert the tube toward the right side of the mouth, keeping the laryngoscope steady. Note helper pulling the cheek and providing cricoid pressure.

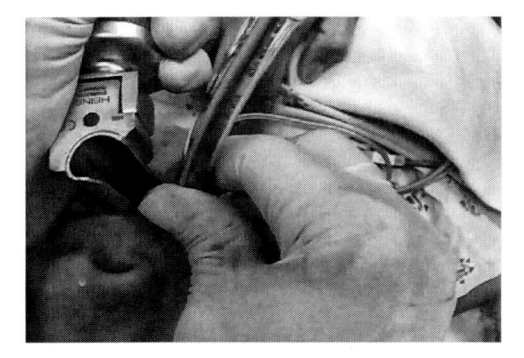

Keyframe 5-6h. Optimize your view of the larynx.

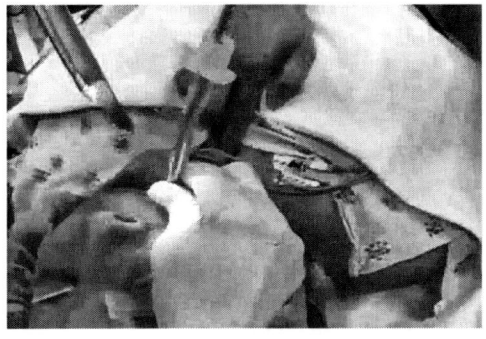

Keyframe 5-6i. Hold tube close to face for stability until secured.

Practice with both blades on the easy patients. That way, when a difficult intubation comes along you control the anatomy rather than letting the anatomy dictate to you.

The Use of Cricoid Pressure to Improve the View

Cricoid pressure is one of the most valuable techniques to help you during intubation. We often use it to improve visualization of the so-called anterior airway, where the view of the larynx is hidden behind the back of the tongue. Often used during difficult intubation, cricoid pressure can also help with the routine intubation if the patient's positioning is not optimal or if the blade you have chosen is not providing the best view.

Cricoid pressure can also be used to protect against aspiration, as this action pinches off the upper esophageal sphincter in patient's with full stomachs or a history of gastric reflux.

To apply cricoid pressure, place your thumb on one side of the cricoid ring and your index or ring finger on the other. Push down firmly to force the cricoid ring against the

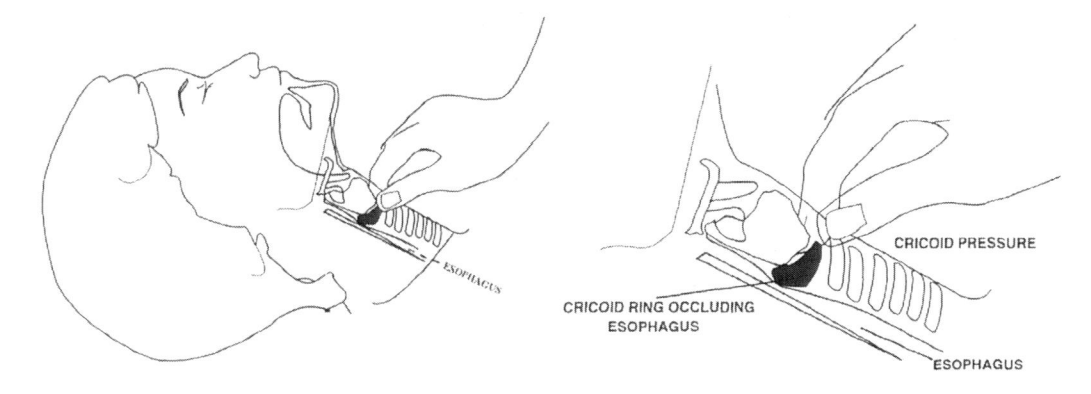

Fig. 5-19. Cricoid pressure is one of the most useful aides there is to improve visualization of the larynx during direct laryngoscopy.

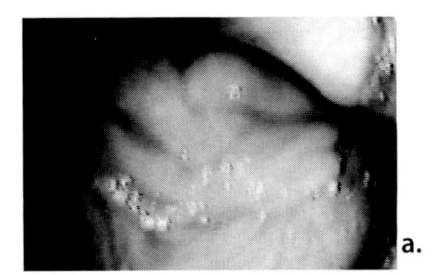

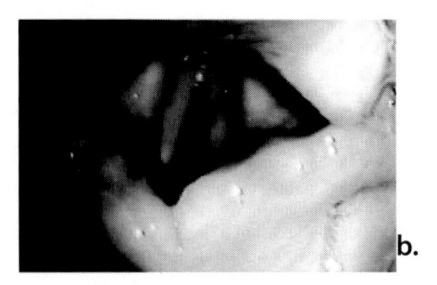

Fig. 5-20. Cricoid pressure. The photo in "a" was the original view during laryngoscopy. Photo "b" shows view after application of cricoid pressure.

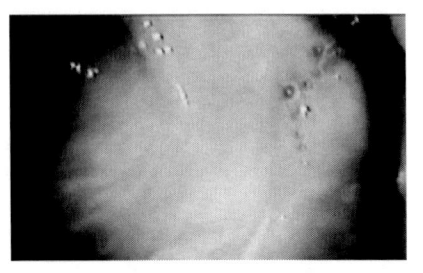

Keyframe 5-7a. When you can't see landmarks, and you feel that your blade is not too deep, then have your assistant give cricoid pressure.

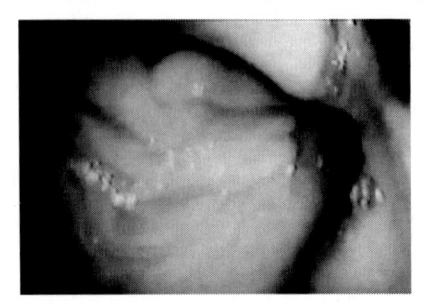

Keyframe 5-7b. As the larynx is pushed downward, landmarks often appear.

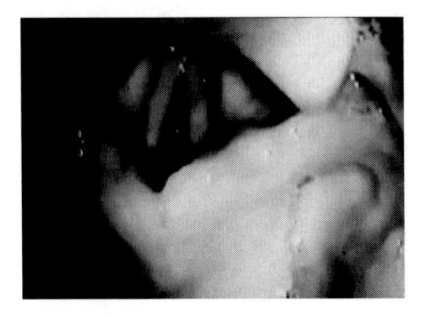

Keyframe 5-7c. View of the larynx with cricoid pressure being held.

vertebral column and effectively seal the esophagus. Cricoid pressure also forces the vocal cords downward and into the field of view (Fig. 5-19, 5-20, Mov. 5-7, KF. 5-7abc).

Many experienced intubators start by placing their own cricoid pressure with the right hand while doing laryngoscopy with the left. Once they see the larynx, they have their helper to mimic their finger position. Your helper must pay close attention to both the placement of your fingers as well as the angle of pressure or your view may worsen when they take over the pressure. Don't hesitate to use your own right hand to either show them again where and how to press, or to reposition their fingers. Avoid moving or rocking the laryngoscope as you do this.

To help protect from aspiration, the pressure must be applied to the cricoid ring. While very effective against passive regurgitation, you should immediately release cricoid pressure if the patient actively vomits. The obstructed esophagus might rupture because of high pressure.

If pressing down on the cricoid fails to improve the view, have your helper press on the thyroid cartilage, a maneuver is called B.U.R.P (Mov. 5-8, KF 5-8abcd). :

B.U.R.P.:
- **B**ackward against the vertebral column,
- **U**pwards toward the head,
- **R**ightwards to the patient's right side, as a constant
- **P**ressure.

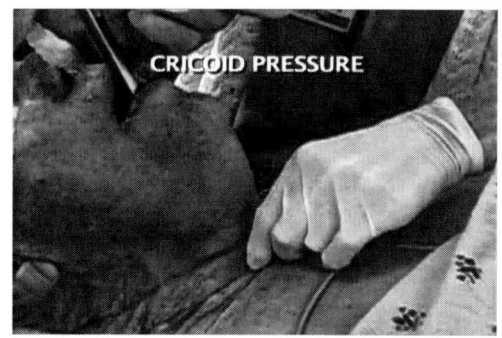

Keyframe 5-8a. The assistant gives cricoid pressure using thumb and forefinger to push down on either side of the cricoid ring.

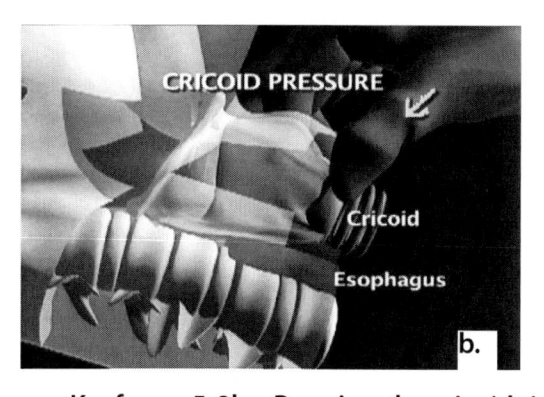

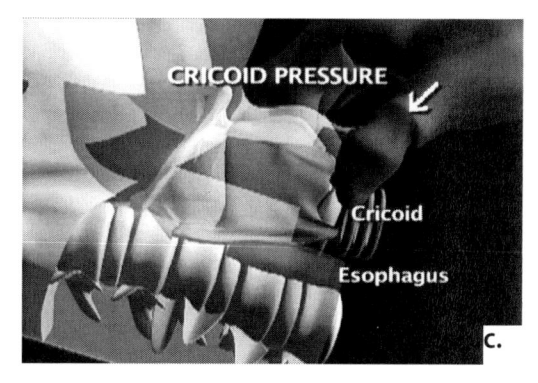

Keyframe 5-8bc. Pressing the cricoid ring downward pushes the larynx downward, but it also compresses the esophagus. This action can help prevent passive reflux.

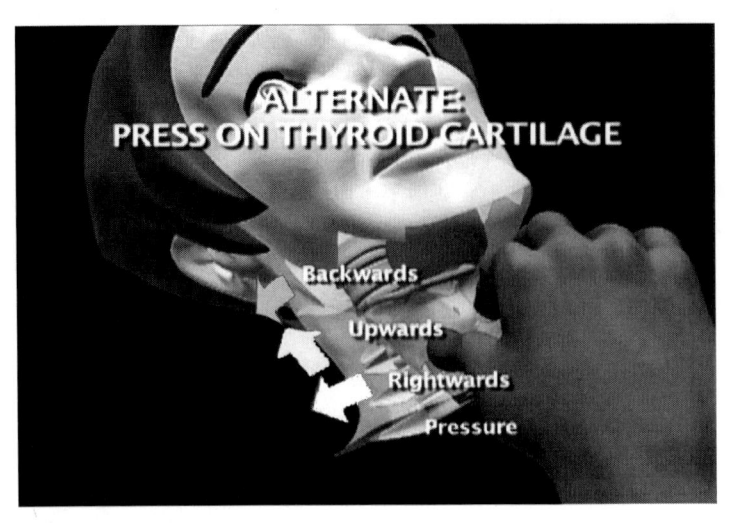

Keyframe 5-8d. Alternatively, pushing the thyroid cartilage backwards, rightward (patient's right), and upwards toward the head is sometimes more effective to bring the larynx into view.

Cricoid pressure and BURP should be used cautiously, if at all, when there is an upper airway foreign body or if there is risk of cervical spine injury

Pulling the Cheek Can Help

If you don't have enough space to maneuver the tube past the blade, it often helps to have your assistant pull the cheek back as far as they can to allow you to insert the tube. Your assistant must be careful not to get in your way, and also not to give you a moving target. As your assistant pulls the cheek have him press gently with the rest of his hand on the maxilla (see Fig. 5-21). This counter pressure prevents him from either pulling the head laterally or

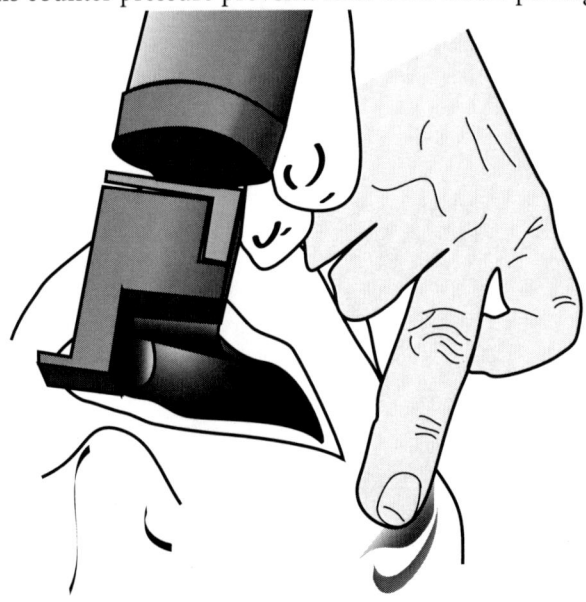

Fig. 5-21. Pulling the right corner of the mouth.

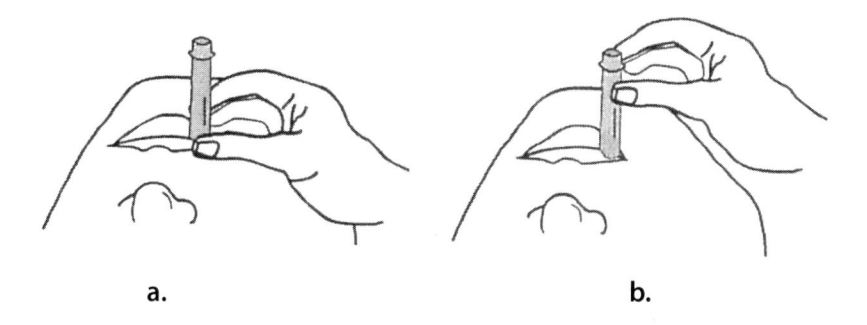

Fig. 5-22. Holding the ETT where it exits the mouth as in "a". Extubation is more likely if you hold the tube as in "b".

rotating it away from you. Make sure they don't "jiggle" the head, which could cause your blade to rattle against the teeth, possibly breaking them.

Securing the Tube

After intubation, you need to stabilize the endotracheal tube before taping it, and also every time you move the patient. Hold the tube where it exits the mouth, resting your hand on the cheek (Fig. 5-22). Extubation is more likely if you hold the adapter end because it's less secure in the event of unexpected movement.

Tape the tube securely to prevent extubation. Notice the depth of the tube by looking at the numbers that lines up with the front gum line: typically 21 cm for a woman, 22 cm for a man. For a child the depth in centimeters should equal the age in years divided by 2 plus 12. For example a four y.o. child should have the ETT inserted to a depth of 14 cm (4 divided by 2 plus 12).

Unless there's a need to place the tube midline, tape it toward the side of the mouth. Most of us tape it on the right since the tube already exits from that side.

There are many acceptable ways of taping the tube. Figures 5-23 and 5-24 show two ways. These methods have several factors in common. First, having the tube in the exact corner of the mouth is more comfortable for the patient. It avoids the patient pushing the tube out with the tongue. It also makes it easier for others to suction the mouth and place oral airways if needed. Second, you don't leave a tape tether. Tape extensions let the tube slide in or out of the mouth, risking either mainstem intubation or extubation. Finally, you avoid taping over the vermilion border or edge of the lip. You can tear this border when you remove the tape, especially in babies and geriatric patients. In addition, tape over the lips gets wet from saliva and loses its adhesion.

Don't pinch the lip in the tape wrap. Avoid taping the skin under tension, which can cause a tape burn or blister. Once the tube is taped, check again that the tube still lies in the trachea.

If you need the tube on the left side of the mouth, then you will have to move it. Hold the tube securely with your right hand where it exits the mouth. Take a tongue blade with your left hand and open the mouth. Push the tongue firmly down. Under direct vision move the tube from the groove on the right side of the tongue to the groove on the left.

Don't let the tube overlie the tongue as this position allows the patient to push it out with

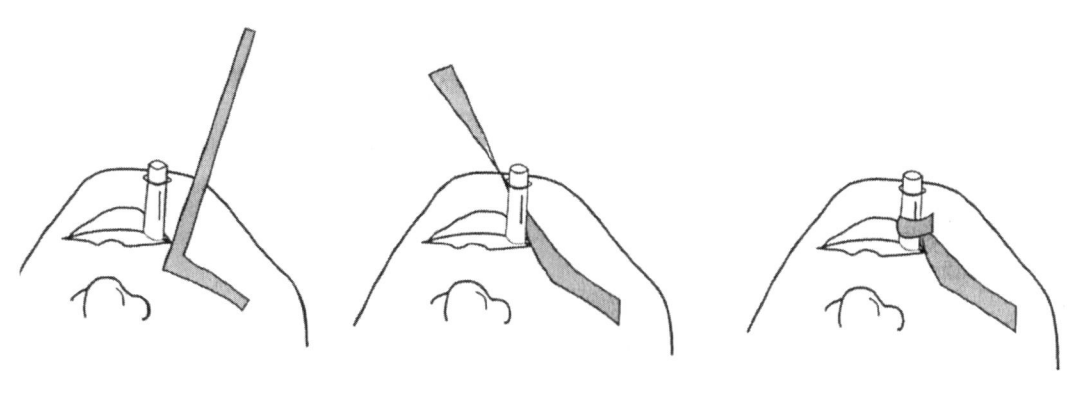

Fig. 5-23. One method to tape the tube. Split a 1 inch wide, 8 inch long piece of tape lengthwise for about 3 inches. Place the unsplit portion over the maxilla. Bring one limb of the split over the upper lip. Wrap the other limb around the tube. The tube is usually taped to one side of the mouth or the other. Avoid tension on the skin.

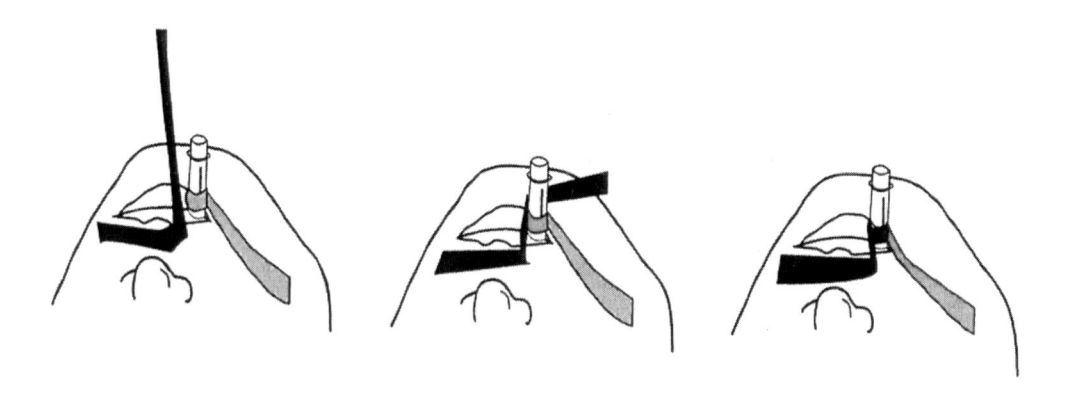

Fig. 5-24. Another way to tape the tube using single thin strips. Don't leave a tether. The tube will slide in and out of the mouth, making it less secure and more likely to lead to potential extubation or mainstem intubation.

their tongue. A tube overlying the tongue also means that there is less tube in the trachea than you would expect by the depth indicator on the tube because there is more hidden inside the mouth, where you can't see it.

Hold the tube securely with either hand and immediately check that the tube is still in the trachea before taping. **I can't emphasize strongly enough that you must verify good breath bilateral sounds anytime the tube or the patient moves.** Extubation and mainstem intubation can occur at any time.

Tape sticks poorly to hair. Taping endotracheal tubes in patients with beards and mustaches requires an alteration in technique. One can use the above methods after applying benzoin to the hair. A more secure method uses an "around the neck" tape as in Fig. 5-25. You can use this method whenever you need greater tube stabilization, for example, during prone positioning or transportation. Don't tape too tightly because your tape might constrict the neck like a tourniquet and cause facial swelling.

Specialized devices exist for tube stabilization during long-term intubation. Refer to their instructions for use.

Oral Intubation of the Adult Patient   117

1. Apply short strip of tape, sticky side down to long piece

Tape: sticky side up

2. Place tape under neck with long piece sticky side up

3. Tape first side as suggested in previous diagrams

4. Pull first side taut. Tape second side. Make sure that tape is not tight enough to act as a tournequet.

Fig 5-25. Taping an endotracheal tube in a bearded patient.

The Keyframe (KF) sequences in this chapter are taken from video clips that are available on-line, for free, from anyonecanintubate.com at:

For Chapter 5 video clips go to:
http://bit.ly/XMjIu8

All video chapter files appear on Anyone Can Intubate Portfolio at:
http://bit.ly/U7EV7f

6
COMMON ERRORS & HOW TO AVOID THEM

Inexperienced intubators often make several fairly common errors. This chapter will describe the most common errors as well as the ways to avoid them.

Describing The View You See

It's helpful to have terminology to describe the view you see during intubation to other providers in order to get their help, as well as to alert them to future problems. (Fig. 6-1 a-d) With a Grade I view, you can see the entire laryngeal outlet. With a Grade II view some, but not all of the vocal cords are visible. With Grade III you can see the back of the epiglottis, but not the cords. With a Grade IV view, the most difficult, the epiglottis can't be seen.

If you look at the figures, you can see that the higher the Grade, the more "anterior" the larynx appears to your field of view. Let's look at some techniques used to bring the larynx back down into your field of view during laryngoscopy.

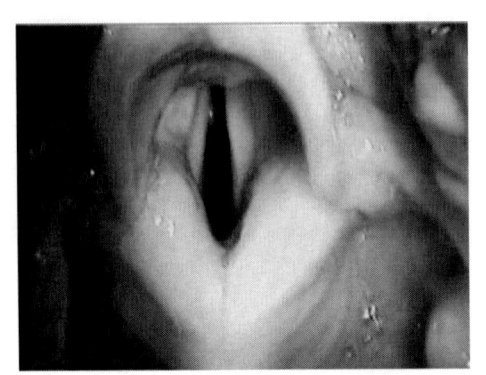

a. Grade I View

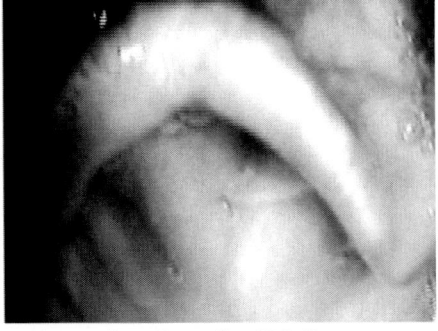

b. Grade II View

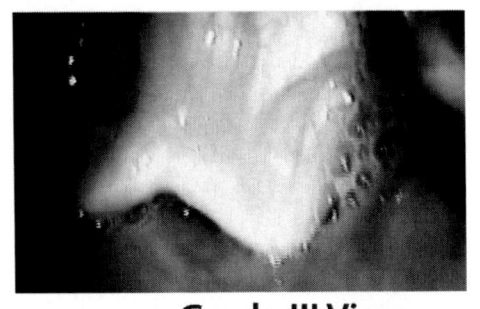

c. Grade III View

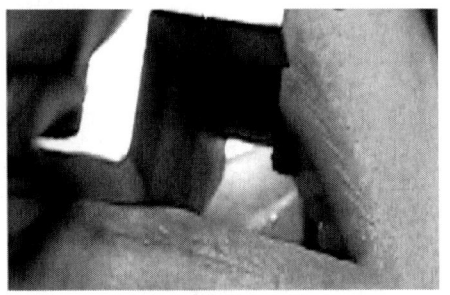

d. Grade IV View

Fig. 6-1. Grading the view during intubation.

Errors

Patient Positioning

Poor head placement is a common error. Sometimes you can't avoid it, such as during cardiac arrest with the patient on the floor. Overextension of the head, even in the average patient, makes the larynx appear more anterior on laryngoscopy.

You can optimize head and neck position with folded sheets or pillows. The goal is to have the mastoid process in line with the top of the chest. Optimal position is achieved with slight elevation of the head, neck flexion relative to the chest, and extreme atlanto-occipital extension. The "sniffing position", with the head elevated about 10 cm (4 in.) off the bed is the optimal height for the typical patient.

Having an assistant stabilize or lift the head, or changing the bed height, can also be helpful. These changes are fast, easy to perform, and often forgotten in the heat of battle. They make intubation easier and therefore less stressful and more likely to succeed. However, when an assistant lifts the head, he must keep the head absolutely stable as any wobble could break teeth. Have the assistant make a fist, and rest the patient's head on that upright fist as it sits immobile (Fig. 6-2a,b).

Unfortunately the standard sniffing position may not be adequate for the morbidly obese patient because the broad chest and large breasts are often positioned higher than the chin, interfering with laryngoscopy. (Fig 6-3a)

For the obese patient, successfully placing the patient in the optimal position may require a "ramp", where the patient's ear is horizontally aligned with the sternal notch. The ramp can be made either by strategically placing folded blankets under the shoulders and the head or by adjusting an OR table. The "ramp" has been found to be superior to the standard "sniffing" position's 10 cm occiput elevation during direct laryngoscopy in morbidly obese patients.[1] (Fig. 6-3b)

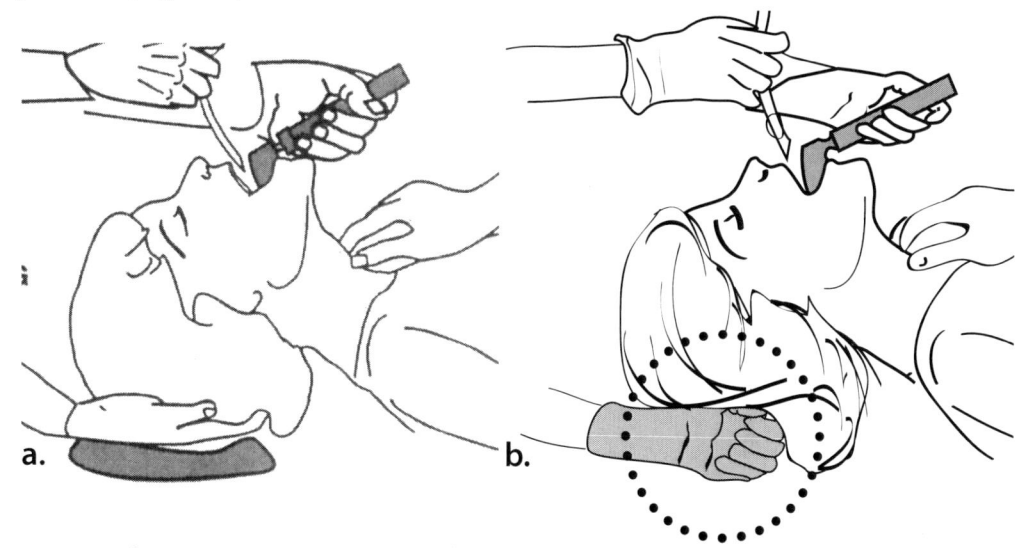

Fig. 6-2 a,b. Having your assistant lift the head can sometimes be helpful. However, it's hard to keep the head steady using outstretched hands as in "a". Any movement, however slight, can interfere with intubation or cause you to damage teeth. Having your assistant place a fist under the head and then rest it on the intubating surface, as in "b", is more stable.

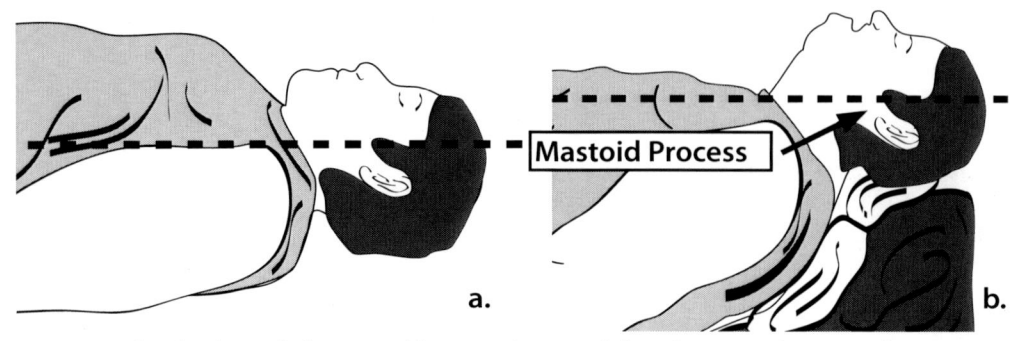

Fig. 6-3 a,b. The broad chest and breast tissue of the obese patient can hamper placement of the laryngoscope and make visualization difficult (a). Ramping the patient makes laryngoscopy easier. Make sure you can still tilt the head back.

A word of caution, however. If the ramp under the head is too high and/or too stiff, you may not be able to tilt the patient's head back. If you are having trouble tilting the head back then consider removing a layer. Before elective intubation, test the ability to tilt the patient's head *before* induction of anesthesia.

Finger Placement

The orbital ridge is a convenient, though incorrect, place to grab and pull. In their preoccupation and rush to extend the patient's head, the novice intubator will frequently place fingers over the patient's eyes (Fig. 6-4). The eyes are also vulnerable to name badges, stethoscopes, and anything else hanging around your neck.

When opening the mouth, inexperienced fingers grab the middle teeth — forcing the insertion of the blade toward the left where control of the tongue is lost. Place your fingers on the far right to allow better control of the tongue. Use the finger positioning shown in Fig. 6-5 and use a pushing rather than a spreading motion. Open the mouth as widely as you can. You are far less likely to damage teeth or gums if you give yourself room to maneuver and see.

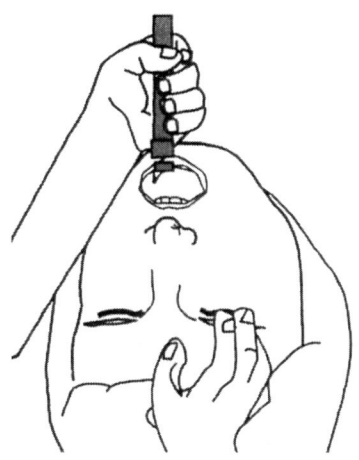

Fig. 6-4. Don't press on the eyes. Corneal abrasion occurs easily

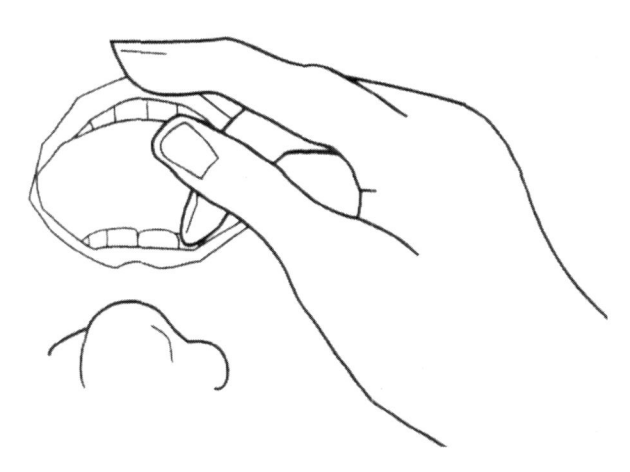

Fig. 6-5. Don't place your fingers in the middle. Place them as far to the right as possible.

Fig. 6-6. Don't hunch over the patient.

Body Posture

Keep your back as straight as possible and left arm rigid. Hunching over the patient, a common mistake, makes intubation more difficult because it impairs your mechanical advantage (Fig. 6-6). You won't have strength to lift and it almost forces you to use the teeth as a fulcrum.

Problems With Cricoid Pressure

Head position and movement of surrounding tissues shifts cartilages and may affect your ability to see the vocal cords. Sometimes the larynx lies anterior to your field of view during laryngoscopy. This view is often described as an "anterior larynx" and it commonly occurs with poor head positioning, as well as in patients with obesity, larynxes located higher in the neck than average, and in patients with poorly developed mandibles or weak chins. Ask your assistant to provide cricoid pressure when you can't see the larynx during intubation.

Cricoid pressure is one of the most valuable aides to use when you can't see the larynx, regardless of reason (Fig. 6-7). It not only improves visualization, but also helps to prevent aspiration because it pinches the esophagus closed and traps contents in the stomach.

No matter how useful cricoid pressure usually is, it will occasionally prevent passage of the endotracheal tube. Cricoid pressure will sometimes pinch a child's soft airway closed. Sometimes the angle created by the downward displacement is too acute, preventing entry of the tube. This is especially true when inexperienced helpers push the cricoid off to the side. If you are having a great deal of difficulty intubating, consider releasing part or all of the cricoid pressure to see if it helps. If something isn't working, don't be afraid to change it.

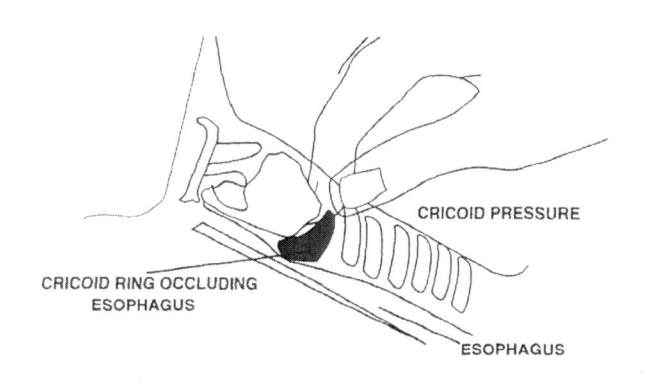

Fig 6-7. Cricoid pressure is one of the most useful aides there is. However, too much can occasionally make intubation harder.

Left-handed Intubation

Most people are right handed and instinctively reach for the laryngoscope with their right hand. They discover their mistake when they find themselves with their right hand blocking their view and with no way for their left hand to pass a tube over their right. Standard laryngoscopes are held in the non-dominant left hand because this hand merely provides a stable platform. The dominant right hand needs all the coordination and dexterity to manipulate the tube. Unfortunately, left handed intubators are left in an awkward position. As just pointed out, the standard blades are held in the left hand. Reversing them doesn't work.

Although the left-handed provider can purchase a left handed blade, which is a mirror image of the standard blade, I don't recommend this. It is far better for you to train yourself to do it "backwards." Training yourself on left handed tools puts you at a major disadvantage when only right handed tools are available. Most hospitals only stock right handed instruments. It may not be fair, but it's definitely more practical. Most left handed intubators use the standard blade, just like they learned to use right handed scissors when children. It's a matter of practice.

Problems with Laryngoscopy Technique

Inserting the blade too deeply and into the esophagus is a common beginner mistake. If you can't identify any landmarks, slowly pull the blade back. Often the larynx will fall into view.

A straight blade can "tent" the esophagus and make it look like vocal cords if you haven't actually seen both (Fig. 6-8ab, Mov. 6-1, KF. 6-1abc). Suspect it's the esophagus if there are no identifiable landmarks.

As mentioned earlier, a blade placed in the center of the tongue produces a mound of tissue that blocks the view (Fig. 6-9). Make sure that you slide the blade as far to the left side of the mouth as you can to move the tongue out of your way. This movement typically places the blade close to the midline, a very stable position for lifting and balancing the head.

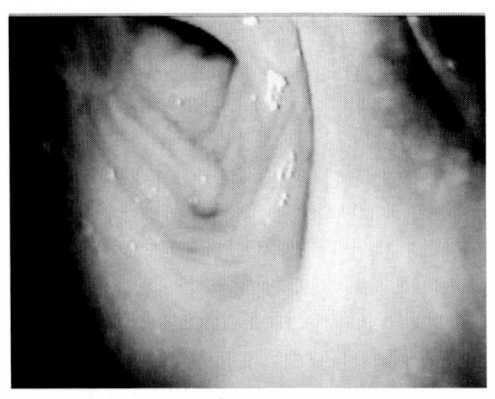

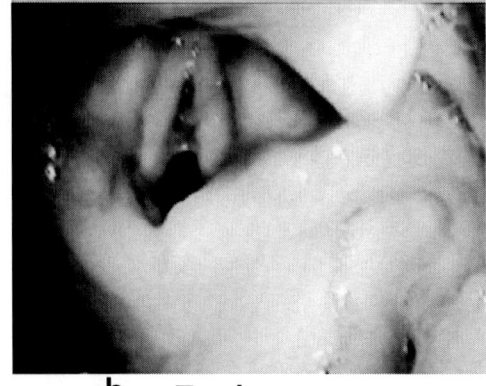

a. Esophagus   b. Trachea

Fig. 6-8ab. In "a", on the left, the blade has been inserted too deep. This is the esophagus. Don't be fooled by that slight triangular tenting at the bottom of the opening. In "b", on the right, the larynx dropped into view after pulling the blade.

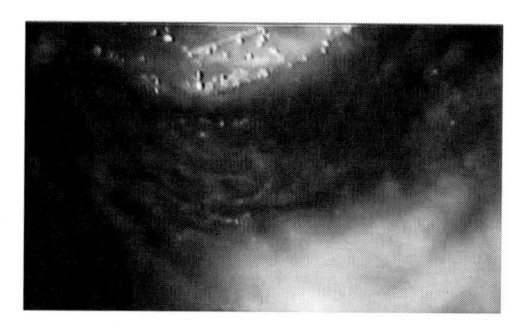

Keyframe 6-1a. When the laryngoscope is too deep, you may not recognize landmarks.

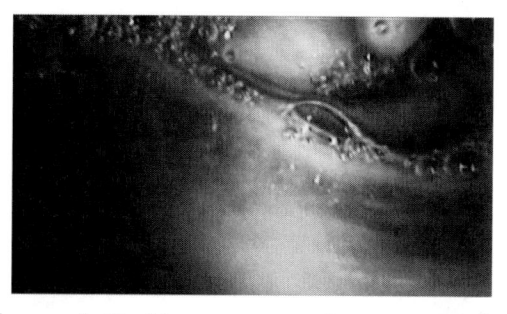

Keyframe 6-1b. Here you can just see the back of the arytenoids at the top of the image.

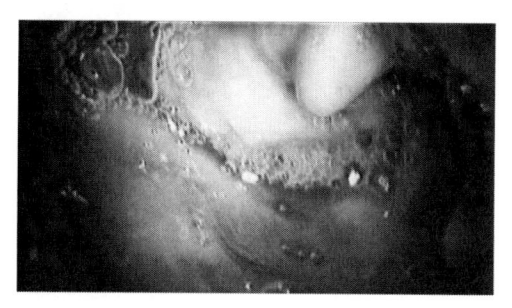

Keyframe 6-1c. The laryngoscope is still too deep, but you see arytenoids. The view is distorted because the larynx is twisted under the blade.

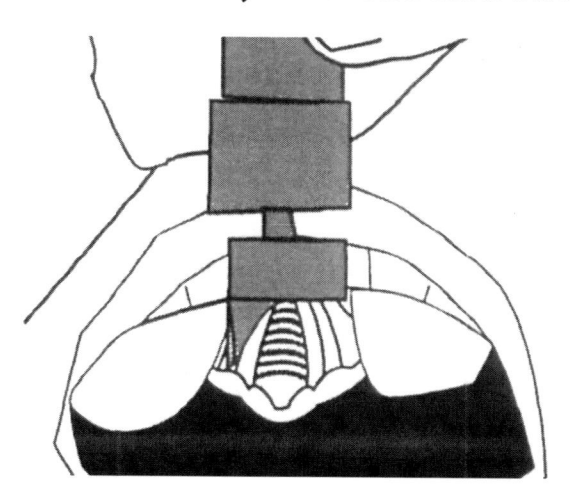

Fig. 6-9. Don't place the blade in the middle of the tongue.

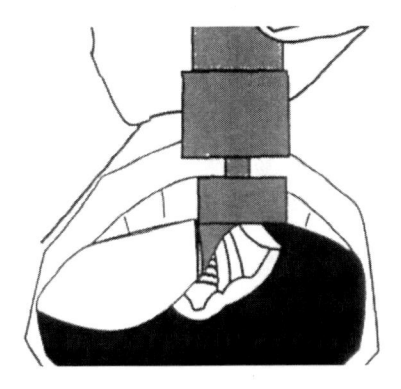

Fig. 6-10. Don't leave the blade on right. Slide tongue to the left.

Leaving the blade too far to the right can provide a good view of the cords but no room to pass the tube (Fig. 6-10). Sometimes you can't even get the tube into the mouth. If you routinely have to ask an assistant to pull the right corner of the mouth out of the way consider sweeping the tongue further left.

Inexperienced intubators place their blade gently, and then barely lift the jaw out of fear of hurting the patient. Without lifting, they don't see the larynx. Failing to see anything, they then use the blade like a lever on the front teeth to lift the epiglottis, placing the teeth in danger. (Fig. 6-11). Always lift. Properly done, you can lift the head off the bed without hurting the patient.

Fig. 6-11. Don't rotate your blade. Lift upward. Like tennis: keep your wrist stiff and your elbow fairly straight.

Edentulous patients, or those missing their front teeth, frequently fool the intubator into thinking he or she has lifted enough (Fig. 6-12). Without front teeth you see a great view of the larynx without lifting the jaw. Without the lift, however, the mouth is barely wide enough to pass the tube. The absence of teeth on the mandible sometimes changes the angle of the blade during lift. Usually, however, the change in "feel" and balance is minimal. It is often offset by the relief of the intubator about not having to worry about the teeth. Intubation is easier without teeth if you lift enough.

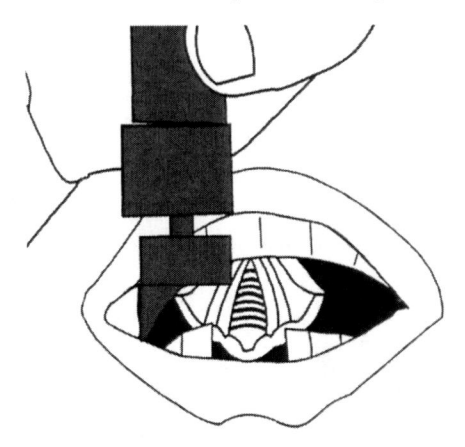

Fig. 6-12. Don't forget to open the mouth as wide as you can with the laryngoscope. Gaps in the teeth can give you a good view but not leave room to pass the tube.

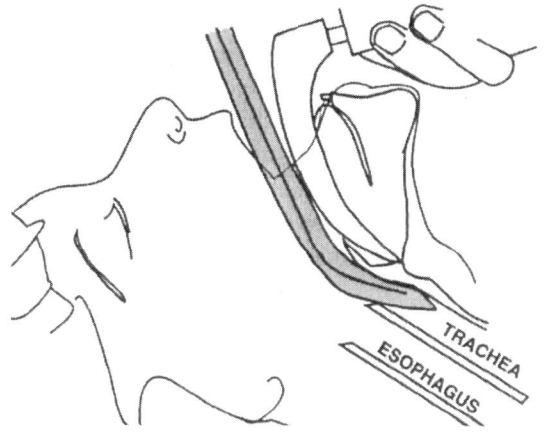

Fig. 6-13. A stylet can sometimes prevent insertion.

The Excessively Bent Stylet

The tube may not advance easily if the stylet is too sharply bent. (Fig. 6-13). If you can't advance the ETT into the trachea, fix your tube firmly in position and either back the stylet out with your thumb or have an assistant slowly remove the stylet 1-2 cm. The tip becomes more flexible, allowing you to advance it.

Slowly rotating the tube often allows the bevel to slip off the anterior commissure and slide down into the trachea when it's caught (Fig.6-14 a,b).

You can always change the shape of your stylet. Sometimes a curved stylet will let you maneuver inside the mouth better (Fig. 6-15). Don't be afraid to change the shape. Stylets make the endotracheal tube more rigid. Be gentle when using one.

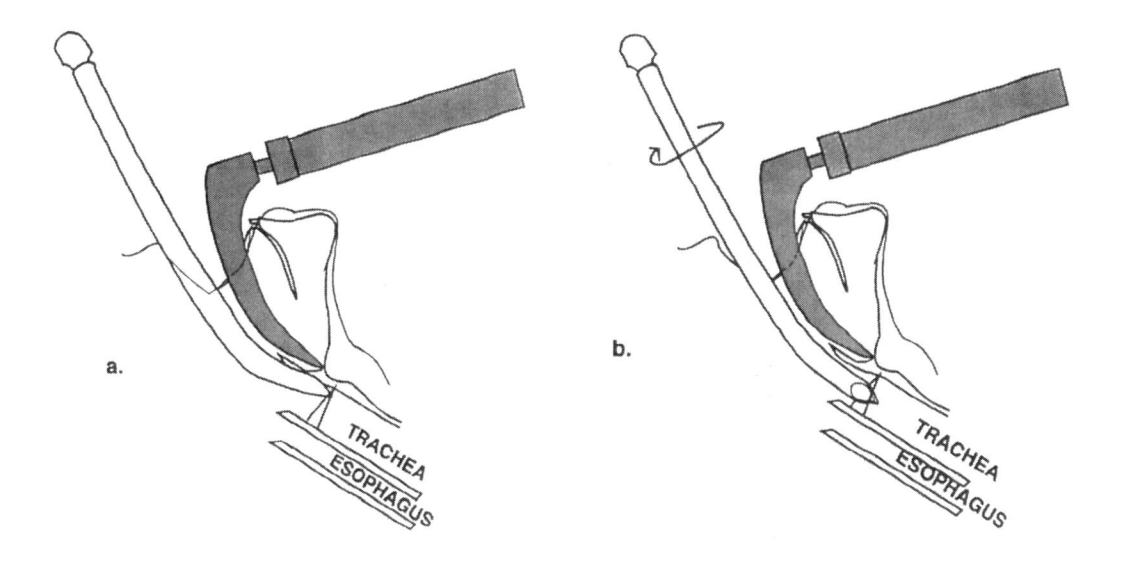

Fig. 6-14. The tube tip in "a" is caught on the anterior commissure. Rotate the tube, as in "b", to allow it to pass.

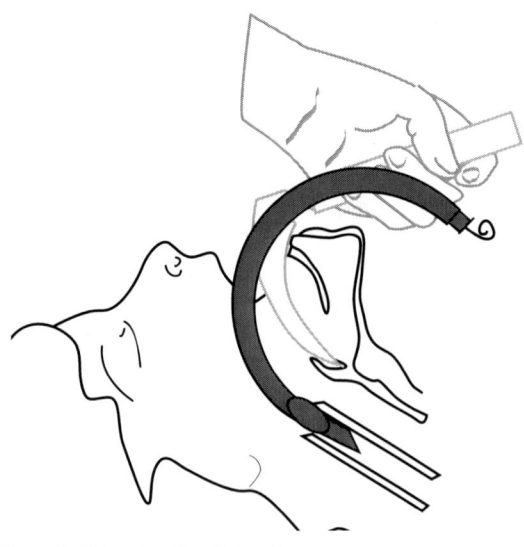

Fig. 6-15. Alter stylet shape as needed. Note the more curved the stylet, the harder it can be to pull out.

Don't Pinch the Lips!

While everyone is rightfully paranoid about damaging teeth, they are often less careful about protecting the lips. Upper and lower lips commonly get pinched between the blade and the teeth and will get cut unless you are take care. While the cut may be small, cut lips are painful and swell impressively. In that last second before you place the weight of the head on your blade by lifting, check the lips and use a finger to push them free if they are trapped. Keep rechecking the lips as well as the teeth during prolonged attempts.

It's also possible to trap part of the lip in your endotracheal tube taping and cause a blister from tape burn. After taping the tube recheck the lips and relieve any pressure or tension if necessary.

Light Bulbs and Flanges Block Tube

Occassionally you will have a great view with a straight blade but can't pass the tube. Older Miller blades have the light bulb on the right. When the light bulb is angled toward the right it often deflects the endotracheal tube away from the glottic opening. If you simply rotate the blade slightly to the left, you will raise the bulb out of the way, allowing the tube to pass (Fig. 6-16).

You won't experience this problem with a fiberoptic straight blade. However, some fiberoptic straight blades have a curved metal rim that extends further down and closer to the tip of the blade than others. This curved metal piece can also deflect the tube, but it's on the opposite side from the light bulb. Therefore, for the fiberoptic blade you often have to slightly rotate your blade toward the *right* to relieve the obstruction.

Once you have an understanding of the intubation procedure and the purpose of each step, you can easily avoid the common errors.

Common Errors and How To Avoid Them   127

a.

b.

c.

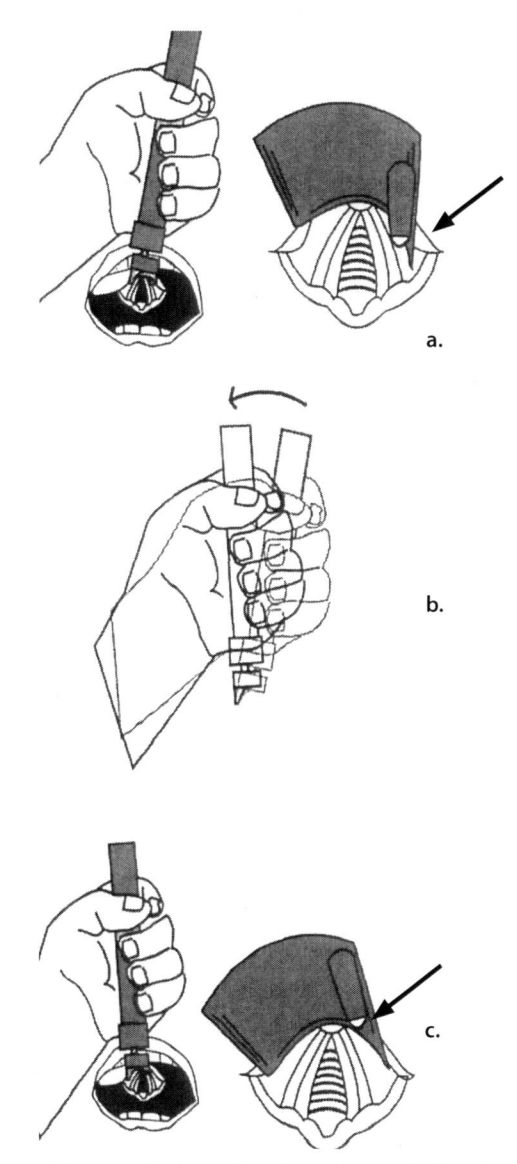

Fig. 6-16. If you can see the cords, but the light bulb deflects your tube, as in "a", then rotate your hand slightly to the left as in "b". This often allows the tube to pass without difficulty as in "c".

The Keyframe (KF) sequences in this chapter are taken from video clips that are available on-line, for free, from anyonecanintubate.com at:

For Chapter 6 video clips go to:
http://bit.ly/W30hzE

All video chapter files appear on Anyone Can Intubate Portfolio at:
http://bit.ly/U7EV7f

7
VERIFYING PLACEMENT

After intubation, check immediately that the tube is positioned correctly in the trachea and not a mainstem bronchus or the esophagus or (Fig. 7-1, 7-2). Even expert intubators occasionally intubate the esophagus. This is not a problem as long as you recognize the error and correct it at once.

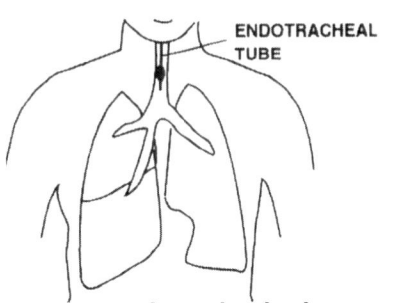

Fig. 7-1. Endotracheal tube properly positioned mid trachea, above carina.

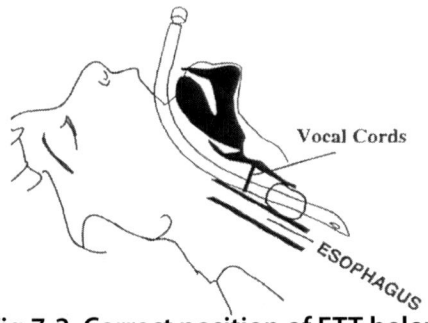

Fig 7-2. Correct position of ETT below cords and cricoid ring, tip approximately midtrachea.

Seven Steps for Correct Tube Placement

One of the first ways to be sure of tube placement is to see the endotracheal tube pass between the vocal cords. Remove the blade slowly while looking for visual confirmation. Next, perform the following tests.

1. Listen over both sides of the chest for breath sounds. A tube placed too far down the trachea will lie in one mainstem bronchus and block the other. In this case you will hear breath sounds only on one side of the chest.
2. Listen over the stomach with a stethoscope. A gurgling sound indicates an esophageal intubation.
3. Look for condensation forming inside the tube with each breath. This indicates tracheal placement.
4. Watch for the chest to rise each time you give a breath.
5. The awake patient will no longer be able to speak once the cuff is inflated.
6. If breathing spontaneously, you will feel air movement with your hand placed over the opening of the tube.
7. If you have an end-tidal CO_2 apparatus, check it. CO_2 won't be detected after several manual breaths with an esophageal intubation.

Esophageal Intubation

Gurgling over the stomach and lack of breath sounds over the chest means the tube is in the esophagus unless proven otherwise. Calmly remove the tube, having your suction ready. Removal of a tube from the esophagus can cause either passive regurgitation or active vomiting so be prepared. Next, ventilate the patient by mask until the patient is adequately oxygenated. The color of the lips, nail beds, and conjunctivae of the eyes are pink if the patient is oxygenated. Try again.

The risk of passive regurgitation is higher due to the increased volume of air now in the stomach. Also the passage of the tube into the esophagus opens the esophageal sphincters and may decrease their tone. I have a helper maintain cricoid pressure until after I place the final tube in the trachea.

Usually there's no doubt about whether the tube lies in the trachea or the esophagus. Unfortunately, there are rare instances when you can't easily tell.

If the stomach is distended with air, you may not hear gurgling. Insufflation of the stomach sometimes transmits muffled air flow sounds to the chest which may be misinterpreted as faint breath sounds. However, the chest will rise poorly if at all. Ventilatory compliance will be bad. Condensation will not form in the tube. It will be hard to keep you bag filled with gas.

After prolonged ventilation with gas in the stomach, there may be initial CO_2 on an end-tidal CO_2 apparatus. However, end-tidal CO_2 will quickly disappear.

Patients with severe bronchospasm start with extremely faint breath sounds and very stiff lung compliance. Their chest barely rises. The endotracheal tube may be correctly placed but you sometimes can't tell by listening to the chest alone.

Having and using an end-tidal CO_2 measuring apparatus will help detect esophageal intubations. The continued presence of CO_2 in the exhaled breath can only mean placement of the tube in the trachea. Although there is some difference in brands, the typical detector is purple or blue if no CO_2 is present and yellow or gold when CO_2 is there. Thus the mnemonic yellow/yes, gold/good, purple/problem usually works.

CO_2 detectors aren't perfect, however. There are several scenarios where the CO_2 detector can sometimes fail to detect CO_2:

- Neonates weighing less than 2 kg, especially with poor perfusion: detector not sensitive enough
- Cardiac arrest: CO_2 can't get to the lungs to be exhaled
- Large pulmonary embolus: CO_2 can't get to the lungs to be exhaled

These real life situations make detection of esophageal intubations more difficult. If you have any doubts about the correct placement of your endotracheal tube don't hesitate to look with your laryngoscope.

Tube Too Deep: Mainstem Intubation

Louder breath sounds on one side of the chest may mean a mainstem intubation. A mainstem intubation occurs when the endotracheal tube is inserted too deeply and extends down one mainstem bronchus, ventilating one lung but obstructing the other (Mov. 7-1, KF. 7-1ab). Usually the tube advances down the right side because the right bronchus is straighter. To cure a mainstem intubation, pull the tube back until you hear breath sounds on both sides of the chest. Secure the tube to prevent it from sliding back down the trachea.

One word of caution. Before you reposition the tube look at the numbers and see if the depth of insertion is appropriate. If the depth seems correct, consider pneumothorax, pneumonectomy, or pleural effusion as possible causes of unequal breath sounds.

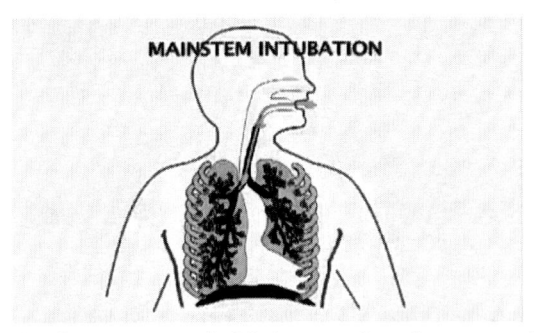

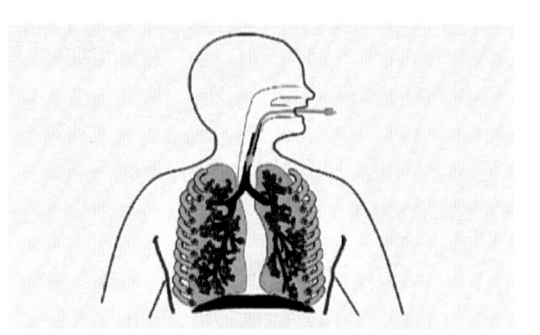

Keyframes 7-1a,b. Mainstem intubaton on left is resolved by withdrawal of the ETT to mid trachea. Breath sounds will become equal and the chest will rise symmetrically.

If you believe the tube is too deep, then slowly back the tube out until you hear equal breath sounds. However, if the breath sounds remain unequal stop withdrawal. Recheck the depth of tube placement by laryngoscopy (to ensure the cuff is below the cords), get an X-ray, and look for other reasons for inequality.

Cuff Too High

In addition to ensuring that the tube is not too deep, also make sure that the cuff is not too high, and that it's *below* the cricoid ring. Suspect the cuff is too high if you hear a leak around it, although there are several other situations, that will cause a leak around the cuff. These are:

- the cuff needs more air to make the seal
- a hole in the cuff
- a faulty pilot balloon
- a cuff above the cords: risk of unplanned extubation high

If adding a little more air to the cuff fixes the leak, there is no problem. With a faulty cuff or pilot balloon, reinflation of the pilot balloon temporarily fixes the problem, but the pilot balloon becomes soft again as the cuff deflates. If the pilot balloon is faulty, attaching a closed stopcock after reinflation will often solve the problem. If the cuff itself is leaking, the tube will need replacement.

If the cuff is above the cords, however, there is a persistent leak despite repeated cuff inflation (Fig. 7-3). Adding more air to the cuff often makes the leak worse. The pilot balloon becomes increasingly distended, tense, and holds pressure. The cuff is above cords on laryngoscopy. You can ventilate the patient because the tube tip lies in the trachea, but there is significant risk of extubation because only the tip of the tube is through the glottis.

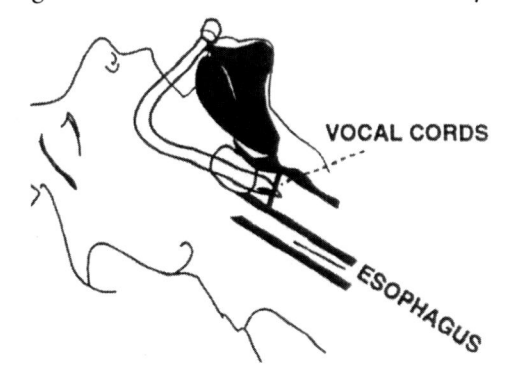

Fig. 7-3. Tube bowed in the pharynx, the cuff is above the cords. This position places the patient at high risk of extubation.

If you have a cuff above the cords:
- Make sure you have the equipment for reintubation immediately available.
- Suction the patient's mouth.
- Untape the tube and deflate the cuff. It may take several aspirations if the balloon has become overdistended with the attempts to seal the leak. Hold the tube firmly during this process.
- Gently advance the tube to the proper depth.
- Immediately reverify proper placement. The tube can sometimes slip off the back of the larynx into the esophagus with the manipulation.

Cuff Inside the Cricoid Ring

If the cuff sits partially inside the rigid cricoid cartilage, it can press on and potentially injure the recurrent laryngeal nerves, causing transient, possibly permanent, vocal cord paralysis (Fig. 7-4). Cuff overdistention increases risk.

Failure to insert the tube to the correct depth for that patient increases risk. Using a smaller tube, such as a 5 or 5.5 cuffed tube for an adult to facilitate oropharyngeal surgery or to accommodate patient pathology can place the cuff too high in the larynx. Pediatric tubes are shorter than standard adult tubes, so they appear to be inserted to the correct depth. Often longer Microlaryngeal Tracheal Tube (MLT) style tubes are chosen to avoid this situation.

If the tube is overlying the tongue, the tube may be taped at the correct depth at the teeth, but the fact that several cm of it are overlying the tongue means that less of it is inside the trachea. Not only does this position risk leaving the cuff inside the cricoid ring, the patient can push the tube out more easily with their tongue.

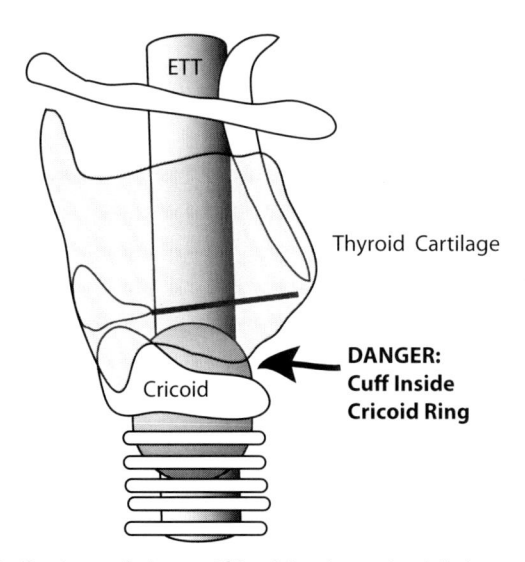

Fig. 7-4. Inflation of the cuff inside the cricoid ring places the recurrent laryngeal nerves at risk, risking transient or permanent vocal cord paralysis and hoarseness.

Cuff Leaks

The differential diagnosis for a cuff that's too high and won't hold a seal is a cuff that really is leaking. An endotracheal tube with a leaky cuff should be changed. However, there are times when changing a leaking tube in an intubated patient may be difficult. For example, a cuff leak that develops in the middle of head and neck surgery or brain surgery can be hard to treat. You lack easy access to the patient's airway. A ventilator dependent patient in the intensive care unit is another example. Occasionally these patients won't tolerate even limited interruption in ventilation without becoming cyanotic. Change the tube if you can.

If you can't, first check the pilot tube. Inflate the cuff until the leak stops and keep the pilot balloon sealed with a closed stopcock or syringe. If the cuff retains air with the pilot tube plugged, then the pilot tube is probably leaking. To keep the cuff inflated use a closed stopcock, a syringe with the plunger firmly taped, or a clamp on the pilot tube itself. I usually avoid clamping the pilot tube itself, which permanently seals the balloon and prevents addition of more air in the future.

When the cuff itself leaks, you can temporarily pack the posterior pharynx around the tube with gauze to plug the leak and help prevent aspiration. Always remember to remove the pack when you remove or change the tube. Packs left in the pharynx cause potentially fatal airway obstruction upon extubation. Please view these tricks as temporary measures and not long-term solutions.

Acute Desaturation in the Intubated Patient

When an intubated patient who has been stable suddenly decompensates and desaturates you need to evaluate him or her quickly. A useful mnemonic is D.O.P.E which stands for:

- **D**isplacement: either extubation or mainstem intubation
- **O**bstruction: tube may be kinked inside the mouth or obstructed by secretions or blood clot
- **P**neumothorax: can occur at any time when positive pressure ventilation is being performed, especially if lung pathology exists.
- **E**quipment: disconnects, failure, incorrect settings

Immediately take the patient off the ventilator and manually ventilate him with 100% oxygen. If the patient's condition improves, there may be an equipment problem.

Listen to breath sounds to ensure the patient is still intubated.

If breath sounds are present but unequal, with asymmetric chest movement, quickly check the depth of tube insertion. If the tube has slid in too deep there may be a mainstem intubation. Reposition the ETT as previously described.

If the depth of the tube has not changed there may be a pneumothorax. A hemodynamically stable patient can probably tolerate waiting for a chest X-Ray verification before treatment. An unstable patient may need emergent chest decompression for a tension pneumothorax. Either way minimize inflation pressures.

If breath sounds are equal, then suction down the endotracheal tube with a flexible suction catheter. If you can't insert the catheter fully check to see if the ETT is kinked where it makes the bend toward the larynx in the back of the pharynx. If not there may be a mucous plug or blood clot. If you can't clear the ETT enough to ventilate through it then you need to replace it.

When To Re-Verify Tube Placement

You should verify tube placement immediately following intubation. Since endotracheal tubes easily slip out of position you should re-verify every time:

- you move the patient from one location to another,
- you change the position of the patient,
- you reposition the endotracheal tube,
- you retape the endotracheal tube,
- a cuff leak develops,
- if the oxygen saturation, ventilation status, or lung compliance changes,
- at the onset of hemodynamic instability.

Do not hesitate to check the endotracheal tube placement if you have any suspicions that it may have moved.

The Keyframe (KF) sequences in this chapter are taken from video clips that are available on-line, for free, from anyonecanintubate.com at:

For Chapter 7 video clips go to:
http://bit.ly/14AtjLQ

All video chapter files appear on Anyone Can Intubate Portfolio at:
http://bit.ly/U7EV7f

8
VENTILATING AND INTUBATING THE CHILD

Children are not miniature adults. From infants to teenagers, the anatomy and physiology of the child is continuously morphing into adult form. These differences make managing the airway and intubation more challenging.

Anatomy: Children Are Not Small Adults

There is a reason why most providers are more nervous taking care of children less than 2 years of age. The differences in pediatric airway anatomy and physiology are most marked in infants and toddlers (Table 8-1 and Figs. 8-1, 8-2). As the child grows, not only do the laryngeal and pharyngeal structures get larger, their shapes and relationships change. Sometime between the ages of 6 and 8, the laryngeal anatomy, although smaller, resembles the adult.

Many aspects of the young child's airway anatomy predispose to airway obstruction and respiratory distress. The newborn's neck is shorter than the adult's. With the head flexed forward, the infant's chin often rests on the chest, reaching the second rib. The infant's larynx lies higher in the neck opposite cervical vertebrae 2-3, instead of opposite the adult C 5-6. It's easier for the tongue and pharyngeal soft tissue to cause obstruction with the larynx higher in the neck.

In the human infant, the larynx can be elevated allowing the epiglottis to slide up behind the soft palate to effectively lock the larynx into the nasopharynx. With the soft palate fitted snugly around the larynx, a constricted passage is formed on both sides of the elevated larynx, allowing liquid to pass around the larynx into the esophagus. The tongue is larger relative to the mandible and fills the mouth, angled slightly forward to cover the gum line. These features allow the nursing human newborn to suckle effectively and breathe while swallowing liquid. The ability to breathe and swallow at the same time results in "obligate nose breathing." Unlike newborn infants, adult humans are not obligate nose breathers.

A newborn infant breathes through his nose and can suffocate if the nose is obstructed. The only time newborns breathe through their mouths is when crying. A congenital defect known as choanal atresia, occurs when the nasal passage is narrowed or blocked by tissue. Choanal atresia blocking both sides of the nose causes acute breathing problems with cyanosis and breathing failure. Infants with bilateral choanal atresia may need resuscitation at delivery.

The baby's relatively large tongue more easily obstructs the airway. When supine, the large occiput flexes the infant's head forward, collapsing the tongue and soft tissues over the larynx and blocking the airway.

The trachea is shorter. The cartilage composing the trachea is soft and easily compressed.

Ventilating And Intubating The Child   135

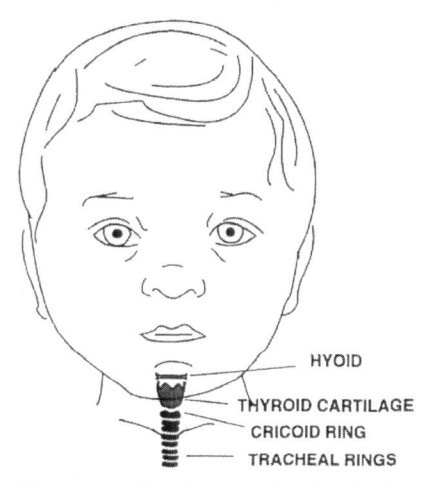

Fig. 8-1. The larynx in the infant is much higher in the neck — opposite C 2-3 rather than C 5-6 as in the adult.

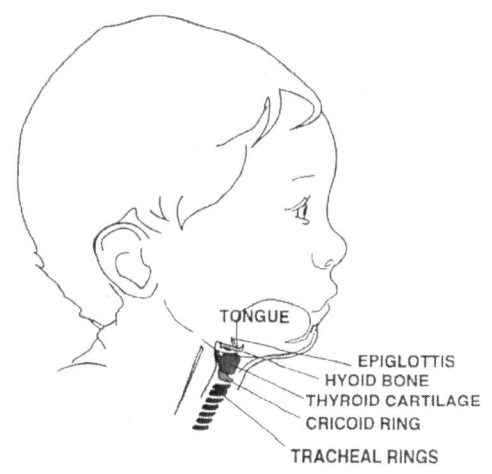

Fig. 8-2. The tongue is large relative to the jaw. The neck is short. The larynx is more easily obstructed.

Table 8-1. Comparing Infant and Adult Airways		
	Infant	Adult
Tongue	relatively larger	relatively smaller
Larynx	opposite 2nd and 3rd cervical vertebrae	opposite 4th and 5th cervical vertebrae
Epiglottis	"U" shaped short	flat, erect, flexible
Hyoid/Thyroid separation	very close	further apart
Glottis	1/2 cartilage	1/4 cartilage
Arytenoids	inclined inferiorly	horizontal
Vocal Cords	concave	horizontal
Cricoid	plate forms funnel	plate is vertical
Smallest Diameter	cricoid ring	vocal cord aperture
Consistency of Cartilage	soft	firm
Shape of Head	pronounced occiput	flatter occiput

Extreme extension or flexion of the child's neck can obstruct the airway. In fact, pressing on the soft tissue under the chin to get a good mask fit can also obstruct the airway.

The infant larynx is not only smaller than the adult's, it's also anatomically different. The epiglottis is shorter and more "U" shaped, making it harder to pick up with the laryngoscope. It's softer and more easily deformed (Mov. 8-1, KF 8-1ab). The higher position of the larynx in the neck makes the larynx appear more anterior during intubation, since it's harder to displace the surrounding soft tissue forward out of the line of sight.

In the adult larynx, the gap through the vocal cords is the smallest diameter. However, in a young child the smallest diameter is the cricoid cartilage, *below* the vocal cords. Therefore, you can occasionally pass an endotracheal tube through the vocal cords — but then not

Adult

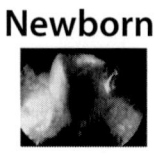

Newborn

Keyframes 8-1a,b. As the larynx grows not only its size but its anatomy changes. Relative sizes of adult vs. newborn larynx.

through the cricoid ring into the trachea. Never force a tube to pass. Instead switch to a smaller tube.

The cricoid's narrow, rigid, ring shaped, bottleneck also increases the risk of airway obstruction when swelling occurs. Minimal swelling can cause tracheal obstruction because the larynx and trachea are small. One mm circumferential swelling in an adult with a 10 mm trachea causes only a 44% decrease in cross-sectional area. The same 1 mm circumferential edema in an infant with a 4 mm trachea causes a 75% decrease (Fig. 8-3). Thus swelling from infections or trauma can have a much more devastating effect.

However, another important concept is airway resistance. Resistance changes proportionately to the inverse of the radius to the 4th power. A small decrease in radius can produce a large increase in resistance. It's worth noting that due to size, a normal infant's 4 mm larynx has 16 X the resistance to flow of a normal adult larynx of 8 mm. The infant has less ability to compensate for increased resistance to air flow.

The vocal cords of the child have a concave upward shape, rather than the horizontal shape of the adult. While this difference in shape doesn't affect our ability to intubate a child,

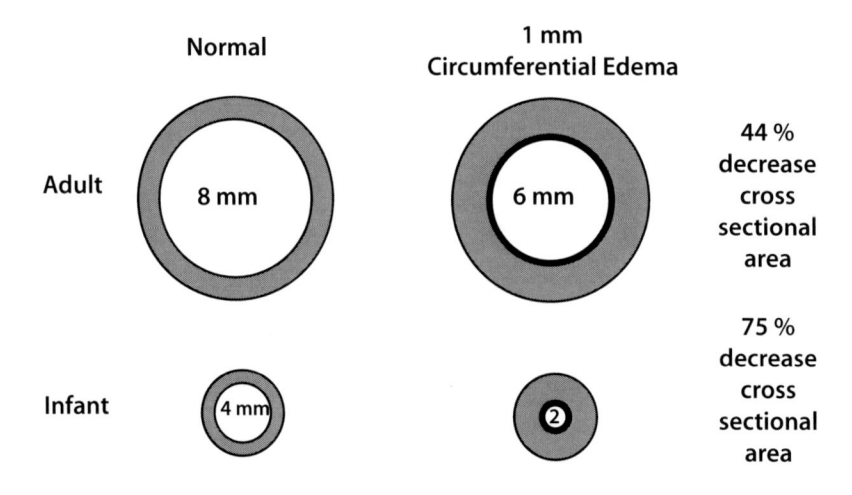

Fig. 8-3. Comparison of effects on 1 mm circumferential edema on both the adult and the infant larynx. For this example, airway resistance increases 3 times for the adult but 16 times for the infants.

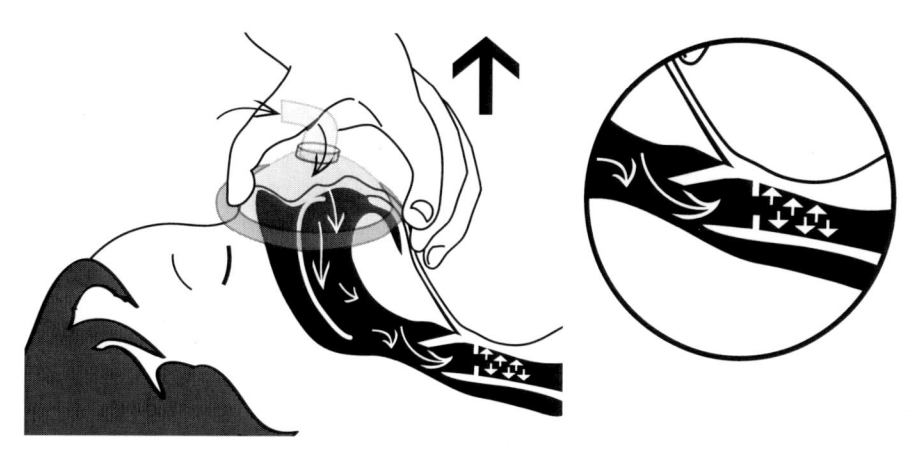

Fig. 8-4. Breaking laryngospasm in a child usually requires lifting upward on the jaw in addition to positive pressure.

it can effect our ability to ventilate him. We often use positive pressure with bag and mask to treat airway obstruction or laryngospasm. The positive pressure pushes the vocal cords downward and slightly apart.

Once the vocal cords separate even a little bit, the positive pressure expands the space below them, forcing the vocal cords apart and opening the airway. Horizontal cords should separate more easily than concave cords, which might overlap more forcefully when pushed downward. To break laryngospasm in a child, we combine positive pressure with chin thrust. Thrusting the chin forward puts tension on the arytenoid cartilages, and pulls them apart. The gap produced allows pressurization of the space below and the spasm usually breaks (Fig. 8-4).

Between 2 and 6 yrs, the larynx gradually descends to a lower neck position. At the same time, the posterior part of the tongue descends, gradually forming more and more of the anterior wall of the oropharynx. By 6 to 8 yrs, the upper respiratory system assumes the adult configuration and the epiglottis can no longer reach the soft palate, even with maximum elevation.

The nasal passages of older children are often filled with adenoidal tissue. Hypertrophied tonsils can fill the dead space in the back of the pharynx, making assisted ventilation more difficult.

It's currently estimated that 1-3% of children suffer from obstructive sleep apnea, or O.S.A., a condition more often thought of as an adult disorder. O.S.A. is now one of the most common reason to remove pediatric tonsils and adenoids.

Part of the reason for the increased incidence of O.S.A. is awareness of the condition. But part is related to the childhood obesity epidemic. According to a recent study, in the United States, over 17% of children and adolescents are overweight. Over 32% of adults were obese[1].

Pediatric sleep apnea typically appears between the ages of two to six, but it can occur from infancy to adolescence. It is believed to affect girls and boys equally, and it's often undiagnosed. Untreated O.S.A. in children has been linked to behavior problems, impaired growth, learning difficulties, poor school performance, bed wetting, high blood pressure, and heart disease. Airway management can be more challenging when such a child loses consciousness or develops airway obstruction from other causes.

Pediatric Physiology

In addition to anatomical predispositions for airway obstruction, children physiologically develop hypoxia faster than adults. Their smaller lungs and higher metabolic rates leave them with fewer oxygen reserves. The basal metabolic rate of a sleeping infant, per kg of body weight, is approximately double that of an adult. The much higher energy requirements relate to differences in body proportions. Major organs such as brain, liver and kidneys contribute to higher energy use in infants. These organs consume more oxygen than lean muscle mass, which makes them the highest energy users. Other contributors to higher infant metabolic rate are rapid growth rate, and temperature control because of the higher surface to volume ratio. These higher metabolic rates depend upon faster heart and respiratory rates for adequate O_2 delivery.

Regardless of age, a normal resting tidal volume is about 8 ml per kg of lean body weight. However this can mean a difference in tidal volume from 15 ml for a 2 kg premie, 40 ml for a 5 kg baby, 160 ml for a 20 kg toddler or 800 ml for a 100 kg man. In the face of such small tidal volumes and their higher oxygen consumption, the infant or toddler must breathe more rapidly than the adult to compensate. (Table 8-2) However, a child's immature lungs and heart are not as efficient at providing this O_2. In addition, the muscles of respiration tire more easily. The combination of high metabolic demand and poor reserve places the child at higher risk of cardiorespiratory failure.

To breathe effectively, the intercostal muscles and diaphragm contract, increasing chest volume and lowering intrathoracic pressure. Air is pulled into the lungs through the unobstructed airway. Normal elastic recoil of the chest wall then increases intrathoracic pressure and pushes air and carbon dioxide out through the unobstructed airway. The chest rises with inspiration as the lungs expand. It falls with expiration as the lungs deflate (Fig 8-5a).

The pediatric lung is stiffer or less compliant than the adult lung. It contains less elastin, the substance that promotes elastic recoil of the lung after inflation. The smaller caliber airways create higher resistance to breathing. Both factors increase the work of breathing at rest and leave less reserve if the child becomes sick or injured. A rocking chest wall motion is very common in children with even partial airway obstruction (Fig 8-5b).

The pediatric chest wall is more box-like in shape compared to the adult's, with ribs more at right angles to the vertebral column. This structural difference makes the chest wall

Table 8-2. Average Respiratory and Heart Rates Change With Age		
AGE	RESPIRATORY RATE (Breathes per minute)	HEART RATE (Beats per minute)
Infant (birth to 1 yr)	30-60	110-160
Toddler (1-3 yrs)	24-40	90-150
Preschooler (3-6 yrs)	22-34	80-140
School age (6-12 yrs)	18-30	70-120
Adolescent to Adult	12-16	50-100

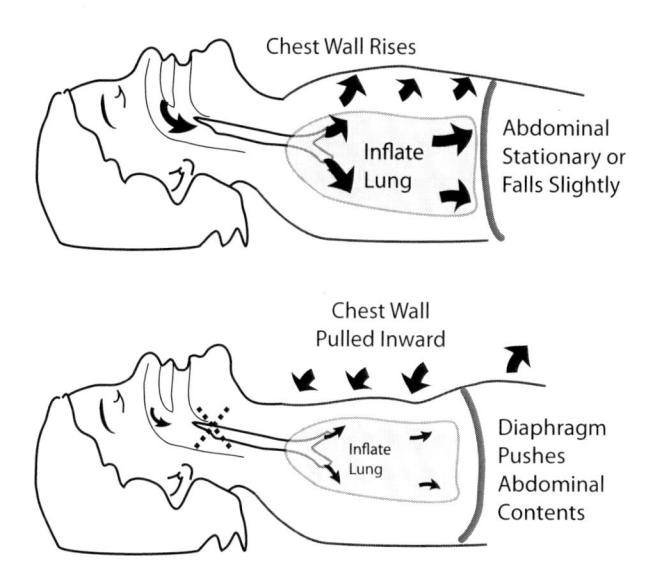

Fig 8-5 (a) Shows the chest rising and abdomen falling with normal breathing. (b) With airway obstruction, the negative intrathoracic pressure pulls the chest wall inward and pushes the abdomen outward — creating a rocking motion. The child's soft, flexible rib cage shows this very easily, even with mild obstruction.

mechanically less efficient and limits potential lung expansion. The child can't increase tidal volume as effectively and must rely on rate increases to compensate. Less reserve places the child at increased risk of respiratory failure when stressed.

In addition, the pediatric chest wall is much less rigid because its structure contains more cartilage and less bone than the adult. When airway obstruction develops, the highly compliant chest wall gets sucked inward as the diaphragm drops, limiting lung expansion and decreasing optimal air exchange. The harder a child tries to breathe, the less efficient breathing can become.

Many things can disrupt the respiratory system and cause it to fail, such as:
- altered mental status, due to medications, underlying illness or trauma
- upper airway obstruction, such as snoring, foreign body, or swelling
- lower airway obstruction, such as asthma or emphysema
- impaired diffusion of gas from alveoli to capillaries such as pneumonia, tumor, radiation or burns
- abnormal pulmonary blood flow such as shock or heart failure
- chest wall or diaphragmatic injury
- impaired chest wall and lung motion such as extreme obesity
- impaired nerve or muscle control such a spinal cord injury, paralytic drug effect, muscular dystrophy, or stroke

Infants and young children are especially vulnerable to respiratory failure. Cardiac output in the young child is rate dependent because the child's heart muscle and sympathetic nervous system are immature. The need for more O_2 is met by increasing heart rate, *not* contractility. Pediatric cardiac output drops dangerously with bradycardia because stroke volume cannot effectively increase to deal with increased demand.

To make matters worse, children, unlike adults, develop bradycardia more easily. Hypoxia in an adult initially triggers a sympathetic response, producing tachycardia. Hypoxic adults remain tachycardic for a long time before this compensatory mechanism fails, and bradycardia begins. Bradycardia rarely develops unless hypoxia is extremely severe and prolonged.

In infants and young children, however, things are very different. In children bradycardia may be the *first* sign of hypoxia — not the last, because their sympathetic nervous system is immature and easily overwhelmed. Hypoxia in a child triggers a vagal response and slows the heart. Bradycardia delivers less oxygen, hypoxia and hypercarbia worsen. Acidosis develops and the myocardium becomes depressed. Cardiac arrest can occur quickly. Always assume bradycardia in a child means hypoxia and treat the child with oxygen and improved ventilation first. You must recognize and treat bradycardia and hypoxia immediately or cardiac arrest can occur rapidly. Good airway management is therefore critical.

Opening the Airway

Look, listen and feel for air movement. When simple arousal doesn't improve respiration, then you must open the airway yourself. The following maneuvers assume no cervical spine injuries. If cervical spine precautions are needed, use jaw thrust only and maintain a stable neck position.

With the head in a relaxed and flexed position, the tongue and soft tissues tend to collapse over the larynx and cause obstruction. A child younger than 2 has a relatively large occiput and a short neck. The larynx is higher in the neck right behind the tongue. A pillow placed under the head of the infant/toddler will tend to force the head forward over the chest, force the tongue back, and worsen airway obstruction. It will also make it hard to tilt the head back to open the airway. Instead, place a small folded towel under the *shoulders* in children younger than 2 to better align the pharyngeal and laryngeal axes and start to open the airway (8-6 a,b).

In a child older than 2 years, the anatomical relationships have started to change as the child grows. Placing the towel under the head, as in the adult, is usually more effective Fig 8-7a,b), but avoid flexing the head forward.

Tilt the head back. Pull the angles of the jaw upward to put tension on the base of the tongue and soft tissues and lift the epiglottis off the trachea, aligning the axes. Further thrust of the jaw opens the mouth and fully opens the airway.

Extreme extension or flexion of the child's neck can obstruct the airway. In fact, pressing on the soft tissue under the chin to get a good mask fit can also obstruct the airway. To avoid obstruction, keep the head in a more neutral, slightly extended position. And keep your fingertip pressure on the bony mandible when opening the airway, not the soft tissue under the chin.

Because young children often have nasal obstruction from hypertrophic adenoids, you can use the hand grip shown in figure (8-8a,b). Since the child's face is small relative to your own hand, it's often possible to maintain a good mask seal while also holding the mouth open under the mask. This maneuver mimics the action of an oral airway without inserting one into a patient too awake to tolerate it.

Look, listen, and feel for evidence of good ventilation.

Ventilating And Intubating The Child 141

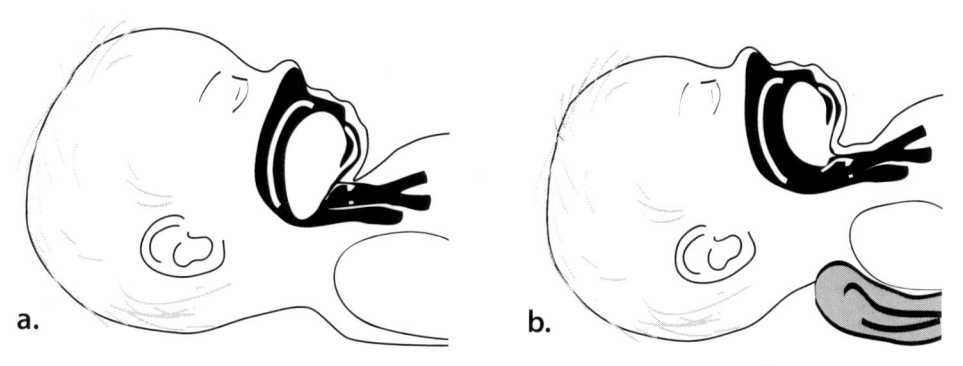

Fig. 8-6. (a) Children younger than 2 yrs have a relatively large occiput which flexes the head forward to cause obstruction. (b) These children may benefit from a small roll under their shoulders to open their airways.

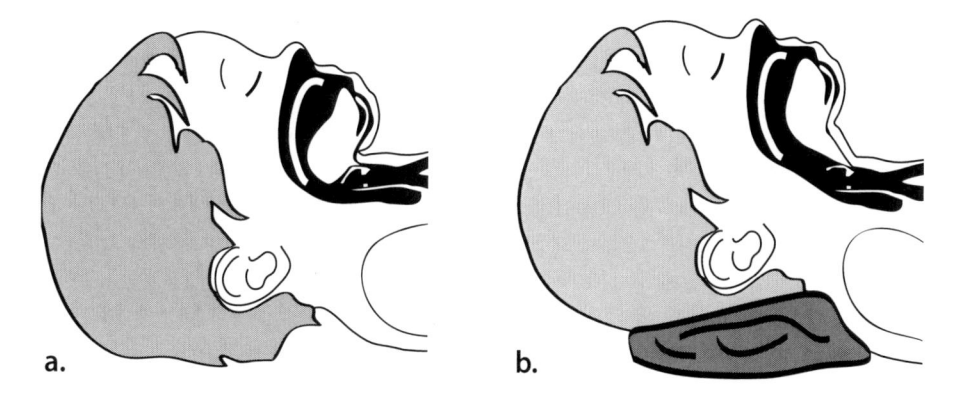

Fig. 8-7. (a) Children older than 2 yrs still have a large occiput that tends to tilt their head forward. (b) Use your judgement regarding placing a small roll under the head rather than the shoulders.

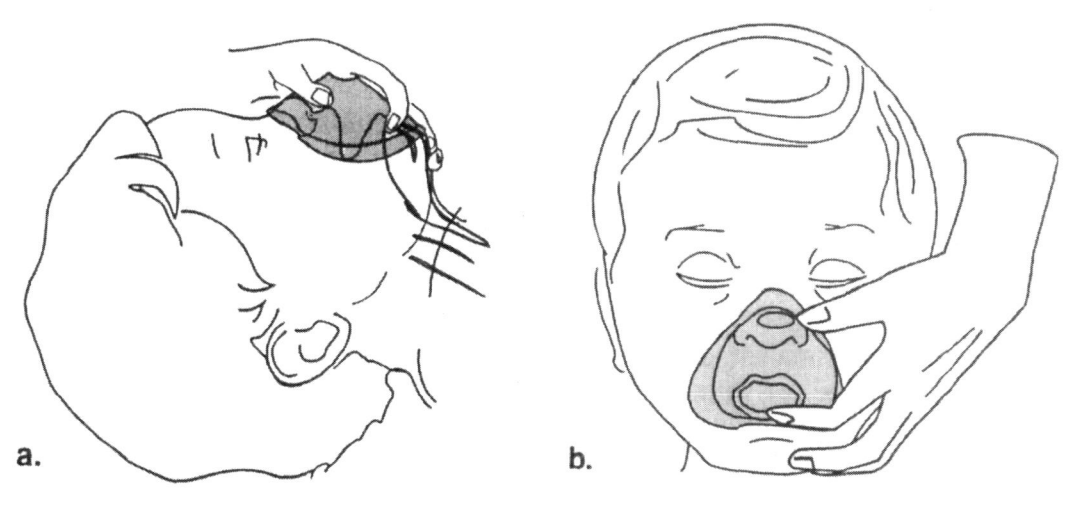

Fig 8-8 a,b. Technique to hold the mouth open under the mask. Pull the lower jaw upward and slightly downward toward the feet by hooking the your fingertips under the mandible. Keep force on the bones, not the soft tissue under the chin. Maintain the seal with your thumb and index finger.

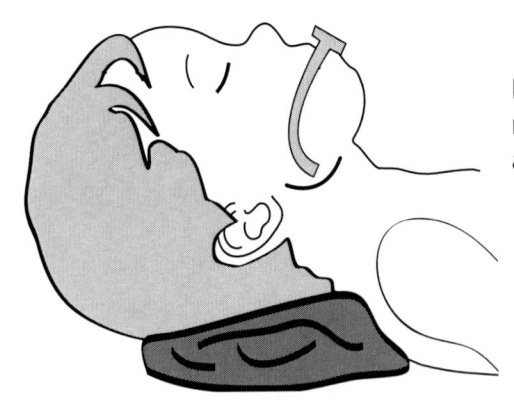

Fig 8-9. The correct size oral airway should reach from the mouth to just above the angle of the jaw.

Use of the Oral Airway

If obstruction persists, insert an oral or a nasal airway. An oral airway is often a better choice in unconscious children. Nasal airways can injure hypertrophic adenoids and cause nosebleeds. However, oral airways placed in conscious or semiconscious patients risk vomiting, aspiration, and tissue damage.

The length of the correct size oral airway puts the flange just outside the teeth and gum line and positions the tip near the vallecula. "Too short" pushes the back of the tongue over the larynx, worsening airway obstruction. "Too long" extends outside the mouth and interferes with mask fit. To estimate the correct size place the oral airway next to the patient's jaw and judge where the tip will lie (Fig 8-9).

A correctly placed oral airway pulls the tongue forward and opens the mouth. If placed incorrectly, oral airways increase airway obstruction by pushing the tongue back over the larynx (Fig 8-10). Infants, who have a large tongue relative to the size of their jaw, are especially at risk of obstruction from improperly sized or positioned oral airways (Mov. 8-2, Mov 8-3, plus KF.s 8-2ab, KF8-3abcd).

Children often have loose baby teeth. If you have time, check for loose or missing teeth before you start. Always recheck the teeth after you've placed an oral airway or intubated. If a tooth is newly missing, and you can't find it, get a chest X-Ray. Teeth lost in the airway can be aspirated.

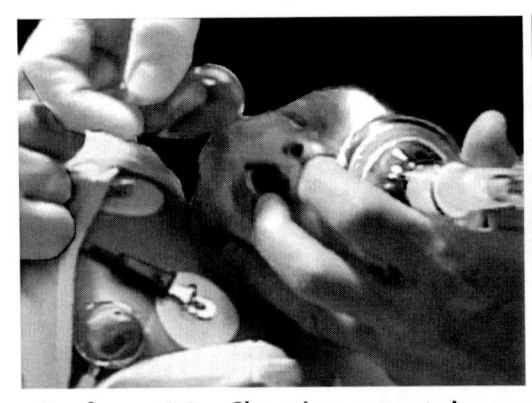

Keyframe 8-2a. Choosing correct size oral airway is especially important in an infant. The size difference between your hands and the baby's face can feel awkward.

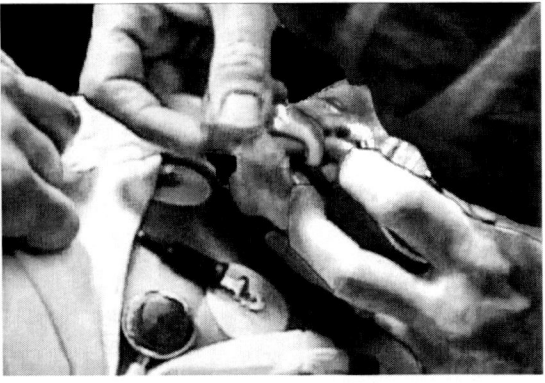

Keyframe 8-2b. Gently slide the oral airway into position over and then around the tongue.

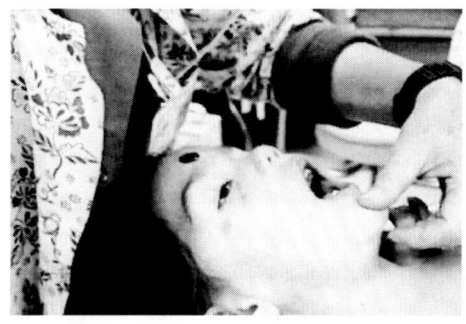

Keyframe 8-3a. Open the mouth. Look at the teeth, which may be loose or missing in children.

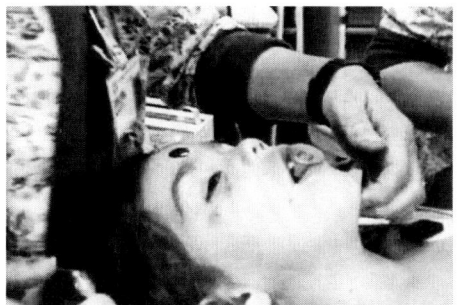

Keyframe 8-3b. Place the oral airway. The flange should be just outside the teeth ad gums. Make sure it's not pinching the lips.

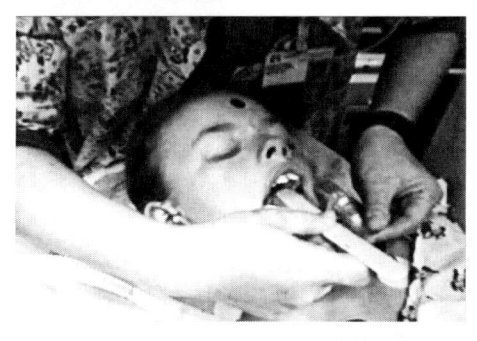

Keyframe 8-3c. You may need to use a tongue blade to open the mouth and pull the tongue forward. Slide the oral airway down the blade into position.

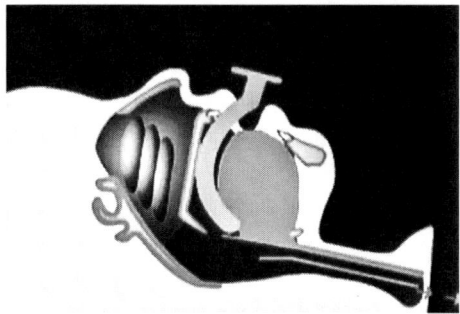

Keyframe 8-3d. The oral airway tip should rest near the vallecula. The flange is just outside the gums, teeth, and lips.

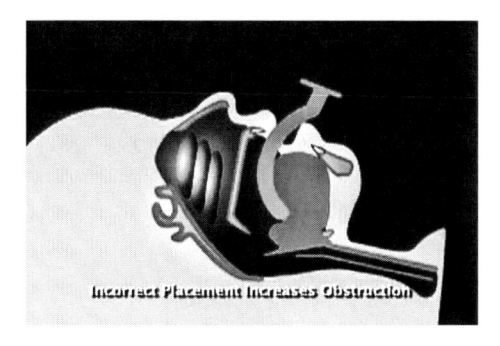

Keyframe 8-3e. Improperly sized or placed, an oral airway can increase airway obstruction.

Use of the Nasal Airway

A nasal airway is better tolerated in semiconscious patients because it won't stimulate the gag reflex as much. However, nasal airways can cause nosebleeds, especially in 3-6 year old children with hypertrophied adenoids. Insert gently (Mov. 8-4, KF 8-4abc).

Estimate the correct size by measuring the nasal airway against the distance from the nostril to the ear canal. Once inserted, it should not be so large that it makes the skin around the nostril blanche from compression.

Always lubricate well. Use gentle technique. Direction of insertion is very important. Don't thread the nasal airway upward toward the frontal sinus. Instead, advance it along the *floor* of the nose, perpendicular to the plane of the face.

Never force a nasal airway during insertion. If you meet an obstruction try rotating the nasal airway as you advance. Adenoidal tissue can plug nasal airways, causing obstruction and potential aspiration of tissue. If it appears plugged, suction the nasal airway to clear it.

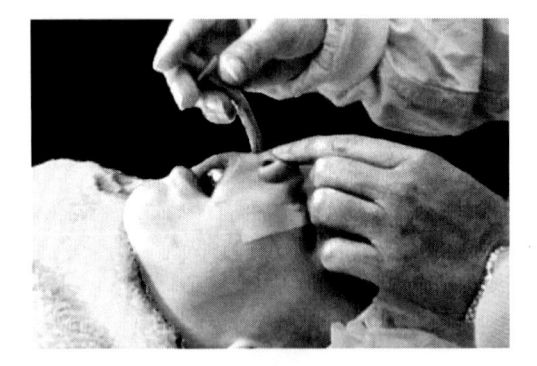

Keyframe 8-4a. Slide the nasal airway perpendicularly to the plane of the face.

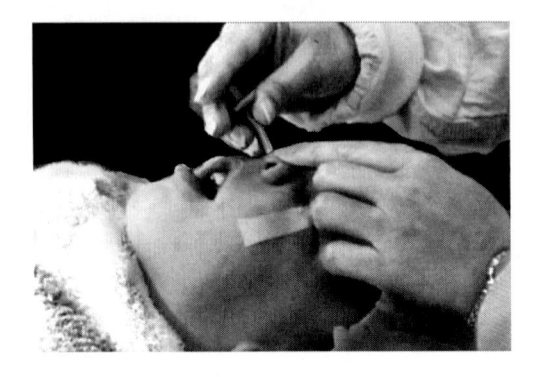

Keyframe 8-4b. Never force it. Gently twist it if needed. Add more lubricant or choose a smaller size.

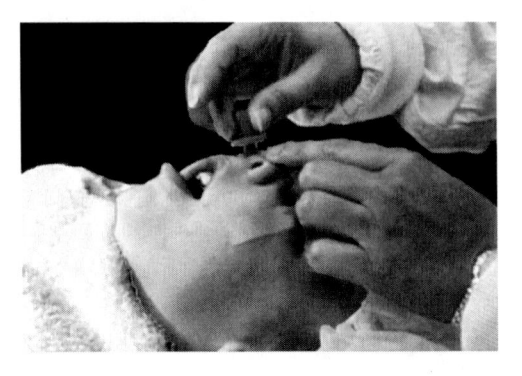

Keyframe 8-4c. The flange will typically rest against the nostril. You may need to withdraw it slightly if it's too long and irritating the posterior pharynx.

Ventilating With Bag-Valve-Mask

As with adults, ventilation is more important than intubation. In the care of pediatric patients, the size of your hand relative to the child's small face forces you to modify your technique with bag-valve-mask compared to the adult. The child's smaller and more delicate lungs require you to be especially mindful of appropriate tidal volumes and inflation force.

Placing and Holding the Mask

To ventilate a child, first choose the correct size mask. The proper size covers the space between the bridge of the nose and the crease of the chin. Wrong sizes prevent a good seal.

For the older child, as in the adult, the thumb and forefinger press the mask against the face and form a "C" shape. The remaining fingers grip the bony mandible and pull upward, forming an "E". The mask seal is created by the opposing force of the thumb and index fingers pushing down, against the force of the other three fingers pulling up (Mov. 8-5, KF abc).

For the infant and toddler, the face is a lot smaller relative to your hand. While the thumb and index finger still form the "C", you will often find room only for your middle finger or middle and ring fingers to grasp the bony mandible. Don't press on the soft tissue under the chin with the remaining finger(s) because pressure here can increase airway obstruction by

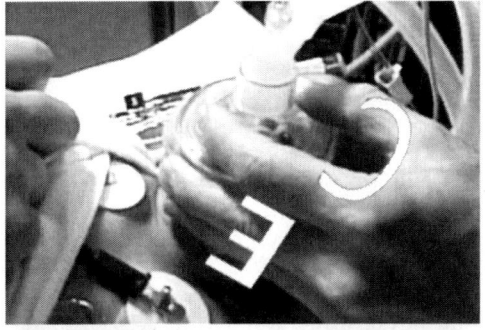

Keyframe 8-5a. The technique to seal the mask is the same, although the size difference of infant face and adult hands can be challenging.

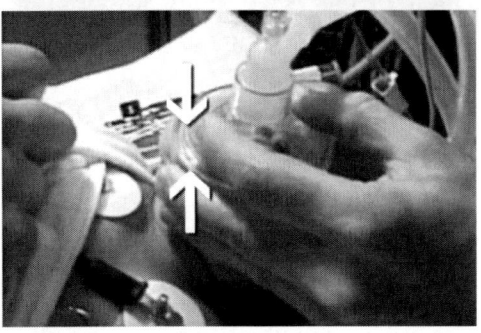

Keyframe 8-5b. Don't just push the mask down to seal. Instead pull the face into the mask by pulling up on the mandible.

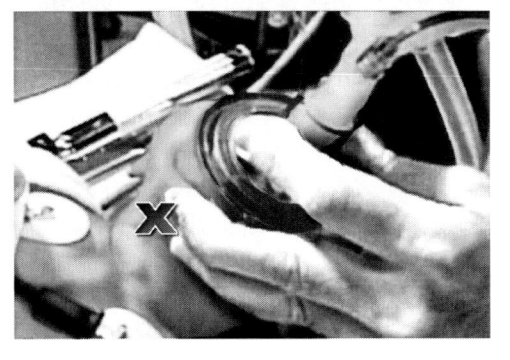

Keyframe 8-5c. Avoid pressing on the soft tissue under the chin. Such pressure can worsen obstruction.

pushing the tongue and epiglottis back over the laryngeal outlet.

Protect the eyes. It's easy for the mask to push open the eyelids, exposing the eyes to corneal abrasion. Consider taping them closed before applying the mask if the patient is unconscious.

Ventilating the Lungs

To ventilate, squeeze the bag, watching the chest rise with each squeeze.

Both children and adults have a tidal volume of about 8 ml/kg of body weight. A 10 kg child has an 80 ml tidal volume. A 2 kg baby has a tidal volume of about 16 ml. Obesity is becoming more common in children, so you may need to adjust your tidal volumes lower for the overweight child. Watch the chest rise as you squeeze the bag to gauge the volume of breath you are delivering and the resistance to ventilation.

Children need a faster respiratory rate to supply O_2 to support their higher metabolic rate and to eliminate an increase in CO_2. Ventilate infants at 35-40, children at 20-30, and teenagers at 10-20 breaths per minute.

Pay attention to the resistance you feel as the lungs inflate. Obstruction makes squeezing the bag more difficult, whereas a leak in the ventilation system makes squeezing the bag very easy. In both these cases, however, the chest won't rise.

When in doubt, have a helper listen to the chest as you ventilate. You should hear breath sounds. Although there are some medical conditions where breath sounds are hard to hear, the absence of any breath sounds almost always means inadequate ventilation. If an end-tidal CO_2 device monitors the patient you should see evidence of exhaled CO_2.

Always use the least force required to effectively inflate the lungs. It takes a lot less force to give a 50 ml breath versus a 900 ml breath. Too large a tidal volume risks pneumothorax, especially with children. You can better judge the size of the breath you deliver by using a half to one liter bag rather than an adult bag.

Slow, steady inflation is more effective than rapid, jerky puffs because the gas is more likely to expand the chest and less likely to distend the stomach. Stomach distention pushes the diaphragm up into the chest cavity, impairing lung inflation and increasing the risk of vomiting and aspiration. If stomach distention impairs your ability to ventilate a child, you may need to pass a small bore, flexible suction catheter, such as a size 10 French, into the stomach to decompress it.

Relax the left hand slightly for the few seconds it takes for the bag to refill. Gripping the mask too tightly can cause your hand to cramp. If your fingers spasm, you'll lose fine motor control and may have difficulty maintaining a seal. If you have a good mask seal, little or no air will escape around the mask. You can tolerate some leak as long as you can ventilate the patient.

You may need to combine jaw thrust with positive pressure breaths, especially when treating laryngospasm.

Hypoxemia rapidly causes bradycardia in children. When a child develops bradycardia treat for hypoxia first. Recheck your hand position and oxygen source. Increase the depth and rate of ventilation. The heart rate usually returns to normal quickly, although atropine may also be needed.

Pediatric Intubation

Intubation in children requires the same basic equipment as in adults, but the technique used must take into account the anatomical differences.

Always have the equipment you need to ventilate the child in case the intubation attempt is difficult or prolonged. The size variation between premature infants to older teenagers is vast. You must plan ahead to ensure that you have the appropriately sized equipment immediately available for the child you are treating. An oral airway or mask that is too big, or too small, is useless.

Equipment

A pediatric laryngoscope handle is thinner and lighter, making it easier to manipulate the smaller anatomy. Pediatric intubating equipment should include Miller or straight blades in size zero for infants, size 1 for 1-2 years, and size 2 for older children. You may want to have a MAC 2 available as well.

Although you can intubate an infant or toddler with a larger blade, it's technically more difficult. The larger blade can interfere with both visualization and passing the tube. It also carries greater risk of injuring the oropharynx.

We often use straight blades in children because the larynx is located higher in the neck than an adult. The smaller separation between the hyoid and the thyroid cartilage also makes displacing the tongue and associated tissues forward more difficult. A straight blade lifts the epiglottis, allowing a clear view of the cords.

A curved blade, like a MAC, is designed to fit into the vallecula and displace the soft tissue forward to provide a view of the larynx. However, in a child, the MAC will sometimes fold the child's epiglottis down over the larynx, blocking your view of the cords (Fig. 8-10). If this happens when using a curved blade in a child, consider using it like a straight blade to lift the epiglottis.

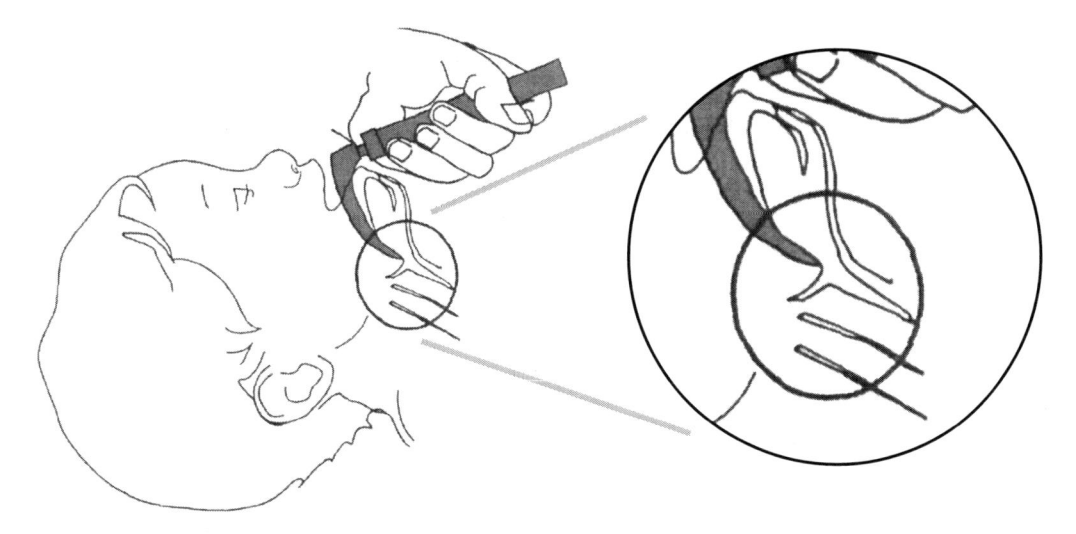

Fig 8-10. A curved blade will sometimes fold the epiglottis down in a pediatric patient, hiding your view of the cords. If this happens, use the blade to pick the epiglottis up instead.

Table 8-3. Suggested Uncuffed Endotracheal Tube Sizes
(Pediatric Cuffed Tubes: use half size smaller)

Age	Size mm I.D.	Depth (cm)	Miller	Mac
	$\frac{\text{age in yrs}}{4} + 4$	$\frac{\text{age in yrs}}{2} + 12$		
Premature	2.5-3	8	0	0
Newborn	3-3.5	9-10	0	0
3-12 mon.	4	10.5-12	0	0
1 yr.	4	12.5-13.5	1	1
2 yrs.	4.5	13.5	2	2
4 yrs.	5	14	2	2
6 yrs.	5.5	15	2	2
8 yrs.	6 cuffed	16	2	2
10 yrs.	6.5 cuffed	17	2-3	2-3
12 yrs.	6.5-7 cuffed	18	2-3	3
Adolescent	6.5-7 cuffed	21	2, 3, 4	3
Adult	6.5-8 cuffed	21	2, 3, 4	3-4

Endotracheal Tubes

The endotracheal tube has two openings on the patient end. The side opening, called a Murphy eye, prevents obstruction when the tip of the endotracheal tube is up against the tracheal wall. The beveled tip also prevents obstruction when the tube tip is against the carina. The larger the tube you insert, the less resistance to breathing and the easier it is to keep free of secretions. Pediatric tubes come either with or without a cuff, for reasons that are discussed below.

Premature infants take a size between 2.5 and 3 mm internal diameter (ID). Neonates usually take a 3-3.5. Infants from 3-13 months usually take a 4.0 and those between 1 and 2 years need a 4.5 (see Table 8-3). Above the age of 2 years, the formula *the age in years divided by 4 plus 4* provides a fairly good estimate of the correct tube size. For example a 4 year old would take a size 5. See Table 8-3. If the child's age is unknown, the correct size tube is often the same diameter as the child's little finger.

The variation in growth rate between children can sometimes make it harder to predict the correct size tube for a specific child. Have at least 3 endotracheal tubes immediately available: the predicted size, one size larger and one size smaller. You lose valuable time looking for a different tube if you have difficulties.

Cuffed or Uncuffed Tubes?

Positive pressure ventilation depends on providing enough pressure to inflate the lungs. If there is a break in the pressure seal, such as through a leak back out the glottis around the endotracheal tube, then ventilation may be inadequate and the patient can potentially aspirate around the tube.

Cuffed endotracheal tubes are used to provide this seal in adults, but uncuffed tubes in infants and children younger than about 8 years have historically been used because their larynxes are anatomically different. In a child younger than 8, the smallest diameter of the airway is the cricoid ring. A properly sized round endotracheal tube was felt to seal this round opening, making aspiration around the tube less likely. Cuffs were felt to place the youngest children at risk of tracheal mucosal injury and post extubation croup.

As the child grows and becomes more adult like at the age of 8 years, the anatomy changes. Now the triangular vocal cord opening becomes the smallest diameter, and an ETT cuff is now needed to seal the larger tracheal diameter below the cords.

Newer research, however, has found that the cricoid ring is more elliptical in shape than round[2]. This means that a round ETT placed into a non-round hole can put more, and potentially excessive, pressure on parts of the tracheal mucosa than expected given the presence of a leak.

This discovery makes use of uncuffed tubes less compelling given the fact that cuffed tubes do offer advantages. Cuffed ETTs protect better against aspiration. They allow higher ventilation pressures in patients with poor pulmonary compliance. Changing an ETT can be avoided when too small a tube is initially inserted. Monitoring ventilation and tidal volume is more accurate. During anesthesia, there is less pollution from anesthesia gas leaking around the tube.

On the other hand, there are potential disadvantages to using cuffed tubes in small children. Cuffs take up space and force use of a smaller tube. Suctioning smaller tubes is more difficult. Decreasing the tube radius a little greatly increases resistance and significantly decreases flow. This relationship is described by the Hagen-Poiseuille equation:

$$Q = nPr^4/8l$$

Where Q = Flow in Liters/second
n = Viscosity in Pa.s
P = Pressure in Pascals
r = Radius of the tube in meters
l = Length of the tube in question in meters

A cuff takes up space and forces use of a tube one-half to one size (0.5-1mm I.D.) smaller than calculated size. A 4 yo will normally take a 5.0 uncuffed tube, and a 4-4.5 I.D. *cuffed* tube. A 4.0 cuffed tube has 59% increased resistance to flow compared to the 5.0. Therefore, use of the larger uncuffed tube significantly lowers resistance and thus the amount of force required for breathing.

The second concern about cuffed tubes in small children stems from the risk of damaging mucosa, potential post-extubation croup and the late appearance of tracheal stenosis. Years ago, cuffed tubes were a high pressure-low volume type that exerted more point pressure on a limited area of mucosa, potentially interrupting capillary blood flow. The newer low pressure-high volume cuffs spread that pressure over a larger surface area. Studies using modern low pressure-high volume cuffs have shown no increase in post-extubation croup between cuffed and uncuffed tubes[3,4,5,6]. These studies have also not shown an increase in the rate of complications between cuffed and uncuffed endotracheal tubes in terms of long term complications such as tracheal stenosis.

Choose a cuffed tube one-half to one size I.D. smaller than calculated size to allow room for the volume of the uninflated cuff. Check for a leak before inflating. You may find that you don't need to inflate the cuff to obtain an adequate seal.

Because the tip of the endotracheal tube rises within the trachea with head extension, the cuff when rise into the subglottic areas, risking injury to these areas as well as to the recurrent laryngeal nerves. A cuffed tube may need to be repositioned if the head will be in extension for a prolonged period[8].

You can use a cuff in infants and children younger than eight if you follow precautions:

1. Be meticulous with choice of tube size, tube depth, and stabilization.
2. Don't overinflate the cuff to greater than 20-25 cm H_2O to avoid pressure induced injury of the mucosa. Inflate the cuff to minimum seal—the cuff volume where air leak around the tube just stops during constant pressure held at 20-25 cm H_2O. Monitor pressure if possible.
3. Make sure that the cuff is below the cricoid cartilage.
4. N_2O used during anesthesia will accumulate in any closed air filled cavity, including ETT cuffs. As N_2O collects, pressure increases over time and distends the cuff. Check the cuff tension periodically — you may have to repeatedly remove a small amount of air to return the cuff to minimum seal.
5. During aerial transport of a patient, the air in the cuff will expand at altitude and compress the mucosa. Repeatedly remove air to restore minimal seal. Note that as the aircraft descends, you may have to add a bit of air to the cuff as the cuff loses pressure. Inflating the cuff with saline avoids pressure changes. You will need a lot less saline than air so be careful not to over pressurize.

The Hagen-Poiseuille equation also shows that resistance increases as tube length increases, so a shorter ETT has less resistance to breathing. It's common practice to cut the length of the endotracheal tube in an infant so that it extends no more than 1-2 cm from where it exits the mouth.

Endotracheal tubes have depth markings in centimeters. Insert an uncuffed tube until the lowest most prominent mark is level with the vocal cords. Insert cuffed tubes until the cuff just passes through the cords, and is below the cricoid ring. See Table 8-3 for suggested depths.

Make sure any stylet does not extend beyond the tip or through the Murphy eye where it could damage the trachea. Pediatric stylets are smaller and more flexible. Because a pediatric stylet may not be stiff enough to adequately assist with an ETT size 6 or greater, consider using an adult stylet for larger pediatric tubes. Lubricate well.

Have your suction ready for use. In addition to a usual yankauer suction tip, have soft suction catheters small enough to suction inside the smallest endotracheal tube you intend to insert.

Intubating The Infant And Toddler

The infant's head lies naturally in the sniffing position due to the pronounced occiput. In fact, the height of the occiput can make the larynx difficult to see. For easier visualization, the ear canal should be roughly level with the anterior shoulder. Placing a small folded towel or similar thickness object under the infant's shoulders raises the rest of the body and straightens the airway path.

The infant occiput tends to roll, making the act of balancing the baby's head on your blade a challenge. Have an assistant steady the head for you if the infant's head is hard to steady. A small cloth or foam "donut" under the head or a rolled towel placed on either side of the head serves the same purpose but care should be taken to avoid raising the head too much. With practice, balancing the head becomes second nature (Mov. 8-6 KF. 8-6abcde).

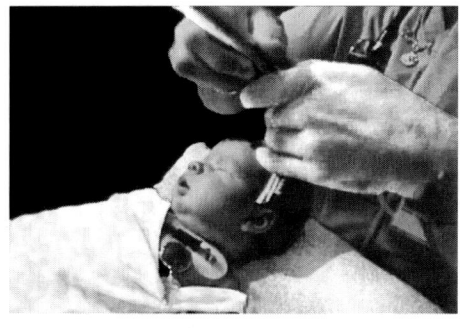

Keyframe 8-6a. Open the laryngoscope blade of an appropriate size for the child.

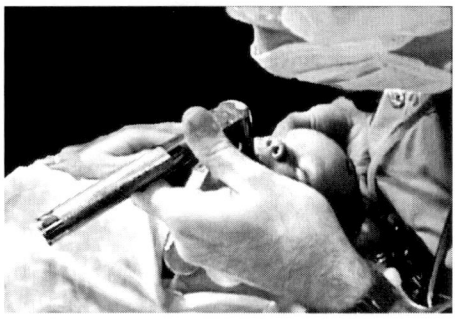

Keyframe 8-6b. Sweep the tongue to the left and visualize the larynx.

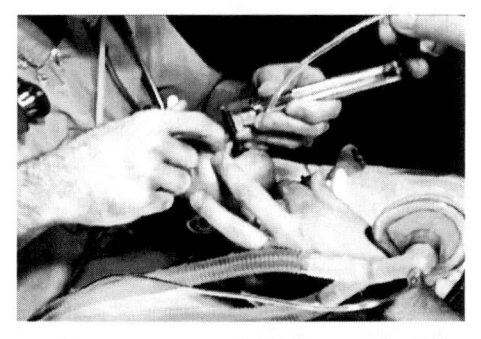

Keyframe 8-6c. Balancing the head of an infant can be harder due to size of the laryngeal structures. The rounder head tends to roll and may need to be stabilized.

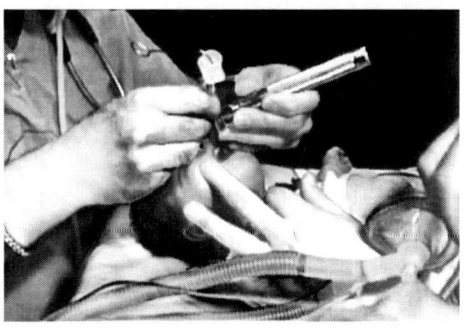

Keyframe 8-6d. Insert the endotracheal tube. Never force a tube. If it won't slide in easily choose a smaller size. A helper is giving cricoid pressure. In an infant, pressing too hard on the cricoid ring can distort the airway and compress the trachea.

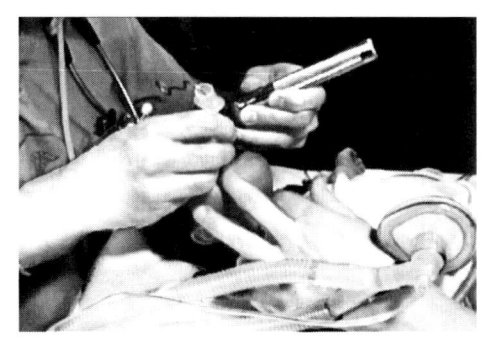

Keyframe 8-6e. Once intubated, carefully remove the blade while holding the tube. Extubation is easy when the patient is small.

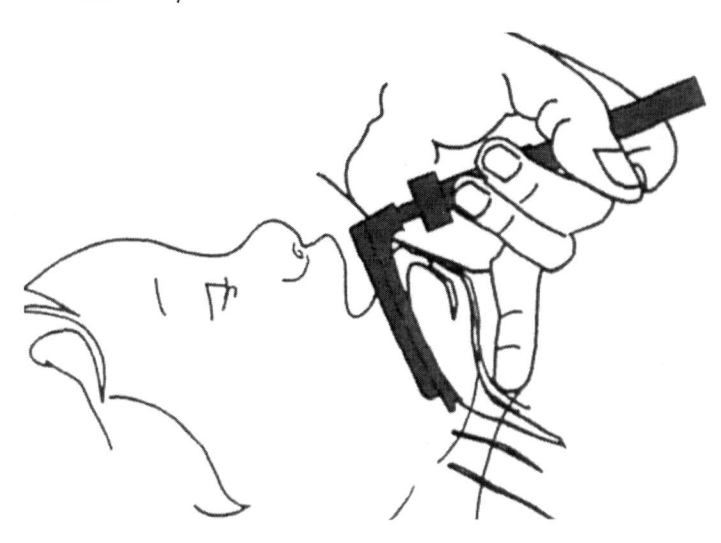

Fig. 8-11. Place the head in a neutral position. If needed, you can often apply cricoid pressure with your little finger. However, don't hesitate to ask a helper to provide cricoid pressure.

During the intubation, avoid hyperextension which can obstruct the pediatric airway. Open the mouth with your right index finger and thumb as far to the right side of the mouth as possible. The infant's mouth is small compared to the size of your hand. Failure to place your fingers far to the right can block your view and prevent insertion of the blade.

The infant tongue is much larger relative to the mouth and mandible than the adult. Failure to sweep the tongue to the left with your laryngoscope blade will leave no room for visualization or tube passage.

Slowly lift the mandible upward as you advance the blade. Don't pinch the lower lip between the teeth and the blade as you lift. Avoid using the upper gum line or teeth as a lever. Watch out for loose teeth.

Continue to lift the mandible upward until you see the larynx. Because your hand is much larger relative to the size of the head and neck, you can often use your left little finger to provide your own cricoid pressure (Fig. 8-11). However, don't hesitate to ask for help. Make sure your helper knows to press gently — too heavy pressure on the child's soft structures can distort the anatomy.

It's very easy to insert the blade too deeply and into the esophagus of such a tiny patient. If you can't identify anatomy, then pull the blade back. Often the larynx will fall into view.

Picking up the epiglottis with the blade tip in a child less than two years old can be hard due to its short, stiff, "U" shaped form. Meticulous placement of the tip of the blade is necessary. Be gentle. Traumatic intubations can cause swelling, which can be especially dangerous in the child's small larynx. Use suction as needed.

The arytenoids and vocal cords in the infant and young child incline. This slant can cause the pediatric tube to hang up on the anterior commissure during insertion. Rotating the tube to the right or left allows the tip to slip off the anterior commissure and pass. While there may be a blind spot at the moment of intubation, you can often see the arytenoids behind the tube.

Remember, the cricoid ring is smaller than the opening between the vocal cords. Forcing a tube can cause traumatic swelling. If the tube won't pass, use a smaller one. Stop insertion when you see the lowest marker ring on an uncuffed tube pass the cords. Carefully remove your laryngoscope blade.

Be gentle. Pediatric airways are small, delicate and prone to edema.

Children can't hold their breaths as long as an adult before the onset of hypoxia. If you

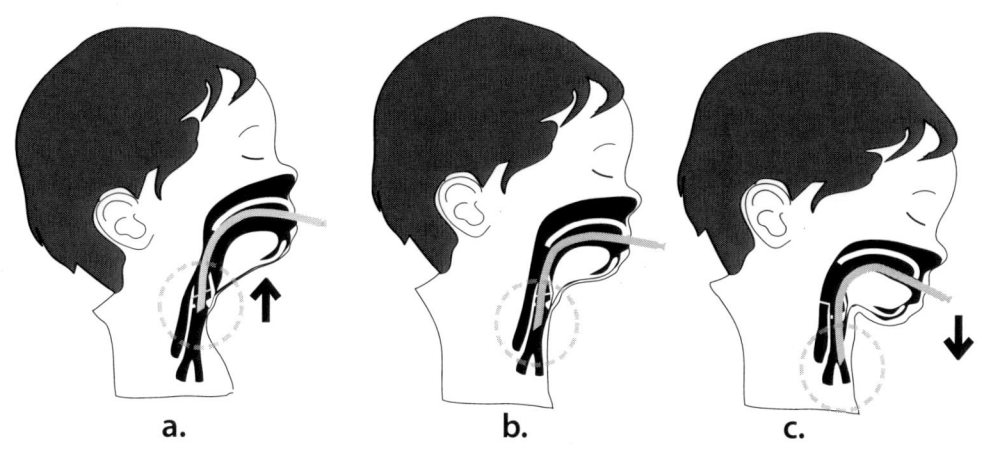

Fig. 8-12 a,b,c. Extension and flexion of the patient's head will move the tip of the tube up and down the trachea, potentially leading to mainstem intubation or extubation.

have trouble intubating, stop and ventilate before trying again. During awake intubations let the patient rest and breathe oxygen. *Lack of ventilation hurts patients, not the lack of an endotracheal tube.*

Always verify tracheal placement by listening over both axilla and the stomach. Easy transmission of sound makes esophageal intubation harder to detect in the child. Breath sounds should be equal and chest movement symmetrical. Stomach distention may indicate esophageal intubation.

Depth of tube placement is critical because the trachea is very short. The tip of the tube should be midway between the larynx and the carina. Extension of the neck causes the endotracheal tube to rise within the trachea. Inadvertent extubation can occur of the tube is too high. Flexion of the head causes it to descend, possibly causing mainstem intubation (Fig 8-12 a,b,c). "The hose follows the nose" is a useful memory aide.

Continue to hold the tube with your fingers at the lips until its secured. Note the depth marking on the tube and compare it to the calculated depth of insertion. A good guideline for the initial depth of insertion is to use the formula:

$$approximate\ ETT\ depth = (age\ in\ years\ /\ 2) + 12$$

For example, according to the formula, a 6 year old would need an ETT depth of 15 cm. (See Table 8-3).

Listen at the infant's mouth for a leak. Unlike in the adult, we want to hear a leak around an uncuffed tube at about 20 cm of water pressure, after the child's lungs are fairly well inflated. The absence of such a leak means that the tube is pressing on the inside the cricoid ring. Excessive pressure inside the cricoid can damage the mucosa. Excessive pressure can also potentially injure the recurrent laryngeal nerves, causing transient or permanent vocal cord paralysis.

A leak is too large if it prevents effective inflation of the lungs. Consider switching to a more appropriate tube size when the situation permits.

When you can't change the tube, as might be the case in an emergency, you can often compensate for a large leak by increasing gas flows or by using a gauze pad to seal the airway. Attach a string or tape long enough to extend outside the mouth to avoid it being forgotten. *It's essential to remove any such padding prior to extubation to avoid airway obstruction.*

Intubating The Older Child

Children, unlike infants, have teeth, often in varying degrees of attachment. If you have time, check for loose or missing teeth before you start. If you notice a tooth is newly missing after intubation or other airway manipulation, then you must make sure the tooth is not in the pharynx where it could be aspirated. If you can't find the tooth, you may need to get a chest X-Ray to be sure the tooth is not in the trachea or a bronchus. A tooth in the stomach will eventually pass.

Children frequently have enlarged tonsils and adenoids. If the tonsils meet or "kiss" in the midline, visualization of the larynx is a challenge. Tonsils are friable tissue and bleed easily. Avoid traumatizing the posterior pharynx.

Most children younger than nine years old do not need a head roll to lift their head into the sniffing position because their occiput is still large proportionate to the rest of their head. The older the child, the more like an adult he or she will be and, at some point, will benefit from a roll under the head. Assess each child individually. Try to place the ear canal level with the anterior shoulder.

If you can't intubate with the first attempt, withdraw, and ventilate the child. Analyze what went wrong and correct it with the next intubation attempt.

After intubation, if you are using an uncuffed tube, check for a leak of about 15-20 cm of water pressure. In children older than about eight years, we usually use cuffed tubes. When using a cuffed tube, check for a leak before inflating the cuff. When there is no leak, leave the cuff deflated. If there is a leak, inflate the cuff until the leak just stops. Checking for a leak before inflating the cuff avoids overinflation of the cuff, which can also injure the mucosa.

Always re-verify equality of breath sounds after taping since the tube can slip deeper. If they are no longer equal remove the tape, reposition, and listen again.

Even after it's taped, hold the tube securely when moving the patient. Tubes frequently slide further in or out during transport. Re-verify optimal tracheal placement after any move.

Movie 8-7, and keyframes 8-7abcdef show a child being intubated.

Pediatric Airway Emergencies

It's easy to see that managing a pediatric airway is challenging compared to the adult in the best of times. When complicated by infection or foreign body aspiration, the situation becomes even more intense. Even for the experienced intubator will be tested. Let's look at 3 of the more common pediatric airway emergencies, remembering that although epiglottitis, croup and foreign body aspiration occur predominately in children, they can also occur in adults.

Epiglottitis

Epiglottitis is infectious inflammation of the epiglottis and supraglottic structures. It typically presents with fever, difficulty swallowing, drooling and stridor. Patients can present with minimal distress, but as swelling progresses the situation worsens. The child often appears acutely ill, leaning forward in the tripod position and drooling because their throat is too sore to swallow. Epiglottitis is commonly caused by the *Haemophilus influenza* bacterium.

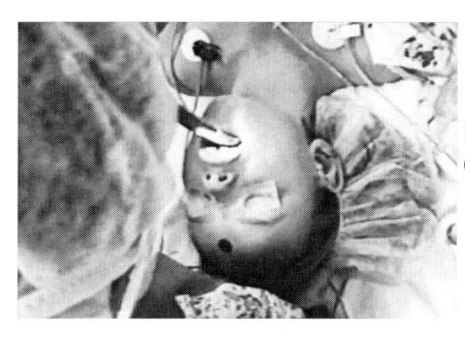

Keyframe 8-7a. Insert the laryngoscope blade. Careful not to pinch the lips against the teeth.

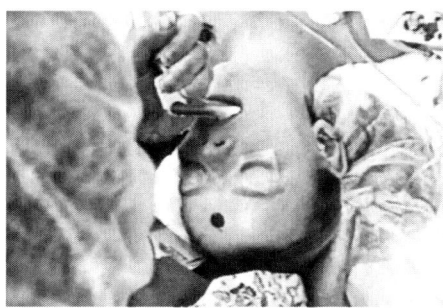

Keyframe 8-7b. Sweep the tongue to the left while inserting and lifting in one smooth gentle motion. The larynx should come into view.

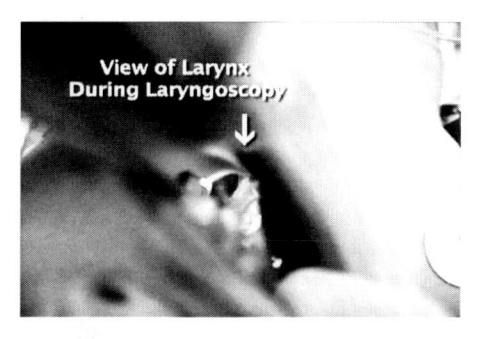

Keyframe 8-7c. You can maneuver gently to optimize this view. You can see that a helper is pulling the cheek to the right. Your helper must be careful not to move the head or rock your blade against the teeth.

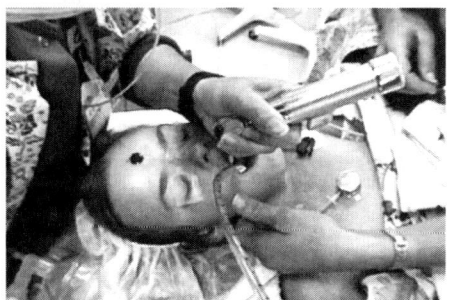

Keyframe 8-7d. Hold the head steady on the blade as you insert the tube. Try to maintain a view of the larynx as you insert if possible.

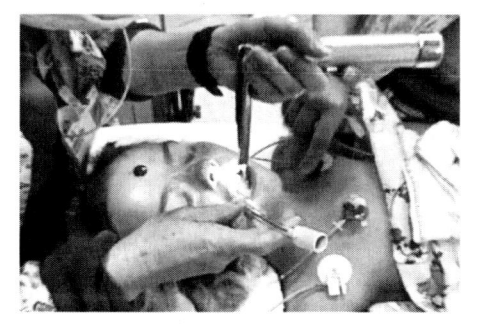

Keyframe 8-7e. Stabilize the tube while you remove the blade, being careful of the teeth and lips. The tube will tend to slide in or out until secured. Note the depth and recheck it after taping. Always verify placement.

Decompensation often develops slowly as the child tires from breathing against the increased resistance of the swollen supraglottic structures. Crying further increases airway resistance and obstruction and can precipitate failure. Once the diagnosis is made, the child should be accompanied at all times by someone skilled in airway management. Decompensation from fatigue can occur suddenly and without warning. Keep the parent with the child to avoid crying and agitation, which will worsen swelling.

Manually ventilating these children, or adults, is usually possible but may take two people — one holding the mask with both hands and using maximal jaw thrust, and the second squeezing the bag.

Treatment includes antibiotics and intubation, usually performed by an experienced intubator. Intubation is preferably done under controlled situation in the OR, often under inhalational anesthesia allowing the child to breathe herself to sleep spontaneously, thus avoiding muscle relaxants. Obviously if the child deteriorates before arriving in an OR setting, waiting may not be possible.

Adults and older children who are capable of cooperation, are often intubated awake to minimize the risk of loosing the airway from loss of pharyngeal muscles tone due to deep planes of anesthesia.

During intubation, the epiglottis is often described as a red cherry due to the swelling and it may hide the glottic opening. Having your assistant press abruptly on the chest often releases a bubble in the secretions in the oropharynx that indicates the location of the trachea.

Use an endotracheal tube size at least one size smaller than the expected size and have smaller tubes available in case swelling is more severe. Place a stylet in your tube to maximize your success on the first pass.

Use gentle technique to avoid adding traumatic swelling to the edema.

Croup

Unlike epiglottitis, the swelling from croup is *sub*glottic. It typically occurs in children less than 6 years. Croup occurs from a variety of infections including laryngotracheitis, laryngotracheal bronchitis, and diphtheria. Croup is characterized by a "barking" cough, often described as like a seal bark. Stridor and hoarseness are also present. Croup is most commonly caused by the parainfluenza virus.

The disease process progresses slowly and deterioration is usually caused by fatigue. Severe croup, with chest retractions and respiratory distress, may require emergency room treatment and ICU observation. Treatment is with steroids, inhaled racemic epinephrine, and humidified oxygen. If the child develops lethargy or decreased level of consciousness then intubation may be needed.

You can usually ventilate children with croup because positive pressure props open the airway, helping to overcome the obstruction, but you may need to use slightly higher pressures. Make sure to open the airway as much as possible to avoid distending the stomach, which will decrease your effective tidal volume and increase the risk of vomiting and aspiration.

Unlike epiglottitis, croup patients rarely need to be intubated and can usually be managed medically by decreasing swelling and treating infection. However, like epiglottitis, if intubation is needed, it's usually performed in the OR by the most experienced team available.

Suction the airway well before intubation. Since the swelling is subglottic, the upper airway will look fairly normal on direct laryngoscopy. Use a tube at least 1 size smaller and use a stylet to maximize first pass success.

Needle cricothyroidotomy can be helpful if intubation has failed and ventilation cannot be performed.

Foreign Body Aspiration

Children are notorious for putting anything into their mouths that fits, including peanuts, coins, balloons, and toy parts. Aspiration of foreign body is therefore a serious risk — one that is optimally managed by keeping such small objects away from the child. The object can be can be supraglottic, subglottic or within the larynx. It can also cause obstructive symptoms from inside the esophagus if it is large enough to compress the trachea.

Unlike either croup or epiglottitis, where decompensation is usually slow, foreign body aspiration can cause acute airway obstruction that can progress quickly and unpredictably. That's because the object is free to move and can change from partial to total obstruction without warning. If the object is soft and absorbent, such as a peanut or a piece of popcorn, progressive expansion of the object can increase obstruction. Some objects can be extremely sticky like gum.

Keep the child calm until you can transport to a location where the object can be removed safely. This usually means keeping a parent with the child, sometimes transporting both in the same wheelchair or gurney. Provide extra oxygen.

If airway obstruction occurs, use maneuvers to remove the foreign body if appropriate. These include looking inside the mouth and grabbing the object with a Magill forceps or your fingers, and using the Heimlich maneuver.

Avoid using bag-valve-mask ventilation until you have attempted to remove the foreign body because you may push it further into the airway, precipitating complete obstruction.

Anesthesiologists typically use a gentle inhalational induction allowing the child to breathe spontaneously until deep enough to perform laryngoscopy or to allow bronchoscopy to be performed to remove the object.

As a last resort, if you have been unable to ventilate the patient, intubation can be used to both establish an airway as well as to push the object further down the trachea and into a mainstem bronchus. This will allow at least partial ventilation and the foreign body can be removed later by bronchoscopy once the crisis has passed. The risk is blocking the carina but if you can't ventilate at all it may be a risk worth taking.

If the patient has inhaled soft material like peanut butter or marsh mallow, it can plug the endotracheal tube. You may need to extubate and reintubate with a new tube if obstruction persists after the intubation.

Cricothyrotomy may or may not establish a viable airway in a foreign body aspiration depending on where the obstruction lies.

For Chapter 8 video clips go to:
http://bit.ly/WB5mAG
or
http://bit.ly/U7EV7f

9
PREINTUBATION EVALUATION

Now that you know the technique of ventilating and intubating you can better appreciate what would make those tasks harder. Performing an airway assessment allows the provider to make an educated guess at how difficult a patient will be to ventilate or intubate. The greater the number of factors that indicate the potential for difficulty, the more likely airway management will be challenging.

Unexpectedly difficult and failed intubations are a significant cause of morbidity and mortality in anesthesia as well as in all emergency care. Frequency of inability to ventilate and intubate has been estimated at 1.15%-3.8% in controlled OR settings, to 3% -5.3% in the Emergency Department setting[1,2]. The higher incidence occurs particularly in the obstetrical patient and the obese patient. Intubation that is difficult but ultimately successful occurs more frequently.

The American Society of Anesthesiology defines a difficult airway based on either ability to ventilate or ability to intubate using the following definitions [3].

- *Difficult ventilation*: inability of a trained provider to maintain oxygen saturation greater than 90% using face mask ventilation and 100% oxygen provided that pre-ventilation oxygen saturation was within normal limits.

- *Difficult intubation*: need for more than 3 intubation attempts by a trained provider or attempts at intubation that last > 10 min.

Both of these definitions assume that the provider is experienced. As good as these definitions are, there are some caveats. If one of my residents (who certainly has some expertise) tries unsuccessfully 3 times, after which I intubate on the 4th attempt without problem, that's not necessarily a difficult intubation. If it takes 2 trained providers to mask ventilate a patient using every ounce of experience, its still a difficult ventilation even if the saturation remains 100% the entire time.

The three requirements to successful laryngoscopy are being able to:
1. adequately open the mouth in order to insert the blade and look inside
2. align the 3 axes sufficiently to bring the larynx at least partially into view
3. have enough room to move the tongue out of the way

When we can't do these things, the view we get during laryngoscopy is limited. The patient is often said to have an "anterior larynx". These patients don't have a larynx anatomically more anterior when looked at in profile. But during laryngoscopy, the larynx looks anterior to your field of view (Fig. 9-1 a,b).

A simple medical history and physical exam will often alert you to potential problems. That's not always an option in emergency or combat situations. Don't forget to ask medical care providers already at the scene for information.

Medical and Surgical History

Whenever possible, review the medical and surgical history before intubation. Anything that obscures the view, alters the anatomy, or which interferes with the ability of the

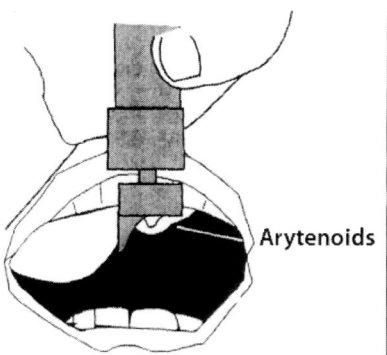

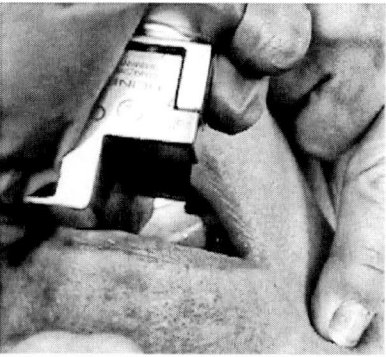

Fig. 9-1 a,b. The view seen with an "anterior larynx", in illustration and with a real patient. The view can vary from just seeing the arytenoids to having no view at all.

laryngoscope to displace the tongue and soft tissue forward, or optimally position the head and neck, can make intubation challenging.

Operations in and around the airway can produce distortion by either changing or removing normal anatomical landmarks. Recent surgery, trauma, tumor, and infection often produce edema or hematoma formation, potentially causing airway obstruction and difficult ventilation. Old nasal fractures often deviate the septum, hindering nasal intubation.

Past surgery or irradiation of the neck create scar tissue, limiting range of motion of the larynx, fixing it in position. It can also limit range of motion of the head and neck.

Potential acute cervical trauma or chronic disease, such as arthritis, can significantly impair your ability to position the patient.

Even in the normal airway, the presence of blood, secretions and emesis in the mouth make visualization more difficult, as well as increase risk of aspiration.

If the patient is awake, don't forget to ask if there has ever been any problem with placing a breathing tube with any past anesthetics. Unfortunately, however, patients are not always told if there has been a problem.

Physical Signs

Over the years, none of the many parameters which have been evaluated to try to predict difficult intubations have been perfect. They are most commonly accurate when multiple predictors are present. In one study looking at 18,500 intubations, where tracheal intubation was difficult, 34.3% of patients had one or more abnormal airway characteristics preoperatively[4].

Common signs to predict difficult laryngoscopy are:

- Limited mouth opening (< roughly 3 finger-breadths)
- Limited jaw protrusion
- Prominent overbite (maxillary incisors anterior to mandibular incisors)
- High arched, narrow palate
- Poor visibility of the uvula, with Mallampati Score 3 or 4
- Thyromental distance (space between thyroid prominence and most anterior part of the chin with head fully extended) < roughly 3 finger-breadths

- Poor compliance of the content of the submandibular space (stiff, indurated, occupied by mass, including the tongue)
- Limited neck mobility, typically looking at the maximum extension of the head on the neck
- Neck circumference > 45 cm
- Tracheal deviation
- Vocal cord abnormalities, stridor, or hoarseness
- Elevated Body Mass Index or B. M. I.
- History of Sleep Apnea or significant snoring

Let's look at these parameters and see how each could impair intubation.

Oral Exam

Limited Mouth Opening or Limited Jaw Protrusion

Laryngoscopy requires two motions: opening the hinge joint on a vertical axis and then sliding the angle of the jaw forward.

To evaluate these two motions, first check opening. Normally, adults can open the mouth at least three cm (or three finger-breadths). When she can't open that broadly, you may not be able to insert the blade, maneuver it, and see. (Fig. 9-2).

Second, check the ability to displace the mandible by having the patient push his lower jaw forward to place lower teeth in front of upper teeth (Fig. 9-3). In other words, "bite the upper lip". If he can't, you might not be able to pull the mandible forward far enough to see the larynx. Temporomandibular joint arthritis often causes loss of forward jaw glide before loss of the ability to open the mouth.

Arthritis, scar tissue, and masseter muscle spasm can impair either motion.

Fig. 9-2. Can the patient open the mouth wide enough for 3 fingers?

Fig. 9-3. Can the patient "bite" their upper lip?

Overbite and Condition of the Teeth

First, look at the condition of the teeth. Notice teeth that are loose, chipped, or missing before you start. The presence of an overbite (the protrusion of the incisor teeth due to relative overgrowth of the premaxilla) hampers intubation. There is less room to maneuver your blade past the upper teeth. In these patients it's especially important to lift the mandible and extend the head to avoid hitting teeth. A straight blade might be easier to use due to its lower profile.

Shape of the Palate

High arched palates with narrow mouths make passage of the tube difficult because the blade itself takes up so much room.

Equally important is the relative size of the tongue in relation to the palate and the rest of the mouth. Young children have relatively large tongues. Sometimes, patients with oral tumors or trauma have a swollen or enlarged tongue. The blade cannot easily manipulate a tongue that is stiff, non-compliant, or fixed.

Visibility of the Uvula

Finally, have the erect patient open his mouth as widely as possible and look at the posterior pharynx. Visibility of intraoral structures using Mallapati's signs and classification system[5,6] correlates with ease of viewing with a laryngoscope. Patients in categories I and II are typically low risk (Fig. 9-4). Patients in category III and IV are at high risk for problems[7].

The Mallampati Signs are useful. However, they are not infallible. Tse et al.[8] reported that the Mallampati Signs were most accurate when they were negative. In other words, having a Mallampati 1 or 2 class airway correctly predicted no problems with intubation in 92% of patients. However, in their study, having a Mallampati Class of 3 only predicted 66% of the difficult intubations. And of those that had Mallampati 3, 78% did not have difficult laryngoscopy. They speculated that the difference in results may have stemmed from the fact that Mallampati himself may have been grading Class 3 differently from the authors.

The take home message, however, is that seeing a Mallampati class 3 and particularly a class 4 should raise your concern, especially when paired with other findings.

Class I: soft palate, uvula, fauces, pillars visible

No difficulty

Class II: soft palate, uvula, fauces visible

No difficulty

Class III: soft palate, base of uvula visible

Moderate difficulty

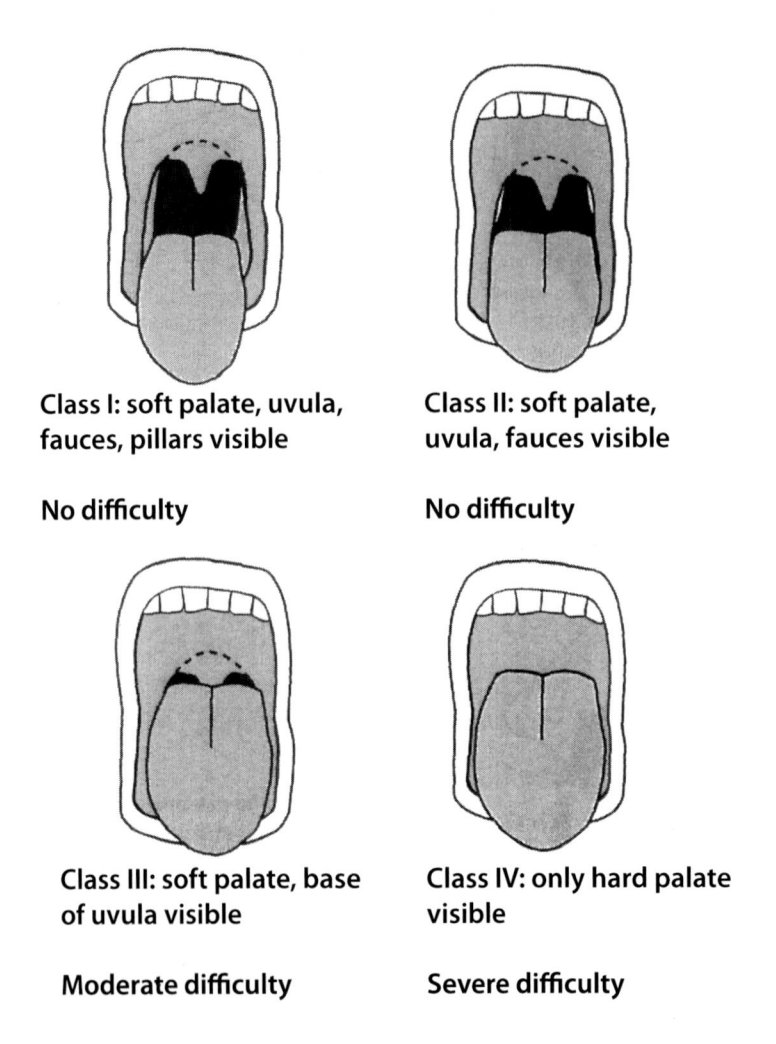

Class IV: only hard palate visible

Severe difficulty

Fig. 9-4. Mallampati Signs as indicators of difficulty of intubation. (Adapted from Mallampati and Samsoon and Young)

Thyromental Distance: The Receding or Small Chin

The thyromental distance is the distance from the tip of the chin to the thyroid notch. Patients with receding chins have hypoplastic, or smaller than normal, mandibles. There is less room to displace the tongue and epiglottis forward — making it hard to see the larynx. Pierre Robin malformation, a congenital syndrome associated with severe mandibular hypoplasia, is an extreme example of a patient who may need awake intubation for anesthetic care. Not every patient with a receding chin needs an awake intubation, of course, but when you see a receding chin you need to be prepared for a challenge.

Identify these patients by looking at their profile and noting the chin line. Spot them also by measuring the distance from the inside of the mandible to the hyoid bone with your fingertips. This distance is normally at least three fingers breadths in the adult (Fig. 9-5a.b.). Less than three indicates possible difficulty. Two or less almost assures it. Have these patients extend their necks. A distance from the lower border of the mandible to the thyroid notch of less than 6 cm alerts you to potential problems.

Beards can obscure these features so examine the chin under the beard.

Fig. 9-5a.b. a: Measuring the distance from the mentum of the chin (inside rim of the mandible) to the hyoid bone — 3 fingers-breadth in typical adult. b: Patients with hypoplastic mandibles, or receding chins, often have very "anterior" larynxes.

Poor Compliance of the Submandibular Space

Intubation depends on bringing all of the axes of the larynx into alignment. Just as a sword swallower needs to align everything to allow the sword to pass unhindered into the esophagus, so too does the intubator needs to align everything for the endotracheal tube to enter the larynx. When the contents of the submandibular space are stiff, indurated, swollen, or fixed, you can't manipulate those structures with your larygoscope blade. Obesity, tumor, hematoma, trauma, infection such as a retropharyngeal abscess, burn/inhalational injury, or radiation can all produce this type of condition. Angioedema, swelling associated with a severe allergic reaction, can make the larynx feel fixed and immobile.

Patients who have received large amounts of intravenous fluids during resuscitation or treatment of conditions such as sepsis can also have significant swelling and induration of their pharyngeal soft tissues. Patients who were easy to intubate before may now be difficult to intubate, or reintubate after extubation.

Approach patients with reduced submandibular compliance with caution. Consider awake intubation.

Macroglossia or Large Tongue

Intubation depends on your ability to move the tongue out of the way. If the tongue is enlarged relative to the size of the mouth for any reason, from congenital anomaly to traumatic swelling, intubation will be challenging.

To begin your examination, view the patient's profile. Have them stick out their tongue. Look at the neck and submandibular space.

Flexion and Extension of the Neck

Have the patient touch his chin to his chest (normal 45°) and to both shoulders in turn (normal 40°). Then have the patient extend his head back as far as possible (normal 55°). Normal range of motion decreases about 20% by 70 years of age.

Limited range of motion impairs your ability to bring the airway axes into alignment. If the atlanto-occipital joint cannot fully extend, then marked extension of the head on the

Fig. 9-6. Gently move the larynx from side to side to check for masses and mobility. You can also ask the patient to swallow so that you can feel vertical movement.

neck increases the anterior cervical spine convexity. The increased convexity pushes the larynx further anteriorly, impairing the view. Maximal sniffing position with a more neutral head position can help.

Tracheal Mobility

Place your hand over the larynx and gently move it from side to side. Feel and watch as the patient swallows to see if the trachea moves up and down normally.

A larynx fixed to the midline by tumor or scar is often hard to lift with the laryngoscope. It looks anterior during the intubation making the vocal cords and arytenoid cartilages very hard to see (Fig. 9-6).

Tracheal Deviation

Look at the trachea and the external laryngeal structures. Are they midline in the neck or deviated to one side? Can you feel the larynx? Some pathology covers the larynx and makes assessment difficult. If you can't feel the larynx it may be shifted out of position or compressed. Tumor, trauma, hematoma, and scar tissue can deviate the trachea. Movement of the larynx from the midline makes identification of landmarks and alignment of axes more difficult.

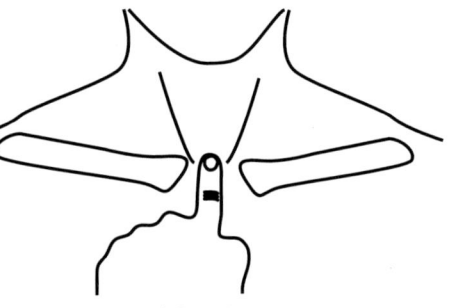

Fig 9-7. Feel for the trachea in the sternal notch to check for deviation.

Feel for the trachea in the sternal notch relative to the ends of the clavicles (Fig. 9-7).

Deviation of the trachea can make insertion of the endotracheal tube harder. It's possible for the larynx itself to remain midline while the trachea shifts to the side (Fig. 9-8). This shift can be obvious, or subtle and require CT or X-Ray to see (Fig 9-9).

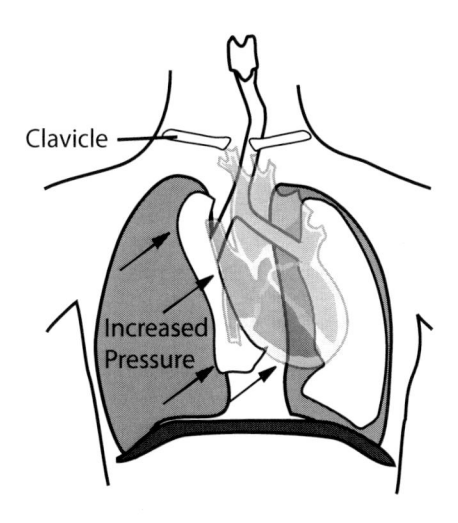

Fig. 9-8. Tension pneumothorax, as well as tumor, or hemothorax, can deviate the trachea inside the chest, in this case to the left.

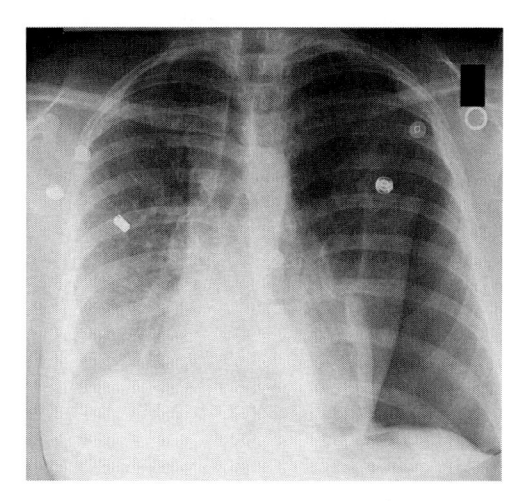

Fig. 9-9. Tension pneumothorax showing tracheal deviation to the patient's right[9].

Elevated Body Mass Index or Morbid Obesity

Obesity is defined as having a Body Mass Index, of B.M.I., greater than 30. B.M.I. is calculated by using the formula:

$$B.M.I. = weight\ in\ kilograms\ /\ height\ in\ meters^2$$

Morbid obesity is defined as a B.M.I greater than 40. Super-morbid obesity is a B.M.I greater than 50. The higher the B.M.I, the more likely a patient is to have multiple medical problems and a tendency to airway and possible respiratory compromise. Short neck, poor neck mobility, and significant submandibular and pretracheal soft tissue are all very common in the morbidly obese. There is also a higher association of difficult intubation with obstructive sleep apnea[10].

However, weight is not distributed evenly about the body in all patients. Even popular magazines talk about obese individuals who are "pear shaped" and "apple shaped." In my experience, "apple-shaped" patients tend to have shorter necks, more limited neck extension, and more pre-tracheal fat than "pears."

When faced with the obese patient, pre-positioning can be absolutely key. We'll talk about strategies for intubating the obese patient in Chapter 10.

Short, Muscular Or Obese Neck

Extreme obesity generally increases the risk of difficult intubation. While B.M.I. alone poorly predicts difficulty, the additional presence of a neck circumference > 45 cm, with an abundance of pretracheal soft tissue at the level of vocal cords is a good predictor of difficult laryngoscopy in obese patients.[7]

Pretracheal soft tissue limits the ability to displace the larynx forward and move the tongue out of the way. Curved blades can be more difficult to use in these patients because they rely on displacing soft tissue forward. Obese patients often require a straight blade and cricoid pressure.

Since we don't routinely measure neck circumference, you must learn to recognize the suggestive body shape or a short thick, neck.

Vocal cord abnormalities

Indirect exam of the vocal cords entails listening to the voice. The presence of hoarseness can mean edema, tumor, paralysis, or arthritis. Stridor implies narrowing obstruction. When I hear voice abnormalities or stridor, I will start with a smaller tube because I expect a smaller than normal opening. Especially true in emergencies, I don't want to risk inability to pass the tube on the first try — which is often your best visualization if swelling is actively worsening.

In the elective situation, direct vocal cord examination or performance of soft tissue X-rays and other studies may also be helpful.

Nose

Check the nose if you plan a nasal intubation. Has the patient ever broken his nose or had nasal surgery? Is the septum deviated? Check to see if he can breath equally out both sides or if one side is more patent. Is there a history of nose bleeds or sinusitis? Is the patient anticoagulated, which would increase the risk of nosebleed.

If there is an acute nasal fracture, nasal intubation is relatively contraindicated due to the potential risk of introducing the endotracheal tube through a broken cribiform plate at the back of the nose.

Lingual Tonsillar Hypertrophy

Lingual tonsils are nodular lymphoid tissues distributed on the posterior surface of the tongue, often symmetrically present on either side of the glosso-epiglottic folds. Large lingual tonsils can occupy the entire vallecula and overly the borders of the epiglottis. Lingual tonsillar hypertrophy (LTH) cannot be identified during a routine oropharyngeal exam and can lead to unexpected difficult intubation as well as can't intubate/can't ventilate scenarios.

LTH is usually asymptomatic but the patient may report a lump in the throat, obstructive sleep apnea, snoring and a history of recurrent tonsillitis or sore throat. It is thought that recurrent pharyngeal inflammation may contribute to growth of enlarged lingual tonsils as a compensatory mechanism after tonsillectomy and adenoidectomy since two thirds of patients have a history of having had tonsils and adenoids removed.

Unfortunately LTH is often diagnosed only after a patient has had a difficult intubation. It is possible to identify lingual tonsils using a pharyngeal mirror to do a more detailed oropharyngeal exam if you have suspicions.

Quickly Evaluating The Emergency Patient

When you've been called to intubate a patient, ask the following questions.

1. **Why does this patient need intubation?** The answer to this question will let you know how quickly you need to proceed. Cardiac arrest victims and patients dying from lack of oxygen require immediate action. Progressive respiratory failure in an asthmatic who is tiring, but still ventilating, allows more time for analysis.
2. **Is someone ventilating this patient?** Regardless of the reason for intubation, your first duty is to be sure that the patient is being ventilated and oxygenated. Ventilation takes

priority over everything else. If you are the only one capable of ventilating the patient, do so. Have an assistant prepare your equipment.

3. **What important medical problems does this patient have?** Knowing that an awake patient with respiratory failure also has unstable angina is important if you are to minimize hypertension and stress during intubation. Knowing that a patient suffers from AIDS or hepatitis is important to protect yourself. Nasal intubations are relatively contraindicated in immunosuppressed patients and those with diabetes because of the risk of sinusitis.

4. **Is this patient anticoagulated?** Intubation techniques in the anticoagulated patient must be especially gentle to prevent airway bleeding. Avoid nasal intubation in the anticoagulated patient due to the risk of nosebleed.

5. **Is there any problem with the airway?** If the patient has a history of surgery, trauma, tumor, radiation or infection of the airway it may influence your choice of equipment.

During this exchange, quickly choosing what you feel is the appropriate laryngoscope blade and tube. Check the cuff on the tube for leaks and inserting a stylet. Ask for suction, with a yankauer suction tip if possible. Suction is often a low priority item for the resuscitation team. It is a high priority item for you because you need to see the larynx and you need to clear the airway.

A quick look at the patient identifies such signs as a receding chin, an overbite, facial trauma, a deviated trachea, and a short, thick neck. Ventilating the patient before the intubation identifies problems with neck and jaw mobility. It took less than the 2-4 minutes you needed to prepare your equipment to do a simple evaluation of the patient's airway.

Many of the signs for evaluating an airway prior to intubation are highly predictive of success if they are *negative*, but have a significant number of false positives. In others words, the signs predict the patient will be difficult to intubate when indeed they are not difficult. The flip side is also true. The patient may look easy to intubate, but they're not — meaning we always have to be prepared for the unexpected.

10
TRICKS OF THE TRADE
COMMON DIFFICULT INTUBATION SCENARIOS

Most intubations proceed without difficulty. Certain patients, however, are difficult to intubate by virtue of their anatomy or the circumstances of the intubation. Unfortunately, such patients can also be difficult to ventilate.

With experience you learn to anticipate these potentially difficult intubations. You can often avoid problems by altering technique at the start. Let's look some of the tricks of the trade that allow you to intubate common challenging patients using conventional laryngoscopy equipment. We'll talk specifically about trauma, the challenges associated with pre-hospital settings, and some important alternative means of ventilating and intubating in later chapters..

Difficulty in intubation, especially when accompanied by difficulty in ventilation, is a life-threatening situation. Even experienced intubators seek help when they have trouble. If you believe an intubation may be difficult, consider having another experienced intubator available during the intubation to save precious time in an emergency.

Cardiac Arrest

Cardiac arrest victims are often challenging intubations because of the circumstances surrounding the intubation. Excitement and apprehension accompany this life saving effort. If you don't intubate often, you're likely to be nervous. Even experienced intubators get excited in emergency situations, but we control our excitement and let the adrenaline work for us, rather than against us.

Step one, therefore, is to remain in control of your own sense of alarm. The leaders, which includes the person in control of the airway, must stay calm. If you appear panicked, the rest of your team will follow your lead.

Step two is to quickly assess the situation. Is the patient being ventilated? Is there suction available? What help do you have? What position is the patient in and how can you optimize that position?

You usually find the patient in one of two awkward positions: on the ground or in a bed. When the patient lies on the ground, you must get down on the patient's level. One technique is to kneel. Mechanical advantage is more difficult from this position. You must rely more heavily on your arm strength to lift the head rather than your upper back and shoulder muscles. The natural tendency to lean forward and bend your arm will make it hard for you to balance (Fig. 10-1). The weight of the patient pulls you forward when you try to lift.

Instead, keep your left arm and your back as straight as you can, leaning backward. Tense your lower back and thigh muscles to form a firm base of support. Lift upward (Fig. 10-2). Position your head and shoulders over the patient's head to improve your center of gravity. Straddling the head with your knees allows you to steady the head, steady yourself, and

Fig. 10-1. Awkward positioning

Fig. 10-2. Position your center of gravity over the patient's head.

improve your angle or approach. A folded sheet under the head can lift it into the sniffing position.

You can also sit to the patient's right side, facing the feet. Your hips should be level with the back of your patient's head. Bend your knees slightly to allow you to maintain balance while shifting your weight to optimize the position of your outstretched left arm doing the laryngoscopy. (Fig. 10-3). This position gives you good leverage without pressing on the upper teeth. Pass the endotracheal tube with your right hand.

Unfortunately, having the patient lie in the typical hospital bed is also awkward (Fig. 10-4, 10-5). Most hospital beds have a fairly high headboard which prevents easy access to the patient's head. Have someone remove the headboard while you prepare your equipment.

Fig. 10-3. Sitting to the right of patient's head.

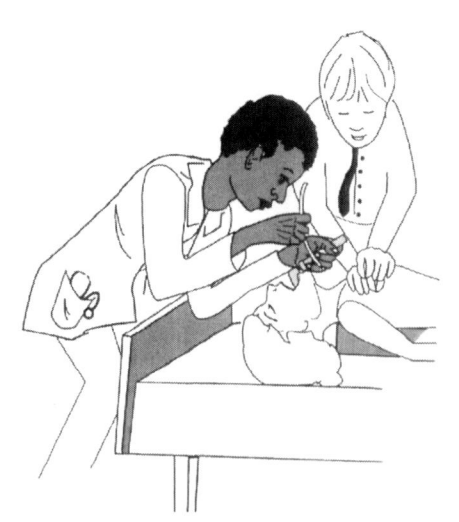

Fig. 10-4. Problems with intubation in the bed:

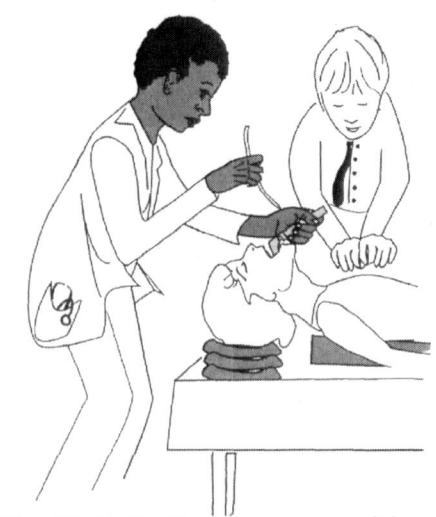

Fig. 10-5. Optimize your position for intubation during CPR.

Second, if you can't easily reach the patient, pull him toward you. Small individuals like myself will have more effective control because you don't have to lean forward.

Third, you'll often find the patient on a soft hospital mattress with the hard cardiac arrest board under his back. Because the backboard allows effective CPR, we take this position for granted. We often fail to notice that the patient's head now hangs fully extended off the back of the board, forcing you to lift the patient's head much higher to straighten the airway (Fig. 10-6).

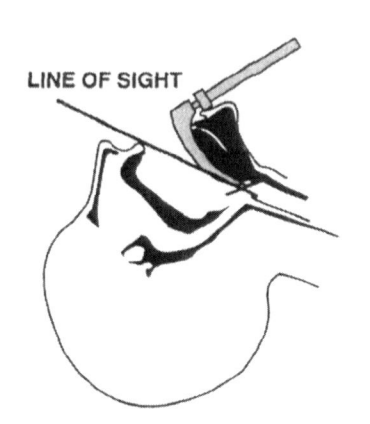

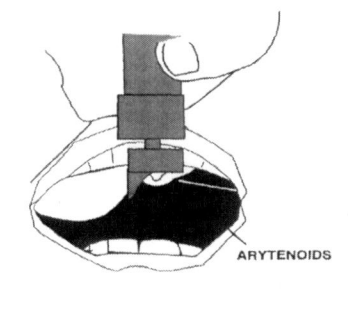

Fig. 10-6. Overextension of the head (a.) makes the larynx appear more anterior on laryngoscopy (b).

Lifting a heavy head high during CPR is difficult. Use pillows to put the head in the sniffing position and decrease the lift needed. Don't hesitate to ask for help in lifting while you place the tube. Cricoid pressure to push the larynx down can also help. (Fig. 10-7).

Fourth, CPR means that someone is rhythmically and forcefully pushing on the patient's chest. The patient and bed are both moving up and down. Moving targets are hard to hit at the best of times.

In emergency situations, I often choose a Macintosh curved blade. In my opinion, its broader flange is more forgiving of less than perfect placement and awkward positioning, conditions common in the emergency intubation. It also makes balancing the patient's head easier in those circumstances.

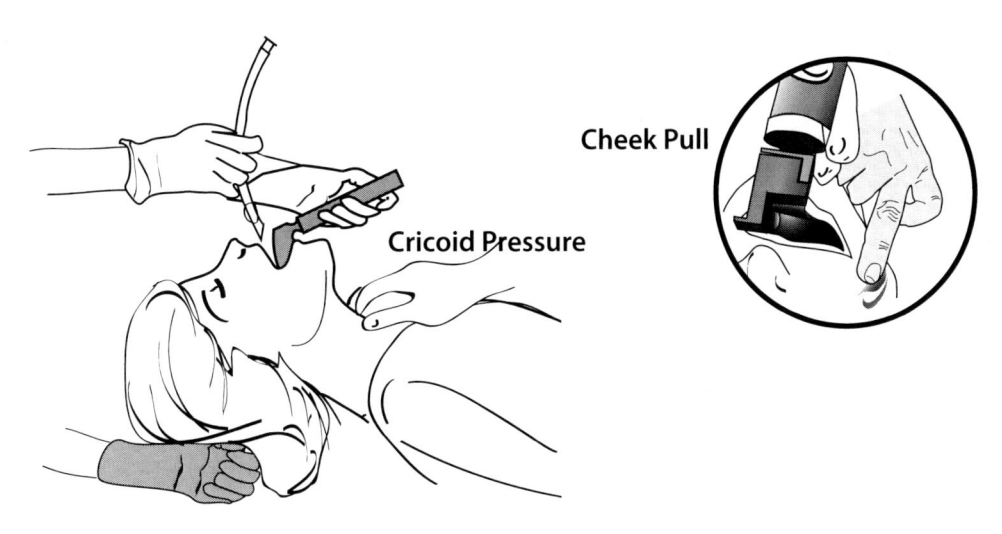

Fig. 10-7. The use of helpers can be key in optimizing the patients position and improving your view.

I usually get in position, visualize the larynx, and try to pass the tube. If movement prevent intubation, I say the command "stop CPR." Pass the tube. Command "begin CPR." This attempt should take no longer than 15 to 20 seconds, usually less. If you have any difficulty passing the tube have your associates begin CPR again. Remove your blade, and ventilate the patient. Ventilation is the priority. Try again.

Never delay CPR for an extended period because of an intubation attempt. Adequate ventilation is more important than intubation. If you have difficulty, stop and ventilate the patient while you decide what to try next. Be prepared for emesis, which can sometimes be massive under these circumstances.

Following intubation, suction the tube and trachea carefully to remove any possible secretions and blood aspirated during the resuscitation.

Obesity

Patients with obesity or with short, muscular necks can sometimes be hard to intubate (Fig. 10-8). Short, thick necks and double chins mean that obese patients have excess soft tissue around, and in front of the larynx.

The curved blade sometimes won't give good visualization in obese patients because soft tissue prevents the blade from displacing of tissue forward. The larynx remains hidden. You might consider starting with a straight blade, or switching to one if your first attempt with a curved blade is unsuccessful. The straight blade doesn't displace the tissues of the hypopharynx forward — it flattens and lifts them.

The straight blade has another advantage.

Fig. 10-8. The obese patient often has a short, thick neck and much soft tissue under the chin.

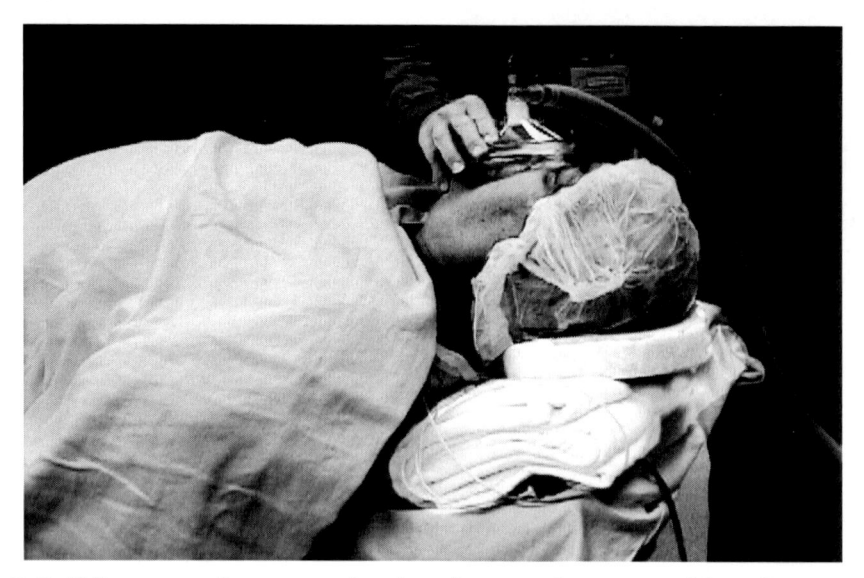

Fig. 10-9. Building a small ramp under the obese patient to position the mastoid fairly level with the anterior chest. Make sure that the ramp is not so high nor so stiff that it prevents you from tilting the patient's head back.

Inserting the curved blade can be difficult in the obese patient. The chest and breasts can get in the way of the handle and prevents rotation of the blade into the mouth. The straight blade bypasses this problem by entering directly without the need for rotation.

Patient position can be key to intubating the obese patient. When you have the time and the opportunity, place the obese patient on a "ramp" of folded blankets or sheets[1]. The optimal final position slightly elevates the shoulders and further elevates the head to place the ear canal fairly level with the anterior shoulder or top of the chest. The head should be tilted slightly back in the sniffing position — don't build the ramp so high or so steep that you can't tilt the head into extension. Use of the ramp makes it easier to get the patient into that "sword swallower" position (Fig. 10-9).

Alternatively, if the patient is on an OR table, the table can often be reconfigured into a ramp by flexing the back upward an then tilting the head platform slightly downward.

The higher the BMI, the more useful the ramped position appears to be[2]. When using patients as their own controls, views of the larynx improved in 88% of patients with BMI less than 25 kg m^2, 91% in patients with 30 kg m^2, and in 100% of patients than 45 kg m^2.

Morbidly obese patients desaturate more quickly when apneic than patients with a normal BMI — even after preoxygenation. You can help prevent this early fall in oxygen saturation by placing the patient in a 25° head up position during preoxygenation. This elevation can be part of the ramping process. Applying about 5 cm H$_2$O of PEEP with a tight face mask for 5 minutes will also allow for maximum oxygenation.

Be prepared to ventilate the patient should the intubation attempt be prolonged. Excess soft tissue collapsing over the laryngeal structures may make manual ventilation difficult. Have an alternate means of ventilation available such as an LMA. Alternate techniques for ventilation are discussed in Chapter 12.

When the equipment is available, considering alternate means of intubation such as the GlideScope® or LMA Fastrach® or having this equipment standing by should direct laryngoscopy fail is prudent. These and other advanced intubation devices are discussed in Chapter 17 and 18.

Receding Chin

Patients with receding chins, caused by hypoplastic mandibles, often have very "anterior airways" (Fig. 9-5b). There is frequently not enough room to displace the tissue forward when you intubate. You should anticipate the need for cricoid pressure and a straight blade. Using a shorter straight blade, such as a Miller 2, increases your ability to maneuver the blade.

Use of cricoid pressure and a sharply bent stylet can also be helpful. As always, make sure head position is optimized.

The GlidesScope and alternate intubation devices have been very useful in this group. These and other advanced intubation devices are discussed later.

Consider awake intubation if the chin is extremely hypoplastic, especially when the patient's ability to open the mouth is limited. Any condition or injury that limits the patient's ability to open their mouth should suggest awake intubation.

Overbites

The upper teeth in a prominent overbite can get in the way of a Macintosh blade (Fig. 10-10) which must follow the curve of the tongue into the mouth. The higher vertical profile of the MAC may bump into the teeth if you don't open the mouth wide. Straight blades avoid these problems. Lift the jaw upward in the presence of overbite. Don't use the teeth as a lever.

If you can't see the larynx, there are two tricks to try. The first is cricoid pressure, a handy standby anytime you have difficulty seeing the larynx. The second is to insert a Miller 2 straight blade into the far right side of the mouth. Instead of shifting the tongue as far to the left as usual, leave the blade slightly to the right so that it enters the mouth at an angle. The tip of the blade is inserted just a bit deeper using this side approach rather than the midline where the overhanging teeth are in the way. You won't have much space. Have your assistant pull the cheek back to allow you to insert the tube. You will probably need cricoid pressure to manipulate the larynx into line.

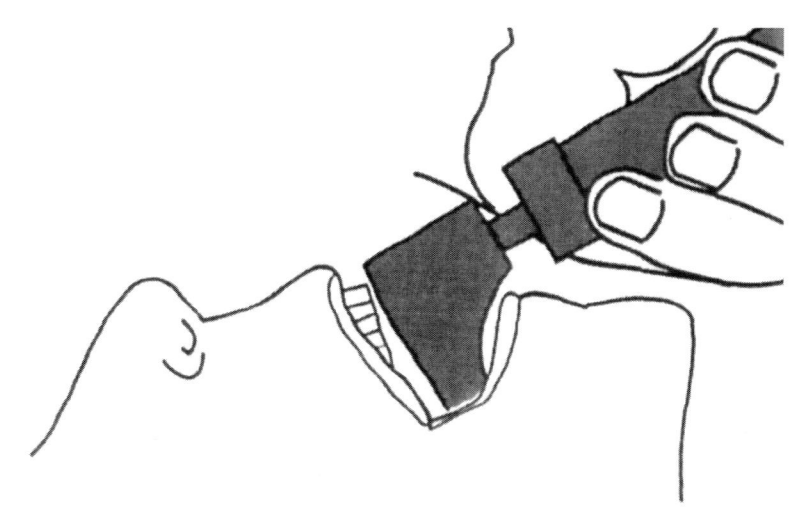

Fig. 10-10. In the presence of overbite be careful to lift upward instead of rotating the blade on the teeth.

Poor Neck Mobility

Poor neck mobility can occur for a number of reasons. Arthritic fusion of the vertebrae in older individuals can be so severe that no extension or flexion of the head can occur. Torticollis or wryneck prevents full range of motion and may pull the neck to one side. Finally, after neck trauma your patient may have a cervical collar or other restraint to prevent damage to the spinal cord.

Sometimes it's safest to intubate these patients awake using fiberoptic laryngoscopes and awake blind-nasal intubations. Some of the newer video laryngoscopes are another option. Sometimes the only safe choice is a tracheostomy. We'll discuss awake intubations and advanced specialty equipment later.

For the moment, let's assume that you have an apneic patient with limited neck mobility in need of intubation and all you have is a laryngoscope. In this scenario there is no risk of spinal cord injury. He's unconscious or perhaps in cardiac arrest. What options do you have?

If the larynx looks very anterior during laryngoscopy lift the head as far off the bed as you can, suspending the head from your blade. This maneuver may be enough to bring the arytenoids into view. If it is, aim for the space immediately above the arytenoids, where the gap between the vocal cords lies. By aiming your tube at the likely location you can sometimes pass the tube into the larynx without seeing the vocal cords. If you do pass the tube blindly, make absolutely certain that you immediately verify proper tube placement. Esophageal intubation occurs easily.

Straight blades often work better than curved blades with poor neck mobility. Forceful cricoid pressure may push the larynx down into view.

Make sure the stylet in your endotracheal tube has a bend on the end, shaping the tube like a hockey stick. Aim your tube anteriorly at the point where you think the larynx lies. Be gentle.

In the event that you can't intubate the patient, ventilate the patient by mask between attempts. Periodically suction the mouth and oropharynx. Ask other intubators to try. Try a bougie (see later in this chapter).

When faced with the trauma patient in a halo, cervical collar, or other restraining device you face a difficult responsibility. You must secure the airway without injuring the patient. Have a knowledgeable assistant hold the head and neck in a neutral position while you intubate. Lift the mandible upward, not the head and neck (Fig. 10-11) See also Chapter 13.

Usually you can see enough anatomy to allow for intubation. If you can't intubate quickly, consider emergent use of an advanced ventilation device such as an LMA or Combitube (see Chapter 12). Remember, ventilation always comes first.

Newer intubation techniques such as video laryngoscopy and the LMA Fastrach have revolutionized management of the unexpected difficult intubation. These advanced techniques are discussed later.

A cricothyroidotomy is also a quick means of securing the airway. More extensive discussion of the management of the patient with potential cervical spine injury is found in Chapter 13.

Fig. 10-11. When intubating the patient with possible cervical spine injury, have an assistant stabilize the head and neck. Lift only the mandible. Don't extend the head.

Fixed Airway Obstruction

Airway obstruction is a life-threatening emergency. If you are an inexperienced intubator, you should seek the advice of any available experienced intubators. Multiple prolonged or traumatic intubation attempts may worsen existing airway obstruction by causing bleeding and increasing edema, leading to a potentially fatal situation. We often bring such patients to an operating room where they are either intubated awake or under deep inhalational anesthesia with spontaneous ventilation. The personnel and means to perform emergency tracheostomy are immediately available and ready. Have plenty of help available.

The most common emergencies involving airway obstruction include epiglottitis, croup, foreign body, trauma, and tumor. Epiglottis, croup, and foreign body are most common in the pediatric population but can occur in the adult.

If your patient is breathing more comfortably sitting up allow them to do so, as long as vital signs are stable. A patient who is sitting has a larger functional residual capacity than one lying down — about 1 liter larger in the adult. A larger FRC provides a larger volume for oxygen exchange. When a compromised patient lies down, soft tissue in the oropharynx tends to collapse over the airway, possibly increasing obstruction. Elevating the head may slow development of any edema.

Give supplemental oxygen. If the patient must be sent to another location, ensure that someone who can manage airway obstruction accompanies them. This intubator must take all required airway equipment with him or her.

If your patient is a child, don't subject the child to unnecessary laboratory exams, or separate him prematurely or unnecessarily from parents. Crying and screaming increases airway edema. Keep him calm. Don't sedate him. Sedation may cause him to lose what airway tone he has. Placing the parent in a wheelchair and the child in his or her lap may be the best choice for transporting a frightened child with airway obstruction around the hospital setting. Read more about pediatric difficult airway scenarios in Chapter 8.

If the patient is in danger of immediate death, and you can't wait for more specialized help, proceed with caution. Call for the tools to do cricothyroidotomy or tracheostomy just in case you need them. Never paralyze or sedate a patient with airway obstruction unless in your judgment paralysis is the only way to proceed safely. The muscle tone of the larynx may be the only factor maintaining the airway. The use of sedatives and muscle relaxants carries very high risk in the patient with fixed airway obstruction. If used they must be titrated extremely slowly and to effect. Use of agents, such as narcotics that can be reversed can be prudent.

Gently visualize the larynx by direct laryngoscopy. Use the largest ETT that will fit the swollen airway. Have a variety of sizes available because the patient may need a tube that is few sizes smaller than the size typically needed. Have pediatric tubes as well. I once used a toddler sized # 5 ETT to intubate an 80 kg, 72 inch adult with epiglottitis because that was the only tube that would fit. This small tube was replaced by a surgical airway once the situation stabilized.

If you can't identify anatomy, look for air bubbles coming from the larynx to direct you to the cords. If the patient is apneic, have an assistant push on the chest while you look for bubbles.

When the patient is breathing, continue to blow oxygen into the mouth. Advanced techniques to insufflate oxygen include placement of a cricothyroid catheter or the use a jet ventilator.

Blood in the Oropharynx

Blood in the oropharynx predisposes the patient to aspiration and hypoxia. Fresh post operative cleft palates and tonsillectomies, severe nosebleeds, massive G.I. bleeders, and trauma victims are examples. In the worst case scenario, the patient is unconscious, unable to protect their airway, and is bleeding so badly that you can't see any landmarks at all. It's a frightening experience.

Handling the situation in an operating room where there is lighting, equipment, personnel, and experienced intubators makes sense. If you're a paramedic, or corpsman, in the field or have to intubate someone on the ward, you don't have this option. Life threatening emergencies sometimes force less than optimal circumstances.

Suction the airway frequently or continuously. You can leave the suction catheter in the corner of the mouth or have your assistant suction while you are attempting intubation. If you can tip the patient into trendelenburg (tilted head down) and turn him or her to the left side, the blood will pool away from the larynx and drain from the mouth, giving you a clearer view. Turning the patient to the left side is preferred as opposed to right side because the tongue will naturally fall to the left, which is where you want it to go anyway. This topic is presented in more detail when we discuss trauma.

Pregnancy

Maternal airway complications are among the leading causes of obstetric morbidity and mortality.[3] Failure to ventilate or intubate in the pregnant patient risks not one life but two or more. Never forget the intrauterine patients.

There are multiple changes to a woman's body during pregnancy that increase the risk of failed intubation and failed ventilation.[4,5] The typical woman gains 12 kg (26 lb.) or 17% of her body weight, or more, during pregnancy.[6] The associated increase in breast size can cause the breasts to fall against the neck when the patient lies supine, blocking the insertion of a curved laryngoscope blade. A short laryngoscope handle can be helpful. Use of a straight blade is often easier.

In addition there is engorgement of the nasal, laryngeal and tracheal tissues and generalized water retention that leads to edema of the oropharyngeal mucosa and some swelling of the tongue. Airway edema, plus fat infiltration of the pharyngeal tissue with weight gain, tends to worsen the Mallampati score, with an increase toward 4 in some pregnant women between 12 and 38 weeks gestation. Difficult visualization during laryngoscopy can lead to failed intubations. And since ventilation using bag and mask can itself be a challenge because of elevation of the diaphragms, and decreased chest compliance, the risk of "can't intubate/can't ventilate" increases.

A smaller than average endotracheal tube, such as a 6.5 or even a 6 may be necessary. Because of capillary engorgement, it's easy to traumatize the oropharyngeal mucosa and cause bleeding during laryngoscopy.

Other physiologic changes place the mother at increased risk of hypoxia during intubation related apnea and hypoventilation. There is a 30 - 60% increased oxygen consumption due to fetal needs. The enlarging uterus displaces intra-abdominal organs and pushes the diaphragm upward, decreasing the mother's resting FRC. All of these changes significant impair her ability to tolerate apnea.

Increased intragastric pressure, lowered gastric pH, and decreased gastric emptying increase the mother's risk of vomiting and aspiration, so prepare.

Optimal positioning is important for laryngoscopy success. In the obese pregnant woman, use of the "ramp" (Fig. 10-9) can be very helpful. Make sure that there is left uterine displacement by either having a folded blanket or IV bag under the right hip, or have your assistant push the uterus to the left side. Left uterine displacement improves venous return and cardiac output, which would otherwise be hindered by the weight of the uterus and baby on the great vessels. Improving blood flow improves oxygen delivery and oxygenation.

Remember to hyperventilate the patient between multiple attempts at intubation and minimize any apneic periods during laryngoscopy. You have two patients using the oxygen "supply", not one.

The Use of Cricoid Pressure

Chapter 5 mentioned how valuable cricoid pressure is to improve visualization during a difficult intubation so it's worth another mention. Use cricoid pressure to improve visualization of the so-called anterior airway and also to help prevent aspiration, as pressure on the cricoid pinches off the upper esophageal sphincter. When you're having trouble passing the tube, cricoid pressure can often change the angle of the larynx enough to allow the tube to slide forward.

To apply cricoid pressure, place your thumb on one side of the cricoid ring and your index or ring finger on the other. Push down firmly to force the cricoid ring against the vertebral column and effectively seal the esophagus. It also forces the vocal cords downward and into the field of view (Fig. 10-12).

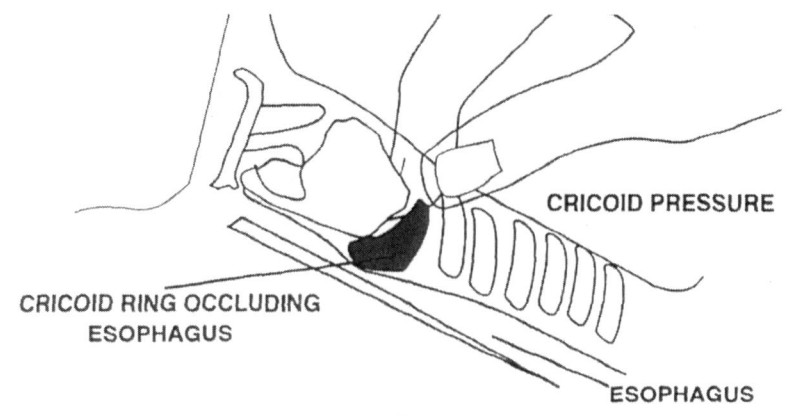

Fig. 10-12. Cricoid pressure is one of the most useful aides there is.

If pressing down on the cricoid fails to improve the view, have your helper press on the thyroid cartilage, a maneuver is called B.U.R.P.:
- **B**ackward against the vertebral column,
- **U**pwards toward the head,
- **R**ightward to the patient's right side, as a constant
- **P**ressure.

Cricoid pressure and BURP should be used cautiously, if at all, when there is an upper airway foreign body or if there is risk of cervical spine injury

Pulling on the Cheek Helps

If you don't have enough space to maneuver the tube past the blade, it often helps to have your assistant pull the cheek back as far as they can to allow you to insert the tube. Your assistant must be careful not to get in your way, and also not to give you a moving target. As your assistant pulls the cheek have him press gently with the rest of his hand on the maxilla (see Fig. 10-13). This counter pressure prevents him from either pulling the head laterally or rotating it away from you. Make sure they don't "jiggle" the head, which could cause your blade to rattle against the teeth, possibly breaking them.

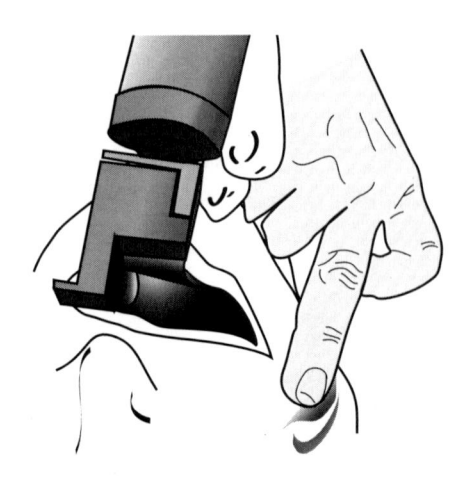

Fig. 10-13. Pulling the right corner of the mouth.

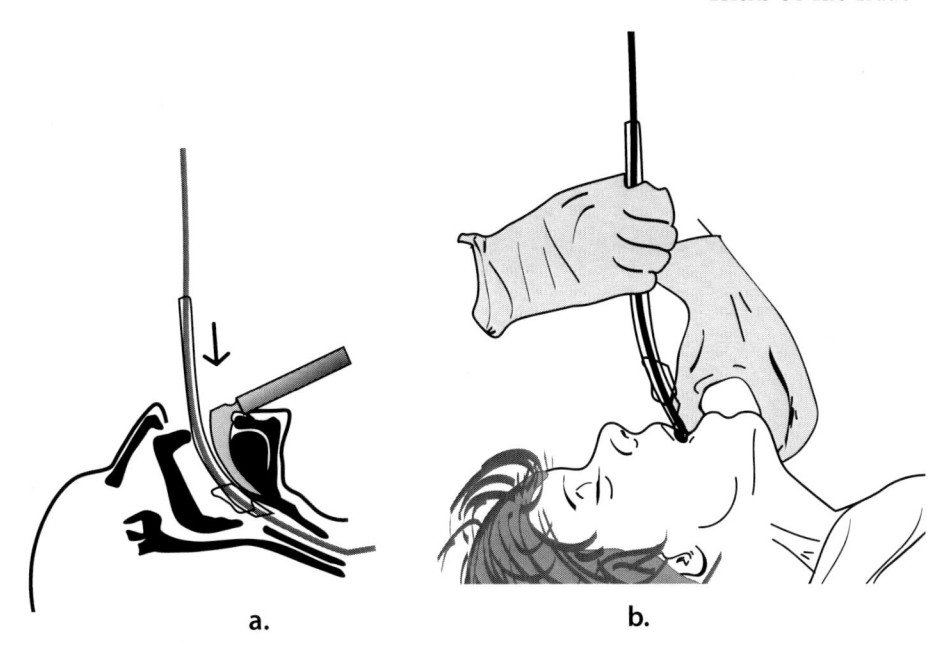

Fig. 10-14 a,b. The bougie is extremely helpful during challenging intubations. You can pass the ETT either with the laryngoscope in place (a) or after having removed the laryngoscope (b).

Use a Bougie

One of the simplest and most valuable adjuncts to intubation is the bougie. The gum-elastic bougie is an endotracheal introducer that is made of a braided polyester base with a resin coating, giving it both flexibility and stiffness at body temperature. The standard size for intubation is 15 Fr, which is 60 cm long. It will retain the curvature given to it, making it very useful for anterior airways.

However, the gum-elastic bougie is stiff enough to cause damage or perforation of the trachea and bronchi and must be used with caution. It should be used in combination with laryngoscopy under direct vision rather than as a blind stent. It is not recommended for use for exchanging endotracheal tubes. A standard tube exchanger should be used for this purpose since the lumen is hollow and will allow insufflation or jetting of oxygen if necessary. The technique described below can be performed using an endotracheal tube exchanger, although the exchanger won't hold a specific curve or shape.

Following laryngoscopy, the bougie is passed forward into the larynx if seen, or toward the probable location of the laryngeal opening under the epiglottis if the larynx is not visible. Correct placement into the trachea is felt as "clicks" as the bougie slides over tracheal rings. The bougie may rotate as it encounters the main stem bronchus or stop when the smaller bronchi are reached. It should not be forced. The bougie and laryngoscope are then fixed in position. Have your helper load the ETT onto the bougie and feed it down to you until you can grab it and continue to push it into the mouth (Fig. 10-14a,b, Mov. 10-1, KF 10-1abc). Keep your eyes on the target. You may need to rotate the tube to allow passage through the vocal cords. Withdraw the bougie and laryngoscope and verify correct placement of the tube.

Pressing the shaft of the bougie lightly against the upper teeth during insertion forces a shallow bend that curves the bougie up toward the larynx. The more you press the more it bends, helping you aim around the corner and easing insertion.

A study[7] of patients requiring cervical spine precautions and stabilization showed that in the neutral position, the view of the larynx on direct laryngoscopy was reduced in 45% of the patients. Of these, 22% had views showing only the epiglottis. The patients in the bougie group were all successfully intubated within 15-20 seconds. On the other hand 5 patients in the laryngoscopy only group subsequently required the bougie and 5 required more than 50 seconds for intubation. Thus the bougie appears to be a good adjunct for difficult intubations. You should practice its use in routine intubations to gain experience before you need it in an emergency.

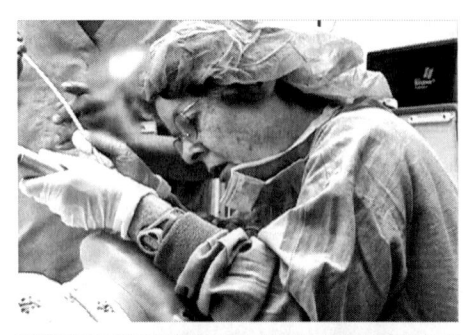

Keyframe 10-1a. Obtain as optimal a view of the larynx as possible. You often cannot see more than the back of the arytenoids.

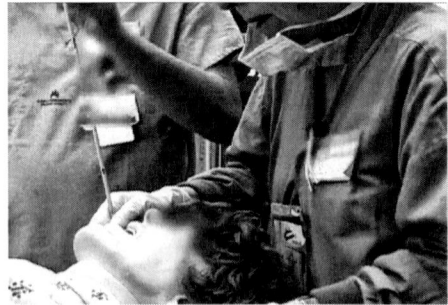

Keyframe 10-1b. Slide the bougie into the trachea. You may feel the tip of the bougie bounce subtly along the tracheal rings.

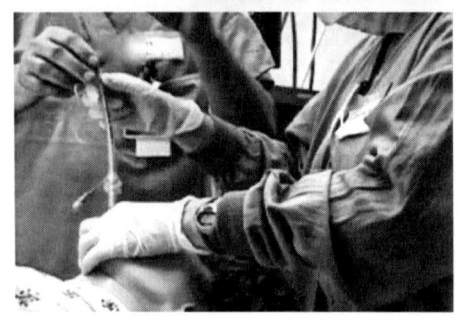

Keyframe 10-1c. Slide the endotracheal tube down the bougie into the trachea. You may need to rotate the tube to pass through the cords. Verify immediately that the tube is in the trachea.

Digital Intubation

You can perform digital intubation on any patient, but it tends to be easier in children or small adults because one major limitation is the length of your own index finger. It is sometimes used in infants with hypoplastic mandibles[8]. You can perform the technique using local or topical anesthesia and I.V. sedation or even general anesthesia. It can also be used on the unconscious patient. Be careful. Your fingers are inside the mouth and can be bitten.

The intubator should stand to the patient's right, facing the head and leaning over the patient. Advance the left index finger, lightly coated with 5% lidocaine ointment, over the surface of the tongue until it overlies the larynx. (Fig. 10-15) You should feel epiglottis and the paired arytenoids. Use of a stylet is optional but can make it easier to guide the tube.

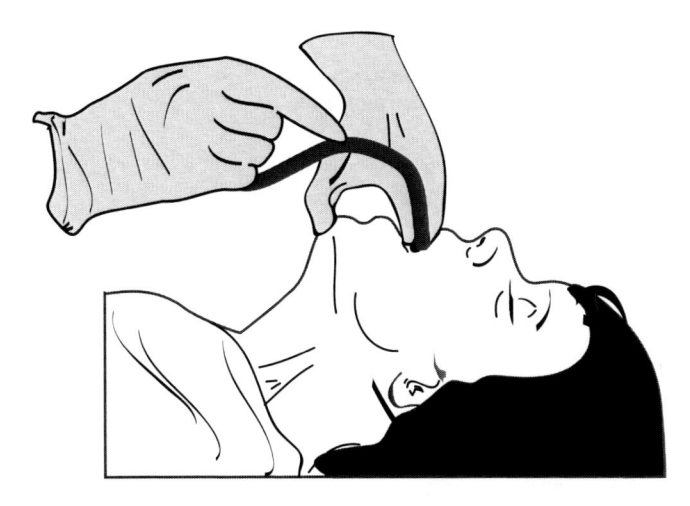

Fig. 10-15. Manual digital intubation, using a stylet to shape the tube, allowing it to be guided around the tongue into the posterior pharynx where the fingers direct the tip into the glottic opening.

Curve the endotracheal tube using a stylet. Hold the endotracheal tube like a pencil in your right hand and advance it along the left index finger until you feel the tube tip slide between the glottis and the left fingertip. You should be able to use your left fingertip to direct the tube into the glottis. You might have to rotate the tube slightly if it hangs up on the cords. Verify immediately that the tube did indeed go into the trachea.

A Difficult Intubation Algorithm

If you anticipate a difficult elective intubation it's may be best to plan an awake intubation from the outset. If intubation fails after inducing general anesthesia, you can wake the patient up and then intubate him awake (Fig. 10-16). The techniques for awake intubation will be discussed in Chapter 17.

Awake intubation may or may not be an option in the emergency situation (Fig. 10-17). If you can adequately mask ventilate the patient, then you have many options and time to explore them.

Call for assistance. Rarely will you be in a situation where you are the only person trained in intubation. Never hesitate to ask for help. That help can be getting equipment ready, aid in holding the head or neck in position, or asking someone else to intubate.

Change your blade, alter the patient's head position, or have someone else try. Bear in mind, however, that the more laryngoscopies you perform, the more likelihood there is of increasing laryngeal edema or bleeding. This can worsen the airway and ultimately make ventilation difficult. Unless you quickly see evidence of impending success, it's better to switch to an alternative method of intubation.

A more serious situation is the "can't intubate/can't ventilate" scenario. You have only minutes until life-threatening complications will occur, including brain damage and death. Try various methods to improve mask ventilation. Try another quick attempt at intubation. Consider the use of a laryngeal mask airway to improve ventilation. If you can wake the patient up, do so. If you can ventilate through the LMA, you may be able to use it as a guide for intubation. This technique is described in Chapter 12.

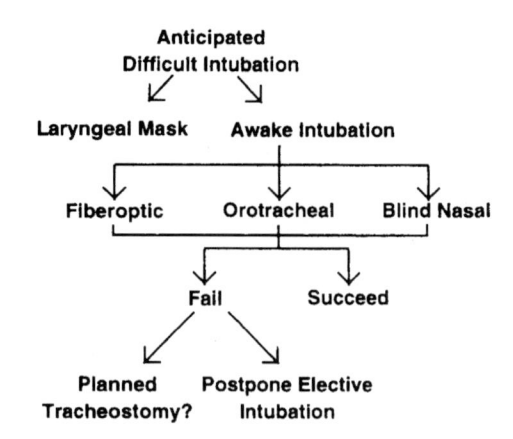

Fig. 10-16. Algorithm for the anticipated difficult intubation.

If ventilation is still poor, place a large bore catheter though the cricothyroid membrane for oxygen administration, optimally by jet ventilator. Once oxygenation is assured limited attempts at intubation can proceed. If these fail, or if you have been unable to establish oxygenation, then a surgical airway is indicated.

By the way, when you do find a patient who is truly difficult to ventilate or intubate, place that information in the patient's chart along with information on why it was difficult and what you did to successfully manage the situation. Also tell the patient and optimally provide the patient with a letter describing the problem. This helps the next provider, and protects the patient.

The Keyframe (KF) sequences in this chapter are taken from video clips that are available on-line, for free, from anyonecanintubate.com at:

For Chapter 10 video clips go to:
http://bit.ly/WDE2RZ

All video chapter files appear on Anyone Can Intubate Portfolio at:
http://bit.ly/U7EV7f

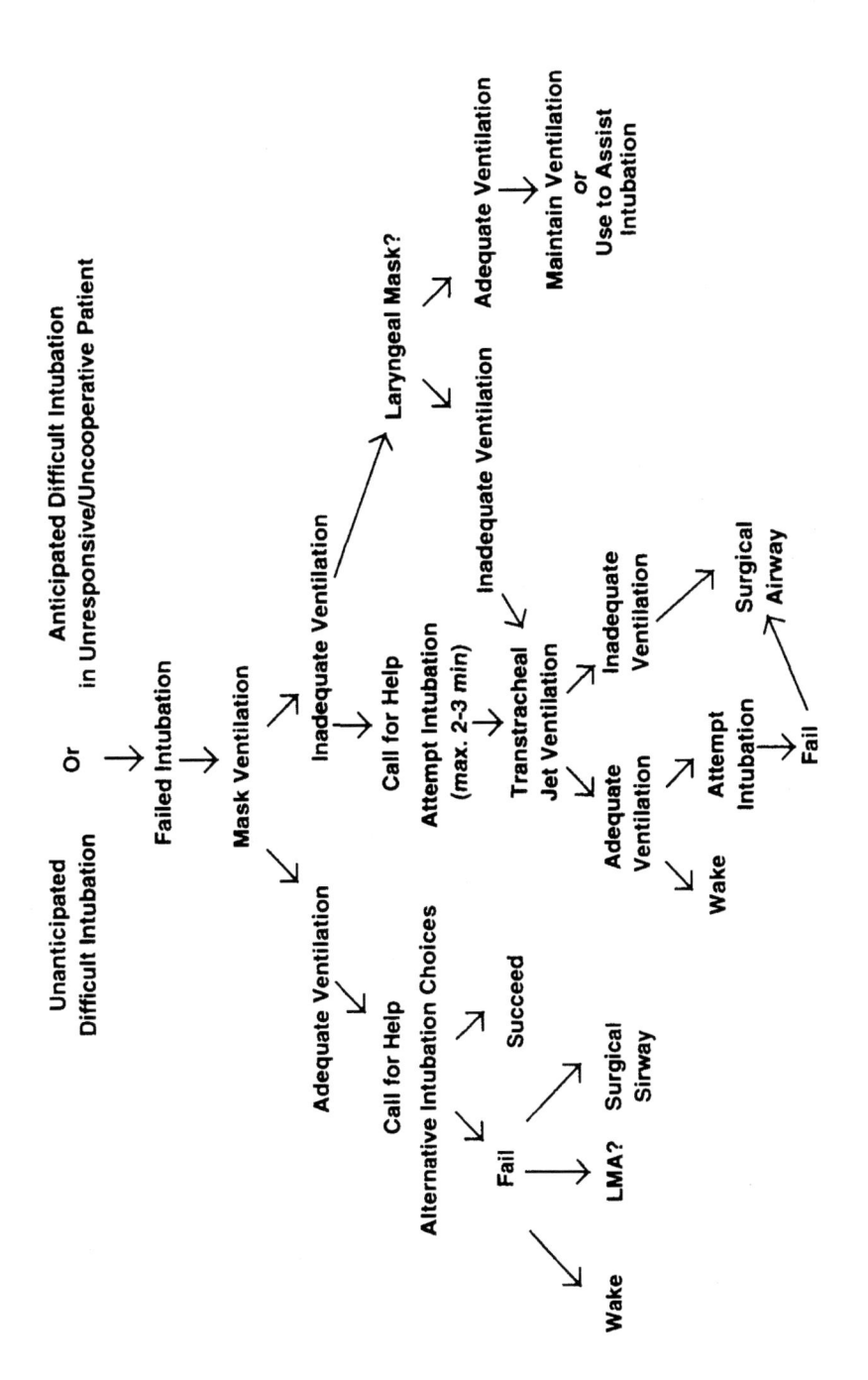

Fig. 10-17. Algorithm for managing the unexpectedly difficult intubation. Based on the American Society of Anesthesiologists Practice Guideline on Difficult Intubation.

11
NASAL INTUBATION

A nasal or nasotracheal intubation is performed through the nose rather than the mouth. Nasal intubation can be especially useful in emergent or difficult intubations because it can be performed without seeing the vocal cords (blind). Nasal intubation is also more easily performed than oral intubations when the patient is in an awkward position.

Blind nasal intubation is less used in the hospital today because of other available techniques. The Glidescope and the fiberoptic bronchoscope are examples of specialized equipment that can be used to intubate a patient with a challenging airway. However, these expensive instruments need specialized training and may not be available. Blind nasal intubation is an important skill to master as is a low-tech solution to a potentially life-threatening airway situation.

Indications

Some of the indications for a blind nasal intubation include:
- The patient with unstable cardiorespiratory status who can't receive medications to induce unconsciousness or who lacks I.V. access
- The anticipated difficult intubation
- Difficult ventilation after induction of unconsciousness (if still breathing)
- With the use of cervical spine precautions to allow a more neutral head position and to allow monitoring of neurologic signs during the intubation
- Intubation with the patient in an awkward position, such as entrapped
- Surgical access — nasal placement avoids surgical site in oral surgery

Nasal intubations are often easier to perform and more comfortable for the awake patient than oral intubations.

Contraindications

Blind nasal intubation may be difficult to perform in the uncooperative or combative patient, or in the young child.

Nasal intubation can offer advantages in a patient with facial trauma because the disruption of facial anatomy interferes with airway management. However, nasal intubation with facial trauma is still somewhat controversial because there is a low but potentially serious risk of passing the tube through a fractured ethmoid sinus and into the cranium. Approach nasal intubation with extreme caution in severe midface fractures or suspected basilar skull fractures.

Since nosebleed is the most common complication, a history of significant nosebleeds or use of anticoagulants are relative contraindications. Use caution in children less than 10 years, who often have hypertrophied, and friable, adenoids.

The nasal route is contraindicated in the patient who is known to be anticoagulated or who has a coagulopathy. It should also be avoided in patients with infected sinuses, or with anatomical abnormalities such as nasal tumor.

Don't use *blind* intubation techniques, if possible, if an oropharyngeal abscess is present to avoid rupture of the abscess with the tube.

Anatomy

The nasal passages are not just open cylinders. Inside each nasal passage there are 3 bones which project inward from the lateral walls like shelves. These are the superior, middle, and inferior turbinates. Each turbinate consists of thin, spongy bone curled upon itself like a scroll and covered with mucous membrane. The turbinates serve to increase surface area to moisten air as it is breathed, and to protect the openings into the sinuses. (Fig. 11-1).

During nasal intubation, the turbinates and the mucosa can be torn or otherwise damaged. Serious nose bleed can result. The nasotracheal tracheal tube must be gently maneuvered past these potential obstructions.

The nasal passages are perpendicular to the plain of the face, parallel to the floor when the patient is upright and the head is in a neutral position.

The nasal passages open posteriorly. The respiratory path then curves downward along the pharyngeal wall leading to the laryngeal opening. Behind the nasal passages lies the mucous membrane of the nasopharynx. This capillary rich bed allows the mucosa to shrink or expand in response to changes in heat, humidity, or allergens to protect the respiratory tract. It will also swell in response to trauma, infection including colds, and from crying. Swollen mucosa is more likely to bleed because the capillaries are engorged.

The protective movements of the larynx during swallowing, gagging, and laryngospasm can hinder blind nasal intubation and must be taken into account in preparing the patient.

When examining the patient prior to nasal intubation evaluate the external anatomy. To detect obstruction pinch off each nostril and feel the amount of air exhaled through the other. Look for septal deviation. In the majority of patients, the right nasal passage is more

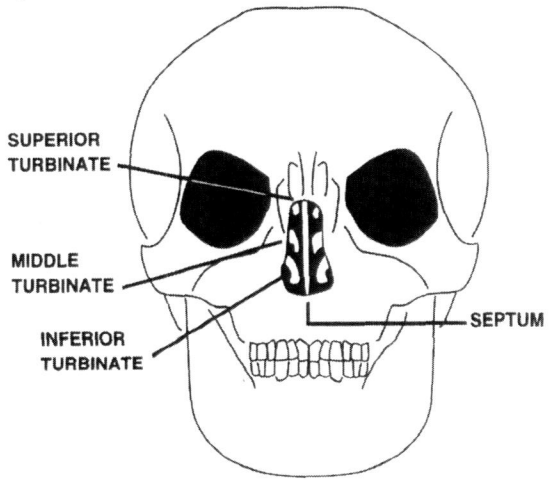

Fig. 11-1. Nasal intubation. The inside of the nose is not smooth. Take care to avoid damaging the turbinates. Be gentle. Nosebleeds easily start and then make intubation more difficult and hazardous to the patient.

patent than the left. When possible avoid the effected side of the nose if there is a history of nosebleeds and sinusitis.

Blind Nasal Intubation, Spontaneous Ventilation

Oral intubation relies on bringing the path from the incisor teeth to the larynx into a reasonably straight line by aligning the oral, pharyngeal and laryngeal axes. Since these axes don't naturally line up, oral intubation depends on optimally by positioning the patient's head and neck and then using the laryngoscope and blade to make the final adjustment. During blind nasal intubation, the path that the nasotracheal tube will naturally tend to

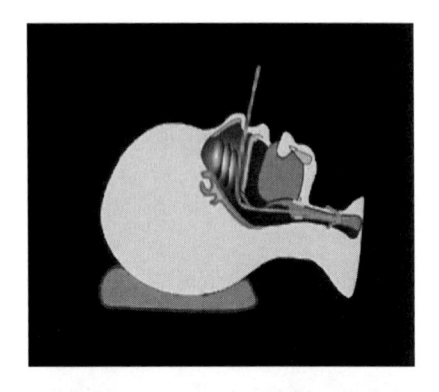

Keyframe 11-1a. A nasotracheal tube must make several turns in the pharynx.

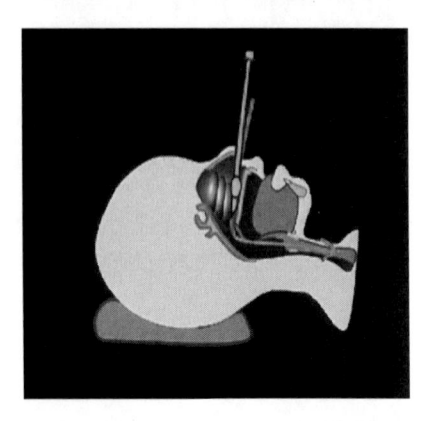

Keyframe 11-1b. Insert the nasotracheal tube perpendicular to the face. As the tube turns into the posterior pharynx you will feel an abrupt "give."

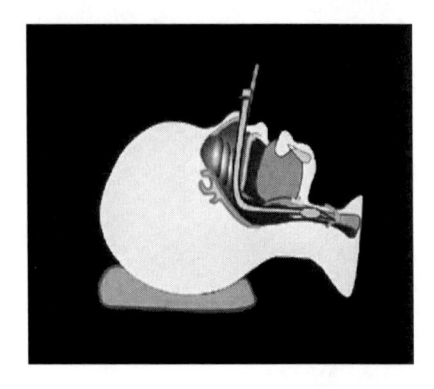

Keyframe 11-1c. Slowly advance during inhalation, when the cords are most open, until the tube enters the trachea.

follow from the nose to the larynx is curved and more easily aligned when the head is in a more neutral position (Mov. 11-1, KF. 11-1abc).

Preparation

You can perform nasal intubations with the patient either awake or asleep. For awake placement, the patient must breathe spontaneously.

Preparation of the patient is extremely important. Nasal intubation is more difficult in a poorly prepared patient because even the semiconscious patient may reflexively protect their airway if their gag reflex is intact. Detailed recommendations for awake intubation and the safe use of drying agents, sedatives, and local anesthetic numbing techniques are described in Chapter 15.

Blind Nasal Insertion Technique

You can use a standard endotracheal tube for nasal intubation. Another option is the nasal Rae tube, a specialty molded tube often used for head and neck surgery since its curve brings the adaptor up over the forehead and away from the surgical field. Additionally, a nasal tube is available with a flexible tip that allows the curve of the tube to be varied by pulling on a control ring. Regardless of the type of tube, the basic technique is the same.

Choose the largest tube size that will provide the least resistance to breathing, while sliding non-traumatically into the nose. We typically choose a nasotracheal tube 0.5 to 1 size smaller than for oral intubation. Alternatively, select a tube just slightly smaller than the diameter of the patient's nostril. Avoid using a tube that is too small. Depending upon height, an adult nose can usually take between a 6.5 and an 8 tube. Check the cuff for leaks before you start.

Warming the tube in hot water, if available, makes it more pliable and easier to pass. Coat the tip of the tube with local anesthetic ointment. If none is at hand then any water soluble lubricant or plain water can serve. Make sure the lubricant does not enter the tube itself.

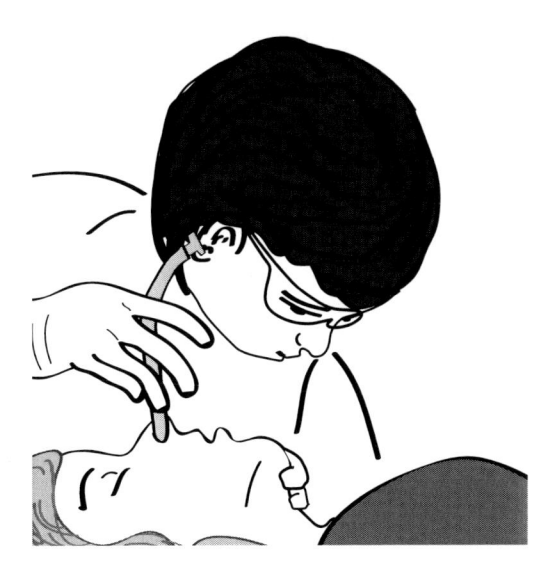

Fig. 11-2. Listening at the end of the tube for breath sounds during nasal intubation. Eye protection from the patient's secretions is recommended.

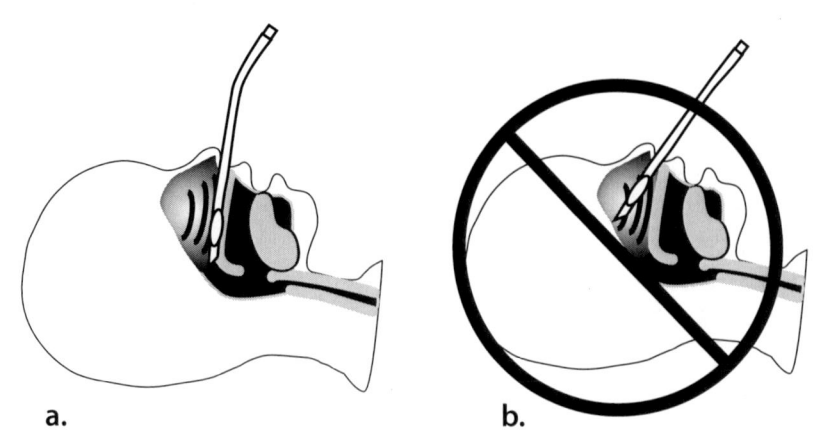

Fig. 11-3 a,b. Thread the nasal endotracheal tube along the floor of the nose (a). Never thread it toward the frontal sinus! (b)

The success of blind nasal intubation depends on positioning the head to align the larynx with the natural path of the tube as it curves through the nasopharynx. Optimally the patient should be breathing spontaneously. The patient's breath sounds are used to guide slight changes in head position and tube angle (Fig. 11-2) in order to aim the tube tip at the larynx.

Stabilize the patient's head with your non-dominant hand and use your other hand to slide the tube straight back into the nose, perpendicular to the face, and parallel to the floor of the nose (Fig. 11-3a). Use the same motion used to insert a nasal airway. Avoid the common tendency to thread the tube into the frontal sinus, a painful maneuver likely to cause a nosebleed. Be gentle, because the middle turbinate is fragile in most patients and can be fractured or torn.

Keep the bevel turned toward the septum. This orientation will make it less likely to tear the mucosa or damage a turbinate.

Gently advance the tube until you feel a give or loss of resistance: the tube has just turned the corner into the posterior pharynx (Fig. 11-4b). Unless your patient is too exhausted or weak, they will be startled. Calmly explain to them what is happening. Loss of resistance is often quite abrupt and may be accompanied by a crunching sensation as the tube passes the turbinates. If you meet resistance, slowly twist the tube while applying gentle forward pressure. The tube will often slide past the obstruction. Never force the tube or the tube tip may dissect under the mucous membrane into the retropharyngeal space or rip a turbinate.

If you can't pass the tube easily, and gentle twisting of the tube fails to solve the problem, then either switch to the other nostril or try a smaller tube.

Now slowly advance the tube during the patient's inspiration, when the vocal cords are most open. If you're using a right sided tube, direct the tube towards the opposite (left) shoulder. This trajectory will help you place the tip of the tube near the midline. For a left sided tube direct it toward the right. Listen to the breath sounds through the tube. As long as the tube and the trachea are aligned you will hear hollow, loud breath sounds and see condensation inside the tube. Continue to advance the tube. If the tube continues to advance and you still hear breath sounds the tube is in the trachea (Fig. 11-4c,d). Successful placement often makes the patient cough. If cervical spine precautions are used, your assistant needs to steady the head and upper torso to prevent movement.

a.

b.

c.

d.

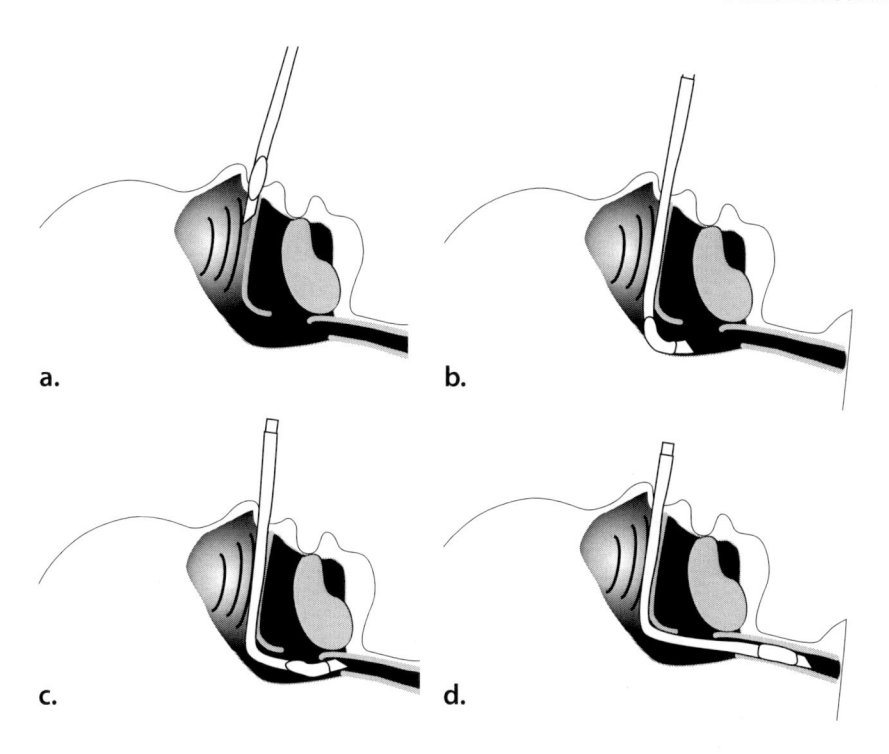

Fig. 11-4 a,b,c,d. Blind nasal intubation. Note the curve that the tube must follow to enter the trachea. Advance the tube during inspiration, when the cords are open.

Check immediately to ensure that you have actually intubated the patient. If the tube has bowed in the posterior pharynx it's possible that the cuff is still above the cords even though you can hear breath sounds continuously. The tube will have a tendency to back out of the nose because, with the cuff above the cords, the tube is bowed in the posterior pharynx.

Inflate the cuff and check for the presence of bilateral breath sounds. With the patient breathing spontaneously, you will feel the air moving in and out of the tube. When she ventilates spontaneously you'll feel the bag collapse with each breath. She won't be able to speak once the tube passes between the cords and the cuff is inflated. Condensation will form inside the tube as she breathes. When you ventilate the patient the chest rises as you squeeze the bag.

Make sure that the breath sounds are bilateral and equal. If there is a mainstem intubation slowly pull the tube back (after suctioning the mouth and deflating the cuff) until bilateral breath sounds reappear. Depth markings on the tube for a nasal intubation will be about 27-28 cm at the nostril in the average adult.

The cuff should always be inflated once the patient is intubated. The tube holds the cords apart and defeats the normal protective mechanisms. Secretions can dribble down the outside of the tube into the trachea.

Movie 11-2 and KF. 11-2abc show a nasal intubation sequence.

Once you verify endotracheal placement, suction down the tube to clear any secretions, blood, or tissue that may be present. Aspiration can occur during nasal intubation, even in awake patients. A suction catheter should pass easily through the gentle curve of the nasotracheal tube. If it doesn't, the tube may be crimped in its path through the posterior pharynx (Fig. 11-5).

190   Anyone Can Intubate

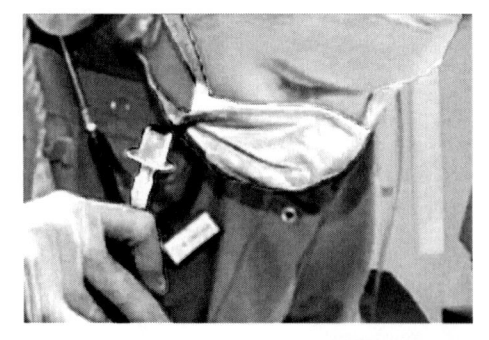

Keyframe 11-2a. Listen for breath sounds. Advance during inhalation. Wait and verify strength of sounds during exhalation.

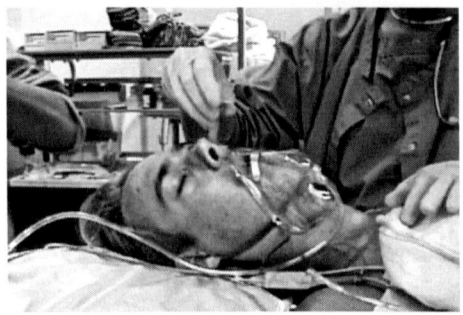

Keyframe 11-2b. Advance the tube into the trachea.

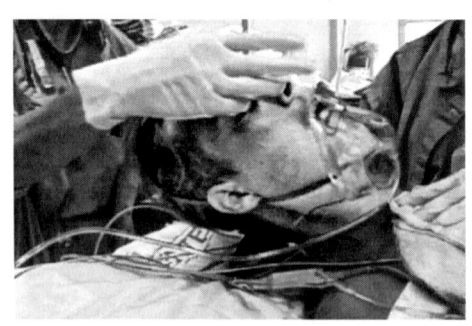

Keyframe 11-2c. As the tube enters the trachea, the patient may cough and buck. Be prepared. If the neck must be protected make sure you immobilze the patient to prevent this abrupt movement.

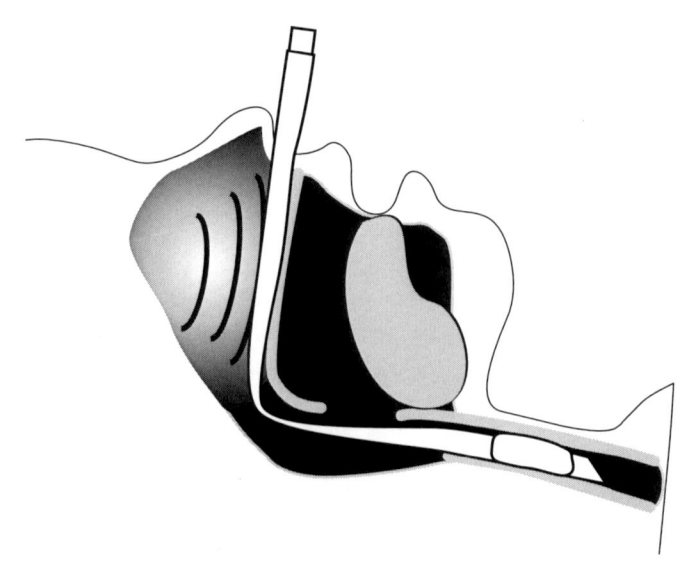

Fig. 11-5. The tube can kink in the posterior pharynx. Pulling the tube out or pushing it in slightly can often smooth out the angle.

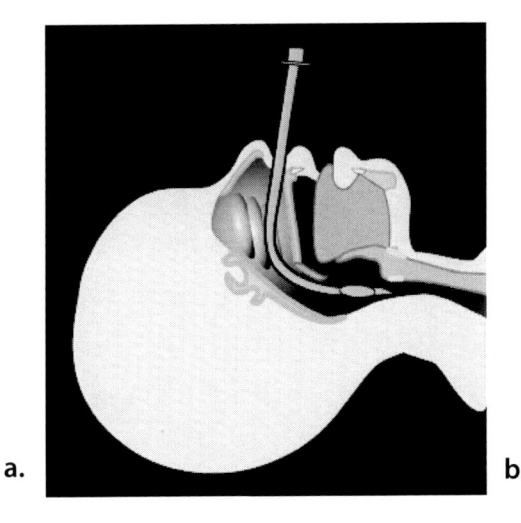

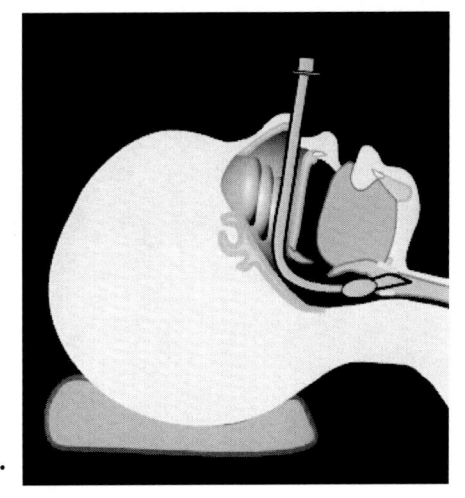

Fig. 11-6. Avoid hyperextension of the head as this can direct the tube toward the esophagus (a). Neutral or slight flexion is better (b).

Crimping partially obstructs the tube, increasing the resistance to breathing. It also impairs the ability to keep the tube cleared of secretions. If the tube is crimped, pulling it out or pushing it in a small amount will sometimes allow it to curve more smoothly. Be careful to avoid extubation or mainstem intubation.

If the tube still won't allow passage of a suction catheter consider replacing it with either a larger tube or an oral tube at the earliest safe opportunity.

Managing Difficult Passage

The two main problems with nasotracheal intubation tend to be difficulty passing the tube through the nose into the posterior pharynx and problems getting the tube to pass into the trachea.

Use a bit more flexion than extension. Extreme extension makes the angle that the tube must turn to enter the trachea more acute and the tube is more likely to enter the esophagus (Fig. 11-6a,b). Placing the patient in a sitting or semi-sitting position, if not contraindicated, prevents tongue and soft tissue from falling over the larynx and can make intubation easier. The patient will also breathe better.

When passing the tube into the nose, never force it if you feel significant resistance. The tube tip could dissect under the mucous membrane into the retropharyngeal space. Choose an appropriate size. Make sure the tube is well lubricated. Try to gently twist the tube between the turbinates. Alter its angle slightly. The tube will often slide past the obstruction.

If the tube still won't pass, switch to the other nostril or try a smaller tube.

Sometimes the tube won't pass into the trachea easily. As long as the tip of the tube is aligned with the trachea then breath sounds are present as you advance the tube. If the tube passes into the esophagus, breath sounds vanish. The patient frequently gags. Stop, pull the tube back until you hear breath sounds again, then slowly advance once more.

If the tube tip catches in the vallecula or one of the pyriform sinuses, you'll hear good breath sounds, but won't be able to advance the tube. Changing either the angle of the head or the angle of the tube will often bring the tube into alignment with the trachea. Gently twist the tube a bit as you advance. Try flexing or extending the head. These maneuvers change

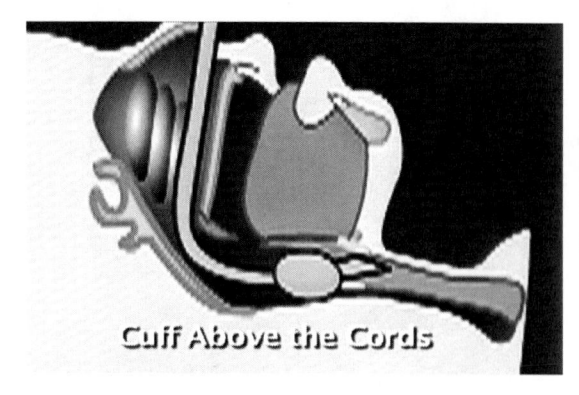

Keyframe 11-3a. When the cuff is above the cords the tube tends to keep backing out of the trachea, and the nose.

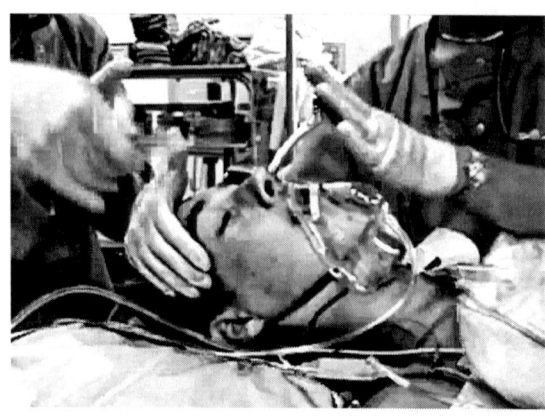

Keyframe 11-3b. Here the patient is breathing through the tube, it would be easy to assume that the tube is well placed in the trachea. However...

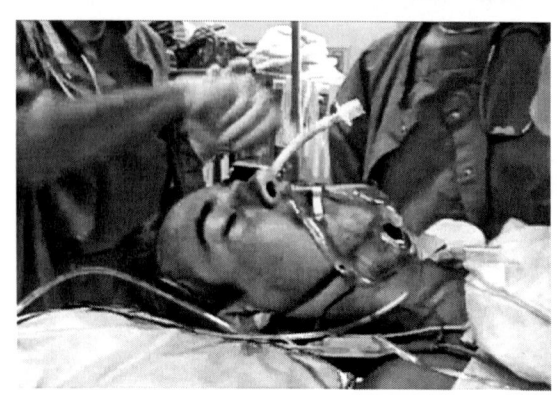

Keyframe 11-3c. ...the tube kept backing out. See how far it has moved out of the nose. Don't ignore this warning sign if you see it.

the angle of the endotracheal tube and frequently let the tip slide off the obstruction and into the trachea.

Catching in the vallecula may cause the tube to bow in the posterior pharynx. Even though you can hear breath sounds, the tube usually keeps backing out of the nose as the tube tries to straighten out. If your tube keeps backing out, be suspicious. Don't just accept it as well positioned (Mov. 11-3, KF. 11-3abc).

If movement is not contraindicated by possible cervical spine injury, manipulating the head or neck can often help align the tube tip with the larynx. Try turning the head slightly to the side. If movement in one direction doesn't work, turn it the other way.

Change the degree of flexion or extension. (Fig. 11-7a,b). Have an assistant apply cricoid pressure, by placing thumb and index finger on either side of the cricoid ring and pressing downward.

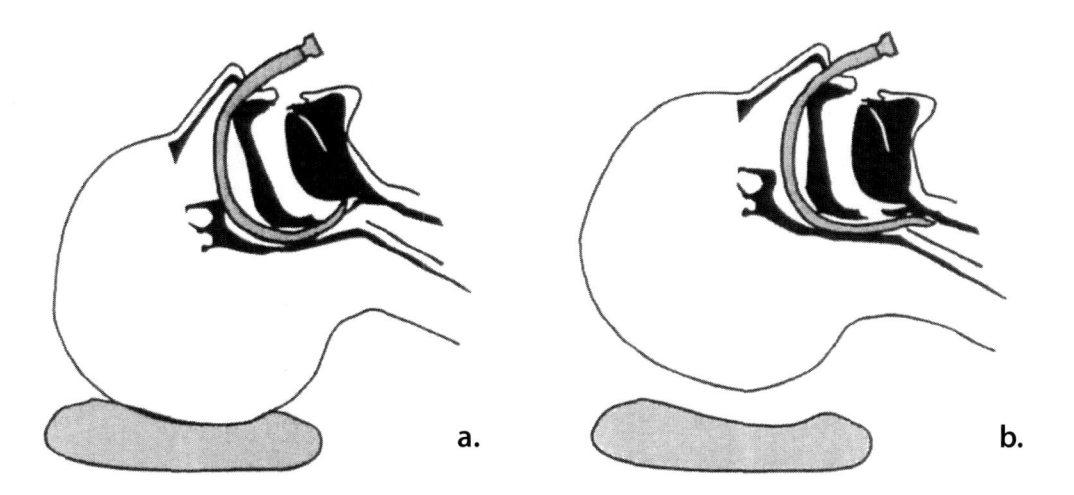

Fig. 11-7 a,b. The endotracheal tube is caught in the vallecula in (a). Flexing, and sometimes slightly rotating the head in addition to manipulating the tube can often allow the tip of the tube to slide into the trachea (b).

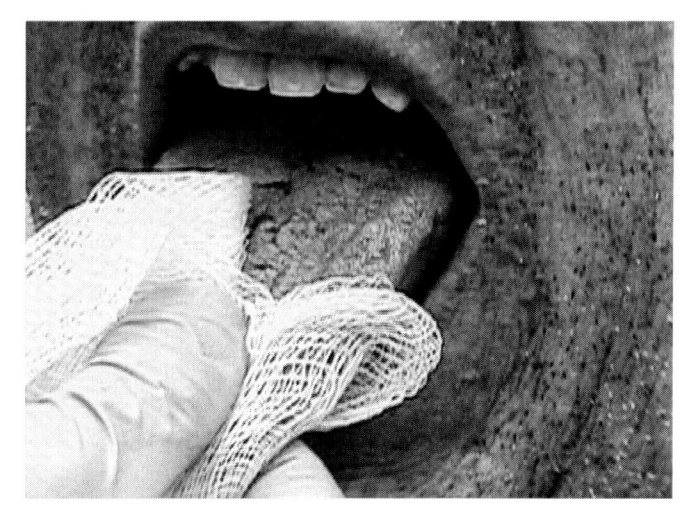

Fig 11-8. Pulling the tongue

Picture where you're aiming the tip of the tube and adjust the head accordingly. A tube placed in the right nostril tends to cross to the left lower pharynx. Therefore, moving the head slightly to the right of midline for a right-sided tube will align the trachea with the tube. For left nasal intubations move the head to the left. Pushing the larynx toward the side opposite the nostril being used can also help. *Any manipulation of the head must take into account the patient's potential risk of existing cervical spinal injury.*

Have an awake patient stick out the tongue (Fig. 11-8) or have your assistant grab the tongue with a gauze pad and pull it out. The gauze will give you a better grip on the slippery surface.

Observe the neck for lateral displacement of the tip of the tube. One trick to help the tube to align itself in the midline is to partially inflate the cuff of the tube after you pass it through the nasopharynx. This may bring the nasotracheal tube in line with the laryngeal

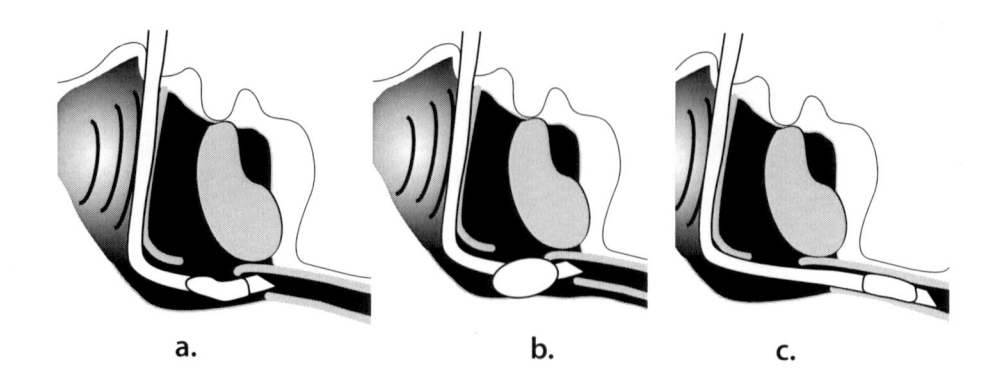

Fig. 11-9, a,b,c. A trick: Use breath sounds to line up the tip of the tube close to the tracheal opening. Partially inflate the balloon in the posterior pharynx to line up with trachea. Advance slightly, then deflate the cuff to advance into the trachea.

opening. While the tube will often start down the trachea, you will need to deflate the cuff to get the tube to completely pass through the cords (Fig. 11-9a,b,c).

If the endotracheal tube still won't enter the larynx, sometimes a firm catheter passed through the tube when it's lined with the trachea can provide a guide to insert the tube. Nasogastric tubes or tube exchangers are useful for this purpose. Soft suction catheters can also serve if long enough. Firmly hold the endotracheal tube at the point where breath sounds are most audible, then pass the catheter through the tube. Slide the tube over the catheter into the larynx. Remove the catheter and check breath sounds (Fig. 11-10).

Natural airway protective reflexes may prevent the tube from passing. Further topicalization or sedation can smooth the intubation. However, you must weigh the risks of these maneuvers against the benefits.

As mentioned earlier, submucosal dissection can occur if the tip of the tube tears the mucosa and slides underneath it. Suspect that this has occurred if you can't hear breath sounds once the tube has entered the posterior pharynx or if you feel a lot of resistance as you advance the tube. The conscious patient often complains of severe pain when this

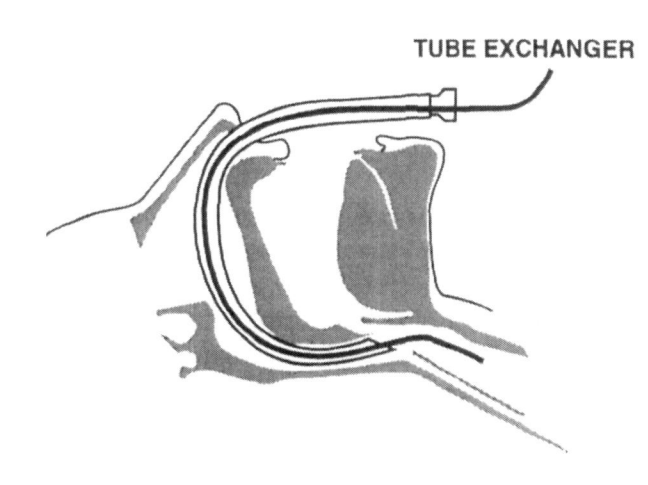

Fig. 11-10. Using a tube exchanger to assist nasal intubation.

happens. With submucosal dissection you won't see the tube in the posterior pharynx but you will see a bulge behind the tonsillar pillars. When a nasotracheal tube is submucosal, remove it carefully. Be prepared for a heavy nosebleed. If nasal intubation is still indicated, try the other side and proceed carefully. You may need to consider postponing elective surgery because of the risk of retropharyngeal hematoma and abscess formation. A patient who already has airway obstruction could have worsening of the obstruction due to the increased swelling.

Adjunctive Techniques to Nasal Intubation

Nasal intubation is sometimes quite challenging, especially in noisy situations when you can't hear breath sounds well or in clinical situations when the patient is not breathing spontaneously. There are some techniques you can use to make intubation easier in these situations.

Endotrol® Tubes

The use of a type of nasotracheal tube called an Endotrol tube can facilitate nasal intubations. Nasotracheal tubes sometimes enter the esophagus because they won't curve forward enough after entering the oropharynx. Endotrol tubes solve this problem with a pull cord attached to a ring near the 15mm adaptor. Pulling the ring turns the tip of the tube anteriorly, allowing you to manipulate the tip with more precise control.

When You Can't Hear Well

Breath sounds can sometimes be hard to hear if the environment is noisy or if the patient is breathing shallowly. There are several ways to make it easier to know the tube is taking the right path when it's hard to hear.

A device called a BAAM, or Beck Airway Airflow Monitor, can make the breath sounds easier to hear even in noisy environments. The BAAM is a small, cylindrical, plastic whistle that fits over the 15 mm adapter for the endotracheal tube. The device is about the same size as an endotracheal tube adaptor and is disposable. A loud whistle is produced whenever the patient inhales or exhales through the tube when the BAAM is attached. Even very low amounts of airflow will produce a whistle. The whistle is said to be loud enough to hear in an ambulance or helicopter.

The pitch varies both with the breathing cycle and with the position of the tube tip relative to the larynx because the airflow velocity through the device changes. The provider can use the loudness of the whistle and the pitch to more precisely guide the tube. If the tube enters the esophagus the whistle sound is lost.

The BAAM has also been used to assist difficult oral intubations. Spontaneous respirations or an assistant's gentle pushing on the chest produce a guiding whistle when the larynx is hard to visualize. The BAAM should not be left in position for more than 2 minutes at a time following successful intubation since its small aperture of 2mm would produce excessive resistance to breathing.

If you don't have a BAAM, you can use an $ETCO_2$ detector on the end of the tube to indicate when you have the tip of the tube close to the glottis. If you see color change you are on the right track. The more intense the color change, the closer you are.

If the patient is hypoventilating, breath sounds out the tube can be hard to hear because

a.   b.

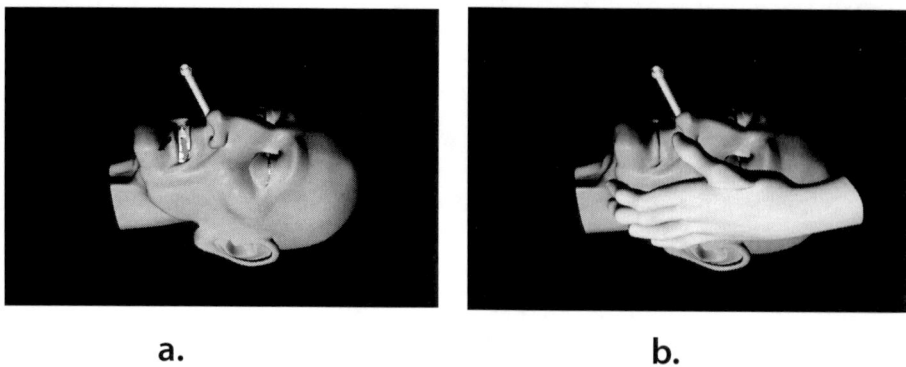

Fig. 11-11. With hypoventilation, airflow can be hard to hear because it is divided among many paths. Closing the opposite nostril and mouth can increase airflow through the endotracheal tube, making sounds louder.

the low airflow is split between the tube, the other nostril and the open mouth. To augment the airflow out of the tube, use your opposite hand to close their mouth and opposite nostril. This will enhance air passage through the tube. Don't interfere with the patient's ability to ventilate! If the patient is not breathing adequately, stop the procedure and immediately begin assisted ventilations. However you can briefly perform this trick and enhance airflow sounds and color change (Fig 11-11).

Combined Nasal with Direct Laryngoscopy

There are times when a nasal intubation is desired in an apneic patient. This situation most commonly arises during elective surgery when nasal intubation is performed after induction of anesthesia.

You can use your laryngoscope to assist (Mov. 11-4, KF. 11-4ab). This combined technique is easier in the unconscious patient because of the absence of a gag reflex. To use

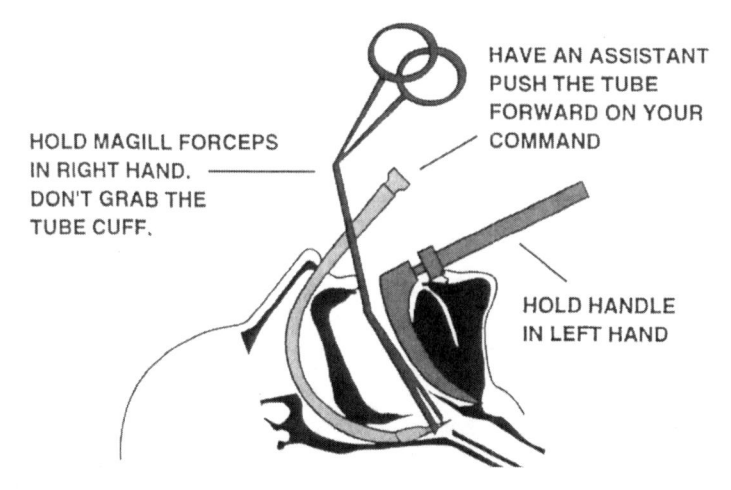

Fig. 11-12. Using Magill Forceps to grab ETT to assist nasal intubation using direct laryngoscopy. Don't grab the cuff or you may rip it.

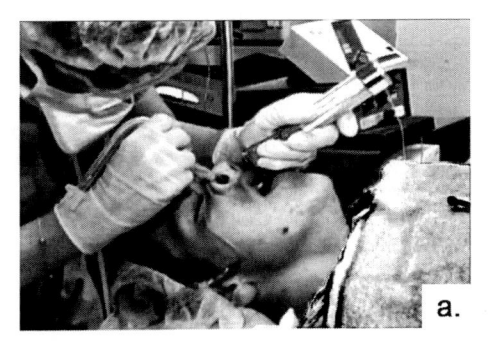

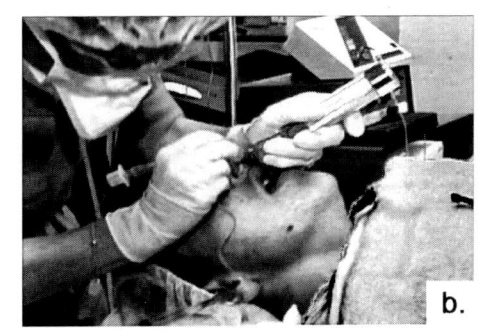

Keyframes 11-4a,b. Visualize the trachea, stabilize the head on your laryngoscope, and advance the nasotracheal tube under direct vision. If all is lined up, the tube will enter the trachea.

this technique in the awake patient, good topicalization, plus glossopharyngeal nerve block is helpful.

Place the nasotracheal tube through the nostril and advance it until the tip is in the posterior pharynx. Visualize the larynx with your laryngoscope. I usually use a curved blade for this maneuver. It gives me more room to manipulate the tube. Once you see the larynx hold the laryngoscope blade firmly in position. Push the tube forward with your right hand into the larynx.

If the tube is still by passing the cords you can have an assistant push the tube into the trachea while you guide the tip of the tube with Magill forceps or some other instrument (Fig. 11-12, Mov. 11-5, KF 11-5abcde). For this maneuver you will need an assistant to push the tube when you are ready. Your assistant must position himself to avoid blocking your view or bumping your arm or the laryngoscope blade. Good communication is key to the teamwork required.

Grab either the *tip* of the tube or the area *behind* the cuff. Never grab the cuff itself with your forceps. You can easily rip it, leaving no way to seal off the trachea. If you damage the cuff then, discard that tube and use a fresh one. If you don't have Magill forceps, you can use a bent stylet or a hook to curve the endotracheal tube anteriorly.

Direct the tube tip positioned directly into the laryngeal opening. Sometimes you are able to feed the tube into the larynx using the Magill forceps yourself. More often you will need to ask your assistant to gently push the tube into the nose while you observe and continue to manipulate it into the trachea.

Fiberoptic bronchoscopy is often combined with nasotracheal intubation. The bronchoscope can act as the ultimate guide since it allows you to enter the larynx under direct vision to direct your tube into the trachea.

One final caveat with the combined oral/nasal technique. Sometimes you can't see the trachea during direct laryngoscopy. If the patient is breathing, listen for breath sounds as you pass the tube. By using their loudness to guide your aim you can blindly intubate a patient during direct laryngoscopy.

198   Anyone Can Intubate

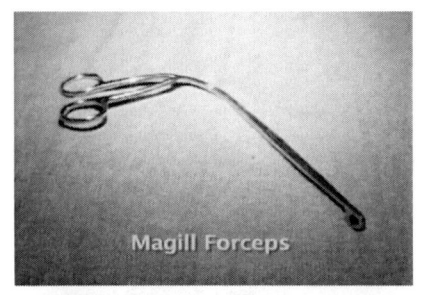

Keyframe 11-5a. Magill forceps are useful during laryngoscope assisted nasal intubation.

Keyframe 11-5b. Never grab the cuff, which tears easily. A torn cuff cannot seal the trachea.

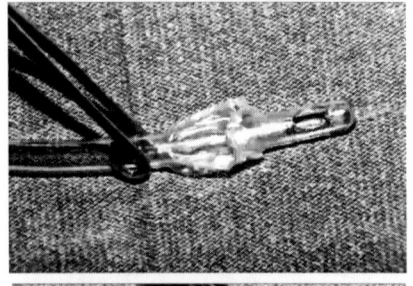

Keyframe 11-5c. Instead, grab the tube either above (c) ...

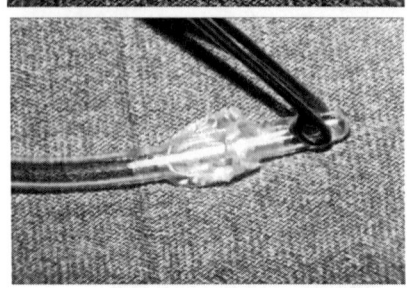

or below (d) the cuff.

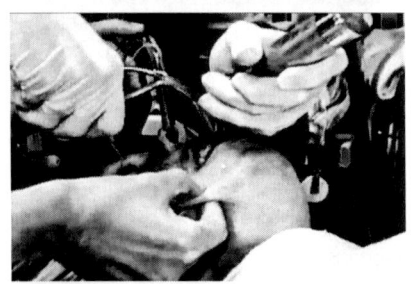

Keyframe 11-5e. Visualize the larynx. Hold the head steady as you grab the tube (not the cuff) with your Magill Forceps.

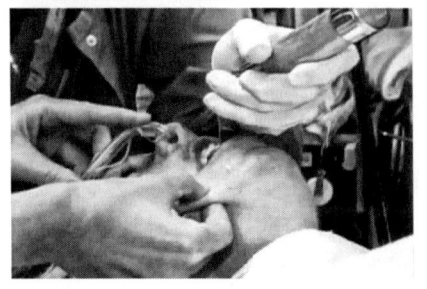

Keyframe 11-5f. Your assistant often has to help advance the tube as you guide it into the trachea.

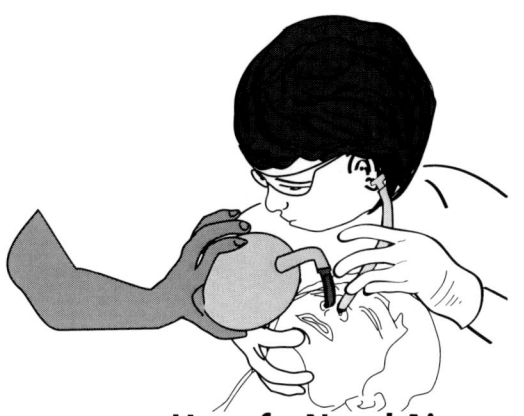

Fig. 11-13. Using a nasal airway to ventilate on the opposite side of the nasal intubation. while the intubator listens for breath sounds and intubates blindly. You must keep the mouth sealed to allow ventilation.

Use of a Nasal Airway to Assist Ventilation

You can assist ventilation using a nasal airway in the opposite nostril during a blind nasal nasotracheal intubation (Fig. 11-13).

First, insert an endotracheal tube adapter into the nasal airway. Place this nasal airway into the opposite nostril and attach it to your ventilation apparatus. Insert your nasotracheal tube using the other nostril and listening to breath sounds, guide the tube to the trachea.

This technique is particularly helpful during blind nasal intubation in young children after induction of general anesthesia for surgery. An adequate depth of inhalational anesthesia is maintained during the intubation process while the patient continues to breath spontaneously. Note that the breathing circuit is open and will allow waste anesthetic gas to escape into the room.

You can use the same nasal airway to assist or control ventilation during the intubation. Close the mouth, occlude the other nostril until you place your nasotracheal tube into it and ventilate. When the assistant ventilates, the lungs inflate. Between breathes the patient exhales and you can hear the breath sounds out of the nasal tube, guiding your placement.

Be aware that the tip of the nasal airway can deflect the tip of the nasotracheal tube away from the larynx if it's long enough. Withdraw both the tube and the airway slightly and try again if this occurs.

While this technique can be used in the emergency situation, the use of a rescue breathing device such as an LMA or Combitube would be more appropriate to minimize the time required to establish good ventilation.

Complications

Oxygenation and ventilation are the top priorities. Good airway management doesn't always mean intubation. It means ensuring an open airway and providing adequate ventilation and oxygenation. Unfortunately, it's easy to develop tunnel vision in an emergency and forget this basic principal. Provide supplemental oxygen. Place nasal prongs, a face mask, or simple oxygen tubing near the patient's mouth. Always be prepared to suction secretions if the patient can't protect their own airway because aspiration can easily occur. Constantly monitor the patient to ensure adequate respiration, airway protection, and hemodynamic stability during nasotracheal intubation. Check blood pressure, pulse rate, and, if you have it, oxygen saturation. Reassure the conscious patient and tell him what you are doing. Use suction frequently. And always be prepared for vomiting.

Prolonged nasal intubation can mechanically obstruct the sinuses, predisposing to infection and leading to sinusitis. Consider switching a nasal intubation to an oral one if prolonged intubation is needed and patient safety allows.

Nosebleed is the most common acute complication of nasal intubation. When a nosebleed occurs the treatment depends on the severity, as well as the clinical situation. If the bleeding is minimal, it may be best to leave the endotracheal tube in place and continue with the attempt. The tube will actually allow you to provide more pressure to the site. If bleeding is severe enough to cause blood to accumulate in the posterior pharynx then remove the tube. Compress the nose on that side firmly against the septum, suction the oropharynx frequently. You may have to position the patient in trendelenburg or on the side, the allow blood to pool away from the larynx. If you haven't already done so apply a vasoconstrictor, such as phenylephrine or oxymetazoline (e.g. Afrin®) spray.

With severe bleeding in the elective situation, stop the intubation attempt.

As mentioned earlier, submucosal dissection can occur if the tip of the tube rears the mucosa and slides underneath it. Signs of a submucosal dissection include:
- No tube visible in posterior pharynx once the tube has turned the corner
- The absence of breath sounds through the tube
- The presence of a bulge behind the tonsillar pillars
- Complaints of pain in the back of the throat in an awake patient
- And significant resistance as you advance the tube

When a nasotracheal tube is submucosal, remove it carefully and prepare for a heavy nosebleed. Consider postponing elective surgery because of the risk of retropharyngeal hematoma and abscess formation. If nasal intubation is still indicated, control bleeding, and carefully try the other side. Watch for airway obstruction due to potential swelling.

Ventilation and intubation attempts will be more difficult, however, securing the airway in the apneic or respiratory distressed patient will be crucial to preventing aspiration or hypoventilation. Other emergency measures to control a severe nosebleed — while awaiting assistance from a head and neck or emergency specialist — include inflating the cuff from an endotracheal tube or the balloon from a foley catheter inside the nose and nasopharynx to compress the site and leaving them in place. Packing the nose can also be done.

A Laryngeal Mask Airway (LMA), ProSeal LMA, or Combitube may be useful in the emergency situation of severe nosebleed in a patient with an unprotected airway who can't be intubated. Since the bleeding comes from above, an LMA can help seal off the glottis and allow ventilation. Suction frequently. An LMA, however, won't prevent aspiration. (See Chapter 12 for more on specialized ventilation equipment.)

Monitor vital signs carefully. Remember hypertension and tachycardia can worsen hemorrhage. Make sure there is good I.V. access. In severe cases a blood transfusion may be needed. Consider sending blood for type and cross match testing.

If bleeding continues, consider consultation from a head and neck specialist. If intubation is not possible and ventilation is inadequate consider a surgical airway.

For Chapter 11 video clips go to:
http://bit.ly/Vy6vLe

All video chapter files appear on Anyone Can Intubate Portfolio at:
http://bit.ly/U7EV7f

12
SPECIALIZED VENTILATION TECHNIQUES

Sometimes, intubation can be technically difficult because of the situation or location, and patient anatomy, trauma, pathology and/or position. It is very important to know alternative ventilation equipment and techniques. These devices are often used in emergency situations when intubation cannot be performed and mask ventilation is felt to be inadequate airway protection. They are also used as adjuncts to ETT intubation.

Supraglottic Airway (SGA) is a generic term for any device that is designed to rest above the glottis and larynx and seal the upper airway in order to allow either spontaneous or assisted ventilation, without intubation or a conventional mask. This chapter teaches two important SGA devices that can used to ventilate: the LMA (Laryngeal Mask Airway™) and the Combitube (Esophageal-Tracheal Combitube®). Another SGA device that is available, but that should used with great care (if at all), is the EOA (Esophageal Obturator Airway).

This chapter will also briefly discuss cricothyroidotomy, an emergency procedure to establish an airway that can be used to ventilate when all else fails.

Laryngeal Mask Airway™

The Laryngeal Mask Airway (LMA) has rapidly gained importance in the management of the difficult airway or the failed intubation. However, use in such patients should optimally occur after the provider has gained experience in patients with normal airways.

The original LMA-Classic was reusable after autoclaving up to 40 times. There is now a disposable PVC version of the LMA, as well as the Proseal LMA™ that allows suctioning of the stomach.

The LMA looks like a short, wide bore endotracheal tube with an elliptical cushioned mask on its distal end (Fig. 12-1). It connects to the breathing circuit with a standard 15 mm adapter.

The LMA was designed using the pharynx of the adult cadaver as a model. The balloon cushion on the mask is inflated after the mask overlies the laryngeal outlet. This perilaryngeal seal allows positive pressure ventilation. A soft, flexible grill that helps prevent entrapment of the epiglottis in the mask opening covers the opening in the mask. It also helps prevent obstruction of the opening by the epiglottis if it folds over the larynx.

When perfectly positioned, the cushion lies with its tip against the upper esophageal sphincter. In this position it acts like a cork to prevent gastric contents from spilling into the hypopharynx. The sides seal against the pyriform sinuses with the upper cushion surface behind and against the base of the tongue. The epiglottis is inside pointing upwards. This ideal positioning occurs about 50-60% of the time. When the epiglottis is within the rim of the LMA, it's folded downward 50-90% of the time and the lateral aryepiglottic folds are folded inward 50% of the time. Although the actual position of the

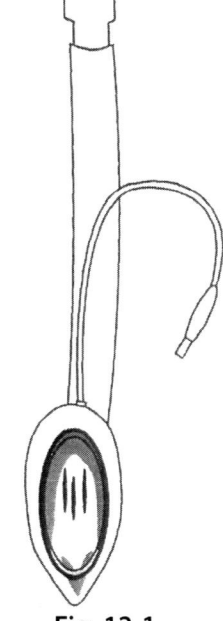

Fig. 12-1. Laryngeal Mask Airway (L.M.A.)

Table 12-1. Laryngeal Mask Airway Sizes & Cuff Volumes		
SIZE	WEIGHT	VOLUME (ml)
Size 1	Neonates & Infants < 6.5 kg	2-5
Size 1.5	Infants 5-10 kg	2-8
Size 2	Infants and children up to 20 kg	2-10
Size 2.5	Children 20-30 kg	2-15
Size 3	Children & small adults over 30 kg	10-25
Size 4	Average adults	20-30
Size 5	Large adults > 80 kg	20-40

LMA may vary from ideal, ventilation is rarely impaired and is judged without difficulty in 95-99% in most studies.

The LMA is inserted blindly, without the use of a laryngoscope. It has been successfully used in emergency situations where intubation has proved impossible. It's also easy for the inexperienced provider to use. One study of paramedical and medical students showed that 94% of the students successfully ventilated the patient on the first try using the LMA while only 69% succeeded in endotracheally intubating the patient on their first try.

Insertion Technique

Choose the correct size mask (Table 12-1). It's worthwhile noting that these are ideal body weights. For example, you will not be able to insert a number 5 LMA into a 4' 11" woman who weighs 110 kg. Use these as guidelines.

Prior to placing the LMA, inflate the cushion on the mask and check for leaks or abnormal bulging. Then deflate the cushion with the cuff gently pressed against a flat surface (Fig. 12-2). It's crucial that the leading edge of the cuff be smooth and wrinkle free to prevent the tip of the deflated cushion from curling. Curling potentially folds the epiglottis down over the glottis during insertion and can prevent a good seal.

Make sure that the rim curves upward, away from the opening. When the flattened cuff is pressed against the palate during insertion, the resultant curve will naturally push it against the palate and help prevent hanging up on the epiglottis.

Lubricate the *posterior* surface of the LMA. Never lubricate the surface where the grill is, because lubricant can obstruct the opening or enter the trachea.

If there are no contraindications, tilt the patient's head into extension and slightly flex the neck.

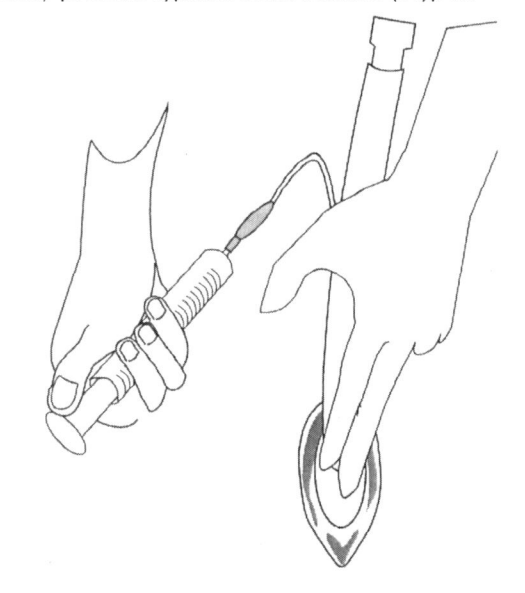

Fig 12-2. Deflate the LMA cushion by pressing it against a clean, flat surface. This typically results in a cuff that curves gently upward.

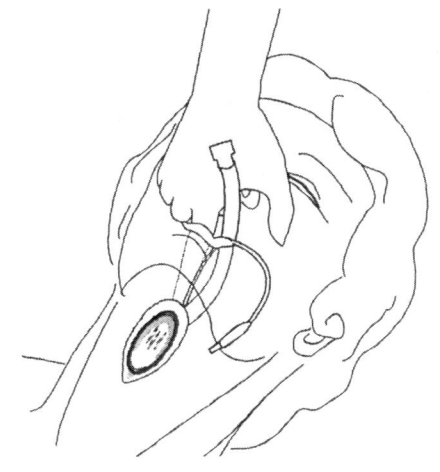

Fig. 12-3. Inserting the LMA. Push device firmly against hard palate and slide inward and downward.

Open the patient's mouth with your left hand and insert the LMA with your right (Fig. 12-3, 12-4). The deflated cushion of the LMA should be directed posteriorly in the midline. The index finger is positioned at the base of the tube. By pressing down at the junction with the cushion, the tip of the cushion can be slid tightly against the palate, preventing the tip from curling under as it slides into position. Insert the LMA until it seats against the upper esophageal sphincter, overlying the larynx. Pressing backwards and downwards helps avoid interference with the epiglottis. The LMA usually seats with the tip of the mask in the hypopharynx with the dark lines on the tube shaft opposite the front teeth.

Occasionally the cuff hangs up on insertion and won't pass. You can use a tongue blade to pull the back of the tongue forward. You may need to insert the index finger of your gloved hand into the mouth to straighten the tip of the LMA if it is curling. Alternatively twisting the partially inflated device sideways is helpful, allowing the LMA to slip around the side of the tongue before sliding into position behind it.

Sometimes the tip of the tongue gets caught in the bowl of the LMA during insertion.

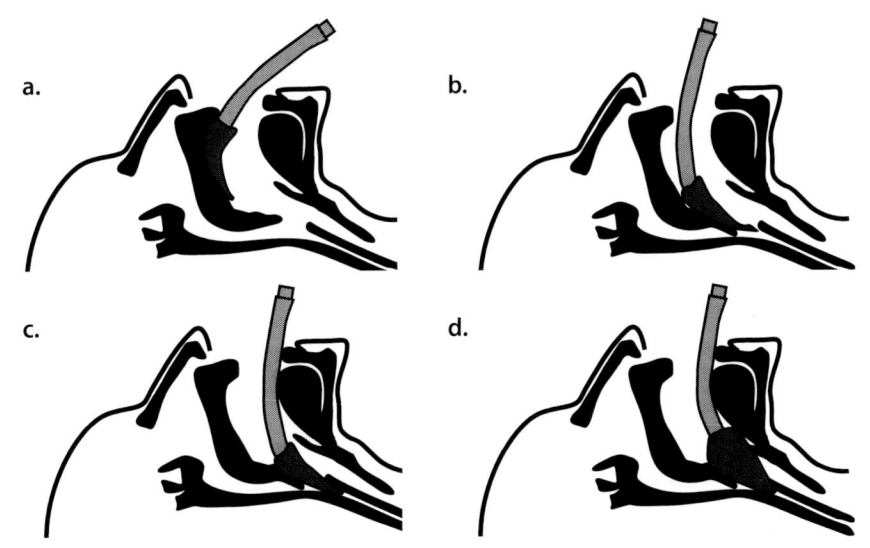

Fig. 12-4. Insertion of the Laryngeal Mask Airway in cross-section. Slide the LMA into the posterior pharynx (a,b) until it seats in the hypopharynx over the top of the larynx (c). Keep pressure against the palate the entire time. Inflate the cuff (d). The pilot tube is not drawn.

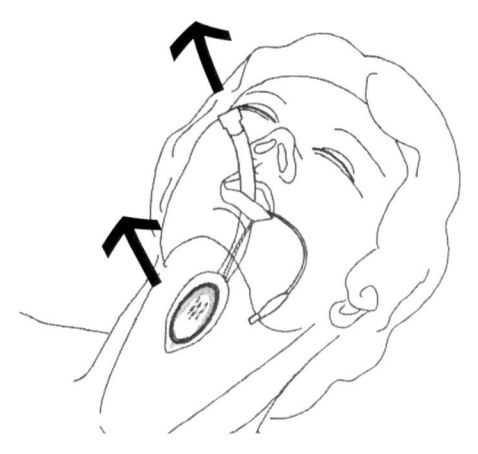

Fig. 12-5. Inflation in proper position will cause the overlying larynx to rise.

It's not uncommon to see even experienced people continue to keep pushing with some force until the tip of the tongue pops out and springs forward out of the way. It's possible to lacerate the lingual frenulum, the cord like tissue tethering the tongue to the floor of the mouth. This is a minor, but very painful injury. It's better to free the tongue with your tongue blade when it gets caught.

Inflate the cushion (see Table 12-1 for suggested volumes) without holding the tube. The tube will typically move outward about 1-2 cm as the cuff centers itself around the laryngeal inlet. Watch the neck — the thyroid and cricoid cartilages rise (Fig. 12-5, Mov. 12-1, KF. 12-1abc). If it's hard to inflate the cushion, check the LMA's position.

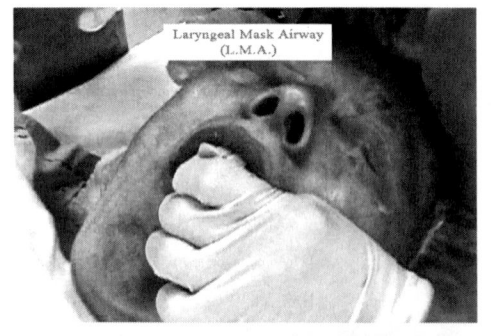

Keyframe 12-1a. Open the mouth. A tongue blade is helpful to pull the tongue forward.

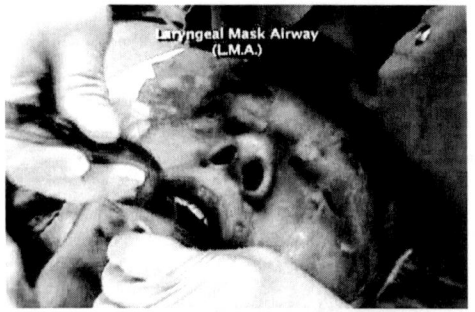

Keyframe 12-1b. Press the LMA against the palate. Slide it along the palate, down the posterior pharyngeal wall.

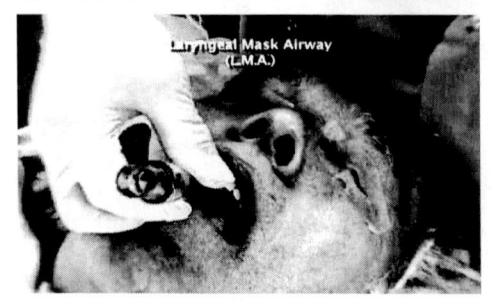

Keyframe 12-1c. The LMA will seat behind the tongue over the larynx. Make sure that you can ventilate through the LMA.

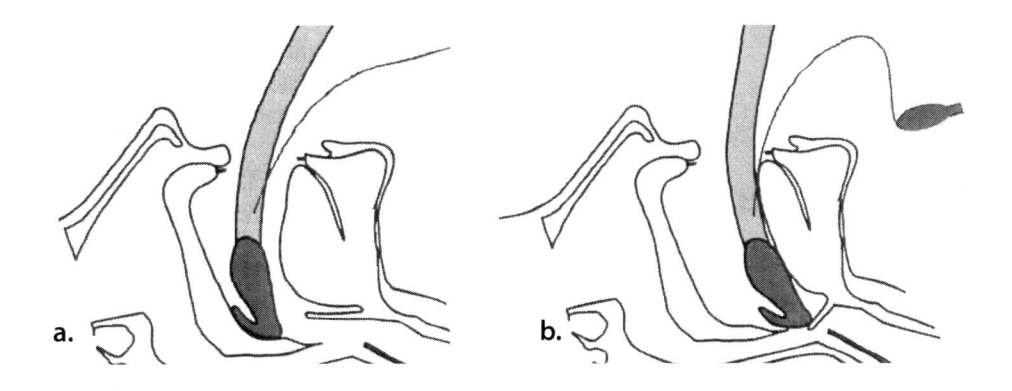

Fig. 12-6 a,b. When the LMA cushion curls under (a) it impairs placement. It may push the epiglottis down over the larynx causing obstruction (b).

Inflating the cushion should provide a good seal around the larynx. It's common to have a leak at 15-20 cm water pressure with positive pressure ventilation. This leak usually disappears with time as the soft tissue molds itself around the cushion. If there is a leak at less than 15 cm then the LMA may be too small or poorly seated.

Cuff over inflation causes it to stiffen and lift away from the larynx, often making the leak worse. One should use "just-sealed" pressures. Ensure that the patient is ventilating well.

If ventilation is inadequate try adding air to the cuff. Sometimes partially removing the LMA and then sliding it back in will free a curled tip or trapped epiglottis. If ventilation is still inadequate, then deflate the cuff and remove it. Ventilate the patient with bag and mask prior to another attempt.

The LMA does come in several sizes, including pediatric sizes, making it ideal for emergency failed intubations. It does not require an effective mask fit on the face or the maintenance of good airway positioning. Thus it can be more easily used when the patient is being moved or is in an awkward position. It frees the provider's hands.

Problems With Positioning the LMA
Most commonly, the tip of the LMA will curl under and prevent it from sliding into the pharynx. It will sometimes force the epiglottis down over the larynx, hindering ventilation (Fig 12-6 a,b). Pulling the LMA outward slightly tends to flatten the tip. Reinsertion with pressure against the palate often allows it to slide into optimal position.

Placement may be more difficult in patients with a large tongue or tonsils, a small mouth, or a "posterior" larynx since these anatomical features can cause malrotation or curling of the LMA.

Rotation of the tube can lead to obstruction. The line on the tube should face upward and be in the midline of the upper lip of the patient. Secure the LMA with the indicator line in the midline.

The LMA can be malpositioned with either down folding or actual trapping of the epiglottis. Signs include obstruction or a poor seal with ventilation in a non-rotated LMA.

Although the insertion technique described has been shown to be most frequently successful, you can alternatively place your index finger behind the lower part of the cushion to straighten the leading edge if it starts to curl.

Partially inflating the cuff may help the LMA make the turn into the lower pharynx, although partial inflation has a higher incidence of folding the epiglottis down over the laryngeal inlet. Additionally, partial inflation may prevent full insertion of the LMA to the level of the upper esophageal sphincter. Failure to seat at the sphincter can lead some gastric inflation with manual ventilation since the esophagus is incompletely sealed.

Some providers insert the LMA upside down and then rotate it 180° while pushing it into the hypopharynx. Alternatively, twist the partially inflated device sideways to allow the LMA to slip around the side of the tongue before sliding into position behind it. Both techniques require a fairly good sized oral cavity to leave room to maneuver. Be careful of the teeth.

After many autoclave cycles, a reusable LMA will get slightly softer and will lose its curvature. This can impair passage of the tube. A stylet can be used to stiffen the LMA and recreate its curvature. Don't let the stylet protrude beyond the grill of the mask or it can injure the pharynx.

Insert the LMA Partially Inflated or Deflated?

The standard insertion technique is to completely deflate the cuff. When the LMA cuff is completely deflated, the provider can slide the LMA slightly deeper into the pharynx before it seats. Once in position, inflation of the cuff places the tip firmly against the upper esophageal sphincter, decreasing the risk of reflux.

Some people find it easier to insert the LMA partially inflated, feeling that this makes it less likely to get caught on the tongue and easier to slide against the palate. However, there are disadvantages to this technique. First, the LMA can't be placed as deep. When the cuff is inflated before insertion, the LMA seats higher in the pharynx and may not seal against the esophagus. Second, the full cuff is more likely to down fold the epiglottis. Finally, an inflated cuff is sometimes too bulky to insert into a small mouth.

LMA Proseal™

The LMA Classic does not protect against aspiration or regurgitation, although when properly seated no air should enter the stomach. There is nothing to prevent emesis from collecting in the LMA bowl if used in a patient with a full stomach. In addition, the higher inflation pressures needed in the obese patient can potentially lead to gastric insufflation and increased risk of vomiting.

To address these issues, a newer variant, the LMA Proseal (PLMA), was developed. The Proseal tube has two separate tracts. The respiratory tract is identical to the classic LMA. The second gastric tract, which sits directly atop the upper esophageal sphincter, allows direct suctioning of the stomach, as well as a channel for venting of any emesis. A second posterior cuff better seals the hypopharynx, allowing higher ventilation pressures.

Properly positioned, no gas should escape through the GI drainage. The PLMA has a pocket for insertion of the index finger to facilitate using the optimal technique of pressing firmly against the hard palate. There's also a reusable malleable blade with a guiding handle that fits into the pocket for this same purpose.

Malpositioning of the PLMA can interfere with ventilation:
- If not inserted deeply enough, the ventilating port is not aligned with the glottic opening. In this case simply push the PLMA deeper into the pharynx until it seats.
- If the PLMA is too anterior, the cuff blocks the glottis. Reinsertion using a lateral approach usually fixes this problem.

- The distal cuff is folded over backward. This positioning blocks the gastric port, losing any protection from aspiration. Partial removal and reinsertion again usually fixes this.

Since the main advantage of the PLMA is protection from aspiration, most providers place a gastric tube through the PLMA after insertion to both verify optimal placement as well as to decompress the stomach.

Cautions in the Use of the LMA

Because the LMA does not seal the trachea and because the esophageal opening may be present within the cushion 10-15% of the time, aspiration is a risk. The LMA is relatively contraindicated for *elective* use in:
- non fasting patients
- morbid obesity
- pregnant patients over 14 weeks gestation
- acute abdomen
- hiatal hernia
- any abdominal condition with delayed gastric emptying
- acute trauma

The LMA Proseal would be a better choice in these patients. Of course in the emergency "can't intubate/can't ventilate" scenario, ventilation must take precedence over fear of potential risk. However, use it with extreme caution when emesis is possible, especially when high ventilation pressures must be used, forcing the LMA cushion to "pop-off" and allowing gastric insufflation.

There is risk of inadequate ventilation when used in patients with:
- thoracic injury
- massive or multiple injury
- poor pulmonary compliance (i.e. status asthmaticus, pneumothorax)

Although better tolerated than an endotracheal tube, placement of an LMA in a conscious or semi-conscious patient can cause gagging and vomiting. The patient can bite and obstruct the LMA. The patient may also bite the provider during insertion.

Because ventilation is dependent on successfully sealing the hypopharyngeal space, the LMA is relatively contraindicated in patients with local pathology of the larynx and pharynx such as tumor, hematoma, abscess, or edema.

The LMA would not be very helpful in improving ventilation in a patient with obstruction below the glottis.

Caveats for the Pediatric Patient

There is less margin for error to correctly place an LMA in a neonate or small child. The larger tonsils of older children can interfere with insertion. Difficulties in placement are more common. The LMA is more easily displaced. Therefore verify the ability to ventilate whenever the child is moved.

Even when ideally positioned, gastric inflation and distention is possible if inflation pressure exceeds the cushion seal of about 20 cm H_2O. Down folding of the epiglottis is more common in children. Delayed airway obstruction has been reported in infants. Interference with ventilation is uncommon but it is recommended that you verify positioning with fiberoptic bronchoscopy, if possible, before using the LMA as a guide for intubation.

Removal of the LMA

Patient's tend to better tolerate an LMA than an endotracheal tube because there is less glottic stimulation. Thus it is better to leave it in place until the patient regains full protective reflexes. Always suction the mouth well in order to clear any secretions on top of the cushion before removing the LMA. Deflate the cushion and remove the LMA. Avoid damaging the cushion on the teeth. Loose teeth or isolated teeth can easily catch on the cuff and be pulled out.

When used under anesthesia the LMA should be removed either with the patient completely anesthetized, or once awake. It should not be removed during Stage 2 of the awakening process when airway reflexes are heightened and laryngospasm may occur.

Use of the LMA to Assist Intubation

You can use the LMA as a guide for blind and fiberoptically directed endotracheal intubation. If good airway anesthesia is provided, the LMA can even be placed in the awake patient for this purpose (Fig. 12-7). You may need to remove the grill from the bowl of the LMA to allow the ETT to exit when using a non-intubating LMA.

The use of the LMA Fastrach®, which is a device specifically designed to perform intubation, is discussed in Chapter 17.

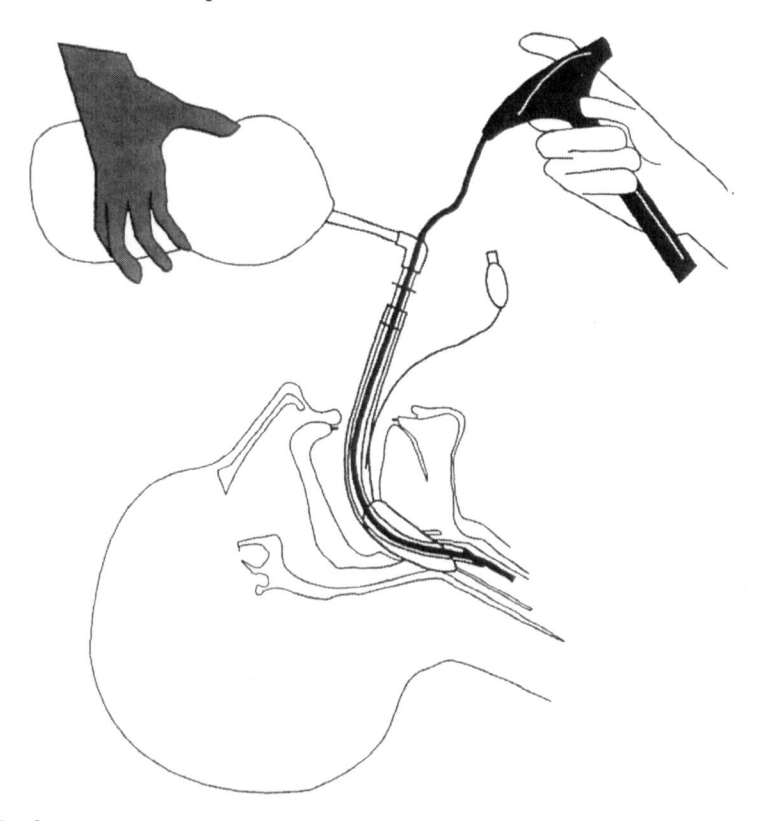

Fig. 12-7. It's always an option to combine techniques. Here fiberoptic intubation is combined with placement of an LMA as a guide for the endotracheal tube.

Care and Sterilization of the LMA

The original LMA was designed for re-use. There are now disposable versions each costing about the same as a disposable endotracheal tube. However, the reusable versions are still in popular use both here in the United States and abroad. Since each reusable LMA costs several hundred dollars, the only economical way to use this type of LMAs is to resterilize them between patients.

Soon after removal from the patient, the reusable LMA should initially be washed with mild soap and water. Use a pipe cleaner style brush to clean secretions from the tube. Be careful not to damage the grill on the mask.

Then autoclave the LMA at a temperature no higher than 134°C for at least 3 minutes. Never use ethylene oxide, glutaraldehyde or formaldehyde. Make certain the cushion and pilot tube are completely deflated before putting the LMA into the autoclave or they may burst from the heat induced expansion of air.

If the drying cycle is omitted, between 100-250 re-uses have been possible, bringing the cost of the LMA per use into the same price range as an endotracheal tube. Discard any LMA if it's discolored, damaged, or if you see abnormal bulging of the inflated cuff. Replacement valves are available if the valve leaks.

Esophageal-Tracheal Combitube®

The Combitube Esophageal-Tracheal (ECT) is a double lumen ventilation tube for use during anesthesia and emergency airway management. The tube has 2 lumens, each with a 15mm airway connector at the proximal end (Fig. 12-8). There are 2 inflatable cuffs. The proximal 100 ml latex pharyngeal cuff seals the pharynx. The second 15 ml PVC cuff near the distal tip seals either the esophagus or the trachea. Either lumen may be used to ventilate depending upon whether the tube lies in the esophagus or the trachea.

The ECT is noninvasive, requires no head or neck manipulations, and is easily inserted blindly by medical providers unskilled in advanced airway techniques. It's very helpful for situations when the patient is trapped in an awkward, even prone, position or who has a mouth full of blood of vomit.

Insertion of the Combitube

The ECT is inserted either blindly or using direct laryngoscopy, entering the esophagus 98% of the time (Fig. 12-9a,b). With the patient's head in neutral position, lift the lower jaw and tongue by one hand and insert the Combitube in a curved, flat movement until the printed proximal black rings lie opposite the front teeth. If there is no risk of cervical spine injury, the head can be flexed forward on the chest or extended slightly — otherwise leave the head position neutral.

Inflate the proximal balloon with 100 ml of air through the blue pilot balloon. Then inflate the distal

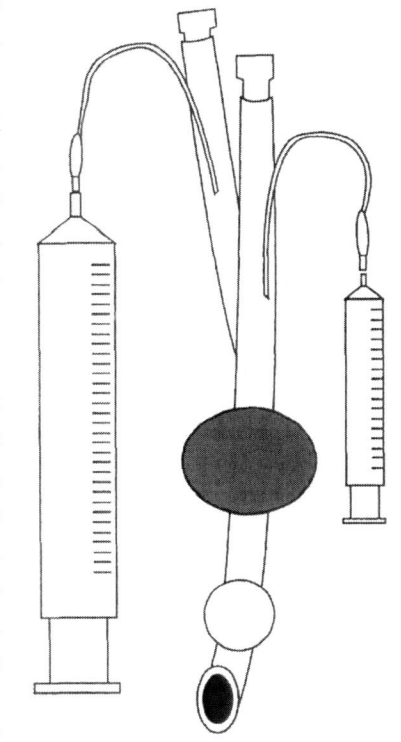

Fig. 12-8. Esophageal-Tracheal Combitube.

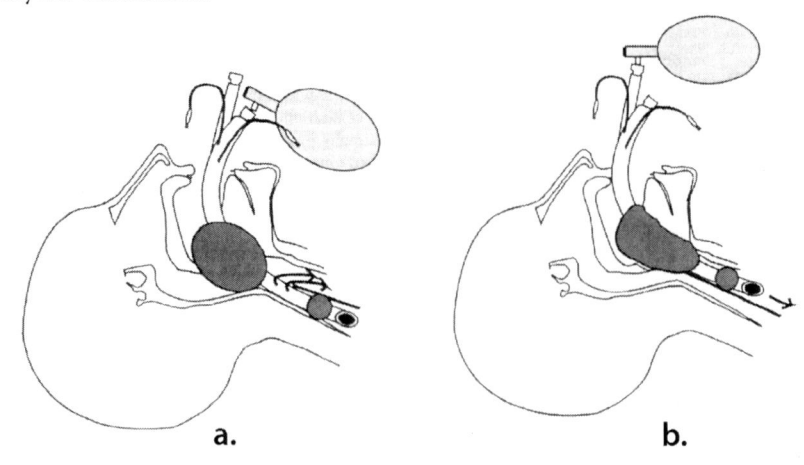

Fig. 12-9a.
Combitube in the esophagus.
Ventilate through lumen #1. Air enters trachea from posterior pharynx.

Fig. 12-9b.
Combitube in the trachea.
Ventilate through lumen #2. Air enters the trachea directly.

balloon with 5-15 ml through the white pilot balloon. Inflation of the proximal pharyngeal balloon secures the tube and normally causes the tube to move outward about 1 cm.

Next verify the location of the tube to determine which lumen should be used for ventilation. Since esophageal positioning is most likely, ventilate the longer blue tube through lumen 1 first. When positioned in the esophagus, air entering through the multiple side ports is trapped between the 2 cuffs and is forced into the trachea, producing the positive pressure for chest inflation.

If ventilation is poor through lumen #1, as evidenced by absent breathe sounds and an expanding stomach, the distal tube may lie in the trachea. In this event try ventilating using the shorter clear tube though lumen #2. Watch for the chest to rise and fall with good breath sounds.

If ventilation continues to be poor then try lumen #1 again after adding more air to the *proximal* cuff since the seal may be inadequate. If the third attempt at ventilation fails remove the Combitube and ventilate the patient by bag and mask before trying this or another technique again.

Occasionally ventilation can't occur through either port because the Combitube, and with it the oropharyngeal balloon, is too deep — obstructing the larynx. Pull the tube out about 3 cm and ventilate again using the esophageal lumen.

There are several advantages of the Combitube over the EOA. Ventilation with the Combitube can occur regardless of whether the tube is in the esophagus or the trachea and the esophagus can be suctioned. Unlike the LMA, the Combitube provides some protection from aspiration.

Intubating With The Combitube In Place

The Combitube can be particularly useful when blood or emesis fills the mouth. Not only can the Combitube help protect the patient from aspiration while allowing ventilation, it can provide a clearer view for intubation under these challenging circumstances.

If intubation is desired once the Combitube is positioned in the *esophagus*, suction the stomach and oropharynx, deflate the oropharyngeal balloon but leave the distal balloon inflated to keep secretions in the stomach. Shift the Combitube to the far left. Intubate as usual.

Once the endotracheal tube cuff is inflated and correct tracheal position verified, deflate the distal cuff of the Combitube and while you are holding the endotracheal tube securely, have your assistant slowly remove the Combitube. If intubation was not successful, reinflate the oropharyngeal balloon and ventilate.

If the Combitube is inserted in the trachea, it must be removed prior to replacement with an endotracheal tube.

Disadvantages of the Combitube

Due to its rigid design and blind technique used to insert the Combitube, airway trauma can occur. A significant disadvantage of the Combitube is the lack of pediatric sizes. Don't attempt to use a Combitube in anyone shorter than 4 feet tall. Also don't use one in patients with intact gag reflexes regardless of their level of consciousness. Don't use one in patients with known esophageal pathology such as those with esophageal varices or patients who have swallowed caustic liquids.

Needle Cricothyroidotomy and Jet Ventilation

Needle cricothyroidotomy is a fast, easy way of providing oxygen to a patient with an obstructed airway who does not respond to more conventional means of opening the airway. It will buy you time to establish a more permanent airway such as an intubation or tracheostomy if the patient is hypoxic.

First identify the cricothyroid membrane by finding the cricoid ring. The membrane lies in the gap between the ring and the thyroid cartilage above it (Fig. 12-10). The membrane is about 10 mm high and 22 mm wide in the average adult. The vocal cords lie 1 cm above. The blood vessels tend to overlie the upper third of the cricothyroid membrane. Making your puncture in the lower third will minimize the risk of hitting them.

You can use any intravenous catheter-over-needle set to puncture the cricothyroid membrane. Use the largest catheter possible, such as a size 10 or 14 gauge in the adult. Attach a syringe to the hub of the needle and aspirate as you advance. Aim the needle slightly caudad. Your insertion should be slow and deliberate to avoid puncture of the posterior tracheal wall. The diameter of the adult trachea averages 18 mm. The aspiration of air verifies intratracheal placement.

Slide the catheter off the needle into the trachea. Again attach your syringe to the hub of the catheter and aspirate 10-20 ml of air to check placement and ensure free aspiration. It's essential that the catheter not be blocked by the tracheal wall or kinked. Jet ventilation against or into the tracheal wall can cause massive subcutaneous emphysema. Have an assistant steady the catheter by the hub to ensure that it doesn't move.

You now need to connect the catheter to a ventilation system. Because of the small diameter, the best means of giving oxygen through this device is a jet ventilator with a Sander's valve. When using the jet it is imperative that the airway be at least partially open above the cricothyroid membrane. If not, the gas pressure will build and potentially cause a pneumothorax. Misplacement of the catheter can lead to subcutaneous emphysema.

If a jet ventilator is unavailable, then there are several ways to connect the catheter to your ventilation system. The connector from a number 3 endotracheal tube fits snugly into the hub of any intravenous catheter. However, this tiny assembly is often difficult to hold while squeezing the bag. I prefer to place the connector from a number 7.5 endotracheal tube into the barrel of a 3 ml syringe.

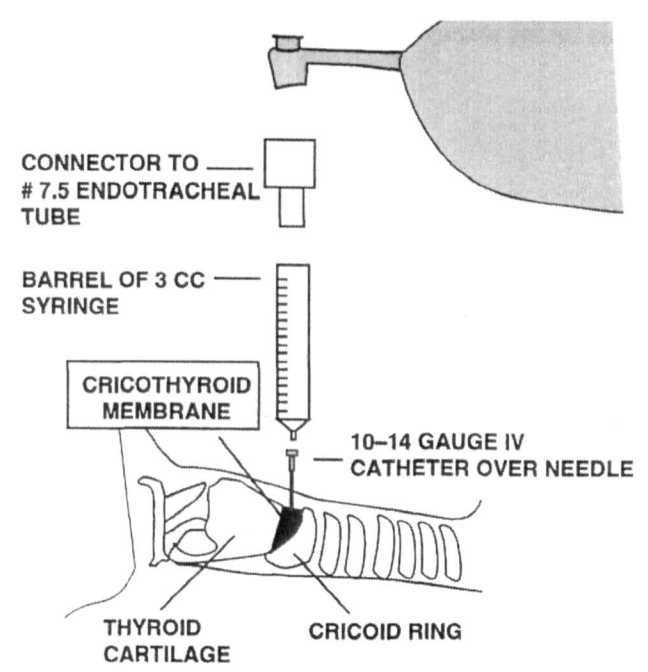

Fig. 12-10. Emergency needle cricothyroidotomy and a simple, though less optimal, means of connecting it to a ventilation system when a jet ventilator is not available. This is a temporary ememrgency measure only as hypercarbia will occur.

The barrel of the syringe now mates to the hub of your catheter and gives you something more substantial to hold. You can also place an endotracheal tube within the barrel of a ten ml syringe and inflates the cuff to maintain the connection. You must ventilate vigorously to pass enough oxygen through the catheter.

Gas will escape through the mouth.

You can attach the barrel from a tuberculin syringe to the catheter hub and connect this to oxygen tubing. If the oxygen tubing can then be connected to the fresh gas outflow from an anesthesia machine a "jet" can be jury rigged.

Reports indicate that patients can maintain themselves for several minutes breathing spontaneously through a 10 g catheter. Although hypoxia is avoided *hypercarbia will develop*. However, any oxygen supplied during emergency treatment of airway obstruction is useful.

Surgical Cricothyroidotomy

Surgical cricothyroidotomy is more hazardous than needle cricothyroidotomy. Unlike jet ventilation, it can be used when total upper airway obstruction is present. It allows for insertion of a larger tube, thus improving ease of ventilation. Suctioning of the airway is possible. Finally, it can be secured and left in place for a longer period, while the transtracheal catheter must be replaced relatively quickly with a more definitive airway.

The indictions for surgical cricothyroidotomy are:
- "can't ventilate/can't intubate" scenario;
- upper airway foreign body or other obstruction;
- severe trauma to face and mouth;
- traumatic C-spine injury where oral intubation not feasible.

Consult an experienced surgeon to perform or to assist you with this procedure unless a delay will jeopardize patient survival. Surgical cricothyroidotomy is beyond the scope of this book.

Several kits are now marketed for non-surgeon providers to allow easy and quick placement of a surgical cricothyroidotomy. Nu-Trake® (Bivone Medical Technologies; Gary, Ind.), Melker Emergency Cricothyroidotomy Catheter Set (Cook Critical Care), and the Arndt Emergency Cricothyroidotomy Catheter Set (Cook Critical Care) are three such devices. These kits contain all of the instruments needed to provide an emergency airway.

Potential complications from this emergency procedure include injury to the larynx, hemorrhage into the trachea, aspiration, pneumothorax, esophageal damage, and subcutaneous or mediastinal emphysema. Death from asphyxia — from failure or from improper placement of the tube — can also occur.

Esophageal Obturator Airway

The EOA is only used in the field as an alternative to bag and mask ventilation. It is less frequently used because of the potential for complications, It does not provide better ventilation than any other properly used bag-valve-mask device. The airway must be maintained open in the same way. The EOA does provide a barrier to minimize regurgitation of gastric contents. The use of the EOA carries risks of patient injury and death if used incorrectly or in a rough fashion. It should not be considered a replacement to intubation, merely an interim form of airway management until intubation can occur.

The EOA consists of a long tube — open at the top and sealed at the bottom — with multiple small holes near the upper end. A special mask fits over the tube and seals against the patient's face in the usual manner. The ventilation bag is then attached to the tube as it exits the top of the mask. The large cuff on the EOA is designed to seal the esophagus, thereby preventing regurgitation and preventing air from entering the stomach.

Insertion of the EOA

To assemble the EOA, place its top through the port in the mask. Check the cuff by inflation with 20-30 ml of air. Deflate the cuff prior to insertion. Lubricate the end with water soluble jelly.

To insert the EOA flex the head slightly and pull the jaw forward (Fig. 12-1). Gently advance the tube down the patient's throat into the esophagus until the mask sits flush against the face. Never force the tube. If there is resistance pull back and re-advance. Try gently twisting it.

Once inserted, check the location of the EOA *before* inflating the cuff by obtaining a good mask seal, ventilating with a ventilation bag, and verifying breath sounds. This sequence is different than endotracheal intubation because inflation of the large EOA cuff, *if misplaced in the trachea*, can lead to tracheal rupture as well as asphyxia if the error is not recognized.

Correct placement of the EOA in the esophagus and with the mask properly sealed will allow you to ventilate the patient. Incorrect placement of the EOA into the trachea will prevent all ventilation because the end of the EOA is closed. Inflation of the cuff in the esophagus seals the esophagus to prevent stomach distention and to prevent aspiration of stomach contents.

If the EOA is in the trachea remove it immediately and ventilate by mask prior to the next attempt.

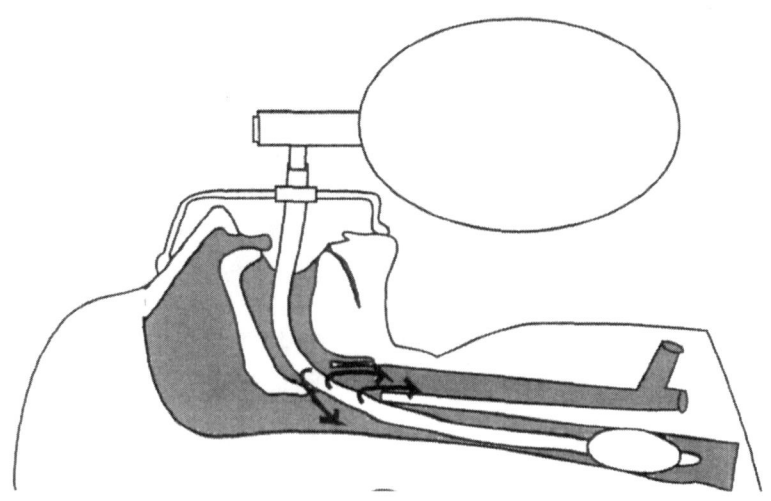

Fig. 12-11. Esophageal Obturator Airway (EOA).

Intubation with the EOA in Place

Prepare your equipment and hyperventilate the patient prior to the attempt. You won't be able to ventilate the patient with the mask removed. To remove the mask, pinch the EOA near the port and slide it off. Push the EOA as far to the left as you can to get it out of the way. Intubate using standard techniques.

Once the intubation is complete immediately verify correct placement — esophageal intubation can occur with an EOA in place. Secure the endotracheal tube well to avoid accidental extubation when the EOA is removed.

To remove the EOA have an assistant hold the endotracheal tube firmly in place no matter how well you feel you have taped it. Prepare for possible vomiting by having suction ready. Then deflate the EOA cuff and gently slide it out of the mouth. Re-verify breath sounds and correct endotracheal tube placement.

Cautions in the Use of the EOA

The esophageal obturator airway (EOA) has long been reported to result in significant complications, and its use is generally discouraged including: unrecognized tracheal intubation[1] and esophageal perforation[2]. Studies indicated that it was no more effective than the Bag-Valve-Mask airway[3]. In a 1983 JAMA review[4], the stated conclusion was that "The use of the EOA to replace endotracheal intubation in airway management is not substantiated in the literature."

A 1993 study[5] compared the incidence of complications of the EOA to intubation in a review of 509 consecutive cardiac arrests. Complications for the EOA included misplacement, kinking, curling, swelling/hematoma, and traumatic extubation; those for intubation included extubation and misplacement. The complication rate for the EOA was higher (11.1% vs. 7.7%). The serious or potentially lethal complication rate was 3.3 times more common with the use of the EOA than with intubation (8.7% vs. 2.6%).

The EOA must be used with caution, if at all — but should be used when necessary. The typical OR has everything you need to intubate, but the EOA may be the only tool available in your environment. If the EOA is all you have, don't hesitate to carefully use it.

Potential EOA complications include:
- Asphyxia and death if the EOA is positioned in the trachea.
- The EOA should be used only in the deeply unconscious patient because it will cause gagging and vomiting in the awake or semiconscious patient.
- Don't use it in children under 16 years old or patient's under 5 ft. tall.
- Don't use the EOA in patients with known esophageal disease such as varices or ingestion of a caustic substance.
- The EOA cannot be suctioned and therefore allows the build up of gastric contents and pressure during use. Never remove the EOA from an unconscious patient until the patient has been intubated. Vomiting and aspiration could occur.

Emergency Airway Cart

Emergency airway situations can occur at any time. It is highly recommended that each provider know at least one alternative method of securing a failed airway. Having a difficult "airway cart" or "tool box" available saves precious minutes since all the needed supplies are together and readily accessible. Needless to say, your assistants also need to know where it's stored so they can fetch it for you in a crisis situation. They should also know how to identify key pieces of equipment.

The Keyframe (KF) sequences in this chapter are taken from video clips that are available on-line, for free, from anyonecanintubate.com at:

For Chapter 12 video clips go to:
http://bit.ly/11kZOhk

All video chapter files appear on Anyone Can Intubate Portfolio at:
http://bit.ly/U7EV7f

13
AIRWAY MANAGEMENT OF TRAUMA

Trauma is a body wound or shock produced by sudden injury, often caused by vehicle and other accidents, or by deliberate violence. The effects of trauma may be immediate, or may not manifest until sometime after the moment of injury (e.g., inflammation, bruises).

Physical trauma can result in obvious physical damage (wounds, bleeding, burns), or the damage can be less obvious (internal bleeding, broken bones). Usually, we are dealing with physical trauma, most often resulting from an accidental fall, a car accident, or by a weapon such as a gun or a knife. However, there is a multitude of other sources of physical trauma, from fisticuffs to flesh-eating bacteria. To put it politely: Hurt Happens.

Chemical trauma results from exposure to toxins, whether natural or man-made. Often, the organs that are compromised by toxins, especially airborne toxins, are the body dermis and/or the lungs, and the damage to these organs is extensive. For example, the chemical weapon known as "Mustard gas" undergoes a chemical reaction in the lungs that produces hydrochloric acid, which rapidly destroys the alveoli. Natural toxins that result in trauma include the necrotic poisons of some rattlesnakes.

Radiation trauma results from radiation of any type. Although nuclear devices can cause such trauma, radiation trauma also includes damage resulting from more common sources, such as ultraviolet (uv) radiation (overexposure to sunlight, welder's arcs) or infrared radiation (IR) (heat from a distance).

Trauma can be, and often is, multifactorial. The burns on a fire victim's skin are the result of 2 different sources of trauma: direct contact with burning or hot objects (physical trauma), and infrared radiation (radiation trauma). To take an extreme example, disaster movie turned real-life drama, an earthquake that produced a tsunami that damaged one or more nuclear power plants could result in victims with severe physical and radiation trauma.

Trauma can happen on a macroscopic or microscopic scale. A broken piece of glass can puncture a lung, and the microscopic glass particles in volcanic ash, if inhaled, can shred alveoli. Either way, respiratory function is impaired.

In addition to primary trauma, physical injury can cause secondary trauma. For example, blunt trauma to the mouth can generate fragments of teeth or bone that cause damage beyond the site of the original injury.

Regardless of its source or type, trauma complicates airway management and intubation in many ways:

• Injury of the airway or other parts of the respiratory system may lead to poor ventilation and oxygenation.

• Damage to, or destruction of, anatomical features may make mask ventilation and intubation difficult or impossible.

• Damage to, or distortion of, anatomical features may affect or hide the anatomical

"landmarks" you would usually use to manage the airway or to intubate.
- Trauma care carries with it a degree of uncertainty. The extent or nature of the injury isn't always apparent when treatment begins, and changes as the body responds to the damage.
- Decompensation can occur at any time, requiring careful monitoring and reassessment.
- In complex or severe trauma, involving multiple injures, attention can be drawn away from the airway at critical moments due to the need to evaluate and treat other injuries. You may have to manage an airway while CPR is being performed. In emergency or military events there may be other distractions as well.
- Finally, there may be some level of risk of personal injury to the provider at the scene. For emergency and military providers, the risk is obviously greater than for others; but disasters like earthquakes or terrorist attacks put fireman and first responders on the front line as well. Risk management procedures should be followed, even if they slow your actions, because they protect the provider as well as the patient.

Good airway management in trauma is essential in order to treat airway obstruction and respiratory insufficiency, avoid aspiration, and improve hemodynamic stability — while at the same time taking precautions to protect the spinal cord and brain from further damage. Secondary injury from such things as shock and anaerobic metabolism can lead to ischemic injury to the brain, spinal cord and other major organ systems.

Any caregiver has to be prepared to help respond to a natural or man-made disaster that results in many injured victims and corpses. In this case, and in combat, you may need to perform triage. I hope you never have to but, if you do, you will need to make very quick assessments of the airways of the wounded. Know and practice the techniques for quickly evaluating respiratory trauma.

Airway and Respiratory Assessment

Trauma can injure any component of the respiratory system and impair oxygen transport. Oxygen delivery depends on:
- air passing through a non-obstructed pharynx and larynx,
- an intact tracheobronchial tree and lung alveolar interface,
- an airtight chest cavity,
- functional bellows action of the diaphragm,
- intact muscle contraction of the intercostal muscles,
- functional phrenic nerve and intercostal nerves,
- brain interpretation of peripheral chemical feedback,
- appropriate nervous system response to chemical feedback,
- efficient heart function,
- adequate circulatory volume,
- adequate Hgb concentration.

Inefficiency or failure of any component in this complex interactive system requires some form of airway intervention. Intervention can be as simple as giving supplemental oxygen and intravenous fluids or, as complex as intubating the patient to provide ventilatory support.

You will need to use a systematic approach to rapidly identify injuries and stabilize the

patient. Using the language of emergency care, this includes:
- *Size up the scene:* what's going on, safety, how many patients, help needed?
- *Initial survey:* consciousness, airway, breathing, circulation (ABCs)
- *Resuscitative phase:* begin stabilization and treatment
- *Secondary survey:* reassess ABCs and consciousness, other injuries
- *Definitive care:* transport as needed, treatment and stabilization continues

This approach has the provider going back to check the patient again after the initial stabilization. Those injuries that are immediately life-threatening may not be the only injuries. Other injuries not immediately apparent may themselves become life-threatening over time. Further systemic deterioration of the patient or internal bleeding can also lead to serious hypoxia, hypercarbia, and shock that can in and of themselves become life-threatening.

Assessment of the airway takes into account:
- urgency of intervention
- initial estimate as to the etiology of the respiratory distress
- state of consciousness of the patient
- presence or absence of facial trauma

Carefully assess the patient to decide if the airway status is critical, urgent, or stable. Critical patients need immediate airway intervention to survive. Urgent patients require airway assistance, but there is more time to optimize both patient and technique. Even patients who appear stable require continued reassessment to identify worsening of their condition.

Respiratory distress in trauma may stem from one or more of the following:
- airway obstruction
- pneumothorax (partial or complete collapsed lung)
- pulmonary contusion (bruised lung)
- aspiration (entry secretions/foreign material into trachea and lungs)
- flail chest (a segment of the chest wall bones breaks and becomes detached from the rest of the chest wall)
- spinal cord injury (cervical or lumbar)
- circulatory shock

Rapid assessment of the cause as well as the degree of dysfunction is essential because treatment will vary. For example, placing a chest tube to treat tension pneumothorax may eliminate the respiratory distress without intubation.

Providing supplemental oxygen increases oxygen availability to the tissues and decreases systemic stress and lactate production. It maximizes hemoglobin saturation, which is helpful in the presence of anemia from blood loss.

Airway patency is key. Obstruction in trauma patients is common and results from swelling, tongue or facial injury, foreign bodies, and blood and secretions.

Ask conscious victims if they are getting enough air. Does their breathing feel normal? Is it painful to breath? Their ability to speak to you is a simple but effective screen for the urgency of intervention. It's a good sign if the patient answers in a normal voice and has no shortness of breath. Not all chemical or physical trauma is visible to the naked eye. If the patient responds in a hoarse or breathless voice, or can't answer at all, then significant respiratory compromise may be present.

Chin lift and/or jaw thrust maneuver, and the mechanical removal of debris are useful in clearing the airway in less injured patients. Avoid neck extension if cervical spine injury is possible. If there is any question of an adequate airway, voice changes, severe facial trauma, severe head injury, cardiac injury, or profound shock then definitive airway control is indicated.

Sedation and loss of consciousness cause loss of pharyngeal muscle tone and can collapse the oropharyngeal space, worsening obstruction. Giving sedation, including pain medications, to any patient with partial airway obstruction carries risk of worse obstruction and death. If you sedate, then titrate light doses of agents such as morphine slowly to effect. Have the reversal agent at hand. Monitor the patient carefully for worsening obstruction.

Unconscious victims are more difficult to evaluate. Cyanosis is a late sign — often hard to see due to anemia, ambient lighting, and skin color. Examining the airway, listening to the chest, and watching chest wall dynamics are methods that while important may miss subtle deterioration. Blood gas analysis, and radiologic exam, when available, are reliable, but take time and aren't present in the field. The loss of protective airway reflexes may go unnoticed. Because of the difficulty, some practitioners routinely intubate the unconscious victim in order to protect the airway, to provide improved ventilation, and to treat possible increased intracranial pressure. When you elect to observe the unconscious victim, frequently re-examine him for evidence of respiratory compromise as well as protective airway reflexes. The patient without gag reflexes is at high risk of aspiration.

Look for the signs of obstruction. Paradoxical chest wall motion, retractions at the sternal notch and rib spaces, accessory muscle use, pursed lips, nasal flaring, respiratory rate, increased or decreased depth of ventilations, and audible gasping, stridor, or wheezing are all signs of respiratory distress.

Be alert. Patients with partial airway obstruction have noisy breathing, but patients with complete airway obstruction may make no noise at all. The *absence* of stridor in a patient showing other signs of severe obstruction may signal impending respiratory collapse because lack of sound implies lack of air movement.

Awake patients with maxillofacial injuries, airway edema, pulmonary edema and even pneumothorax often breathe more easily when sitting, flexed forward, trying to assume the tripod position. Patients should be allowed to stay in a position of more comfortable breathing if other injuries and hemodynamic status permit. The 23% increase in cross-sectional area of the pharynx that takes place when the patient moves from supine to sitting[1] decreases resistance to breathing. The sitting position slows further development of edema, lets blood and secretions drain from the mouth, and lets gravity pull soft tissue forward, out of the airway.

Transporting such patients on their side can also minimize airway obstruction when sitting is not an option and/or intubation has not been possible. In the side position the tongue and other soft tissue tends to fall away from, rather than over, the larynx. The weight of the abdominal contents no longer pushes the diaphragm upward, allowing for a greater lung volume and tidal volume. Consider elevating the head if this position will not place the patient at risk.

Airway Management

In the case of trauma, airway management includes establishing air exchange, decreasing the risk of aspiration, deciding whether or not to intubate, protecting the cervical spine, knowing when to consider a surgical airway, and never forgetting the rest of the patient.

Establish Air Exchange

The first priority is to establish good air exchange. The trauma victim is less likely to tolerate prolonged hypoventilation. Chest wall splinting, altered consciousness, and hemorrhagic anemia can result in hypoxemia and hypercarbia.

Open the airway. Intubation may not be required if the patient rouses sufficiently from relief of hypoxemia. Suction secretions. If available, provide supplemental oxygen. Persistent airway obstruction despite soft tissue manipulation may mean a foreign body is lodged in the airway. Consider the use of oral and nasal airways.

Rarely, intubation may need to precede bag and mask ventilation if the maxillofacial anatomy is destroyed. Attempt to improve ventilation while the intubation equipment is assembled and checked. Changing the patient's position or pulling forward on the mandible, maxilla, or tongue may open the airway enough to improve gas exchange and perhaps give you more time to optimize the situation. Every second counts when the patient is badly injured.

Decrease the Risk of Aspiration

All trauma patients are at increased risk of aspiration, regardless of the timing or amount of the last meal. Delayed gastric emptying and emesis occurs frequently due to pain, shock, ileus, drug effects, CNS injury, and occasionally gastric outlet obstruction. The trauma victim's stomach often contains a large volume of particulate matter with low pH. Conscious patients strapped to a backboard for transport are helpless if they vomit. Aspiration of blood, secretions, or stomach contents can occur at any time due to laryngeal incompetence, diminished or absent cough, and altered consciousness, even if emesis does not occur. When the victim aspirates, aspiration pneumonitis is likely.

When manually ventilating, decrease the risk of aspiration by avoiding gastric distention. In addition to making vomiting more likely, gastric distention pushes the diaphragm upward, impairing ventilation by decreasing lung volume. This is especially true in small children.

If your patient can't protect herself you must protect her. Always be prepared for vomiting, which in the patient in shock can be massive. Hypotension often causes nausea. Watch for repetitive swallowing — often a first sign that the patient is nauseous or about to vomit. Massive emesis can even occur if the patient is in cardiac arrest. Keep your suction ready and close at all times. If your patient is unconscious consider passage of a nasogastric (NG) or orogastric tube to decompress the stomach.

When to Consider Intubation

Deciding whether or not to intubate can be difficult. An adequate airway can quickly disappear because of progressive edema, hematoma, or deteriorating hemodynamic status. One of my instructors used to say that if you are caring for a patient who is so sick that you ask yourself whether you should intubate the patient, it probably means you should.

Clear indications to attempt intubation if possible are:

Table 13-1. Glasgow Coma Scale	
Eye Opening (E)	
• Spontaneous	4
• To speech	3
• To pain	2
• None	1
Best Motor Response (M)	
• Obeys	6
• Localizes	5
• Withdraws	4
• Abnormal flexion	3
• Abnormal extension	2
• None	1
Verbal (V)	
• Oriented	5
• Confused conversation	4
• Inappropriate words	3
• Incomprehensible words	2
• None	1
Coma Score = E + M + V (e.g. 3 to 15)	

- full cardiac arrest
- hypovolemic shock with impending arrest
- apnea
- severe airway obstruction
- inability to ventilate with bag and mask
- deteriorating air exchange with no sign of improvement
- no pharyngeal (gag) reflexes (e.g. can't protect own airway)
- head injury with a Glasgow coma scale less than 7-8 (see Table 13-1)
- potential for increased intracranial pressure with hypoventilation.

Unfortunately, especially in the trauma victim, decisions must often be made before a clear picture of obstruction presents. Symptoms and signs of increasing airway obstruction may be occasionally subtle and one must have a high index of suspicion to identify them.

The common signs of airway decompensation are:
- inability to swallow, drooling
- expiratory snore or fluttering sound — may indicate increasing edema
- altered voice: hoarseness, weak or "strangled" voice

Table 13-2. Risk of Cervical Spine Injury
Risk of Cervical Spine Injury
• Known injury
• Positive C-Spine X-rays or CT scans
• Neurologic deficit
High Risk (> 10%)
• Front end MVA > 35 mph without seatbelt
• Head first fall
• Equivocal C-Spine X-Ray
Moderate Risk (1-2%)
• MVA
• Head injury
• Non-head first fall
• Contact sport injury
• High risk group with negative C-Spine X-Ray
No Risk
• Alert patient without neck pain or tenderness
• Negative C-Spine X-Rays (3 views)
• Negative C-Spine CT scan

- persistent and severe sore throat
- intermittent obstruction
- symptoms worsen with forced ventilation
- inability to make a high pitched "e" sound
- restlessness or disorientation may mean hypoxia and hypercarbia

The decision to intubate in the face of such subtle signs is a judgment call and should be based on proximity to the hospital if in the field, concurrent injuries, progression of symptoms, the mechanism of injury, and the skill and available equipment of the caregiver. Ask yourself what will happen if you do nothing? If you decide to wait, observe the patient carefully, reassess often, and place him as quickly as possible into a hospital setting where continued evaluation — and possibly intubation — can take place if needed.

Intubation Technique: Protecting the Cervical Spine

Any intubation technique must take the potential for cervical spine (CS) injury into account. A review article by Hastings and Marks[1] provides an excellent summary of the risks of CS injury (Table 13-2).

Because even minor trauma may injure the CS, it's imperative to stabilize the head and neck until injury is ruled out. Excessive extension, flexion, or distraction of the CS must be avoided.

Different stabilization devices are used, depending on factors such as the type, location and extent of trauma. Soft cervical collars allow 75% of normal movement; rigid collars allow about 30% flexion/extension and 50% lateral turn. The best method, securing the victim from head to foot on a backboard, with further stabilization of the neck with sandbags and a rigid collar, allows only 5% of normal movement[2].

Awake intubation has been shown to be safe in the patient with cervical spine injury[3]. When immediate airway intervention is not necessary, awake techniques and fiberoptic intubation should be considered. In the stable patient, definitive work-up to evaluate potential CS injury should occur and, if present, the patient should be immobilized as indicated.

Some controversy exists as to the best method of securing the airway in the presence of possible cervical spine injury. Three options exist: (1) nasal intubation, (2) oral intubation and (3), in the case of severe trauma, surgical airway (for example, cricothyroidotomy). The technique chosen depends on:
- urgency
- need for cervical spine immobilization and protection
- aspiration prevention
- severity of airway compromise
- potential for difficult intubation (i.e. "anterior airway," facial trauma)
- associated medical conditions (i.e. angina, head injury, shock)
- conscious or unconscious patient
- cooperative or uncooperative patient
- intubator's expertise with the different techniques

Nasal Intubation v. Oral Intubation in CS Injury

Advanced Trauma Life Support (ATLS) recommends awake nasal intubation in the spontaneously breathing patient, and oral intubation in the apneic patient. Let's review the advantages and disadvantages of each of these.

Nasal intubation is sometimes recommended in the patient with potential CS injury as a means of avoiding neurologic damage. However, nasal intubation in the trauma victim has several disadvantages[4]. The risk of inserting the ETT into the brain contraindicates its use in nasal, midface, or basilar skull fractures because of possible associated cribiform plate fracture. Severe nosebleeds can occur. Tube manipulations in the posterior pharynx may cause retching, which can worsen ICP, and cause bronchospasm or laryngospasm. In addition, cervical spine precautions can interfere with the inability to manipulate head and neck, leading to a prolonged intubation attempt that a hypoxemic patient can ill afford. Prolonged nasal intubations can lead to sinusitis and sepsis.

Blind nasal intubation is difficult in frightened, drunk, obtunded, or combative patients, and in children. In urban settings, studies of samples of hospitalized trauma patients have shown that from 20-86% test positive for alcohol or other drugs[5]. One study performed by emergency medicine physicians comparing safety and efficacy of nasal vs. oral intubations in intoxicated patients showed that oral intubation was preferable. In their study, it had a higher success rate (100% oral vs. 65% nasal), was faster, required fewer attempts, and had fewer complications (0% oral, 69% nasal)[6]. However, it should be noted that they used the muscle relaxant succinylcholine when necessary, a technique which also carries potential hazards to be discussed elsewhere.

Oral intubation, according to the ATLS, is "generally accepted as the more usual method for securing the airway in the trauma patient." In one report[7], three thousand patients were intubated orally with a modified rapid sequence induction (RSI) technique with preoxygenation and cricoid pressure. Ten percent of these patients were found to have cervical spine injury, and none deteriorated neurologically following intubation.

In the critical patient, direct laryngoscopy is the fastest and surest method of intubating, even though it requires some atlanto-occipital extension, even if the CS is immobilized. Accordingly, patients with unstable C1 or C2 injuries might be at more risk from this technique, and manual axial in-line stabilization (MILS) should always be used. While slightly more motion of the cervical spine takes place with oral, as opposed to careful nasal intubation, it has yet to be documented that this potential fracture movement damages the spinal cord[8,9,10,11]. The Cervical Spine Research Society reported a neurologic complication rate of 1% in 5,356 major cervical procedures. Increasing data support the careful use of oral intubation and muscle relaxants in the CS injured patient. Thus, careful oral intubation of critical patients using Manual In-Line Stabilization (MILS) is often a preferable alternative to nasal intubation[12].

Immobilization and Intubation

The assistant stabilizing the neck must balance the need for static immobilization versus active traction, a task that is not always easy. Have your assistant grip the head at the mastoid processes bilaterally and hold it in a neutral position without pulling on the head (Fig. 13-1).

You can also have your assistant pull on the hair to stabilize the head, but the goal is stabilization, not traction. You may need to carefully remove any obstructions to the mouth such as cervical collars prior to attempting oral intubation if they are preventing laryngoscopy.

Stabilizing the patient's head and neck can be awkward with the patient on the ground. It's difficult for the assistant using the MILS to stay out of the intubator's way. It's often easier

Fig. 13-1.
Manual In-line Stabilization or MILS

Fig. 13-2. Cervical stabilization during intubation on the ground using the knees to hold the head.

Fig. 13-3. Sitting to the right of the head and leaning backward to stabilize yourself. Your assistant can stabilize the head in this scenario.

for the intubator to provide her own stabilization by placing the head and neck between her own knees (see Fig. 13-2). Leaning backward provides the distance needed to manipulate the tube and visualize the larynx.

Another strategy is to sit to the patient's right side, facing the feet. Your assistant is behind the patient's head stabilizing it. Your hips should be level with the back of your patient's head. Your knees should be slightly bent, allowing you to maintain balance as your shift back and forth to optimize the position of your outstretched left arm doing the laryngoscopy (Fig. 13-3). This position gives you good leverage without pressing on the upper teeth. Pass the endotracheal tube with your right hand. You will need to twist your body slightly to accomplish this move.

Adjunct Techniques

Cricoid pressure frequently helps visualization and guards against aspiration. However, use this technique with caution in patients with suspected laryngeal or cervical spine injuries. Don't hesitate to omit it if you feel it's contraindicated.

The classic Laryngeal Mask Airway (LMA) should not be a first choice for airway management in trauma victims because these patients are at high risk for vomiting. While the classic LMA does not protect against aspiration, the LMA ProSeal™ does have a channel that allows gastric suctioning. The LMA is a good adjunct when oropharyngeal anatomy is undamaged and no fixed obstruction exists above the glottis.

The LMA is a poorer choice when the anatomy has been distorted by trauma or edema or if fixed upper airway obstruction exists. These latter situations might prevent a good seal and interfere with ventilation. You can also secure the airway with a Combitube™.

Video laryngoscopy, such as with the GlidesScope, or the use of an LMA Fastrach, can be very helpful in performing intubation with the head maintained in a neutral, stabilized position.

Fiberoptic laryngoscopy can also be used to assist both nasal and oral intubations. Its use in trauma is often hampered by its lack of availability of equipment, lack of familiarity with the instrument, blood in the oropharynx, distortion of the anatomy, edema, combative patients, and the need for speed in the presence of hypoxemia.

Intubators need to practice extensively with these instruments prior to using it in trauma victims. Use of the Fiberoptic bronchoscope, GlideScope, and LMA Fastrach will be discussed in Chapters 17 and 18.

When To Consider A Surgical Airway

Trauma victims, with often marginal oxygenation, cannot tolerate prolonged, repetitive attempts at intubation. Make sure you provide supplementary oxygen and suction the airway as needed during your attempts. Have a low threshold for proceeding to a surgical airway if:

- you are unable to clear an upper airway obstruction, *AND*
- have performed multiple unsuccessful attempts at intubation, *AND*
- other methods of ventilation, such as an LMA or Combitube do not allow for effective ventilation and respiration

In addition, in your judgment, the risks of not intubating are greater than the risk of performing the surgical airway.

Some conditions when surgical airway might be necessary are:
- combined bilateral mandibular fractures and Le Forte maxillary fractures
- gross deformity, edema of oropharynx or tongue
- gunshot wounds to the face
- extensive facial burns or crush injury
- cervical spine injury
- penetrating injury to the neck

Use of Sedatives and Local Anesthetics

The advantages and disadvantages of the use of sedatives combined with local anesthetics are discussed in Chapters 14 and 15. Any sedative can cause hypotension when only circulating catecholamines are maintaining the blood pressure. Start low and go slow. Give sedatives time to work before adding more.

Small increments of sedation and topical anesthesia may be all you need to control the unruly patient. However, the line between sedation and apnea, as well as the line between sedation and the loss of inhibition and onset of agitation can be quite slim if hypoxia or hypotension are present.

Don't use injected local anesthetic blocks in patients who are fighting because of the risk of intravascular injection of the drug. Instead use topical anesthesia. Lidocaine ointment or gel down the nose can help make nasal intubation tolerable. A glob of lidocaine ointment on a tongue blade swiped across the back of the tongue provides quick oropharyngeal anesthesia.

Never leave the patient alone once you start to topicalize the airway. Have suction ready to use. Even if the trachea itself is not anesthetized, other protective airway reflexes have been altered.

Spraying intravenous lidocaine (50-100mg) down the endotracheal tube after intubation often allows semi-conscious patients to tolerate the tube better.

Use of Muscle Relaxants and Induction Agents

Since the unconscious, relaxed patient does not struggle, intubation is faster and less traumatic when drugs that relax muscles (muscle relaxants) and agents that induce unconsciousness (induction agents) are used prior to the intubation. Faster intubations cause fewer physiologic changes and allow faster treatment of hypoxia, hypercarbia. They can minimize aspiration risk.

However, muscle relaxants carry risk and should *not* be used when you have any doubt about whether or not you will be able to ventilate a patient using bag and mask. Their use in the field, though valuable, must be carefully considered.

Muscle relaxants and inductions agents are discussed in Chapter 14.

Problems in the Field

Paramedics, nurses, and physicians working at an accident site or battlefield face multiple problems that hospital caregivers never experience. The healthcare worker in the field may face personal injury from vehicles, fire, toxic exposure, and smoke. Distractions abound. An audience of sobbing family members makes dispassionate assessment difficult at best. Care under these circumstances produces more anxiety than caring for the same patient in the emergency room.

Even the healthcare worker accustomed to the sight of blood and trauma may be emotionally repelled by the severity of injury — especially in young, previously healthy individuals vs. multiple trauma victims may force prioritizing of treatment to take place. Salvageable patients with inadequate respiration must receive immediate care to prevent irreversible hypoxemia and death. This priority may mean bypassing, for the moment, patients deemed unsalvageable. During triage you will have to make these assessments quickly.

Noise and sirens drown out breath sounds and heart sounds. Nighttime lighting, headlights, and flashing red strobes hide cyanosis and pallor. Daylight has a bluer cast than indoor tungsten lighting and makes skin color harder to judge. Even feeling a pulse in a vibrating ambulance or helicopter may prove impossible.

Because assessment at the scene is more difficult, the caregiver must be more attentive to the potential for subtle or delayed signs of respiratory embarrassment. Use all the senses. If you can't hear breath sounds because of noise then feel for movement of air out of the nose and mouth with your hand. If you can't see the chest rise, place your hand on the chest to feel it rise in conjunction with air movement. Shining your flashlight on the eye's conjunctiva or inside the mouth may pick up cyanosis when skin color is ambiguous. Placing your ear near the mouth may allow you to pick up stridor that you otherwise can't hear.

Intubation in the field is technically harder. Most paramedic protocols allow three intubation attempts in the field before aborting the procedure. If intubation fails, use nasal or oral airways, mask assistance, advanced airways such as LMAs and Combitubes, and patient positioning to optimize ventilation during transport. Grasping the tongue or mandible with a clamp or suture and pulling it forward can help in mandibular fractures and massive tongue edema. Use an endotracheal tube adapter to attach a nasal airway to the ventilation bag and ventilate by closing the patient's mouth and opposite nostril (Fig. 3-7). For midface fractures, pulling the maxilla forward can open the airway. Suction frequently as needed.

Noise, distractions, anxiety, and awkward positioning make inadvertent esophageal intubation more likely, and more difficult to recognize. Moving the patient repetitively from site of injury to stretcher, to ambulance, to hospital means extubation can occur at any time. Reassess the correct positioning of the endotracheal tube every time you move the patient, regardless of how minor the repositioning. If the respiratory status deteriorates check the position of the tube in addition to ruling out pneumothorax, etc. Always have a high index of suspicion for extubation and esophageal intubation.

Listen to your co-workers. If someone suggests that you are not ventilating well, or that the endotracheal tube may be esophageal don't become defensive. Instead, check the patient and verify the location of the ETT. It's better to perform an unnecessary check than it is to miss a problem because of pride.

Intubating with a Field Airway in Place

Esophageal Obturator Airways and Combitubes are often called field airways because they are placed most commonly in the field by emergency personnel. If the patient has an EOA and requires intubation, place the endotracheal tube *prior* to removing the obturator to avoid aspiration. See Chapter 12.

Don't Become Fixated on One Aspect of the Patient's Care

It's easy in the urgency of establishing an airway to ignore the rest of the patient. Hemodynamic changes associated with intubation can lead to further decompensation. Check blood pressure, pulse, and oxygen saturation frequently. Consider pneumothorax if ventilation is difficult after intubation.

On the other hand, urgent control of hemorrhage, placement of intravenous access and chest tubes, and ongoing diagnosis of the extent and nature of the patient's injuries can allow the team to lose sight of progressive airway obstruction or respiratory failure.

Don't become fixated on one aspect of the patient's care.

Entrapment

Entrapment situations, for example being trapped in a car wreck, can be particularly dangerous for both the victim and the caregivers. In these high risk, intensive situations, the injury usually results from high impact. There are often hidden injuries and potentially uncontrolled bleeding or hypoxia. In addition, there is lack of access to the patient, including visual and physical impediments, and sometimes inability to reach the patient.

To the best of your ability given the conditions at hand assess, stabilize, disassemble the vehicle or debris around the victim, and then extricate.

The temptation is to apply oxygen immediately but oxygen used in an enclosed space where cutting tools are being used increases the risk of fire. If the patient is breathing adequately, protection from dust and debris with a non-rebreather mask or dust mask may be sufficient.

It's important to consider concrete dust a threat because it can combine with moisture in the lungs to form casts in the airway. Concrete additives such as lime can cause chemical burns, bronchospasm, and edema.[13]

Rapid extrication, while perhaps desirable, may expose the patient to increased risk of further injury and should only be done if essential. Haste can be a hazard too. Environmental danger, such as a burning car, would be one obvious indication. Airway compromise or apnea is another common reason. However, alternative means of ventilation, such as an LMA or Combitube can often be used to support ventilation of the victim if extraction is delayed. Nasal intubation or oral intubation, including in the sitting and prone positions, if you have the access may be safer for the patient.[14,15] The caregiver must use best judgment in a suboptimal situation where there may be no good choice.

Patients may be trapped in awkward and precarious situations. If you need to manually ventilate, getting behind the victim in the back seat and using bag-valve-mask is difficult but sometimes possible. Consider use of an LMA device, Combitube, EOA, or nasal intubation.

Nasal intubation in the spontaneously breathing patient is usually easiest in these situations. But in the face of facial or basilar skull fractures, or when a paramedic or nurse is not certified to perform nasal intubations, the need for oral intubations may arise. Orally intubating a patient pinned in a sitting position is certainly difficult, but can often be successfully done. Barring anatomical distortion from edema or direct trauma, the anatomy of the airway does not change when the patient's position changes. If you have access to the airway and room to maneuver you can orally intubate in unusual positions.

You may have room to work from the back seat looking over the patient's shoulder. However, another technique is to face the patient. Have your assistant stabilize the patient's head from the back. You will need about 6 inches of clearance to get a field of view from above the patient's face. Insert the laryngoscope using a MAC blade into the mouth with your right hand with the curve facing the tongue and pull downward. Using your right hand, the blade flange will still hold the tongue to the patient's left. Now pass the endotracheal tube with your left hand into the trachea. Remember, the anatomical relationships will be the same even though your orientation is different.

Practice with a manikin in sitting, lateral, and prone positions to familiarize yourself with the problems of visualizing the anatomy, stabilizing the head, and positioning yourself for best mechanical advantage. Mental rehearsal and practice for difficult situations helps greatly when facing the unknown.

Blood in the Oropharynx

Blood in the oropharynx predisposes the patient to aspiration and hypoxia. It can be frightening in the worst-case scenario when the patient is unconscious, unable to protect the airway, and bleeding so badly that you can't see landmarks.

The patient needs ventilation and oxygen. If they are breathing well on their own give them supplemental oxygen, start intravenous volume replacement, and supply suction for the airway. Ventilate them if they are not breathing adequately. Place these patients in a position that allows the blood to drain away from the airway. For example, place them on their side or sitting up leaning forward. Never let them lay face up and flat. If they must be supine, as during CPR, then place the bed in Trendelenburg to allow the blood to pool in the

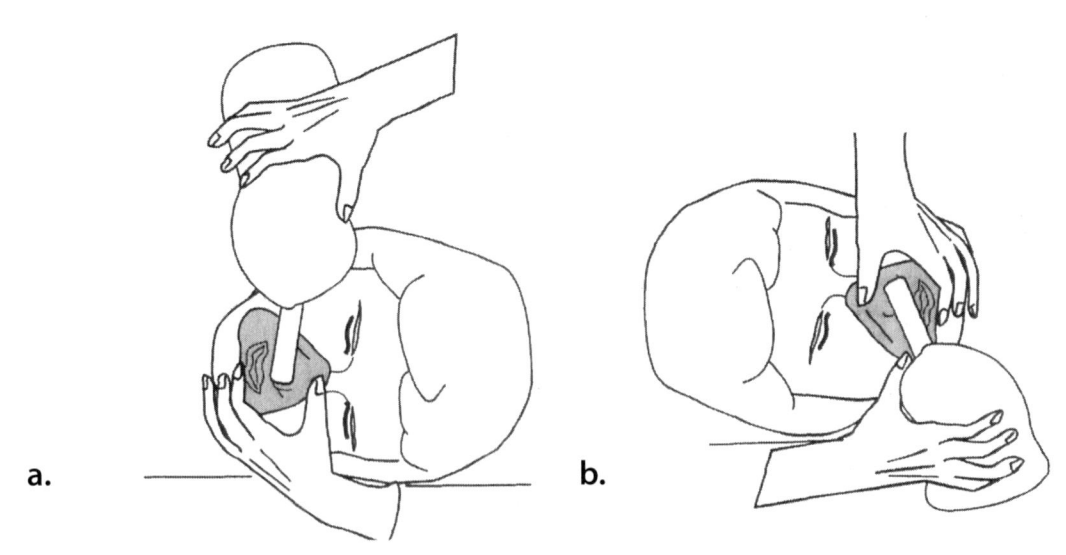

Fig. 13-4. Ventilating the patient on her side. Ventilation with left side down (a) is easiest. The hand squeezing the bag is free is move. With the right side down (b), the angle of the hands is awkward and the bag bumps into the bed unless you switch hands.

Fig. 13-5. Intubation with the left side down. Note helper stabilizing head.

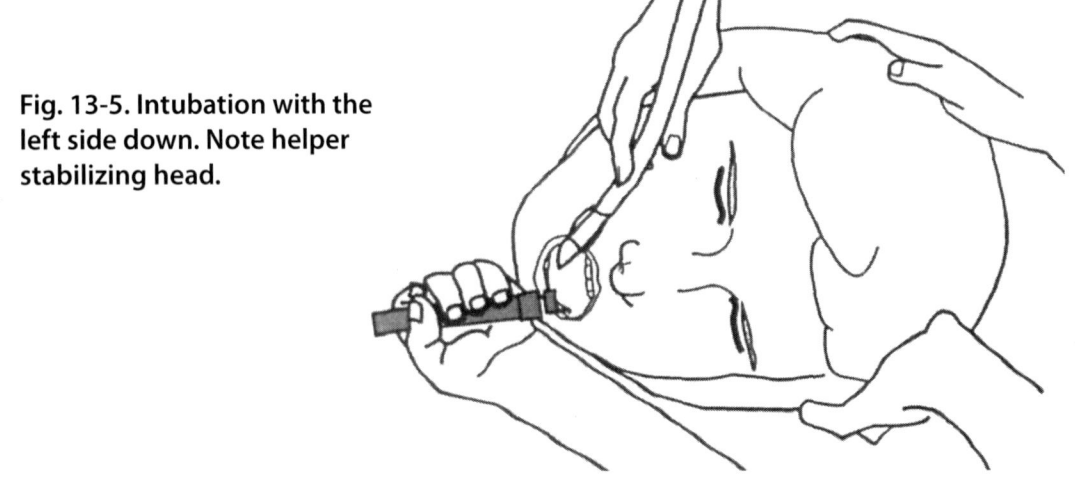

upper pharynx, away from the airway. Suction the mouth frequently. You may need to keep a soft suction catheter or the main suction tubing itself in the mouth to suction continuously. Turn the face to the side if you can. If you hear gurgling as the patient ventilates, then suction the patient. Patients who can't protect their airways need intubation as quickly as possible.

You can manually ventilate patients on their side, if spinal precautions are not needed. You may need help maintaining the mask seal. Have someone check breath sounds. It is far easier to place the patient left side down. The left hand can hold the mask while resting on the bed and the right one can ventilate freely. Right side down points the bag into the bed, forcing you to reverse the equipment (Fig. 13-4a, b) and ventilate with your left hand. Ventilating with opposite hands is easily done but can be difficult for the novice who has not practiced the technique.

If the bleeding is serious, you may prefer to intubate the patient on her side (Fig. 13-5). Again, left side down is optimal. Your left hand pushes the tongue to the left during laryngoscopy. With the left side down, gravity helps pull the tongue out of the way. It also leaves plenty of room for your right arm to maneuver the tube. The anatomy is the same and you should not let the different position unnerve you. You won't have the weight of the head pulling it down during laryngoscopy because the head stays on the bed. The blade may pull the head without lifting the jaw. You can have a helper hold the head steady as you look.

Sometimes a combination of methods is the best technique to use. Place the patient left side down and in slight Trendelenburg to ventilate the patient until everything is ready for intubation. Use cricoid pressure to prevent passive regurgitation of swallowed blood and secretions. Cricoid pressure may not prevent aspiration of the blood pooling in the oropharynx so suction frequently as you wait. Just before intubation clean the airway thoroughly, hand the suction catheter to an assistant, and turn the patient onto his back. Maintain cricoid pressure. Intubate quickly. Have your assistant suction the airway if needed.

If your first attempt fails use judgment about turning the patient lateral or keeping him supine. Whichever you choose, suction the airway well between attempts. When the anatomy is covered in blood, identification of landmarks can be difficult. Look for air bubbles coming from the larynx as a clue to the location of the cords. A gentle, abrupt push on the chest by an assistant can provide bubbles for you if the patient isn't breathing. If the patient is breathing, you will hear breath sounds through the tube. These sounds will stop instantly if the tube enters the esophagus. Use breath sounds as another clue to tube position.

After intubating, thoroughly suction the endotracheal tube, as aspiration of blood is common in these cases. Another danger is blood left in the tube may clot, obstructing the tube and preventing ventilation. These clots can become so solid that the tube must be removed and replaced, sometimes emergently.

If the source of the bleeding is above the glottis, such as nosebleed, the patient is unconscious, and the situation is critical. Placement of an LMA may secure the airway and provide some minimum of airway protection. The LMA may then be used to facilitate intubation, either as a direct conduit or by using the fiberoptic bronchoscope. The LMA would help to provide a clear visual field for the fiberoptic, even in the presence of continued bleeding.

An LMA does not protect against aspiration of gastric contents, although the LMA Proseal does provide a channel to suction the stomach. The patient with bleeding into the oropharynx is at high risk due to swallowed blood. Be prepared for vomiting. You can also use a Combitube® to secure the airway.

Burn Victims

Airway obstruction can occur precipitously in the burn victim. The patient is at high risk if the injury occurred in an enclosed space or involved steam, especially with prolonged exposure. Examine the victim for facial burns, singed nasal hair, and carbonaceous material in the nose or oropharynx. Look in the mouth for blisters on the hard palate, redness or marked inflammation of the oropharynx, and red/dry mucosa. Does the victim complain of hoarseness, dyspnea, or sore throat? Is there carbonaceous sputum or a cough? The combination of any of these in a high-risk patient causes many physicians to intubate prophylactically, rather than waiting for evidence if airway obstruction. Fifteen minutes can make a huge difference in oropharyngeal swelling.

The patient can still be at risk even if none of these signs and symptoms is initially present and should be re-evaluated frequently.

Once airway obstruction occurs, intubation can be extremely difficult and sometimes impossible. Surgical airways in burn victims cause a higher incidence of complications and mortality than intubation, and should be avoided unless absolutely necessary.

Burn victims may also suffer respiratory collapse, independent of airway problems, due to toxic fumes such as carbon monoxide (CO), hydrogen cyanide, and nitrogen dioxide, among other products of combustion in our synthetic filled world. Smoke inhalation can also lead to pneumonia and ARDS. Such failure can occur anytime during the first several days following the injury.

Provide a high FiO_2 (if it's safe to do so in that environment). The four-hour half-life of CO breathing room air can be reduced to one hour when breathing 100% oxygen and half an hour when breathing hyperbaric oxygen.

Severe Facial Injuries

Always assume that the patient with severe facial injuries has a possible cervical spine or brain injury and take appropriate precautions. If the patient has adequate respirations you have time to rule out concurrent injuries. Be aware, however, that airway injuries are often dynamic and severe obstruction can occur at any time. Bleeding or edema formation within the retropharyngeal space can cause abrupt obstruction, as can foreign bodies in the form of bone fragments and tissue. There is little relationship between the external findings and the severity of skeletal injuries.

In bimandibular fractures, the mandible is often pulled backwards by the strong facial muscles. Orally intubating such a patient risks damage to nerves as the fracture shifts.

Blind nasal intubation is relatively contraindicated due to potential cribiform plate rupture and the risk for passing the endotracheal tube or fracture material into the cranial vault or the brain itself. If the need to proceed to intubation is critical and X-rays are not available, a quick exam of the nasal passages with a gloved and lubricated finger can establish whether the passage appears intact. When in doubt use an alternate technique.

Oral intubation may be possible even in the presence of severe facial trauma. You should consider proceeding to a surgical airway in a patient with destroyed anatomy if you have any difficulty providing adequate ventilation.

The patient may be unable to open his mouth for several reasons. Trismus, or masseter spasm, is very common in facial fractures and will respond to the administration of an anesthetic and muscle relaxant (see Chapter 14). On the other hand, temporomandibular joint dysfunction due to injury of the joint itself can also lock the jaw shut and this condition will not respond to muscle relaxants. You will not be able to distinguish between the two entities acutely without radiologic exam. Awake intubation is recommended for these cases until the pathology is known. Trismus lasting longer than two weeks may cause permanent fibrosis and partial freezing of the joint.

Head Injury

Patients presenting with altered mental status may or may not have obvious signs of head injury such as scalp lacerations, postauricular ecchymosis ("Battles" sign), bilateral black eyes ("raccoon eyes"), unequal pupils, or blood behind the eardrum. Any patient with possible head injury should be treated as though they have the potential for increased intracranial pressure (ICP). Even a short noxious stimulus such as laryngoscopy can elevate the ICP

Table 13-3. Signs of Potential Laryngeal or Tracheal Injury

• hoarseness	• muffled voice
• dyspnea	• difficulty swallowing
• painful swallowing	• cervical pain and tenderness
• cervical ecchymosis or swelling	• subcutaneous emphysema

for prolonged periods. Once initiated, elevated ICP can lead to a vicious cycle of increasing cerebral edema, compromising blood flow, and potentially herniating the brain.

Heavy sedation, topicalization of the airway, and muscle relaxants can allow rapid control of the airway with minimal stimulation or increase in ICP. In addition, lidocaine, propofol, pentothal, and etomidate can directly decrease ICP by causing cerebral vasoconstriction. However, one must weigh the benefits of prophylactic ICP treatment against the potential complications such as shock or airway obstruction. Avoid ketamine which can raise ICP and increase cerebral metabolism.

Hyperventilate head-injured patients vigorously both before and after intubation to lower pCO_2. Hypocarbia causes cerebral vasoconstriction and thereby decreases ICP. Hyperventilation also helps treat any hypoxemia. Lidocaine 50-100 mg down the endotracheal tube after intubation can improve tolerance of the tube and avoid increased ICP due to coughing.

Laryngeal Trauma

Signs suggesting laryngotracheal injury after blunt or penetrating neck trauma (Table 13-3) can be non-specific. Patients with suspected laryngeal trauma should be carefully examined with direct and indirect layngoscopy, soft tissue neck X-rays, endoscopy, and possibly CT scan if time permits. However, respiratory distress requires immediate intubation or, if this fails a surgical airway.

Recommendations for airway control differ. In controlled situations when the anatomical derangement is known, and the intubator is experienced, then careful direct laryngoscopy may be tried. However, using a fiberoptic bronchoscope is prudent to directly visualize infraglottic structures.

Have the equipment and personnel immediately available for performing a surgical airway. Blind techniques can potentially complete a partial laryngotracheal disruption and should be avoided if there is any question of laryngeal injury. In severe airway obstruction proceed directly to tracheostomy. Cricothyroidotomy is contraindicated in the presence of blunt laryngotracheal trauma because of the possibility of acute separation of the cricoid from the trachea or the creation of a false passage.

Have a high index of suspicion in the presence of head and neck trauma. Laryngotracheal trauma frequently isn't recognized during initial stabilization and intubation. Conventional intubation, without special precautions, carries the risk of precipitating airway obstruction. Signs include difficulty advancing the tube or the tube tip appearing as a bulging mass in the anterior neck suggesting a false passage.

Traumatic rupture of the trachea and bronchi may produce few initial signs and symptoms if the leak is small. Laryngeal/tracheal injury is more likely to occur with clothesline or handlebar injuries to the neck. These patients are frequently intubated by the time increasing pneumothorax, persistent air leak, and subcutaneous emphysema reveal the injury. If rupture is known prior to intubation, a sterile, single or double lumen tube can be carefully passed, preferably into the uninjured bronchus. Position the cuff below the site of injury. Don't force the tube if you feel any resistance at all. A fiberoptic bronchoscope can be used as a stent to position the tube and minimize the risk of complete tracheobronchial disruption.

Pediatric Patients

Pediatric patients are more prone to airway obstruction and respiratory failure than adults (see Chapter 8) and must be closely observed. Special care must be taken to minimize further insult to their airway. Although awake nasal or oral intubations are common in the adult, these techniques are physically and psychologically traumatic in the infant and small child. They can exacerbate edema and bleeding in an already marginal airway and should be avoided unless absolutely necessary. Intubation is preferable to a surgical airway in the infant or child because tracheostomy is difficult, even in experienced surgical hands.

The incidence of CS trauma is lower in infants (0.5%) and increases with the age of the child and the violence of the accident. It also tends to be higher, at the C1,2 level due to the more horizontal facet joints and laxer ligaments at these levels[16,17]. Thus when intubation is performed in a high-risk victim great care should be taken to stabilize the cervical spine.

Caregiver Safety

My friends and I came across a traffic accident one evening and saw the driver unconscious in the middle of the road. I never hesitated to go into the middle of the road myself to take care of her. My friends, fortunately for me, got out the flares and thought about stopping any traffic that came along until the paramedics got there. Providers concentrate on their patient's welfare sometimes to the exclusion of their own personal safety.

From needle sticks to orthopedic trauma (I personally injured my rotator cuff during a difficult intubation in an awake patient) the risk of provider injury is real. During the SARS outbreak in Canada in 2003, a cluster of health care providers, including at least 3 anesthesiologists, contracted SARS through patient care, despite taking traditional precautions.

What sorts of things do we providers need to worry about?

- Infections (blood born, secretions, and respiratory)
- Needle injuries
- Back injuries
- Shoulder injuries
- Allergy-causing substances
- Trauma from hazards at the scene (fire, explosions, cars)
- Contamination from toxic spills
- Violence (angry family members, people on drugs, gunfire)
- Stress

Who knew our job could be so exciting, or so risky? It's important to be aware of what's going on around you. It's essential to use good body mechanics. Secretions can splash or be spit into your eyes and mouth. You must use protective gear such as gloves, eye protection and cover gowns when appropriate. Wash your hands well and often. Hand sanitizer can be used if soap and water is not available.

In addition to taking care of yourself, you can also potentially injure or infect other caregivers. If you are incautious about how you handle your needles or where you put your contaminated gear, you can unintentionally cause others to suffer.

Stress and the Caregiver

Early therapeutic intervention improves patient outcome and survival. Time pressure puts the burden on caregivers to make rapid decisions, often before all the facts are known. For example, the decision to intubate a minimally symptomatic burn victim is a judgment call which may avoid the potential need for a later emergent tracheostomy — a technique which in burn victims carries a high risk of mortality from infection.

Awkward positioning of trapped victims and the risk of injury to rescuers themselves complicate care at the scene of the accident. Trauma scenes where the caregiver must triage multiple victims and decide who gets care and who does not, can leave the caregiver guilt ridden even for a job well done. The severity of trauma injuries, the need to face the acute grief of a patient's family, and the reminder of one's own mortality, make care of the trauma victim much more emotionally draining for the caregiver than other types of patients.

Unfortunately, it is also true that a patient can develop serious complications or die even if you make all the correct decisions. When dealing with trauma you must do the best you can with what you have, and accept that sometimes even your best isn't good enough.

No matter how skilled you are and how carefully you practice, all of you will participate in one or more cases in your careers where you will question what you did and how you did it. A patient can develop serious complications or die even if you make all the correct decisions. Not being perfect, you can also miss diagnoses and choose what turn out to be suboptimal treatments in hindsight because you have incomplete and rapidly changing information at the time that you are making critical decisions.

Every caregiver faces these difficult emotions and should not face them alone. Sharing your feelings and distress with others can make you a better provider and will help prevent burnout. Therapy should always be considered.

14
RAPID SEQUENCE INDUCTION

Intubation can be a very noxious stimulus — potentially provoking hypertension, tachycardia, ischemia, increased intracranial pressure, bronchospasm and laryngospasm. Seizures, agitation, and struggling can impair the intubation process, causing poor visualization and difficult ventilation.

Use of sedative drugs to induce unconsciousness and muscle relaxants to induce paralysis speeds intubation, is more comfortable for the patient, minimizes the risk of trauma to patient (and provider) and blunts physiologic responses. We use these drugs routinely during general anesthesia.

During an elective anesthetic induction, we typically test our ability to ventilate with bag-valve-mask after induction of unconsciousness but *before* giving a paralytic. In contrast, Rapid Sequence Induction, or RSI, is the administration of induction agent and muscle relaxant *in rapid sequence, without* testing ventilation between. RSI is commonly used in the patient with a full stomach to reduce the window of vulnerability to reflux, vomiting, and aspiration. Cricoid pressure, to avoid aspiration, is held continuously until verification of tracheal placement.

The general order of steps for RSI is: preparation of equipment and patient, cricoid pressure, induction of unconsciousness, paralysis, and intubation. The following discussion gives some guidelines for the use of general anesthesia for intubation, concentrating on the RSI scenario.

Cautions

Don't use induction agents or muscle relaxants if you're not skilled in intubation, ventilation with bag and mask apparatus, and management of complications. These drugs must be used with caution at all times.

Paralyzing a patient during intubation, without testing ventilation first, is betting that patient's life that you'll be able to intubate them—and if needed, ventilate easily. This is a risk benefit equation. If the airway looks normal and the patient is at high risk of aspiration, then it's less risky to do RSI. If you're worried that intubation or ventilation might be difficult, test ventilation as a safety precaution before giving the paralytic. You can still use cricoid pressure.

Muscle relaxants can make fixed airway obstruction worse because of loss of the intrinsic laryngeal muscle tone. If you think intubation or ventilation will be difficult, then seriously consider awake/sedated intubation.

Induction agents can cause myocardial depression, hypotension, and cardiovascular collapse in the hemodynamically unstable patient. They can interact with other drugs a patient has taken. Adjust the dose to the patient's status and monitor vital signs carefully.

Preparing Equipment and Personnel

A useful mnemonic that helps us ensure our equipment is ready is S.O.A.P., which stands for:

- **S** — **S**uction, equipment
- **O** — **O**xygen (and for anesthesia providers "**O**ther gases" as well)
- **A** — **A**irway equipment (laryngoscope, ETT, etc) and **A**ncillary equipment (such as monitors)
- **P** — **P**harmacy (appropriate drugs for induction, resuscitation and ongoing sedation to tolerate the tube)

Before you induce a patient, review S.O.A.P. to check that you're ready.

You need at least 2 people to perform RSI: the intubator and the assistant providing the cricoid pressure. If the patient is unstable, you should consider using a helper to inject the IV medications and monitor vital signs, allowing the intubator to concentrate on the airway. When cervical spine precautions are needed you will need a potential 4th person to stabilize the neck.

Preparing the Patient

Pre-oxygenate as much as time allows. Giving 100% FiO_2 with a tight fitting face mask for 2-5 minutes is optimal. Room air is roughly 79% nitrogen, 21% oxygen. Preoxygenation washes out nitrogen, leaving more oxygen in reserve and allowing a longer apneic period for the intubation process.

If you don't have time to wait, ask the cooperative patient to take 5 maximal breaths of 100% O_2 or hyperventilate the apneic patient with bag-valve mask oxygen. It's optimal to raise the patient's O_2 sat to 100% before you start, although this may not be possible depending on the circumstances and pathology.

Apply the cardiac, oximeter, and BP monitors. Secure intravenous access.

Optimize position as much as possible. Unless contraindicated, place the head in the sniffing position. If cervical spine injury is possible, stabilize the head.

Estimate patient's weight, calculate drug dosages, and draw up into syringes.

Consider premedication with lidocaine or atropine.

Lidocaine (1 mg/kg IV) can blunt the hypertensive response, help protect against increased intracranial pressure, decreases the risk of arrythmias, and weakens the cough reflex. Give it about one minute before induction. It usually doesn't sedate the patient, but it can if the patient is frail or compromised.

Atropie is another common premedication in children. Succinylcholine, a short acting paralytic often used in RSI, stimulates the vagus nerve and can cause bradycardia, most commonly in children less than five years old. Bradycardia in young children decreases cardiac output and can cause hypotension and hypoxia. Premedication with atropine (0.02 mg/kg I.V. or I.M., minimal dose 0.1 mg and maximal up to 1 mg) blocks this reflex, helps dry secretions, and can decrease the risk of bronchospasm. Routine atropine premedication of adults is *not* recommended, unless the patient is bradycardic, because it can potentially cause excessive tachycardia.

Cricoid Pressure for RSI

Patients requiring emergency intubation are at high risk for aspiration. Hypotension often causes nausea and vomiting. Trauma can delay or stop gastric emptying — leading to stomachs full of highly acid and often particulate material, even hours after the meal. Cricoid pressure pinches the esophagus closed against the cervical spine, thereby helping to prevent passive regurgitation. It can also help visualization during laryngoscopy.

Have your helper apply cricoid pressure and hold until patient has been intubated, balloon of ETT has been inflated, position of tube tip has been assured, and ETT has been secured in place. If the patient vomits, release pressure and roll the patient on his side, suctioning to clear the airway. Holding cricoid pressure during active vomiting theoretically risks esophageal rupture.

Sedative Agents

All drugs used for induction of anesthesia must be given by or under the direction of a physician or anesthesia provider knowledgeable of the indications and contraindications of their use as well as skilled in airway management and ventilation. Sedatives used for emergency induction of anesthesia for intubation should optimally have rapid onset (see Table 14-1).

Tailoring the induction agent to the disease state is especially important because the choice of drug can either improve or worsen the symptoms. For example, etomidate and ketamine tend to raise blood pressure, useful in unstable patients, whereas propofol tends to lower it. Ketamine should be avoided in the brain injured patient because it can increase intracranial pressure and cause hypertension. Ketamine, however, is useful in asthmatics because it's a bronchodilator.

Etomidate, Propofol, Ketamine, and Midazolam are the most common agents currently used in emergent RSI. Thiopental is less commonly used today and will not be discussed. Fentanyl is a potent narcotic most often used as an adjunct to intubation as an analgesic to reduce the noxious stimulus.

Etomidate

- **advantages**:
  - good amnestic
  - minimal cardiac depression: tends to maintain BP, P, cardiac output
- **dose**: 0.2 - 0.6 mg/kg IV
  - 0.3 mg adequate for most patients
  - use lower doses in frail/unstable patients
- **onset**: 30-60 sec.
- **duration**: 5 - 10 min.
- **problems:**
  - myoclonic activity: mild to moderate, may appear seizure-like
  - nausea and vomiting

- injection painful, especially in small veins
- 24-48 hr adrenal suppression after induction dose, consider steroids
- **contraindications**: sensitivity to drug

Propofol (Diprivan)
- **advantages:**
  - versatile: low doses for sedation, higher doses for induction
  - continuous infusions for sedation or complete general anesthesia
  - good amnestic
  - short acting: wears off quickly
- **dose**: 1-2 mg/kg IV for induction (lower doses for sedation)
- **onset**: 40 sec.
- **duration**: 5-10 min.
- **problems**:
  - hypotension from myocardial depression and vasodilation
  - short acting (emergently intubated will need sedation with longer acting agent (e.g. midazolam) to tolerate endotracheal tube
- **contraindications**:
  - generic preserved with sulfite: avoid use of generic in sulfite allergy

Ketamine
- **advantages:**
  - good amnestic
  - increases sympathetic tone (BP)
  - bronchodilator
  - minimal respiratory depression as solo agent
  - maintains airway reflexes (but always protect pt. from aspiration)
  - good analgesia
- **dose**: 2 mg/kg IV
- **onset**: 30-60 seconds
- **duration**: 10-15 min.
- **note**: nystagmus common
- **problems**
  - decreases seizure threshold
  - hallucinations: treat with midazolam, quiet reassuring environment

- increased salivation
- increased intracranial pressure (ICP)
- increased intraocular pressure
- **contraindications**:
    - hypertensive crisis
    - leaking aneurysm
    - status epilepticus
    - risk of elevated ICP (closed head injury, brain tumor, etc.)
    - open globe (eye)

Midazolam (Versed)
- **advantages:**
    - good amnestic
    - anti-convulsant
- **dose**: 0.2-0.5 mg/kg IV up to 5 mg initial dose for induction
    - consider decreased dose if systolic BP is 80 – 100 mmHg.
- **onset**: 1-3 min.
- **duration**: 20-45 min.
- **problems**:
    - hypotension (decreased venous return and systemic resistance)
    - apnea with larger doses
- **contraindications**:
    - sensitivity to drug

Fentanyl
- **advantages**
    - excellent analgesic
    - blunts sympathetic increases in BP, P, and mean arterial pressure
- **dose**: 1-3 mcg/kg
- **onset**: 1-3 min
- **duration**:
- **problems**:
    - apnea with larger doses

Which Induction Agent?

The choice of induction agent should be based on the patient's medical problem and hemodynamic stability (see Table 14-2). Each has advantages and disadvantages in certain conditions. If you're performing RSI infrequently, the best plan is to use a routine combination of drugs unless there is a contraindication. That way you will be very familiar with its effects and potential complications.

Table 14-1. Suggested Doses For Induction of Unconsciousness

Drug	Intravenous Dose/Duration	Advantages	Disadvantages Potential Side Effects
Etomidate (Amidate) 2 mg/ml	• 0.2-0.6 mg/kg • onset rapid • lasts 5-20 min	• hemodynamic stability • amnesia	• pain on injection • seizure-like movements • adrenocortical suppression • lowers serum cortisol • high incidence n/v
Ketamine 10-100 mg/ml	• 1-2 mg/kg • onset rapid • lasts 10-20 min	• dissociative anesthetic • bronchodilator • useful in bronchospasm • transient rise BP/pulse • useful in shock • good analgesia	• increased ICP • tachycardia • hypertension • increased secretions • active airway reflexes • hallucinations • lowers seizure threshold
Midazolam (Versed) 1 - 5 mg/ml	• 0.2-0.3 mg/kg • onset 1-3 min • lasts 20-45 min	• amnesia • anticonvulsant • no active metabolites • water soluble • reversal with flumazenil	• hypotension possible • apnea • no analgesia
Propofol (Diprivan) 10mg/ml	• 1-2 mg/kg • onset rapid • lasts 5-10 min	rapid recovery amnesia	• rapid recovery • generic contains sulfite • potential allergen • hypotension • pain on injection • hypotension • myoclonic movements • infection risk • propofol infusion syndrome • no analgesia
Fentanyl	1-3 mcg/kg	• blunts sympathetic response opioid analgesia • short acting	• respiratory depression • hypotension • chest wall rigidity if mask ventilation needed

Paralysis: Muscle Relaxants

Muscle relaxants, or neuromuscular blockers, are medications that produce temporary paralysis of all the patient's muscles. They are commonly used in combination with general anesthetic induction drugs to allow rapid intubation as well as to produce a relaxed operative field during surgery.

Muscle relaxants themselves do not produce loss of consciousness or amnesia. They should rarely if ever be used without an amnestic in the conscious patient. Paralysis and awake intubation could be a horrifying experience for a patient — who would appear peacefully asleep to the health care provider. Hypertension, tachycardia, and possibly increased intracranial pressure could also occur. Muscle relaxants without some form of sedative should only be used in extreme emergencies, when the use of the sedative represents a greater risk to the patient than the failure to use one. In this rare event, continue to reassure the patient — even if you feel they are incapable of hearing you.

There are two types of muscle relaxants: depolarizers like succinylcholine and nondepolarizers like vecuronium, atracurium, and pancuronium. (Table 14-2).

Normal muscle contraction occurs when the electrical signal from the brain reaches the nerve ending and releases the neurotransmitter acetylcholine. Acetylcholine crosses the gap between the nerve endings and combines with its receptor at the neuromuscular junction on the muscle, releasing calcium throughout the muscle. The muscle contracts as the result. Acetylcholine is quickly removed from the receptor by breakdown by the enzyme pseudocholinesterase. Calcium returns to storage, and the muscle relaxes, ready for the next cycle. To use an analogy, it is as though a key (acetylcholine) has entered the lock (or receptor) and then opened the lock (caused the muscle to contract). The key is then rapidly removed and the lock is ready to be opened again by the next key.

A depolarizer like succinylcholine produces paralysis by combining with the acetylcholine receptor. All the muscles in the body contract simultaneously. These massed contractions are called fasciculations. The muscles then become flaccid. The muscles remain paralyzed for many minutes because the enzyme pseudocholinesterase takes much longer to break down the drug than the natural neurotransmitter. In our analogy, the alternate key (succinylcholine) has entered and opened the lock (caused muscle contractions) but then becomes stuck for several minutes during which time the lock cannot be reopened (the muscle remains paralyzed).

Nondepolarizer type drugs, on the other hand, block the acetylcholine receptors but do not fire them, producing flaccid paralysis from their onset. Here our key enters the lock but cannot open it. However, the real key can't enter the blocked keyhole to open it either and the muscle remains paralyzed until the molecule leaves the receptor.

Succinylcholine: a depolarizing muscle relaxant

- **advantages:**
  - rapid onset
  - short acting
  - can be given intramuscular
- **dose**: 1-1.5 mg/kg IV, (2-4 mg/kg deep IM)

- **onset**: 30-60 sec. IV, (2-4 min IM)
- **duration**: 4-6 min.
- **problems**:
  - muscle soreness,
  - bradycardia
  - tachycardia
  - increased intracranial pressure
  - increased intraocular pressure
  - increased intragastric pressure
  - life-threatening hyperkalemia with cardiac arrest
    - in patients with extensive muscle damage or denervation, such as: spinal cord injury, anoxic brain injury, severe muscle injuries or burns, motor nerve injury or tentanus and, rarely, intra-abdominal sepsis. Reaction develops variably from 24 hrs to 2 wks following injury. Most practitioners avoid in acute extensive crush or burn injuries because actual time of onset of increased risk unknown.
  - malignant hyperthermia
    - rare but potentially fatal hypermetabolic state
    - signs include muscle rigidity — often heralded by masseter rigidity
    - unexplained tachycardia, metabolic acidosis, and hypercarbia
    - fever, often rises in excess of 106°F or 41 °C
    - If masseter or generalized persistent muscle rigidity is encountered after the use of Succinylcholine, the drug should not be repeated. Monitor the patient must closely for fever or other instability.

Malignant Hyperthermia Hotline manned 24 hrs per day by MHAUS, the Malignant Hyperthermia Association of the United States (http://www.mhaus.org/).

- **contraindications**:
  - hyperkalemia,
  - paraplegia (potential severe hyperkalemia)
  - pseudocholinesterase deficiency (prolonged paralysis)
  - severe burns (potential severe hyperkalemia)
  - demyelinating nervous system disease (potential severe hyperkalemia)
  - patient or family history malignant hyperthermia
- **Note**: Because of the potential problems with Succinylcholine, use of nondepolarizers during intubation is becoming more routine. They should be used with great caution since their prolonged action can cause problems if intubation is difficult.

MHAUS CONTACT PHONE NUMBERS	
In USA and Canada:	Outside the US call:
1 (800) 644-9739	0011 315 464 7079
1 (800) MH HYPER	
http://www.mhaus.org	

Vecuronium (Norcuron): a nondepolarizing muscle relaxant

- **advantages:**
  - no histamine release or effect on BP or pulse
  - no effect on BP, P, cardiac output
  - no effect on potassium
  - does not trigger malignant hyperthermia
- **dose**:
  - 0.1-0.2 mg/kg IV (higher doses allow faster intubating conditions but last longer)
  - Note: when succinylcholine used, 1/10th of the paralyzing dose can be given as a defasiculating dose, a dose to minimize fasciculations caused by the succinylcholine
- **onset**: 1-3 min.
- **duration**: 45-60 min. (can be reversed in 20-30 min.)
- **problems**: can't be pharmacologically reversed in less than 20 min
- **contraindications**: inability to ventilate patient before use

Rocuronium (Zemuron): a nondepolarizing muscle relaxant

- **advantages:**
  - faster onset than vecuronium
  - shorter acting than vecuronium with lower doses
    - useful for short general anesthetics and in intubations that turn out to be unexpectedly difficult, requiring wake up.
- **dose**:
  - 0.6-1.2 mg/kg IV
  - Note: with succinylcholine, 1/10th of paralyzing dose can be given as defasiculating dose
- **onset**: 1-1.5 min.
- **duration**: 15-150 min. (dose dependent)

- **problems**:
  - rare anaphylaxis
  - tachycardia
  - bronchospasm
  - rare anaphylaxis
- **contraindications:** inability to ventilate patient before use

Never use any long-acting nondepolarizing muscle relaxant if you have any question about your ability to ventilate or intubate. Guard against aspiration with cricoid pressure and suction as necessary. Be prepared to completely support ventilations during the intubation period and for several hours afterward.

Reversal of Muscle Relaxation

Neuromuscular blockade by muscle relaxants will eventually resolve spontaneously, although it may be prolonged in patients with severe liver or renal failure. However, there are many times when it is to the patient's advantage to have the neuromuscular blockade reversed. The end of a surgical procedure, preparation for weaning from the ventilator, and the need to follow neurologic exams are examples.

The drug class used to reverse neuromuscular blockade is called a cholinesterase inhibitor. These drugs temporarily inhibit the function of the enzyme pseudocholinesterase. The result is increased availability of the transmitter acetylcholine at the muscle end plate receptor. If sufficient time has passed for the concentration of the blocking agent to drop, then flooding of the receptor with acetylcholine will allow the muscle to contract.

Only nondepolarizing type muscle relaxants such as vecuronium should be reversed. The use of reversal agents on routine succinylcholine blockade will prolong the block for many hours because the inhibition of pseudocholinesterase will also delay breakdown of the succinylcholine.

The dose used is either 0.035-0.07 mg/kg of neostigmine or 0.5-1 mg/kg of tensilon. Giving too much reversal agent will also cause paralysis, because it then interferes with the natural neurotransmitter, acetylcholine, as well. If adequate reversal of neuromuscular blockade does not occur after the maximum reversal dose is given, then ventilate the patient until the blockade resolves on its own.

It's essential that the reversal agent always be given with either an equal volume of atropine or glycopyrrolate or serious bradycardia will result. The pulse rate should be monitored carefully for the next 10-20 minutes to ensure that late onset bradycardia does not occur. Use of glycopyrrolate, which has a longer half life, can help to prevent this side effect.

The patient should meet extubation criteria prior to removal of the endotracheal tube. Intact strength should be tested. The various tests have differing sensitivity for detecting residual muscle relaxation (see Chapter 16).

It's worth noting that if you must use succinylcholine to reintubate an patient who has recently been reversed with neostigmine, the muscle relaxation may last many hours because the inhibition of pseudocholinesterase prevents breakdown of the succinylcholine.

Table 14-2. Muscle Relaxants

Succinylcholine	• relaxation 1.5-2 mg/kg • onset 1 min • duration of effect 5 min • recovery time: 20 min	• rapid onset • short duration	• increased intraocular P • increased ICP • tachycardia/bradycardia • hypertension • muscle pain • prolonged relaxation in certain conditions • hyperkalemia • cardiac arrest • malignant hyperthermia
Vecuronium	• defasciculation: 0.01 mg/kg • relaxation: 0.1 mg/kg • for quicker onset: 0.15-0.2 mg/kg • onset 2-3 min • duration of effect 30 min • recovery time: 40-60 min	• hemodynamic stability • no dysrrythmia • min cumulative effect	• slower onset • not for difficult airways • longer duration
Rocuronium	• defasciculation: 0.01 mg/kg • relaxation: 0.6-1.2 mg/kg • onset 1-1.5 min • duration of effect 15-150m • recovery time: dose dependent	• hemodynamic stability • no dysrrythmia • short duration • rapid onset	• slower onset • not for difficult airways • longer duration with higher doses • anaphylaxis reported

15
AWAKE INTUBATION

Awake intubation while the patient is spontaneously breathing is sometimes required for patient safety. Awake intubation can be performed using standard laryngoscopy techniques, but it is more commonly done using specialty intubation techniques such as blind nasal or fiberoptic intubation.

Many providers are uncomfortable with performing awake intubations and leave it as a last resort. There are a variety of reasons for this discomfort, including lack of experience and/or the fear that the patient will remember the intubation and think poorly of their care. However, awake intubation can be a safe and comfortable strategy in many clinical situations and all providers should develop expertise with one or more techniques of choice — before an emergency forces them to use one.

Awake or Not Awake? — That is the Question

When should we think about awake intubation? Making that decision is a judgment call. As we saw in Chapter 9, many of the signs for evaluating an airway prior to intubation are highly predictive of success if they are *negative*, but have a significant number of false positives[1]. In others words, the signs may predict the patient will be difficult to intubate when, in fact, they are not difficult. The reverse is unfortunately also true. The patient may look easy to intubate, but they're not. We always have to be prepared for the unexpected.

Questions I ask myself when deciding whether to intubate awake.

1. **Will the patient be difficult to ventilate?** Ability to ventilate is always more important than ability intubate. Try to imagine what might get in the way of a good mask seal. Conditions that may make the patient a challenge to ventilate, especially if occurring together, include:
    a. BMI greater than 30: especially if the neck is short with a large neck circumference
    b. Full beard
    c. Mallampati Class 3 or 4
    d. Edentulous
    e. Sleep apnea or snoring
    f. Abnormal facial anatomy or trauma
2. **Will the patient tolerate the induction medications?** If the patient is in severe shock or respiratory failure, awake intubation may be less stressful and more likely to maintain hemodynamic stability.
3. **Will the patient tolerate any period of apnea** if the intubation *is* difficult?
4. **Is there a history of difficult intubation?** Most patients don't come with this history, but you won't know unless you ask or look at available records.

5. **Is there an obvious abnormality predisposing to difficult intubation or difficult ventilation?** Can the patient open their mouth widely enough to accept the laryngoscope? Is their thyromental distance extremely short? Is there a large tumor or swelling filling their mouth or submandibular space? If so, consider awake intubation.
6. **Is the patient at risk of vomiting and aspiration?** We certainly intubate patients with full stomachs all the time using rapid sequence induction. However, if we have a patient who we are worried may be difficult to intubate, and the patient is actively vomiting or at high risk of aspiration, then awake intubation may be safer.
7. **Is it dangerous to move this patient's neck?** When the patient has an unstable cervical spine, careful awake intubation with neck stabilization and monitoring of neurologic signs may be the safest choice.

Contraindications to Awake Intubation?

Are there patients who should not be intubated awake? Yes there are.
1. **Patient refusal:** A patient who is awake, alert and oriented and therefore competent to refuse treatment after being told the risks and alternatives can refuse awake intubation. However, most patients are initially hesitant out of fear. Approach them with empathy, explain the facts regarding risks, and a plan outlining their safety and comfort and they will rarely refuse.
2. **Inability to cooperate:** Awake intubation absolutely requires cooperation between patient and provider. If the patient can't cooperate, the risks of injuring the patient (or the provider) can be significant. Uncooperative patients include most younger children, most developmentally delayed patients, and the intoxicated or combative patient.
3. **Local anesthetic allergy**: Awake intubation with a *well-anesthetized* airway is not that uncomfortable, even with light or no sedation. If you can't numb the airway safely, then awake intubation would be difficult and painful to perform, leading to loss of cooperation and potentially patient refusal.

Awake Patient Preparation

Awake intubation is more difficult in a poorly prepared patient. Airway anesthesia and judicious sedation are the keys to improving cooperation, minimizing hemodynamic changes, and decreasing gaging and vomiting.

Preparation optimally consists of a series of separate but equally important steps:
1. administering a drying agent,
2. vasoconstricting the nose,
3. numbing the oro/nasopharynx, providing
4. sedation and last
5. communicating with the patient[2].

The clinical situation will dictate how involved a prep you can perform.

Drying The Airway: The First Step

Always consider giving an intravenous drying agent. Normal airway secretions dilute and wash away any topical local anesthetics we apply. Secretions obscure landmarks. Moreover, our intubation attempt will further increase secretions.

Drying agents work quickly to prevent release of new secretions when given intravenously, but they don't dry secretions that are already in the airway. Optimally give them at least 10–15 minutes before the intubation to allow time to work.

Either glycopyrrolate, 0.2-0.4 mg IV, or atropine 0.4-0.6 mg IV are effective. While both have fairly rapid onset IV, there is a delay of 30 min to 2 hours with IM, PO or subcutaneous administration. Glycopyrrolate is often preferred as it is less likely to cause acute tachycardia.

Nasal Vasoconstriction: The Second Step

All local anesthetics, except cocaine, cause vasodilation. Vasodilation causes edema, narrows the nasal passage, and makes nosebleeds more likely.

Vasoconstrictors, such as phenylephrine or oxymetazoline (Afrin), shrink the mucous membrane, thereby dilating the nasal passage. They also minimize bleeding by shrinking capillary beds. You can use nasal spray, drops or add your constrictor to your topical solution. The use of 5% cocaine liquid numbs as well as vasoconstricts, but is often unavailable emergently — even in the OR setting.

Nasal vasoconstrictors takes 10–15 minutes, so give them early. However, any vasoconstriction will help — even if you don't have time to wait for peak effect. Unless contraindicated, prepare both nasal passages to allow you to switch nostrils immediately if insertion on the first side of the nose is difficult.

Consider a nasal vasoconstrictor even when oral intubation is planned in order to allow you to switch to a nasal insertion site immediately if problems occur.

Numbing the Airway: The Third Step

Use of minimal sedation may sometimes be the best way to ensure a cooperative patient safe from aspiration. The key to using minimal sedation, however, is good local anesthesia. Inadequate airway anesthesia leads to coughing, gagging, and vomiting. No amount of sedation can compensate for inadequate airway anesthesia. Let's look at noninvasive as well as invasive numbing techniques.

Noninvasive Numbing of the Nasopharynx

Mucous membrane absorbs local anesthetic rapidly. Topical techniques can be highly effective, allowing you to avoid the need for injections.

The nasal mucosa is supplied by the sphenopalatine ganglion, the network of nerves supplying in part the nose and nasopharynx. The ganglion is located at the very back of the nasal passage.

Filling the nostril with lidocaine is a technique that is easy to perform in the field and requires no special equipment. Lidocaine is readily available in multiple forms. Lidocaine gel is fairly liquid and easily "sniffed," while the ointment is viscous and must be allowed a few minutes to melt. As the gel melts the patient will often aspirate a small amount, numbing the trachea. The patient must be able to tolerate having the nose plugged with gel or ointment for a few minutes.

A more precise way to rapidly numb this nerve network is to place a generous glob of lidocaine ointment on the tip of a cotton tipped applicator.[2] You can also soak the tip with 4% lidocaine liquid. Gently advance into the nose until the patient winces. Stop for 30 seconds

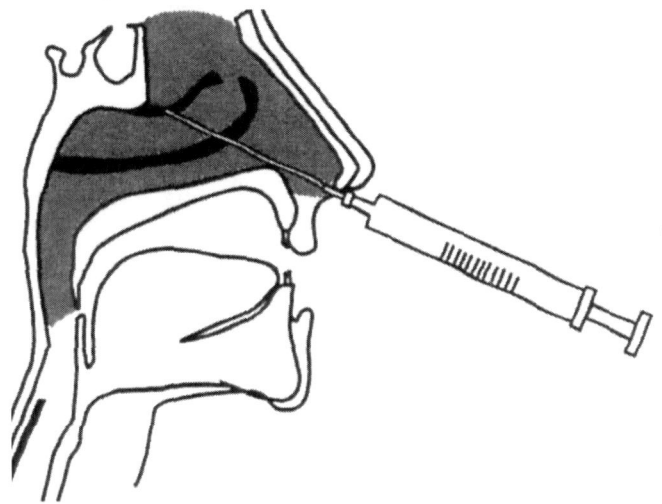

Fig. 15-1. Using an angiocath to numb the sphenopalatine ganglion

until it numbs that area, then advance until he winces again. Keep repeating until the swab is as deep as you can insert. Allow the local anesthetic several minutes to work in contact with the posterior wall.

As an alternative, use a plastic I.V. catheter (Fig. 15-1), such as an 18-20g, to spray 2 ml of 2-4% lidocaine liquid onto the nasopharyngeal mucosa toward the posterior superior aspect of each nasal passage (total 4 ml). This application numbs the back of the nasal passage and sphenopalatine ganglion which can be difficult to reach.

You can use Cetacaine or other local anesthetic spray to numb the nose, but warn the patient that it will sting for about 20 seconds. Always keep track of the total local anesthetic dose since absorption through the mucous membrane is rapid and toxicity can occur. Limit plain lidocaine to less than 5 mg/kg.

Once numbing has started, I frequently pass progressively larger nasal airways coated with local anesthetic ointment. I personally don't believe that this practice further dilates the nasal passage. However, it does enhance numbing and tests the passage for size and signs of obstruction. Meanwhile, the patient becomes accustomed to the passage of nasal tubes, making passage of the larger endotracheal tube more tolerable. Nasal topicalization can be accompanied by other nerve blocks.

Noninvasive Blocking of the Glossopharyngeal

The glossopharyngeal nerve controls the gag reflex, which is the strongest protective reflex. For a noninvasive way to block the glossopharyngeal, have the patient open their mouth widely and stick out their tongue. Use a tongue blade in the non-dominant hand to shift the tongue toward the midline. This traction forms a gutter along the floor of the mouth between the tongue and the teeth. The gutter ends in a "U" shaped cul de sac where the gutter meets the palatoglossal arch. The glossopharyngeal nerve runs under this gutter (Fig 15-2).

Place small sponges or gauzes soaked in 4% lidocaine or covered in lidocaine ointment into the gutters bilaterally for 3-5 minutes[2]. *Don't forget to remove them or the patient might aspirate them.* Using cotton tipped swabs or wrapping a gauze around a tongue blade allows precise placement with little likelihood of misplacing the swabs. Let the patient bite down on the swabs to hold them in position for several minutes, allowing the local anesthetic to soak into the mucous membrane and numb the glossopharyngeal nerves. The patient might gag as this process begins but will soon tolerate the process better as the gag reflex is blocked.

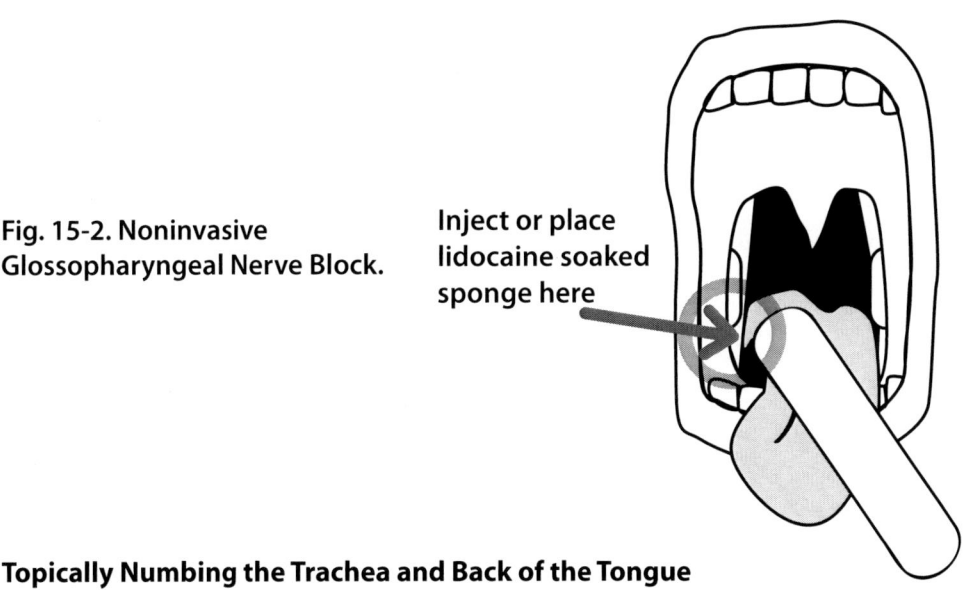

Fig. 15-2. Noninvasive Glossopharyngeal Nerve Block.

Inject or place lidocaine soaked sponge here

Topically Numbing the Trachea and Back of the Tongue

There are several preformed catheters and atomizers designed to allow aerosolyzing local anesthetic liquid around the base of the tongue and into the trachea. However, you can use a simple syringe filled with 5 ml of 2% lidocaine attached to a curved angiocath or IV extension tubing to squirt or drip the local anesthetic on the back of the tongue and into the trachea. You may not need all of the solution. The patient will often cough until the trachea becomes numb.

A glob of lidocaine ointment on a tongue blade can be placed on the back of the tongue and allowed to melt over several minutes. This lidocaine "lollypop" numbs the posterior oropharynx, and blunts the gag reflex. Local anesthetic will dribble over the epiglottis and into the trachea.

Another technique uses a nebulizer, such as an Acorn® nebulizer, to aerosolyze to deposit a fine spray of droplets onto the mucous membranes and larger airways. We frequently use this device to treat bronchospasm, making them common to find in the hospital setting. Place 3-5 ml of 1-2% lidocaine into the nebulizer. Attach the nebulizer to your oxygen delivery system, such as a face mask. Wait until the liquid disappears, usually 15-20 minutes. By this time the entire pharynx, larynx, and trachea of the patient will be numb.

Invasive Nerve Blocks

A few patients may need supplementation to topical local for those nerve endings running deep to the mucosa. There is no single anatomic site where one nerve block can anesthetize the entire airway, however there are several easily performed nerve blocks that carry minimal risk to the patient yet rapidly provide profound analgesia. Such nerve blocks require knowledge of the anatomy and a recognition of the potential complications of each block. While I don't recommend them for the occasional intubator, they're valuable to the experienced intubator.

Transtracheal Block

Transtracheal block anesthetizes the vocal cords, the subglottic larynx and the trachea. It's one of the more common blocks since it's easy to perform.

The ideal patient position is supine with the neck hyperextended. Tell the patient not to talk, swallow or cough. (Fig. 15-3, Mov. 15-1, KF. 5-1abc) Use a TB syringe to raise a skin wheal over but not through the cricothyroid membrane. Use the left hand to stabilize

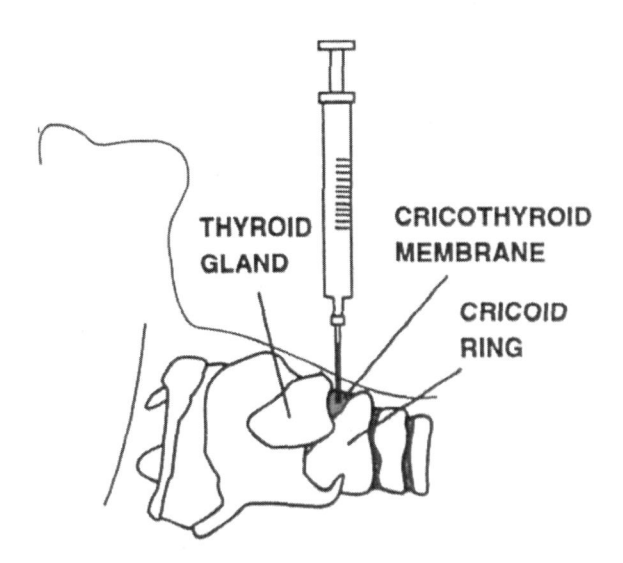

Fig. 15-3. Transtracheal Nerve Block.

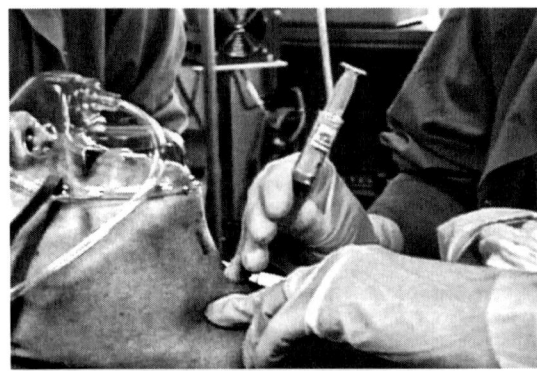

Keyframe 15-1a. Identify the cricothyroid membrane. Puncture the membrane with your needle. You will feel a "pop".

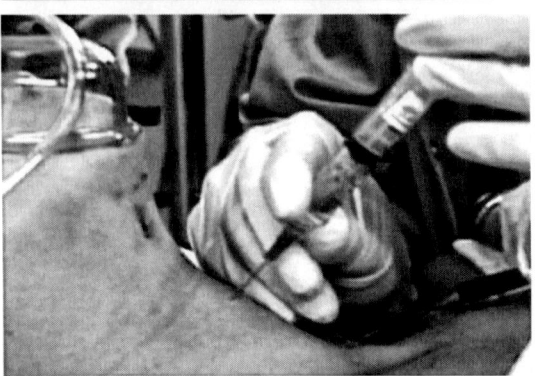

Keyframe 15-1b. Aspirate to confirm that the tip is inside the tracheal lumen.

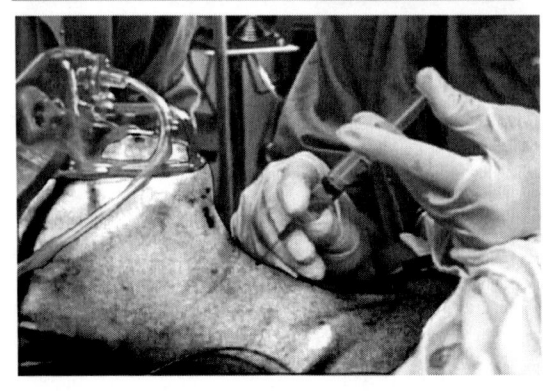

Keyframe 15-1c. Inject your local anesthetic. Be prepared that your patient may cough. Don't injure the patient or yourself with the needle if this occurs.

the trachea by placing the thumb and third finger on either side of the thyroid cartilage. Use the left index finger to identify the cricothyroid membrane in the midline. Pick up the syringe with 4-5 milliliters of local anesthetic with your right hand like a pencil. Aim the 20-22 g needle slightly caudad. You will feel resistance as the needle enters the cricothyroid membrane and then loss of resistance as the needle enters the trachea. You aim caudad so that your needle's point can't traumatize the cords from below.

Some providers use 25-26 g needles. However, slower injection through the smaller needle means holding the needle firmly in place while the patient coughs. You can inject more rapidly through a 21g or 23 g needle.

It's important to verify that the tip of the needle is inside the trachea, not in the soft tissue overlying it or behind it, inside the esophagus. Ensure that you can aspirate air freely before injecting local anesthetic.

Instead of using a needle, you can insert a 22-20 g IV catheter into the trachea using the same technique. Remove the needle and attach your syringe. You may now inject repeatedly without fear of needle trauma when the patient coughs.

The patient will cough during injection so stabilize the head, especially when using cervical spine precautions. Coughing helps nebulize the local anesthetic over the top and bottom of the vocal cords.

A full stomach is a relative contraindication as loss of sensation below the vocal cords makes silent aspiration possible. Other relative contraindications include a fat, short neck, bleeding tendencies, a large thyroid or overlying tumors.

Glossopharyngeal Nerve Block

The glossopharyngeal nerve gives sensation to the posterior third of the tongue, uvula, soft palate, and the rest of the pharynx.

In the majority of patients, topicalization of the oropharyngeal mucosa blunts the gag reflex. However in some patients the gag reflex is so pronounced that blockade of the glossopharyngeal nerve should be considered, since blockade of this nerve anesthetizes the deep pressure sensors in the posterior 3rd of the tongue. A glossopharyngeal block lets you insert an oral airway within about one minute without causing the patient to gag.

Topicalize the oropharynx. Place the patient in a sitting position with the physician facing the patient on the side opposite the one to be blocked. Have the patient open their mouth widely and stick out their tongue. Use a tongue blade in the non-dominant hand to shift the tongue medially. This traction forms a gutter along the floor of the mouth between the tongue and the teeth. The gutter ends in a "U" shaped cul de sac where the gutter meets the palatoglossal arch.

Although you can use a 25 g spinal needle to perform the block, a 23 g tonsillar needle makes the block easier and somewhat safer (Mov. 15-2, KF. 5-2abc). A tonsillar needle has an angulated tip smaller than the rest of the needle to prevent deep insertion. Tonsillar needles are great if you have one. If not, you can use an angled spinal needle and pay close attention to the depth of penetration.

Insert your spinal or tonsillar needle at the base of the cul-de-sac and advance 0.25-0.5 cm. Make sure to aspirate before injecting because the carotid artery and jugular vein are right behind your needle tip. If you aspirate blood your needle tip may be inside a vessel. Redirect the needle more medially. A small dose of local anesthetic into the carotid can cause seizures.

254   Anyone Can Intubate

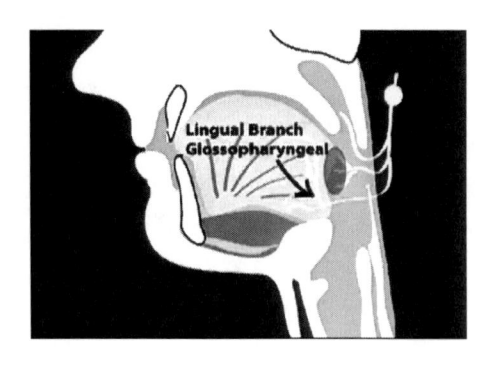

Keyframe 15-2a. The glossopharyngeal nerve supplies the oropharynx and posterior third of the tongue. It also carries the gag reflex.

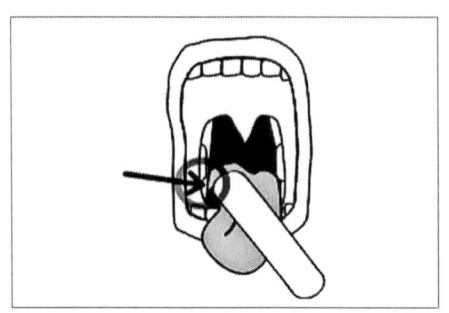

Keyframe 15-2b. You can block this nerve at the gutter where the tongue meets the anterior tonsillar pillar.

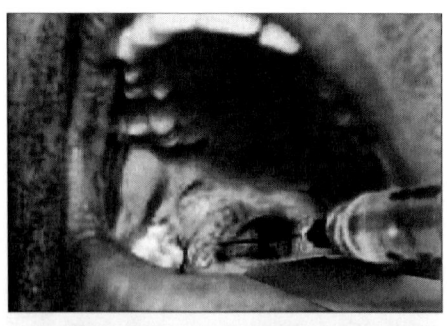

Keyframe 15-2c. The carotid artery and jugular vein lie underneath this gutter. Insert the needle 1-2 mm only and aspirate carefully before injecting.

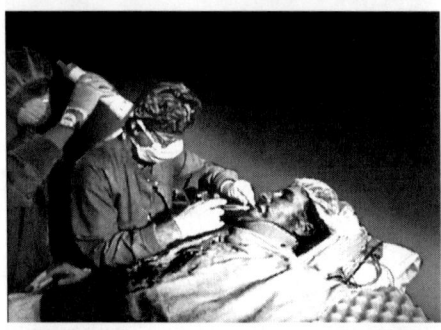

Keyframe 15-2d. Having your patient with the head slightly elevated can make injection easier.

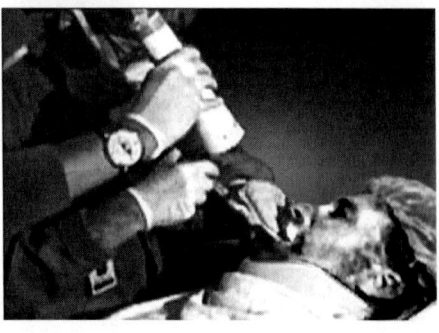

Keyframe 15-2e. This patient is well prepared, and knows what to expect. This is more effective than heavy sedation since your patient is cooperative yet comfortable.

If you aspirate air the needle tip is too deep and has gone through the arch. Withdraw the needle slightly until you can no longer aspirate air. Inject 2-3 ml of 1-2% lidocaine bilaterally. Repeat for the other side.

Combined superior laryngeal and glossopharyngeal blocks give excellent laryngeal anesthesia and depress the gag reflex. You may cautiously use them on patients with full stomachs because they preserve motor function. They preserve sensation below the vocal cords so any secretions or blood falling on or below the cords will still stimulate coughing.

Superior Laryngeal Nerve Block

The internal laryngeal nerve is a branch of the superior laryngeal nerve. It provides sensation over the laryngeal surface of the epiglottis, the larynx above the vocal cords, the vallecula, and the lower pharynx. It penetrates the thyrohyoid membrane midway between the hyoid bone and the thyroid cartilage about 1 cm anterior to the superior thyroid cornu.

Pressing on the opposite side of the larynx makes the landmarks more obvious (Fig. 15-4). Clean the skin with antiseptic. Find the superior thyroid cornu on the block side. The carotid sheath lies beneath your finger and the internal laryngeal nerve lies in front of your fingertip.

Insert a 25 or 26 g needle attached to a 3 ml syringe into the thyrohyoid membrane. You can start by touching the thyroid cartilage itself with your needle tip and then gently walking the needle tip upward until you step off the edge of the cartilage and into the membrane. You will feel resistance when you enter the membrane. Inject 1-2 ml of 1-2% lidocaine on each side. If you can't feel the membrane, advance into the hypopharynx and aspirate air. Withdraw the needle slowly until you can no longer aspirate air. Your needle tip should now lie just inside the membrane. Aspirate before you inject to avoid intravascular injections.

A block here preserves motor control of the cricothyroid muscle.

To avoid injection, it is possible, though not common, to place small sponges or gauzes soaked in 2% lidocaine into the pyriform fossae bilaterally for 3-5 minutes. *Don't forget to remove them.*

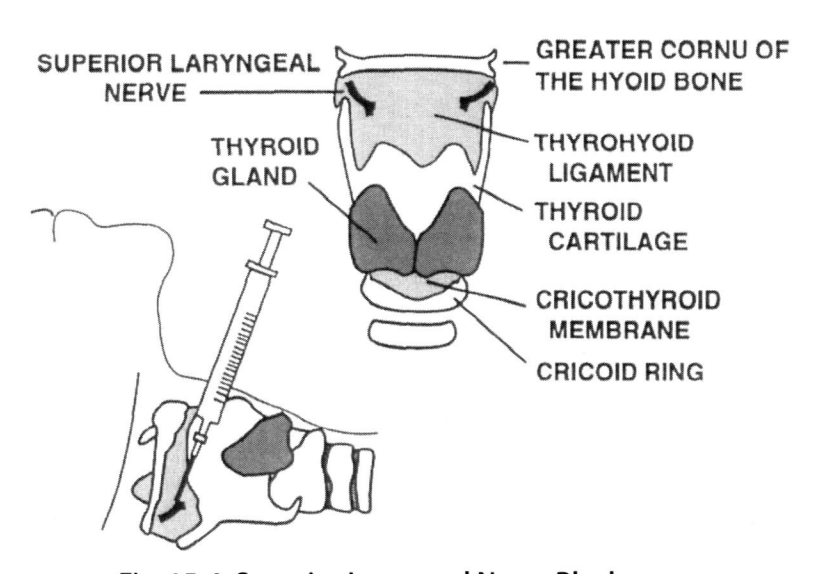

Fig. 15-4. Superior Laryngeal Nerve Block.

Complications of Local Anesthetic Blocks

Potential complications of injections include intravascular injection, bleeding into the airway, hematoma, vocal cord trauma, subcutaneous emphysema, esophageal trauma, pneumothorax, spread of tumor, and infection — although the risk of these is very low. Avoid airway blocks in patients with bleeding tendencies, infection, or tumor in the area of the injection.

Guard against aspiration. Have suction available and use it frequently. Never leave the patient alone after numbing his airway, even if awake and alert. Aspiration can still occur despite precautions. Suction the ETT after placement.

Local anesthetic toxicity is a potentially serious problem. Calculate the cumulative total dose of local anesthetics before use. Limit lidocaine to 5 mg/kg of plain or 7 mg/kg with epinephrine. Remember to consider any local anesthetic, perhaps for surgery, needed after the intubation.

Symptoms of local anesthetic toxicity are:

- sedation
- confusion
- tinnitus or ringing in ears
- apnea
- metallic taste
- loss of consciousness
- seizures
- arrythmias
- cardiac arrest
- heart block

Mucous membranes absorb medications rapidly. Have the patient spit out the local after holding it in the mouth for several minutes rather than swallow.

If your patient shows signs of systemic toxicity then stop giving local, give oxygen, optimize airway and vital signs, and consider the use of midazolam to raise the local anesthetic seizure threshold.

Sedation: The Fourth Step

Although simply telling the patient what to expect improves cooperation, providing some sedation reduces anxiety, speeds the intubation, and often induces amnesia for a potentially unpleasant procedure.

However, sedation must be used with caution in the patient with airway compromise, especially in the field where resources to manage complications are minimal. The hypoxic, exhausted patient may become apneic without warning. Safe use depends on the clinical situation and constant reassessment.

Learning to sedate properly takes practice. Always start with small doses and determine effect before giving more. Remember circulation time may be delayed. Also, circulating adrenalin tends to counteract your sedative until a critical threshold is passed — at which point it all appears to take effect at once.

The Ramsay Sedation Scale (RSS)[5], the first scale to be defined for sedated patients, defines 6 different levels of conscious response to stimuli:

1. Patient is anxious and agitated or restless, or both
2. Patient is cooperative, oriented and tranquil
3. Patient responds to commands only
4. Patient exhibits brisk response to light forehead tap or sound
5. Patient exhibits a sluggish response to light forehead tap or loud sound
6. Patient exhibits no response

With conscious sedation for intubation we typically aim for a RSS of 2.

With good analgesia, one can often intubate awake with no sedation. Under-sedation (RSS 1) tends to be more of a problem if airway anesthesia is not optimal. Under-sedation can potentially lead to poor cooperation raising the risk of physical and mental trauma, aspiration, difficulty performing the intubation, and hemodynamic disturbance.

Over-sedation (RSS 3-6), however, can be even more dangerous than under-sedation. Potential complications include: uncontrolled general anesthesia; hypoventilation (hypercarbia, hypoxia, apnea, cardiac arrest); decreased protective airway reflexes; aspiration; and disorientation. Poor cooperation can occur because the patient loses inhibition, often reacts instinctively and follows commands poorly. You are then faced with the dilemma of whether to give even more sedation and risk making things worse. Better to sedate lightly.

Preferentially use agents that can be reversed. Table 15-1 lists common drugs and doses. Avoid the tendency to sedate heavily to make *you* feel better. You can always add more, you can't remove it. As you gain skill you can often, not always, predict the effect in advance.

We use two types of sedatives: hypnotics and analgesics. Hypnotics, such as Valium, Midazolam, Propofol, or Droperidol cause sleep, decrease anxiety and often produce amnesia. Narcotics like Morphine, Fentanyl, and Demerol give analgesia, but also sedate. Treat anxiety with a hypnotic. Treat pain with a narcotic.

Factors Influencing Drug Effect

Many factors influence how the patient will react to your medications.

Drug potency, dosage, route, and speed of administration — Giving larger doses or more potent drugs will increase sedation. Giving the medication very slowly promotes calm without oversedation. Give the medications a chance to work. As a rule, intravenous drugs sedate more than intramuscular drugs, because levels in the brain rise more rapidly.

Previous drug exposure — Patients who drink heavily or who use narcotics or tranquilizers regularly need more sedation.

Pre-existing sedation — A tired or sleepy patient needs less drug to lose consciousness, even if he doesn't appear sedated at the time. Factors that predispose to over-sedation include:

- other drugs
- exhaustion
- acid/base imbalance
- alcohol
- hypothermia
- shock
- hypoxia
- hyperthermia
- hypercarbia
- hypoglycemia
- electolyte imbalance

Age — Elderly patients and children need less drug for sedation.

Pre-existing disease — Renal or liver failure may alter metabolism or excretion of sedatives, increasing their effect. Also consider:

Emotional state — Fear increases the tolerance for sedatives. Be careful, however. After the intubation the now calm patient may become apneic. Sedatives also release inhibitions. A previously stoic patient may become uncooperative after a sedative.

Pain — Pain decreases the effectiveness of your sedatives. Once the discomfort is gone, the sedatives may suddenly take effect.

Diurnal rhythm — In my experience, it's easier to sedate patients at night than during the day. They often sleep longer once sedated.

Table 15-1. Suggested Adult Starting Doses for Intravenous Sedation.

Sedative Drug	Intravenous Sedative Dose	Advantages	Disadvantages/ Potential Side Effects
Valium (10 mg/ml)	• 2.5-10 mg • (0.035-0.15 mg/kg) • give 1-2.5 mg increments	• amnesia • sedation • minimal resp. depression • reverse with flumazenil	• thrombophlebitis • long acting with active metabolites • no analgesia
Midazolam (Versed) (1.5mg/ml)	• 1-5 mg • (0.01-0.07mgkg) • give 0.5-1 mg increments	• amnesia • short acting (1-2 hrs) • no active metabolites • minimal resp. depression • reverse with flumazenil	• no analgesia • 6X stronger than valium
Propofol (10 mg/ml)	• 10-20 mg (give 10 mg doses to effect)	• amnesia • short acting (min.)	• no analgesia • no reversal • burns on injection
Propofol Infusion	Infusion: • 0.2–0.7 mcg/kg per hr	• induces state of detachment • low dose no resp. depress. • useful *adjunct*: decrease dose other meds • minor analgesia	• with higher dose or fast administration: • nausea/vomiting • bradycardia • hypotension • heart block
Morphine	• 1-5 mg • (0.01-0.07 mg/kg) • give 1-2 mg doses	• good analgesia • some sedation • reversed with narcan	• respiratory depression • nausea / vomiting
Fentanyl (50 ug/ml)	• 25-75 mcg	• good analgesia • reversed with narcan	• minimal sedation • respiratory depression • rigid chest possible (with manual ventilation)

Table 15-1 (continued).
Suggested Adult Starting Doses for Intravenous Sedation.

Sedative Drug	Intravenous Sedative Dose	Advantages	Disadvantages/ Potential Side Effects
Demerol (50 mg/ml)	• 12.5-5mg • (0.02- 0.07 mg/kg) (give 1.25 mg increments)	• good analgesia • reversed with narcan	• respiratory depression • nausea / vomiting • tachycardia • dry mouth • dysphoria
Droperidol (2.5 mg/ml)	• 1.25-5mg • (0.02- 0.07 mg/kg) (give 1.25 mg increments)	• sedation • antiemetic • induces state of detachment	• avoid in Parkinson's • extrapyramidal movements • monitor for cardiac conduction delays • dysphoria
Ketamine (10, 50, 100 mg/ml)	• 10-100 mg • (0.15- 1.5 mg/kg) (give 10 mg increments)	• dissociative anesthetic • bronchodilator • induces detachment • amnesia • active airway reflexes	• hallucinations • increased secretions • tachycardia / HTN • increased ICP
Precedex	1 mcg/kg loading dose, administered over 10 minutes, followed by a maintenance infusion of 0.2–1.0 mcg/kg/hour when used in combination may not need loading dose	• alpha 2 agonist • calm, cooperative state • often doesn't "care" what is going on • less delirium, tachycardia, hypertension	• bradycardia • hypotension • no reversal • high cost • titrate carefully[3,4]: variability in effect on pulse and BP • variability in sedative effect

Evaluating the Effect of Sedation

To judge the need for further sedation, evaluate the following.

Will the patient tolerate any sedation?

Use sedation with extreme caution in shock, airway obstruction, or respiratory failure. The hypoxic or exhausted patient may lose consciousness or become apneic with little warning, so titrate sedation slowly to effect. Heavily sedated patients may lose their inhibitions and become agitated and less cooperative. Consider having reversal agents immediately available. Constantly monitor level of consciousness and adequacy of ventilation and oxygenation. Watch pulse and blood pressure. It's helpful to have an assistant monitor the patient while the operator does the intubation since it's easy to become hyperfocused on the task at hand.

Is this patient at risk for aspiration?
Sedate lightly when there is risk of aspiration. Always have suction available and watch the patient.

Will sedation make the intubation safer?
Patients with hypertension or angina need stress reduction. Struggling patients may injure themselves. Alert patients guard their airways more forcefully.

What is the emotional state of the patient?
Calm, cooperative patients need little sedation. Fearful or belligerent patients may need a lot.

Is ventilation adequate?
Check skin color, rate and depth of respirations, presence of breath sounds, and air exchange. Remember that hypoxia or hypotension cause restlessness and lack of cooperation. Rule these out before giving more sedation (Fig. 15-5).

Safe use of sedation and local anesthetics depends on constant reassessment of clinical status. Your goal is to improve intubating conditions, not make them worse. Never abolish a protective reflex unless you can provide an equally safe substitute. Always guard against aspiration, especially if you anesthetize the larynx and trachea in addition to the nose. Constantly monitor level of consciousness and adequacy of ventilation and oxygenation. Remember, sedation in an exhausted patient suffering from hypoxia and/or airway obstruction can produce apnea with little warning.

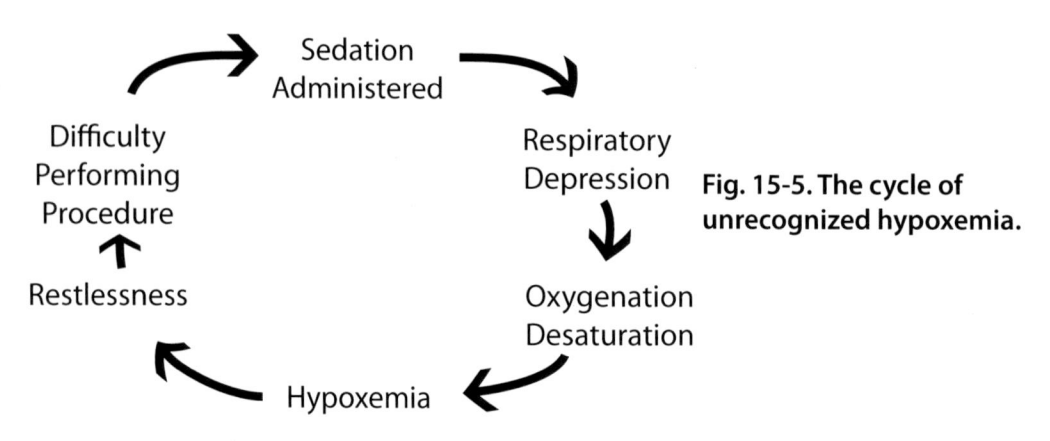

Fig. 15-5. The cycle of unrecognized hypoxemia.

The Keyframe (KF) sequences in this chapter are taken from video clips that are available on-line, for free at:

For Chapter 15 video clips go to:
http://bit.ly/XoVRCu

All video chapter files appear on Anyone Can Intubate Portfolio at:
http://bit.ly/U7EV7f

16
EXTUBATION & EXCHANGING ENDOTRACHEAL TUBES

Removing an endotracheal tube is called extubation. Endotracheal tubes can be removed either because they're no longer needed, or in order to exchange one tube for another of a different type or size. Both activities can have serious potential complications and must be approached with caution and preparation.

Extubation

Learning to intubate includes learning how and when to safely extubate a patient. Since endotracheal tubes are uncomfortable for the awake patient and can also cause trauma — especially with prolonged intubation — the endotracheal tube should be removed as soon as it is no longer needed. However, removing the tube too soon may predispose the patient to respiratory failure or airway obstruction requiring urgent reintubation, which carries its own risks.

Extubation Criteria

Criteria for extubation include:

- recovery of airway reflexes and response to command;
- inspiratory capacity of at least 15 ml/kg;
- no hypoxia, hypercarbia, or major acid/base imbalance;
- no cardiopulmonary instability;
- signs of intact muscle power;
- absence of retraction during spontaneous respiration;
- absence of a distended stomach.

In other words, you want your patient to be stable, able to breathe without help, and able to protect the airway.

"Intact muscle power" can sometimes be hard to assess because the patient's oropharyngeal musculature must be coordinated enough to hold the airway open once the tube is removed. However, with the tube in place, these muscles aren't needed to perform this function. So what signs do you evaluate?

After a general anesthetic the anesthesiologist often uses a nerve stimulator to determine whether the paralytic muscle relaxants given for surgery have worn off enough to let the patient breath on their own. This device uses externally applied electrodes to stimulate the nerves and evaluate the resulting muscle twitch response. Anesthesiologists look at several different tests:

- how many *full strength* twitches can be seen during a rapid fire series of 4 electrical impulses (train of four testing)
- whether or not there is a sustained muscle contraction (sustained tetanus), with no fall off in strength of contraction,

However, the nerve stimulator may not be sensitive enough to measure full reversal of the paralysis. A complete train four response returns when 75% of the receptors are still blocked. If you see a complete train of four you simply can't tell if 75% of the receptors are blocked or none of them are. Sustained tentanus returns when blockade drops below 50%.

In both of these cases, the patient may not have adequate strength to cough or maintain their airway because the test is not picking up the presence of persistent blockade. Anesthesiologists often rely on the patient's ability to lift their head off the bed for a full 5 seconds. A head lift can be sustained for 5 seconds or more only if less than 25% of the receptors are still blocked. This test is a simple and reliable method for testing strength. It also tells you whether the patient can follow commands. However, be aware that abdominal pain and splinting of abdominal muscles from pain may interfere with the patient's ability to cooperate. You should always have the equipment readily available to ventilate or reintubate the patient prior to any extubation.

Routine Extubation Technique

Always suction the pharynx well prior to extubation because oral secretions drain into the trachea when you deflate the cuff. Suction any secretions out of the endotracheal tube. Oxygenate the patient both before and after you suction the tube. Limit the time spent suctioning the tube to less than 10 seconds to prevent hypoxia. Make multiple passes if you have to clear a lot of secretions and oxygenate between each pass.

After you have suctioned and oxygenated the patient, untape the tube, but continue to hold it securely at the corner of the mouth so it doesn't come out until you're ready. Have the patient take a deep breath or manually assist the patient to take a deep breath. Deflate the cuff, and then pull the tube out quickly.

The order of steps is important. When the patient inhales after the cuff is down, they can aspirate any secretions that are pooled above the cuff. On the other hand, if the lungs are *already* inflated, then the initial gas flow is outward. Frequently the initial outward flow of air will blow any secretions sticking to the cuff into the mouth where you can suction them. Squeezing the ventilation bag at the moment of extubation also helps blow secretions out. Deflation of the cuff should immediately precede extubation for the same reason — to prevent aspiration around the tube.

Have suction, oxygen, and the means to reintubate the patient immediately available. Observe the patient carefully (Mov. 16-1, KF. 16-1abc).

There is a high risk of laryngospasm and vomiting following extubation. Other potential complications include post-extubation croup and post obstruction pulmonary edema. These complications are discussed in Chapter 19.

Extubating the Difficult Airway

Extubation of the patient with a difficult airway must be approached with caution due to the potential for problems if the patient fails extubation. Assess carefully the:
- patient with a history of difficult intubation
- patient who may be potentially difficult to ventilate;
- patient who has had airway edema from trauma or infection, which is now felt to be resolved enough for extubation to occur;
- patient in halo traction.

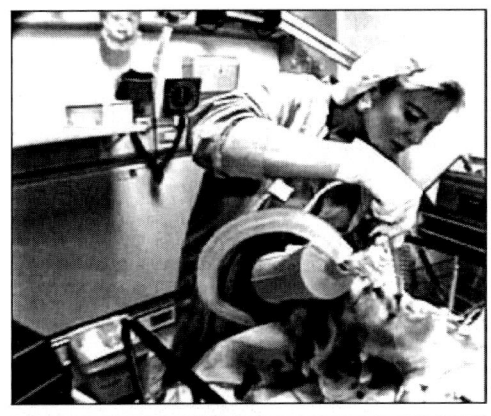

Keyframe 16-1a. Before extubation, suction any secretions well. Assess adequacy of breathing and the ability to protect the airway.

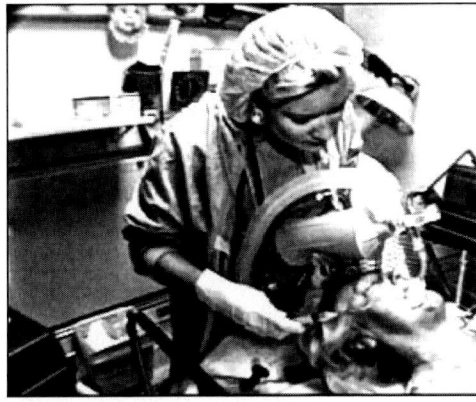

Keyframe 16-1b. Just prior to extubation, have the patient breathe deeply or give the patient a deep breath.

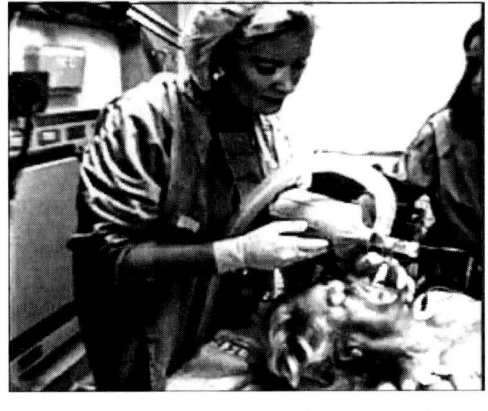

Keyframe 16-1c. Provide supplemental oxygen as you immediately assess adequacy of ventilation.

Determine if there any factors, such as continued infection or bleeding in the oropharynx, which might cause recurrent decompensation. If so, postponement of the extubation should be considered.

Intubated patients have many reasons to have laryngeal edema. Edema present before the intubation may not have had time to resolve. Large volumes of IV fluids often cause upper respiratory and facial edema. Finally, the friction of the ETT against the mucosa can cause edema, which may not manifest until after the ETT stenting the airway open is removed.

Airway edema can cause life threatening airway obstruction after extubation and can predispose to difficult reintubating conditions. Assessing for the presence of continued edema can be done in several ways. Direct examination with laryngoscope or fiberoptic is rarely an easy option but should be considered if the patient had significant preintubation edema and airway obstruction.

More commonly, you can also perform a leak test. First, suction the oropharynx clear of secretions to avoid aspiration. Deflate the endotracheal tube cuff and listen for a leak around the tube as the patient exhales. If there isn't a leak, there may be too much edema to ensure an open airway after extubation. In this case you may wish to postpone extubation.

Have the equipment needed to emergently reintubate at the bedside. An emergency airway cart or tool box serves well.

Monitor the patient's pulse, blood pressure and O_2 saturation. Have a knowledgeable assistant available to help. Tell the patient what to expect.

Monitor the patient following extubation. Avoid extubating the patient at risk for respiratory failure or obstruction during the late evening or night shift, when there are fewer nursing and physician staff available.

Extubation Over A Guide

If you're worried about the potential need to reintubate, and are concerned that reintubation might be difficult, then consider the use of a device such as an endotracheal tube exchanger. The exchanger can be inserted down the endotracheal tube until it is between mid trachea and carina. The endotracheal tube is removed over the top, leaving the exchanger in place as a possible guide for reintubation if needed. Because a tube exchanger is hollow, oxygen can be insufflated or jet ventilated down the tube if the patient develops respiratory distress.

The patient will usually tolerate the presence of the exchanger. You can assist this by injecting 50-100 mg of lidocaine down the endotracheal tube before inserting the exchanger and pulling the tube. Tape the exchanger at the corner of the mouth and note the depth.

Reintubation over an exchanger usually works fairly well, but always be prepared to perform standard laryngoscopy just in case.

Deciding when to remove the exchanger must be based on careful observation of the patient but you can typically remove it in about an hour if no problems have arisen.

The American Society of Anesthesiologist's Task Force on Management of the Difficult Airway has published clinical practice guidelines for managing the difficult airway, including an extubation algorithm (Fig. 16-1).

Extubating Using the Bailey Maneuver

During the wake up process for specific surgical procedures such as brain surgery, we occassionally wish to extubate a patient deep, to avoid coughing or bucking against the endotracheal tube. Such coughing can increase intracranial pressure. Typically the patient is allowed to breath spontaneously and then assisted to breathe with a mask until fully awake.

Alternatively one can use the Bailey maneuver. Toward the end of surgery, and after suctioning the oropharynx well, the provider inserts an LMA behind the ETT and inflates the cuff. The ETT cuff is then deflated and the ETT removed. Verify ventilation. The patient is then allowed to awaken with the LMA in place. The presence of the LMA can provide a more secure airway then mask alone.

Exchanging an Endotracheal Tube

Sometimes it's necessary to exchange one endotracheal tube for another. Perhaps the cuff on the original tube is damaged and won't seal or a larger tube is needed to allow

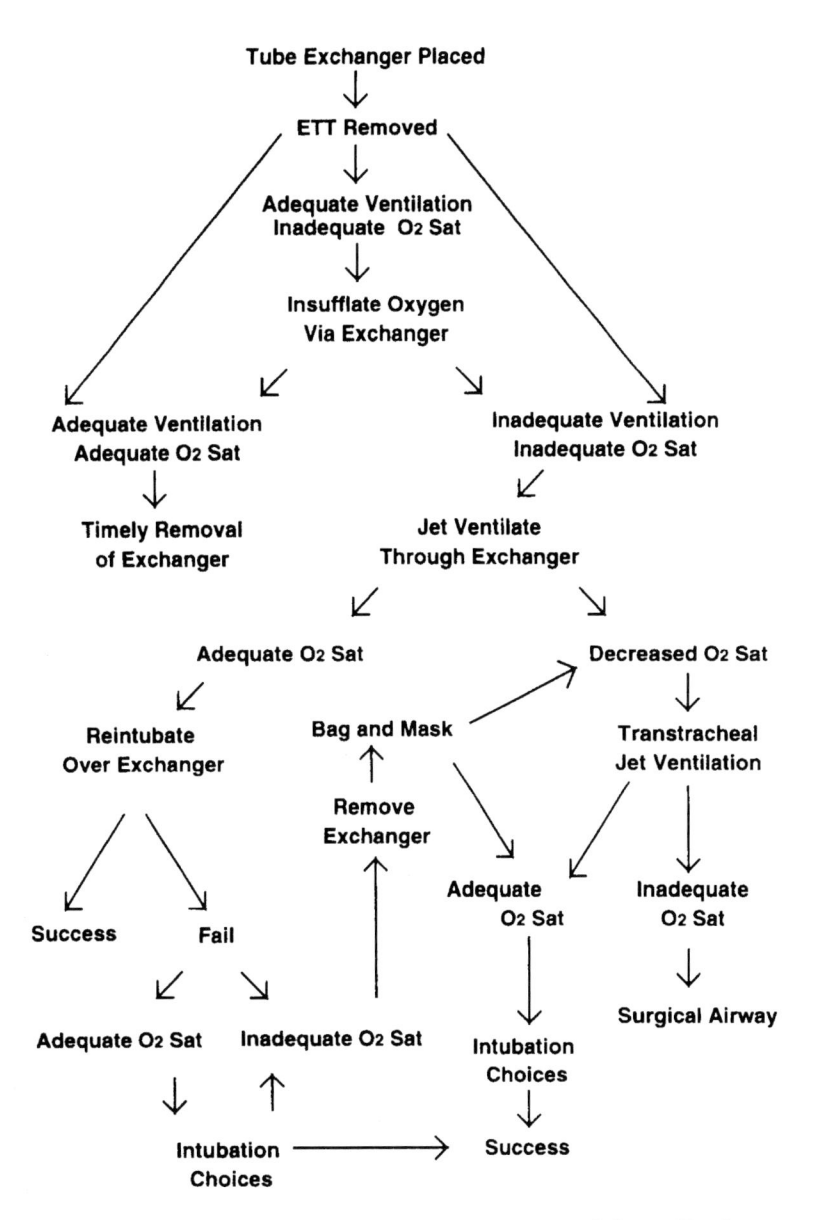

```
                    Tube Exchanger Placed
                              ↓
                        ETT Removed
                              ↓
                    Adequate Ventilation
                    Inadequate O2 Sat
                              ↓
                    Insufflate Oxygen
                     Via Exchanger
```

Adequate Ventilation   Inadequate Ventilation
Adequate O2 Sat   Inadequate O2 Sat
      ↓   ↙
Timely Removal   Jet Ventilate
of Exchanger   Through Exchanger
      ↙   ↙   ↘
 Adequate O2 Sat   Decreased O2 Sat
      ↙   ↓
Reintubate   Bag and Mask   Transtracheal
Over Exchanger   ↑   Jet Ventilation
   ↙   ↘   Remove   ↙   ↘
Success Fail   Exchanger   Adequate   Inadequate
          ↓   ↑   O2 Sat   O2 Sat
                                    ↓   ↓
Adequate O2 Sat Inadequate O2 Sat Intubation   Surgical Airway
      ↓   ↑   Choices
              Intubation   →   Success
              Choices

Fig 16-1. Adapted from ASA's Task Force on Management of the Difficult Airway Algorithm

bronchoscopy for examination or tracheal toilet. If the airway is uncomplicated and there are no contraindications, the patient can have brief general anesthesia induced and the tube changed while they're asleep. The very ill or unstable patient may not tolerate this technique. If the airway is difficult, the possibility of losing the airway under deep anesthesia might be too great a risk. In this case the use of sedatives and local can help.

The main goal is to minimize the interruption of ventilator support because many of these patient's are in respiratory failure.

First, make sure that the tube needs to be changed. Sometimes an endotracheal tube cuff which won't seal is not damaged but is above the cords. Look inside the mouth. A chest X-ray will often show the tip of the tube to be just below the larynx rather than mid-trachea. If the pilot balloon is malfunctioning but the cuff is intact, then sealing the pilot balloon port with

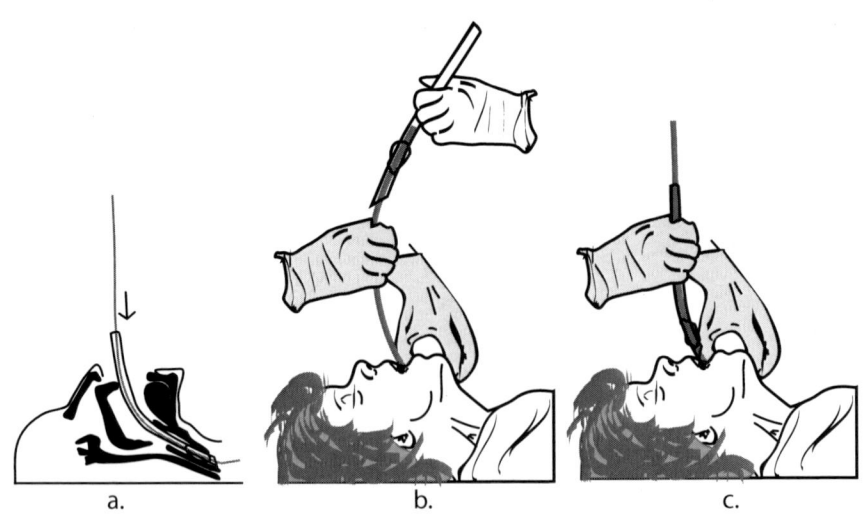

Fig. 16-2. Use of an endotracheal tube exchanger to change a tube. (a) Place the exchanger or bougie into the ETT deep enough to extend beyond its tip. (b) A helper is useful to remove the old ETT while you hold the exchanger firmly in the trachea. Have your helper thread new ETT into the exchanger. (c) Guide ETT into the trachea.

a stopcock can buy time if extubation will occur soon or the patient is unstable.

If the tube does need to be changed, then use of an endotracheal tube exchanger or bougie simplifies the procedure (Fig. 16-2). An advantage of an exchanger is that most are designed to allow jet ventilation or insufflation of oxygen while a bougie cannot. An example is the Cook Airway Exchange Catheter. The bougie, on the other hand, is stiffer and may offer a firmer guide.

You can use exchangers with both oral and nasal intubations. Optimally, attach an angled endotracheal tube adapter with a fiberoptic port to your endotracheal tube to allow continuous ventilation. If one is not available you will need to be mindful of apneic time once the ETT is removed.

Slide the tube exchanger down over the tube through the port into the trachea until it lies just above the carina. Injecting 50-100 mg of lidocaine down the tube before you do this improves patient comfort and tolerance.

Once the exchanger is in position, suction the mouth well. Deflate the cuff and remove the original endotracheal tube by sliding it out over the exchanger. As soon as the ETT exits the mouth, grab the exchanger inside the mouth with your other hand to keep it from backing out of the trachea with the ETT.

Next, slide the new tube over the top of the exchanger and into the trachea. You will probably have to rotate the bevel posteriorly to allow it to pass between the cords. Inflate the cuff, remove the exchanger and check immediately that the tube is in the trachea and not in the esophagus. If it's not in the trachea, you'll have to proceed immediately to the alternative methods of intubation that you prepared ahead of time.

Video laryngoscopy can be very helpful during endotracheal tube exchange because it allows you to see the replacement endotracheal tube enter the trachea over the exchanger. If rotation is needed to get the tip to pass, you can see on screen what maneuvers are needed. You can also assess for laryngeal edema or trauma. Use of a GlideScope or other video laryngoscopic device can add a level of safety in case use of the exchanger fails and reintubation is required.

Reintubation Following Failed Extubation

Occasionally the patient fails the extubation attempt and requires reintubation. If you have a tube exchanger in position, you can either use it as a guide immediately or attempt conventional intubation first. If conventional intubation fails then the exchanger becomes plan "B."

To use the tube exchanger, slide the endotracheal tube down over it into the naso- or oropharynx. Consider the use of a tube smaller than the original to ease passage. Rotate the tube 90° so that the bevel faces posteriorly.

Have one of your assistants monitor the status of the patient and update you regularly. Give oxygen. If you have a tube exchanger in place use it to provide oxygen. While you can simply insufflate oxygen down the exchanger, you will have to attach a jet ventilator if you need to ventilate the patient. See the next section.

If ventilation or oxygenation becomes difficult and there is no tube exchanger in place, apply higher concentrations of oxygen via face mask and positive pressure ventilation. If ventilation fails, then transtracheal jet ventilation should be considered if a "can't intubate, can't ventilate" situation ensues and hypoxemia is significant. If intubation attempts continue to fail, you may need to consider a surgical airway.

Using an Endotracheal Tube Exchanger to Jet Ventilate

You can use a variety of adapters to connect your jet ventilator to an endotracheal tube exchanger, such as a 14g IV catheter, a needleless IV port adapter, or a stopcock — preferably with a luer lock. Cooke makes a tube exchanger set that comes with all of the needed adapters — consider adding one to your emergency airway cart. Don't try to ventilate through the tube exchanger with a ventilation bag —you won't be able to generate enough air flow to inflate the lungs.

You usually need 20-25 psi to jet ventilate the lungs. You must keep the tip of the tube exchanger *above the carina* to minimize the risk of barotrauma and to allow ventilation of both lungs.

Watch the lungs inflate to an appropriate tidal volume and then allow enough time for them to deflate before inflating them again. As with any jet ventilation attempt, the airway above the jet must be open to allow unobstructed exhalation or pneumothorax will occur.

The Keyframe (KF) sequences in this chapter are taken from video clips that are available on-line, for free, from anyonecanintubate.com at:

For Chapter 16 video clips go to:
http://bit.ly/WB65BS

All video chapter files appear on Anyone Can Intubate Portfolio at:
http://bit.ly/U7EV7f

17
SPECIALIZED INTUBATING TECHNIQUES

In previous chapters, we discussed intubation using the standard equipment readily available in operating rooms, emergency rooms, ambulances, and cardiac arrest carts. Specialists occasionally use more specialized equipment to intubate patients with difficult airways.

Safeguarding Patient Safety

Since it's easy to lose track of time when performing any of the following maneuvers, use the following safety precautions.

Monitor the patient's oxygenation. Observe the patient's color. Always provide extra oxygen when available. If you have a pulse oximeter, use it to measure the patient's oxygen saturation. Keep the O_2 saturation above 90%, corresponding to a PO_2 above 60 mmHg.

Have your assistant time any period of apnea occurring during airway instrumentation. If it takes more than one or two minutes to perform any maneuver in the apneic patient, stop and ventilate. If pulse oximetry is available, stop and ventilate when the oxygen saturation starts to drop. Have an assistant monitor vital signs while you concentrate on the airway. High blood pressure and fast heart rates harm some patients as much as the lack of oxygen.

Suction the airway frequently since instrumenting the airway causes saliva formation. After intubation, suction the endotracheal tube well.

Discuss problems with more experienced intubators and ask for their advice and help. Asking for help during intubation should never threaten your ego. Asking for assistance only helps your patient.

It is highly recommended that you practice any of these specialized techniques on healthy patients with normal airways before trying them in an emergency.

Whenever you intubate without seeing the vocal cords, immediately check proper tube placement. Esophageal intubation easily occurs.

Light Wands

Light wands (Fig. 17-1) or stylets trans-illuminate the trachea at the point of the sternal notch. With the trachea thus identified, the stylet is then used as a guide for the endotracheal tube. Typical lighted stylets are self contained, with a small power source the size of a pen flashlight attached to a long, thin, somewhat stiff stylet. Lighted stylets are designed for re-use. To use, make sure the light source is functional. Lubricate the stylet well, then place the stylet into the endotracheal tube. Lock the two together to maintain this relationship. Make sure the tip does not extend past the tip or through the Murphy eye or tissue trauma can occur. Gently bend the tip *90°* (making the need for lubrication clear) .

Uncover the anterior neck and place the bed at a height where it can easily be seen. Because the light wand depends on transillumination of the soft tissues of the neck it works best in a darkened environment and it can be hard to use if the room lighting is bright.

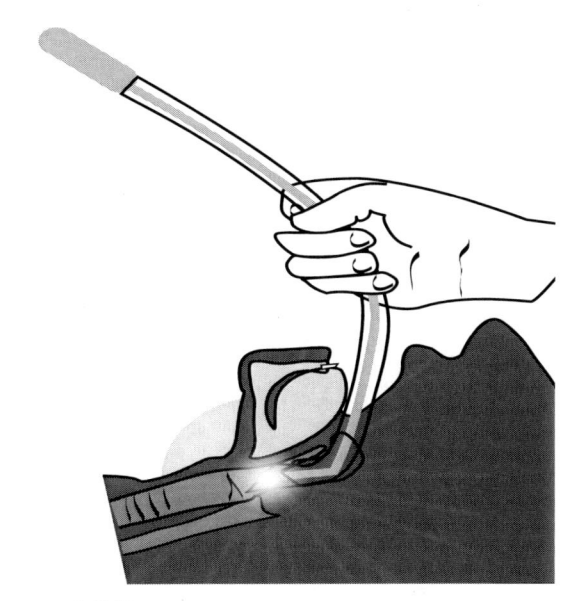

Fig 17-1. Light Wand

Consider dimming room lights to improve visibility.

Open the mouth and pull the jaw forward with your non-dominant hand. Insert the tube/wand unit midline into the mouth with your dominant hand and advance it over and around the tongue.

As the wand tip approaches the larynx you will begin to see a bright red, teardrop shaped glow through the skin of the anterior neck when the tip approaches the glottic inlet. One way to test the expected brightness for a particular patient is to look at the glow through the cheeks.

Once you see the glow, advance and manipulate the tip. Cricoid pressure may help. When the stylet enters the trachea, a bright, discrete light will continue down the midline in a straight line toward the sternal notch where it disappears. Thread the endotracheal tube and remove the stylet.

Relative brightness is important. You may also get a glow with the tip near the pyriform sinuses or submental space. When the wand enters the esophagus, the light will not be seen or will be hazy and dim. Caution: the patient with an extremely thin neck may give a false positive glow with the wand in the esophagus.

When the stylet enters the pyriform sinuses you will see a widespread, diffuse glow on either side of the midline. The goal is to keep the light midline. If you don't have room to maneuver have an assistant pull the tongue forward with a gauze. If the lightwand is stuck in a pyriform sinus or in the vallecula, then advance the lighted stylet over the posterior pharynx instead of base of the tongue.

If the patient is obese, have an assistant spread the skin laterally over the neck, decreasing the distance from the thyroid cartilage to the skin surface

If you can't advance the ETT, the stylet may be stuck in the vallecula, giving impression of a pre-tracheal glow: withdraw and re-advance more posteriorly.

Any blind technique can cause tissue trauma. Be gentle. Since there is no direct visualization of the larynx, avoid this technique in patients with known anatomical abnormalities of the upper airway (tumors, polyps, infection, foreign body, upper airway trauma).

Video Assisted Intubation

This discussion includes only a few of the available video assist devices. A wide variety of instruments provide full color view of the larynx, giving improved visualization of even the difficult or anterior airway without neck manipulation. More appear all the time. However, at present these instruments are too expensive for routine use on every intubation or in the field. Given the recent explosion of inexpensive, miniaturized, high-resolution digital cameras it's only a matter of time before mass production puts some variant of video laryngoscope in every intubator's pocket. Until then, however, knowledge of how to use a few of the more common varieties can be helpful. Hospitals are highly recommended to consider having some version of video laryngoscopy available for the difficult intubation.

Video Intubating Stylets

Clarus Medical and other manufacturers produce several types of fiberoptic intubating stylets that allow direct visualization through an eyepiece of the view at the tip of the stylet. The differences in the models relate to whether or not one looks through an eyepiece, looks through a hand held pistol grip, or uses an attached video screen. The intubator threads the endotracheal tube over the flexible fiberoptic stylet. He or she then directly sees the larynx through the camera at the tip of the stylet, enters the glottis, and then uses the stylet as a guide for tube placement. The stylet is as malleable as a standard stylet and may be curved into the usual shapes used in routine intubation. It should not be bent into sharp angles that would damage the fiberoptic bundles.

An advantage of the device is the simplicity of looking directly through the tip of the endotracheal tube. However, one has to keep the device centered. Introduce it into the mouth under direct vision, not while looking through the eyepiece. Stabilize it at the center of the mouth using your left hand, which should be allowed to gently rest on the chin to keep it stationary with respect to the head.

GlideScope®

The GlideScope Video Laryngoscope distributed by Verathon Medical has a color camera embedded in a curved high impact plastic laryngoscope blade that resembles a Mac blade with a greater curvature (Fig. 17-2). The distal third of the blade angles upward at about 60°. The image appears on a small, color, stand-alone video monitor. The airway is well illuminated with light LEDs. Three models are available: a reusable version with a video monitor on an attached stand, a version with a flexible video baton which inserts into a disposable handle, and a totally portable model that can be easily carried to more remote locations. The technique of use for all three is the same.

While shaped like a longer, more curved

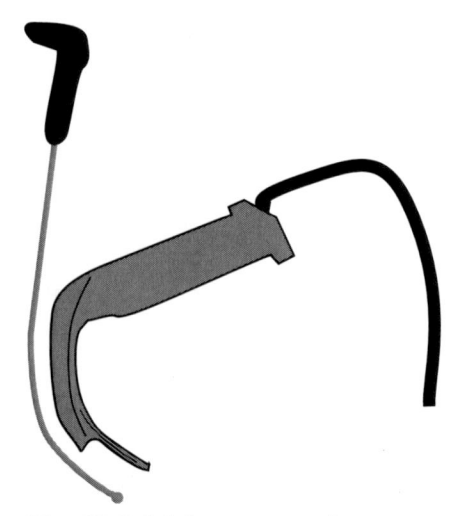

Fig. 17-2. It's important that your stylet be curved to match the shape of the GlideScope blade.

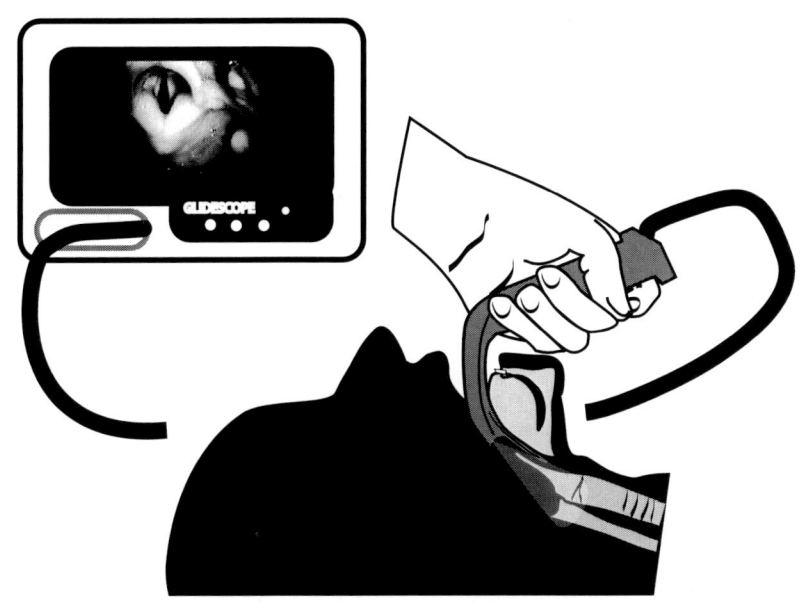

Fig. 17-3. The GlideScope is designed to allow you to "see around corners" at an "anterior larynx and direct your tube tip by looking at a monitor.

Macintosh blade and handle, insertion of the GlideScope is different. Unlike the MAC, which is inserted to the right side of the mouth and used to slide the tongue to the left, the GlideScope must be inserted into the *center* of the mouth and rotated around the tongue in order to line up the tip of the blade that contains the camera lens with the larynx.

Always insert the GlideScope *midline* into the mouth *under direct vision* until its tip has passed the palate. You can glance up at your monitor as you're doing this but this is like glancing in your side view mirror of your car as you are preparing to change lanes — you don't want to take your eyes off the "road" or you'll crash.

Even though you may have a magnificent view of the larynx on the monitor at this point, the larynx isn't in the direct line of sight, as it would be with the MAC. Therefore you have to use a properly curved stylet to manipulate the endotracheal tube into the larynx (Fig. 17-3). Unlike the typical "hockey-stick" shape, the stylet should match the curve on the GlideScope blade. Usually I place the stylet into the ETT and then mold it against the GlideScope blade so that the curves match.

Because a standard stylet is so malleable, occasionally it will straighten during insertion next to the GlideScope, especially if the space it tight, leading to the frustrating situation of being able to see the larynx and not being able to "get there". A stiffer specialty stylet is now available for the GlideScope that is preconfigured to the correct curve. It has a blunt tip to minimize any potential for trauma, however it is very stiff. Do pull it back slightly before fully inserting the ETT into the trachea.

Regardless of which stylet you're using, insert the endotracheal tube with the curve aimed toward the right side of the mouth, 3:00 o'clock position, under direct vision until you start to see it on the monitor. At this point rotate the tube back toward the midline (12 o'clock position) and aim it at the larynx.

Insert the ETT under direct vision as described above until its tip has passed out of view beyond the tonsillar pillars. *Only then* should you look at the monitor. Manipulate the tip of the tube through the glottis. Withdraw the stylet 2-3 cm to effectively soften the tip of the ETT. Advance the ETT into the trachea looking at the monitor. Remove the GlideScope *looking at the patient*, not the monitor.

Switching your focus of attention is comparable to what you do when changing lanes while driving. When changing lanes you are watching the road ahead (to avoid a collision) but you are also glancing into your side and rear-view mirrors so you don't hit anyone around you. Look at the patient to insert the blade while glancing at the monitor until you have a good view of the larynx. Look at the patient while you're inserting the ETT while glancing at the monitor until the tip of the tube appears on the screen. Then you can watch the monitor, occasionally glancing at your patient.

This sounds obvious, *but watch what you're doing*. There is a strong temptation to just look at your monitor while you're inserting the blade and the ETT. There have been case reports of perforating the right palatopharyngeal wall during intubation with the GlidesScope.[1] The most likely cause was blind insertion of a styletted ETT into a taut tonsillar pillar while looking at the monitor for the ETT to appear. You can also damage teeth. Look at the patient during insertion *then* the monitor.

Movie 17-1 and KF. 17-1abce show an intubation sequence using the GlideScope.

A common error is inserting the GlideScope as deeply as you possibly can. If you lack room to maneuver, pull the GlideScope back slightly (Mov. 17-2, KF 17-1abcd, 17-1efg). Ask for cricoid pressure if necessary.

Decreasing the angle the ETT must travel can help. Unlike with the MAC, this typically means placing the head and neck in a more neutral position rather than an extreme sniffing position.

If the mouth is small, it can be helpful to insert the ETT into the mouth first, slide it far to the right side of the mouth, and *then* the GlidesScope blade.

Stortz C-MAC®

The CMAC consists of a laryngoscope that attaches directly to a portable LCD screen via a single cable. The C-MAC has two options for blades.

The first has a thicker "pistol-grip" handle as opposed to the standard round laryngoscope handle but caries the basic shaping of a standard MAC blade. This means that laryngoscopy can be performed either directly, like a conventional MAC blade, or indirectly by looking at the screen. The ability to perform direct laryngoscopy conventionally differentiates it from the GlideScope.

The second type, the D blade, is shaped similarly to the GlideScope and principles of use are the same.

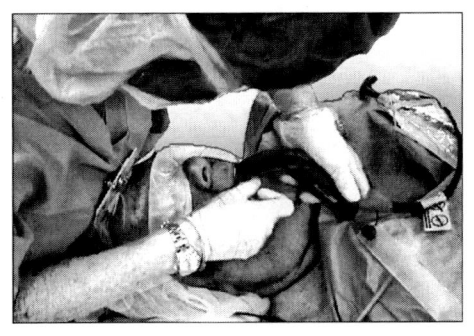

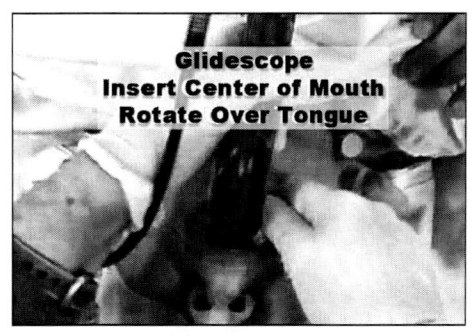

Keyframe 17-1a. Place the GlideScope midline and rotate it into position over the tongue.

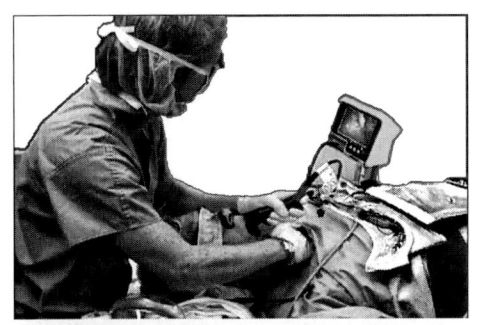

Keyframe 17-1b. Look at the patient, glance at the screen as you insert. As the larynx appears on the screen, lift to optimize the position of the blade to get the best view.

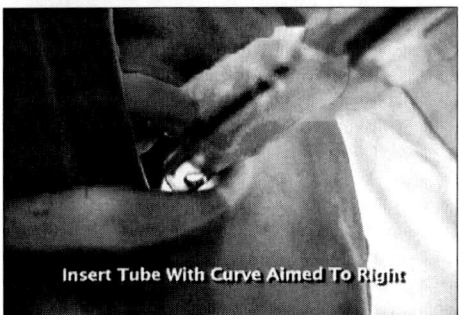

Keyframe 17-1c. Insert the tube, looking at the patient, with the curve toward the right, 09:00 position. This gives you more room since the blade is midline. Glance at the screen until you see the tube appear.

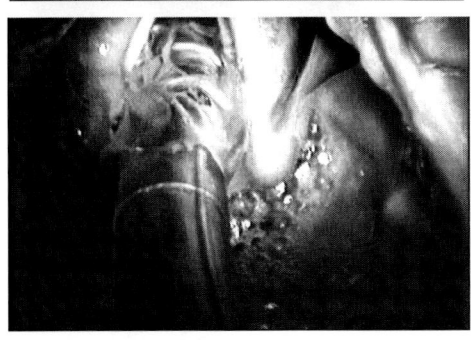

Keyframe 17-1d. Once the tube enters the pharynx and appears on the screen, turn it to the 12:00 position, and maneuver it into the trachea looking at the screen. Keep the blade and head stable.

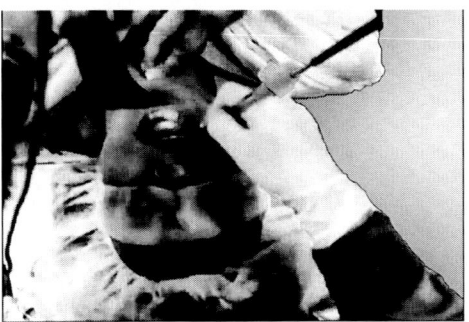

Keyframe 17-1e. The GlideScope is bulky and the dedicated stylet is stiffer. Keep the tube steady as you remove them.

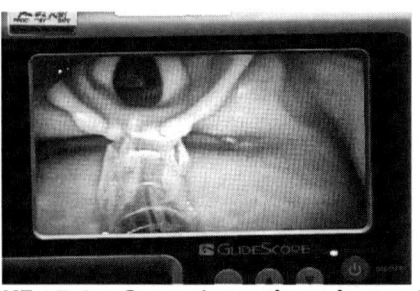

274 Anyone Can Intubate

KF 17-2a. Sometimes the tube can't make the turn into the larynx.

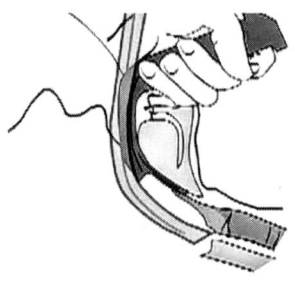

KF 17-2b. Often the tube is too deep, without space to turn.

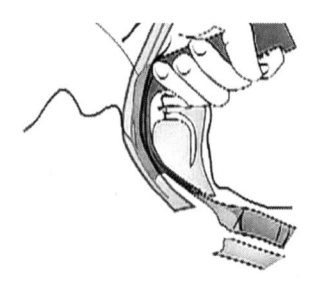

KF 17-2c. Pull the tube back to leave more space to maneuver.

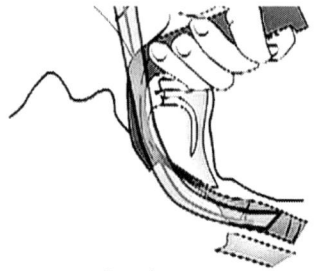

KF 17-2d. When you pass the tube forward it will now be in a higher plane.

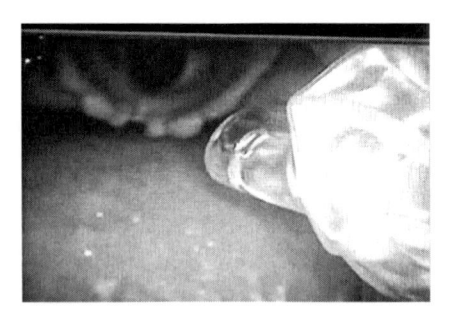

KF 17-2e. Tube tip is too deep. There is no space to maneuver. The short focal length of the camera lens makes the space seem larger than it is, but gives you less room to make the turn than you think you have..

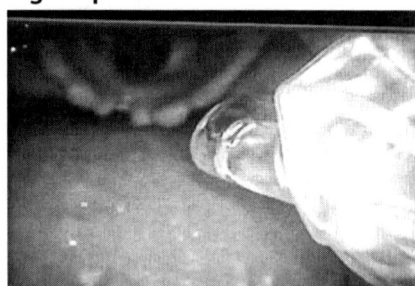

KF 17-2f. Here the tip has been pulled back. This places the tip in a higher plane in the posterior pharynx.

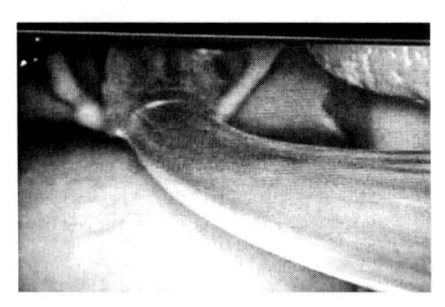

KF 17-2g. The tube swings forward and because it's in the same plane as the glottic opening it enters the trachea.

McGrath® Series 5 Video Laryngoscope

Advertised as the first fully portable video laryngoscope, the McGrath® Series 5 looks and feels like a standard laryngoscopy handle with a curved blade. It looks and feels like a standard Mac, including using AA batteries and not having any attached cables. The difference is that there is a tiny high resolution LCD screen attached to the handle providing a clear view of the larynx at the tip of the blade after insertion. The LCD monitor can be pivoted just like the tiny view screen on your typical camcorder, which it resembles.

Additionally, you can adjust the length of the disposable blade, making it easier to deal with patient variation without having a full assortment of blades.

Like the GlideScope, insert this blade into the midline under direct vision to line up with the trachea. Insert the ETT under direct vision — don't watch the monitor until the ETT is in the mouth and past the tonsillar pillars.

Use of Laryngeal Mask Airway Devices to Intubate

You can use the LMA, as well as the LMA Fastrach™ and the LMA CTrach™ as adjuncts for blind and fiberoptically directed endotracheal intubation. With good airway anesthesia, the LMA awake placement is possible.

LMA Assisted Intubation

If the LMA is placed ideally in the hypopharynx, the grill of the mask is directly over the laryngeal outlet and vocal cord aperture. Up to a size 6.0 cuffed endotracheal tube can be passed down the lumen of a size 3 or 4 LMA and into the trachea. A size 4.5 uncuffed tube can fit through a size 2 LMA. The ETT must be well lubricated and the adapter must be removed. The endotracheal tube must be rotated 15-90° toward the left to allow the bevel to pass through the grill bars on the LMA. Once you feel the tube pass through the bars, at about 20 cm, then rotate it back and advance until the connector touches the LMA.

Cricoid pressure reduces the success rate. If you're holding cricoid pressure to protect against aspiration, consider transiently removing the pressure if you experience difficulty passing the tube.

The LMA can either be left in position around the endotracheal tube or removed. Removal is sometimes difficult due to the tight fit between the tube and the inner wall of the LMA and due to the fact that there is no way to grip the tube as you back the LMA out. One solution is to pass a fiberoptic scope down the tube into the trachea, thus allowing rapid reintubation if the trachea is accidentally extubated. A bougie or tube exchanger can also be used blindly.

Another trick for removal is to take off the endotracheal adaptor. Bundle the pilot balloon and its tubing over the top of the tube and into its shaft. Take the same size or one size smaller endotracheal tube and place its tip into the top of the tracheally placed tube. Use this "pusher" to hold the tracheal tube in place as you slowly back the LMA out over it. Whichever technique you choose, always re-verify continued tracheal placement of your endotracheal tube after LMA removal.

LMA Fastrach™

The LMA Fastrach is a device specifically designed to assist intubation. It's unique from

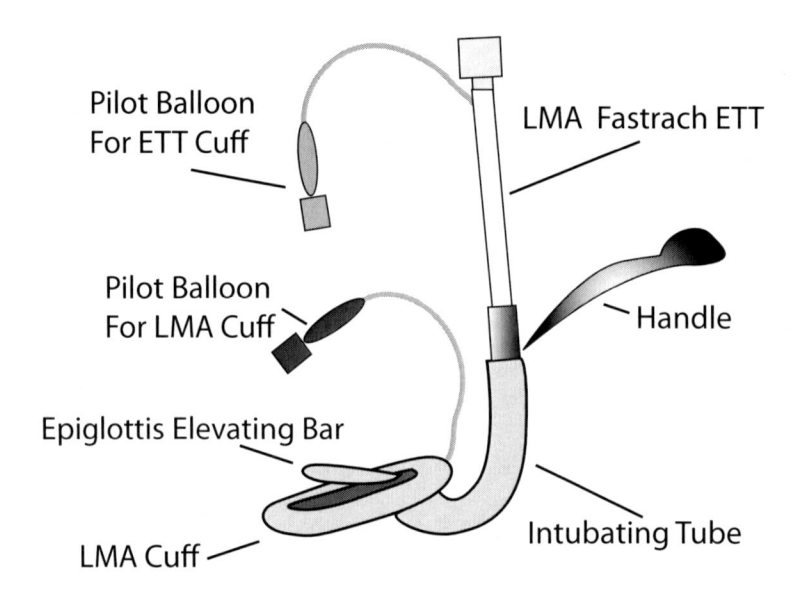

Fig. 17-5 LMA Fastrach Device

other intubation devices because it can also be used to ventilate the patient.

The Fastrach is a rigid, anatomically curved, airway tube that is wide enough to accept an 8.0 mm cuffed ETT and is short enough to ensure passage of the ETT cuff beyond the vocal cords. This tube has a 15 mm standard connector that allows attachment to a breathing apparatus for ventilation. It has a rigid handle to facilitate one-handed insertion, removal, and adjustment of the device's position to enhance oxygenation and alignment with the glottis. Like the LMA, the Fastrach has an inflatable cuff that fits over the glottis and seals the supraglottic space allowing ventilation (Fig. 17-5).

The cuff bowl contains a bar in the mask opening rather than a grill to elevate the epiglottis as the ETT is passed through the aperture. A ramp directs the tube centrally and anteriorly to reduce the risk of arytenoid trauma or esophageal placement. The Fastrach comes in 3 sizes: one size for children, two sizes for adults. It comes with a specially designed reusable LMA Fastrach™ ETT, although it can be used with a conventional ETT if needed. Both a reusable and a disposable Fastrach are available. Both are latex free.

The Fastrach ETT is a wire-reinforced, straight, cuffed tube with a Murphy eye and a standard 15 mm connector. It has a unique molded tip for atraumatic passage through the vocal cords. The distal tip extends approximately 2 cm beyond the wire-reinforced tube.

Preparing the Fastrach

Prior to insertion, completely deflate the cuff using a syringe so that it forms a smooth wedge shape without wrinkles. Like the standard LMA, apply a dab of water-soluble lubricant to the posterior mask tip just before insertion. It's crucial that the leading edge of the cuff be smooth and wrinkle free to prevent the tip of the deflated cushion from curling. Curling can potentially fold the epiglottis down over the glottis during insertion, or prevent a good seal.

Lubricate the posterior surface of the LMA Fastrach™. Never lubricate the anterior surface, where the bar is, because lubricant can obstruct the opening.

Prior to applying lubricant to the ETT cuff, gently fit the connector into the end of the LMA Fastrach™ ETT. The connector should be secure enough to allow adequate ventilation, but don't insert it so tightly that you can't take it out when it's time to withdraw the Fastrach™ after the intubation (Mov. 17-3, KF 17-3abc).

Keyframe 17-3a. Lubricate the endotracheal tube well.

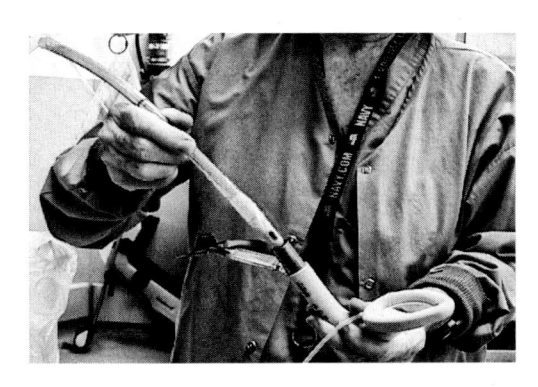

Keyframe 17-3b. Slide the lubricated ETT in and out of the intubating channel until it passes easily.

Keyframe 17-3c. Make sure to lubricate all the way to the epiglottis elevating bar.

Fastrach Insertion Technique

Hold the Fastrach™ by its handle as shown in Fig 17-6a, with the handle approximately parallel to the patient's chest. Position the mask tip so it is flat, not folded against the hard palate just inside the mouth immediately posterior to the upper teeth.

Like the classic LMA, slide the mask backwards following the curve of the rigid airway tube. You might have to pull the lower jaw upward to allow the widest part of the mask to pass into the mouth. Don't use the handle as a lever to force the mouth open.

Insert the curved part of the handle downward into the mouth, pushing against the palate until the straight part of the rigid tube contacts the patient's chin (Fig17-6b). Only at this point in the intubation should you begin to rotate the handle, allowing the mask to slide around the tongue into the posterior pharynx.

Keep the mask firmly applied to the soft palate and posterior pharyngeal wall as you rotate the handle downward, in order to avoid accidental folding of the mask tip.

After insertion, the tube should exit the mouth roughly parallel with the upper teeth, aimed somewhat caudad. Inflate the cuff with just enough air to obtain a seal, corresponding to a pressure of approximately 60 cm H_2O (Fig. 17-6c). Frequently, only half of the maximum volumes are needed to obtain a seal.

Now attach your breathing apparatus and ventilate the patient. If ventilation is difficult The epiglottis may be folded over the glottis or the Fastrach may not be inserted deeply enough. Use of the "up-down" maneuver can be tried. Without deflating the cuff, grasp the handle, swing it outward about 6 cm, and then reinsert it. This maneuver can also be used if you are having difficulty passing the endotracheal tube.

Insert the ETT into the Fastrach™ metal tube, rotating and moving the ETT up and down within the shaft to distribute the lubricant until it travels freely through the entire extent of the tube (Fig 17-6d).

Insert the ETT with the longitudinal black line on the tube facing the handle of up to the 15 cm mark until you reach the transverse line. This line corresponds to the point at which the ETT beveled tip is about to enter the opening in the mask.

Grip the handle firmly and lift the larynx forwards a few centimeters. Don't "lever" against the teeth. This lifting action is called the "Chandy maneuver" and it increases the seal pressure and optimally aligns of the axes of the trachea and the ETT. It will also correct any tendency for the mask to be flexed, which may happen if not positioned correctly. If the mask is flexed, the ETT will not emerge at the correct angle, making esophageal intubation more likely.

Gently push the ETT into the Fastrach past the 15 cm line (Fig 17-6e). If everything is aligned optimally, the ETT will lift the bar that in turn lifts the epiglottis out of the way, allowing the tube to slide into the trachea. Keep inserting until you think you have reached an appropriate depth.

Inflate the ETT cuff and verify tracheal placement (Fig 17-6f).

Failure to intubate may be caused by one of the following four problems:
- Down folded epiglottis or tube impaction on vestibular wall,
- LMA Fastrach™ is too small,
- LMA Fastrach™ is too large, or
- Inadequate anesthesia and/or muscle relaxant. (Pt. is guarding his airway)

Specialized Intubating Techniques 279

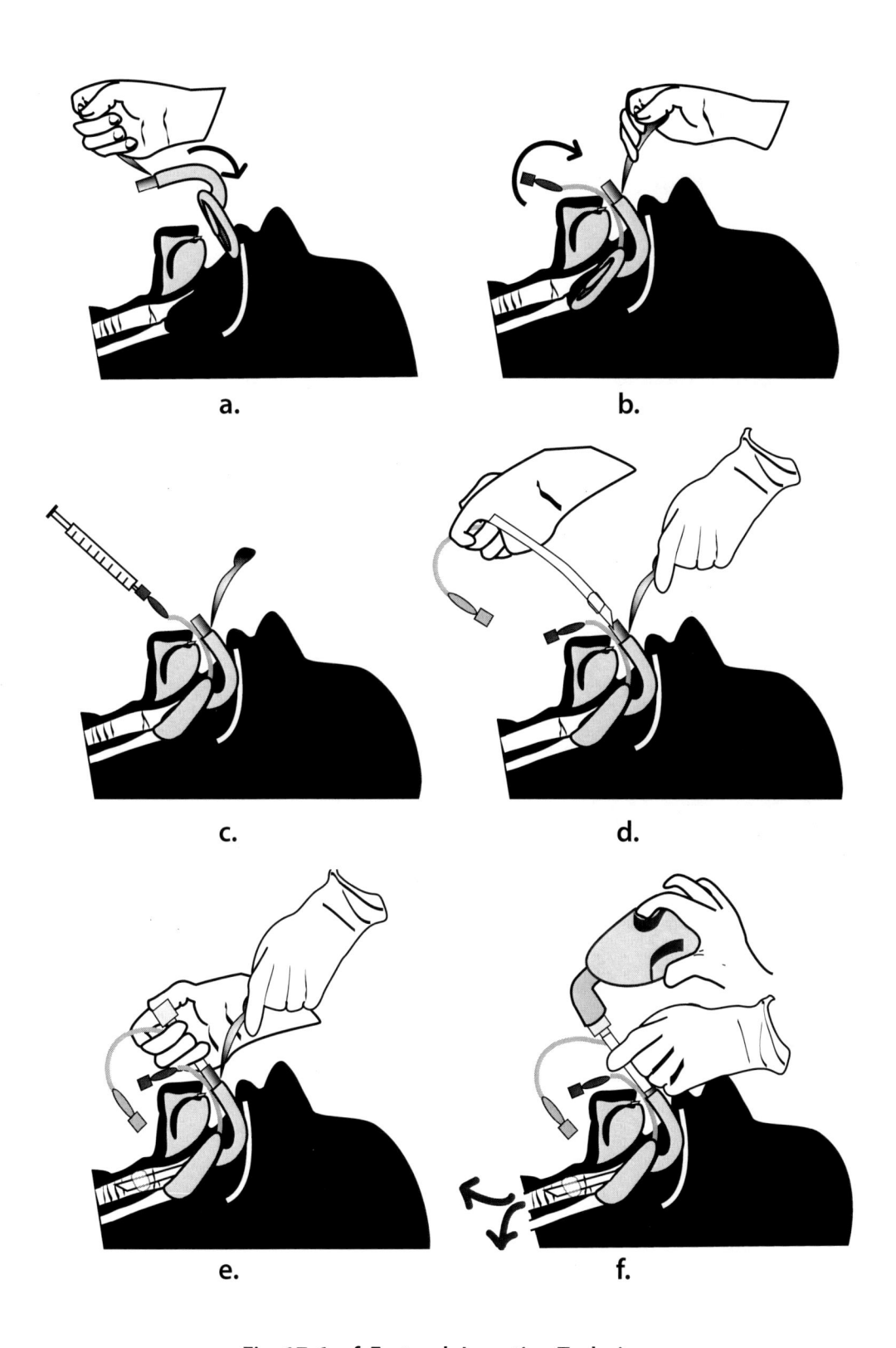

Fig. 17-6 a-f. Fastrach Insertion Technique
(see text for details)

In the event the ETT won't pass try the up-down maneuver or the Chandy maneuver. If the patient is breathing spontaneously or you are ventilating the patient you can judge optimal position of the Fastrach by locating where ventilation is easiest. Hold that position and try again.

Movie 17-4 and Keyframes 17-4a-e show an intubaton sequence using the LMA Fastrach.

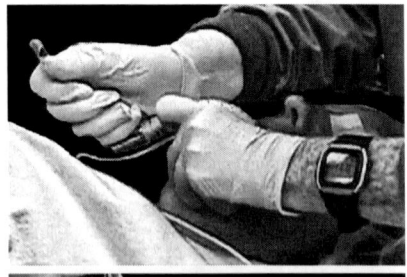

Keyframe 17-4a. Placing the LMA Fastrach is like placing an LMA. Follow the palate.

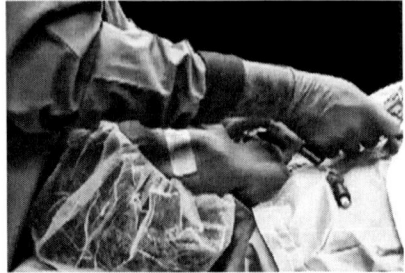

Keyframe 17-4b. Same insertion from the other side.

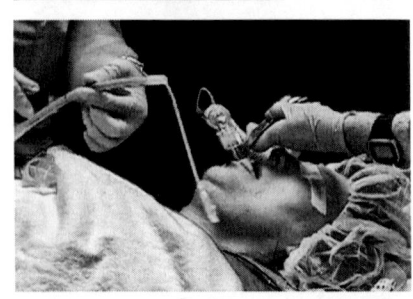

Keyframe 17-4c. Once seated, inflate the Fastrach cuff and use the handle to position the device where ventilation is best .

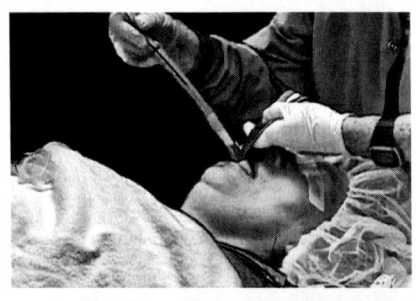

Keyframe 17-4d. Hold the Fastrach at the point where ventilation is best, insert the endotracheal tube to the correct depth an inflate the ETT cuff to minimal seal.

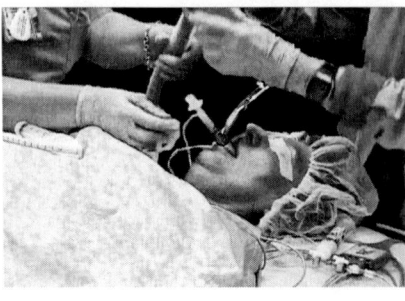

Keyframe 17-4e. Connect your breathing circuit and verify that the ETT is within the trachea before pulling out the Fastrach.

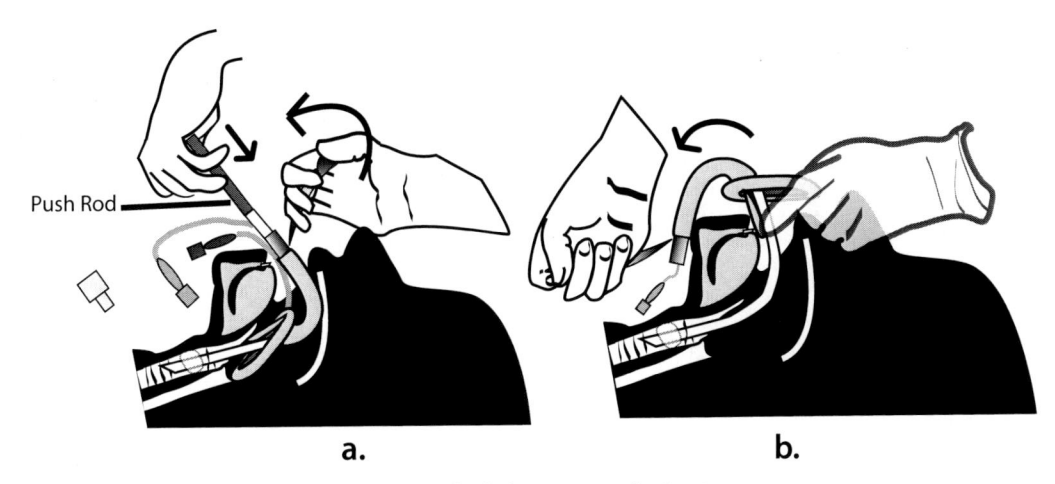

Fig. 17-7a,b. Removal of the Fastrach device.

Removing The Fastrach Device After intubation

Since prolonged presence of the Fastrach can cause swelling, you should remove it after intubation (Fig. 17-7a,b, Mov. 17-5, KF. 17-5abc). After pre-oxygenating the patient, remove the ETT adapter. Deflate the Fastrach cuff but *leave the ETT cuff inflated*.

Hold the end of the ETT firmly as you slowly back the Fastrach out of the mouth. You may have to slightly tap or rock the device as you rotate it around the chin. When the end of the metal tube reaches the end of the ETT use the stabilizer rod to continue to apply counter pressure to the ETT. Once the Fastrach is out, reattach the ETT adapter and immediately verify that you are still intubated.

If you must leave the Fastrach in place after intubation, then deflate the cuff and avoid moving the device inside the mouth.

LMA CTrach™

The CTrach is placed like the Fastrach, however once in place, the intubator attaches a small video monitor which provides a full color view of the larynx. You can then pass the ETT into the larynx under direct vision. The same maneuvers described above are used to obtain good alignment.

Techniques such as the in-out maneuver and the Chandy maneuver for improving ventilation and view/intubating conditions are the same as for the Fastrach. The main difference is that you can see how effective those maneuvers are in a particular situation.

Failure of the CTrach, as well as the Fastrach, have been reported with the presence of lingual tonsillar hypertrophy since the tonsillar tissue prevents elevation of the epiglottis.

Once intubation is confirmed, remove the video monitor, inflate the ETT cuff, and remove the CTrach device using a procedure identical to the Fastrach. Always verify breath sounds and tracheal placement once the device is removed before securing the tube.

Safety First

All of the techniques described above take time. If one is practiced in the technique, then intubation can be quickly achieved. If one uses the device infrequently, it can take quite a few minutes. Always ensure proper ventilation and monitor your patients' vital signs throughout the procedures.

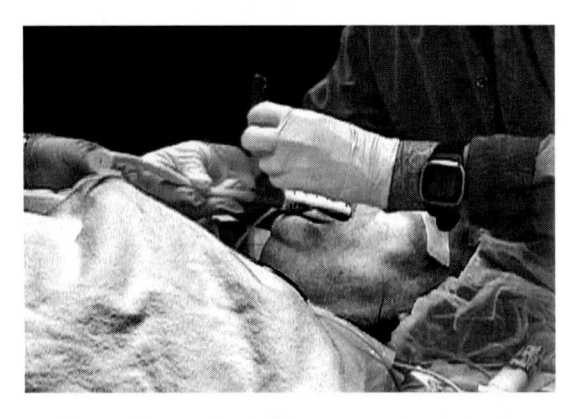

Keyframe 17-5a. To remove the Fastrach, first remove ETT adapter and insert pusher.

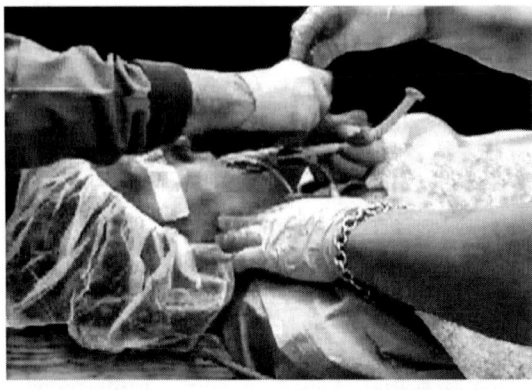

Keyframe 17-5b. Use the pusher to stabilize the ETT while rotating the Fastrach out of the mouth over the tube.

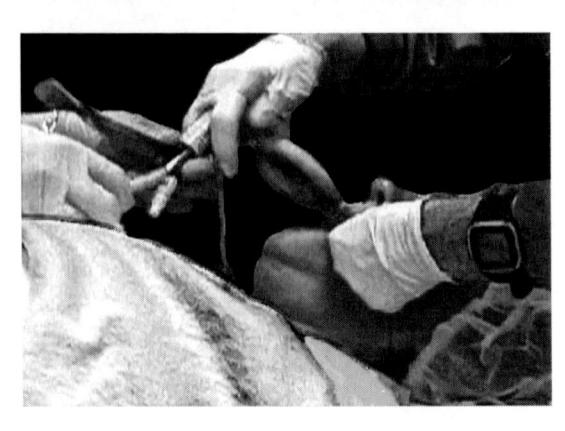

Keyframe 17-5c. Grab the ETT inside the mouth as soon as you can and complete the Fastrach removal. Verify ETT position immediately after removal.

The Keyframe (KF) sequences in this chapter are taken from video clips that are available on-line, for free, from anyonecanintubate.com at:

For Chapter 17 video clips go to:
http://bit.ly/WVoIhZ

All video chapter files appear on Anyone Can Intubate Portfolio at:
http://bit.ly/U7EV7f

18
FIBEROPTIC INTUBATION

The fiberoptic bronchoscope is a specialty instrument used for intubation and examination of the airway. It can maneuver past obstacles into the trachea under direct vision without moving the neck, making it very useful for intubations that are too difficult or dangerous to perform using direct laryngoscopy. Examples include the unstable cervical spine, morbid obesity, inability to open the mouth, mandibular hypoplasia, rheumatoid arthritis, or oropharyngeal tumor. Fiberoptic bronchoscopy allows intubation of both conscious and unconscious patients. Awake intubation lets patients breathe and protect their own airway.

Use of the fiberoptic can be difficult in the patient with severe tracheal or laryngeal stenosis, copious blood in the airway, active vomiting, large amounts of secretions, severe upper airway edema, radiation therapy, and severe cellulitis. Given the availability of the newer video assisted tools, the fiberoptic may or may not be the first instrument of choice in these situations for two reasons:

1. Small amounts of blood or secretions can obscure the view of the tiny lens.
2. Placement of the fiber is under direct vision, however, the endotracheal tube is then railroaded over the fiber and into the larynx *blindly*. There is some risk of traumatizing the anatomy, especially if abnormal.

Preparing The Fiberoptic Bronchoscope

The device consists of a long cable containing bundles of threadlike glass fibers connected to a handle holding the control knobs. The handle attaches to a portable light source (Fig. 18-1). Light travels down the glass bundles with minimal loss in brightness because of the internal reflection within the glass threads. The image returns along the same route.

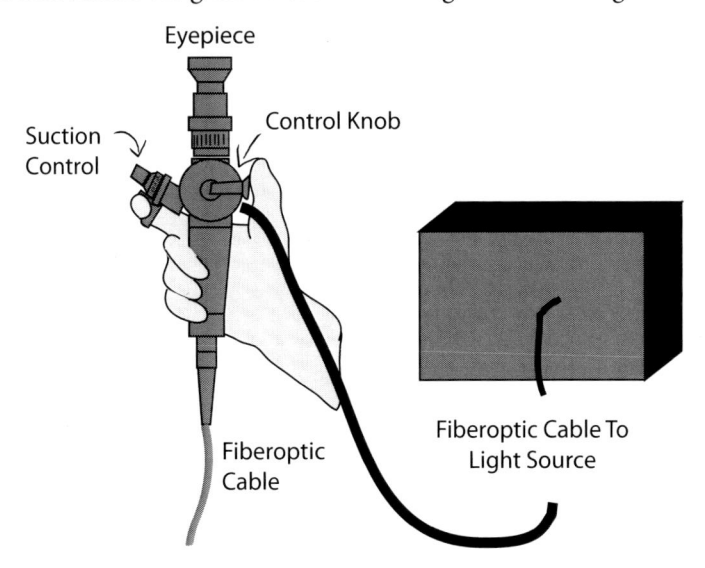

Fig. 18-1. The fiberoptic bronchoscope. Some scopes have a small battery powered light source attached to the hand grip freeing the instrument from the light cable.

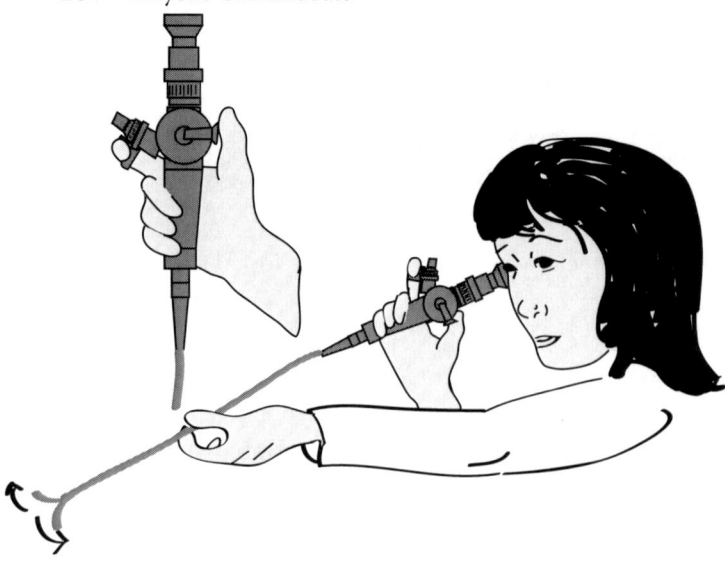

Fig. 18-2. Practice with the controls *before* inserting the bronchoscope.

Since the fiberoptic bundles are glass, *never* bend the cables or wrap them tightly around your hand. Holding the cable in a single loose coil avoids breakage. *Never* pile equipment on top of the scope. Train anyone who has to clean the scope how to avoid breakage. Fiberoptic scopes are very expensive and can cost thousands of dollars to repair if the glass fibers are damaged.

It's paramount to check your equipment before use. If it doesn't work well when you're checking it out, don't expect it to work in your patient. Attach the light source. Make sure it's bright. Obtain a clear image. Look through the viewfinder and focus the lens by aiming the tip at some printed text. Note the distance of the object from the tip of the cable when the image focuses.

The unprepared lens will fog. Use an anti fogging solution or warm the lens. D*on't* use solvents which can dissolve the glue holding the bundles together. Dry the tip carefully to avoid scratching.

Gently turn the control knob and confirm that the tip moves cleanly up and down, a motion called deflection. Memorize which way the cable deflects when you turn the knob (Fig. 18-2). Most viewfinders have an asymmetric mark on the perimeter of the image. Check the orientation of this mark to the intended movement of the tip before each use. You absolutely need to know which directions are right and left, or up and down.

It's important to realize that the way you hold the scope, with either the control knob on top or on bottom of the handgrip, changes the direction of the deflection of the tip *with relationship to the patient*. This is especially true if you have a camera attachment on the eye piece allowing you to project the image onto a video screen. The camera attachment can freely rotate around the eyepiece. If the camera has rotated you may not notice that right, left, up and down have reversed.

Attach working channels to O_2 or to suction.

Don't forget to load the endotracheal tube onto the scope *before* you start. It would be embarrassing, at best, to be looking at the tracheal carina through your eyepiece and realize your endotracheal tube is still on the cart behind you.

Choose the largest tube reasonable for that patient. Too small a tube may wrinkle the cable's plastic covering. However, a pediatric cable may not be stiff enough to guide a very large tube. An adult scope will fit any tube 6.5 mm (26 Fr.) or larger. A pediatric scope will fit inside a 4.5 mm (20 Fr.) or larger tube.

Lubricate the cable with lubricant jelly or ointment, spreading it back toward the handle with a gauze pad from a point about 5 cm (2 inches) from the tip. *Don't lubricate close to the lens*. Lubricant on the lens blurs the image.

Having two suction devices is helpful to allow attachment to the suction port of the bronchoscope as well as direct suctioning of the airway. Suction frequently during intubation. Instrumentation of the oropharynx, sedation, and local anesthesia of the airway predispose to aspiration — even with an awake patient.

Patient Preparation

Preparation of the patient is important. Recommendations for the safe use of sedatives, local anesthetics and nerve blocks are described elsewhere in the book , but an abbreviated list of preparation steps is provided here.

1. Administer an IV drying agents such as glycopyrrolate as your first premedication. It takes time for drying to start so give it as early as possible.
2. Administer a nasal vasoconstrictor such as neosinephrine even if you plan oral intubation. If you have to change route of insertion you're prepared.
3. Topicalize the patient. While advanced nerve blocks can be used and are extremely helpful, in a pinch you can apply a good glob of 5% lidocaine gel at the base of the tongue with a tongue blade and let it melt. Topical spray can also be liberally applied. Never leave the patient alone once numbing begins. You are blocking the patient's protective reflexes. Have suction available.
4. Provide judicious sedation while closely monitoring response.
5. Adequate topicalization is key. Inadequate airway anesthesia leads to coughing, gagging and vomiting. No amount of sedation can compensate for inadequate airway anesthesia and heavy sedation may makes things worse — either because of release of behavioral inhibitions or from respiratory depression. Sometimes minimal sedation is key to a cooperative patient.
6. Tell the patient what sensations to expect to improve cooperation.

Insertion Technique

How you insert the fiberoptic bronchoscope into the trachea depends on many variables. Factors that affect the technique that you use include your position relative to the patient, use of the oral vs. the nasal approach, and whether the patient is spontaneously ventilating or apneic. This section details the various options available to you, and when they are most appropriate to use.

Where To Stand

Either stand at the head of the bed, in the usual intubating position, or to the side of the patient, facing back toward the head. There are advantages and disadvantages to each. (Fig. 18-3a). Standing at the head gives the operator the anatomical relations in the standard intubating position. Left and right, up and down are unchanged. The disadvantage is that the multiple angles that the bronchoscope is forced to make in its journey through the oropharynx hamper the maneuverability of the tip if you're looking directly through the eyepiece.

On the other hand, if there is a camera attachment on your eyepiece and you're projecting

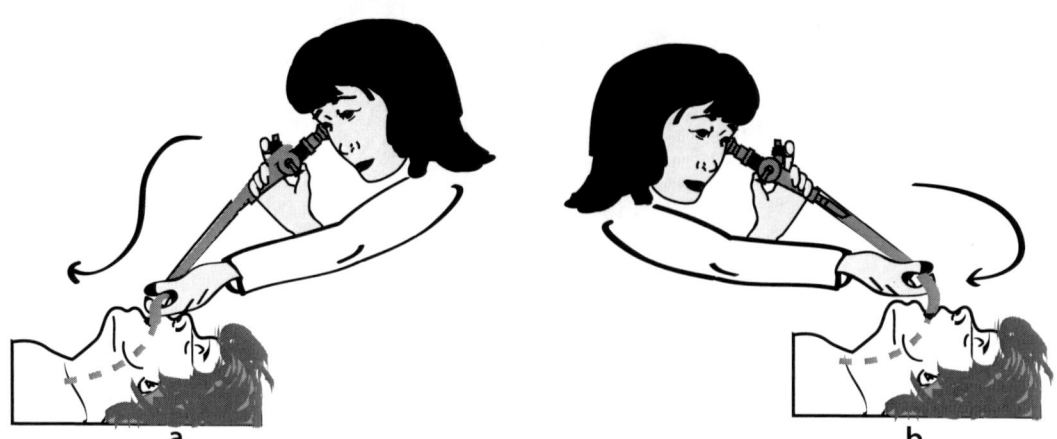

Fig. 18-3 a,b. Stand at the head (a) or the side (b). Keep your back and arm fairly straight for bronchoscope positioning. Note the difference in fiber path with both approaches. Avoid coils in the fiber which will decrease your control.

the image onto a video monitor, you can hold the control grip of the scope directly above the patient's head, eliminating a major bend and simplifying the intubation. In this instance, however, you're looking at the video monitor, not directly at the patient. Using the monitor requires a little practice to master the altered eye hand coordination.

When you stand at the patient's side facing the head (Fig. 18-3b), the directions for controlling the tip are reversed. Aiming toward the patient's left means turning the cable tip to your *right*. Aiming anteriorly (toward the front of the patient) means deflecting the tip down instead of up. Using the asymmetric marker visible in the viewfinder to keep you oriented becomes very helpful.

Once the directional changes are mastered, it's often easier to perform fiberoptic bronchoscopy from the side position because the cable doesn't have to make as many turns. It's therefore easier to manipulate the tip.

Use of Fiberoptic Guides

Because of the flexibility of the cable, rigid guides are often used to help direct its movement. Two types of oral airways, the Ovassapian and the Airway Intubator, are commonly used. These airways have a large channel down the center that holds the endotracheal tube and the enclosed fiberoptic cable steady so that the tip can be manipulated. These airways also protect your expensive cable from the patient's teeth. All are designed to move the tongue forward, providing more space behind the tongue to improve visualization. The pitfalls of oral guides include:

- Failure to move the largest tongues anteriorly
- May still need to pull the tongue forward manually
- Must be perfectly aligned with the center of patient's airway

Off center placement delivers the fiber tip laterally. Even if you can see the larynx, aiming from a lateral position may prevent you from directing the tip toward the opening. You must control the guide in addition to your fiberscope.

During nasotracheal intubation, the nasotracheal tube can act as the guide. Never be afraid to turn or reposition the guide. The guide plays an active role in the intubation and its placement can bring success or failure.

The basic technique is the same whether doing oral or nasal intubation. However, the site of insertion does dictate some differences.

Oral vs. Nasal Route

Flexible fiberoptic intubation can be performed either orally or nasally. There are advantages and disadvantages to both routes.

Although the oral route is often preferable, nasal intubation is technically easier because the fiber makes a smoother curve in the posterior nasopharynx and takes a more direct path to the larynx. Redirection is less necessary. You bypass most of gag reflex because you can usually avoid the tongue. The patient cannot bite the fiber or you during the intubation. However, the big risk is epistaxis — which can then make the entire intubation process more difficult by obscuring the view. Use of a nasal vasoconstrictor is very important. You may need to use a smaller tube because of septal deviation or to avoid prominent turbinates.

Oral intubation avoids the nose and nosebleeds, but it can be more difficult due to the more curved path through the mouth and into the larynx. It's more difficult with a large tongue, short thyromental distance, short or long hyomental distance because the tongue can't be pulled forward as easily in these condition to allow the fiber and the tube to pass. Oral fiberoptic intubation often requires some type of intubation guide/airway. The gag reflex is more likely to be stimulated making good topicalization essential. Since the fiber passes through the mouth the patient can accidentally bite it, and possibly you, if precautions aren't taken.

Insertion Technique: Oral Route

Allowing the patient to sit, when possible, let the tongue fall forward away from the larynx. Insert the cable into the endotracheal tube. Removing the endotracheal tube adaptor may improve fit and prevent bunching or wrinkling of the covering which can damage the glass fibers. Don't lose the ETT adapter.

For oral intubations the tube may be slid up the cable out of your way, or placed within the mouth or airway guide. Use of the endotracheal tube as part of your guide can improve control, but be aware of where it is pointing.

There are 3 coordinated motions to master:
1. rotation of the *entire* scope, avoiding twisting the fiber;
2. deflection of the tip along the 6 o'clock to 12 o'clock flexion plane;
3. advancement and withdrawal of the fiber.

You will need all 3 motions to succeed.

Hold the cable in the left hand and the pistol grip control in the right, using either your right thumb or index finger to turn the control knob. Hold it with both hands to let it to turn as a unit. You can reverse your grip if you are left-handed.

Dimming the room lights slightly may improve your image — if lower lighting doesn't compromise patient safety. The light will shine through the neck as the tip nears the larynx and disappear as the fiber enters the trachea. Failure to see the light as the cable advances may mean esophageal placement.

Put the cable into the patient's mouth. If the tongue is in the way, have the patient stick his tongue out or have your assistant gently pull the tongue forward.

Place the fiber in the center of mouth or through any guide *by looking at the mouth/guide*

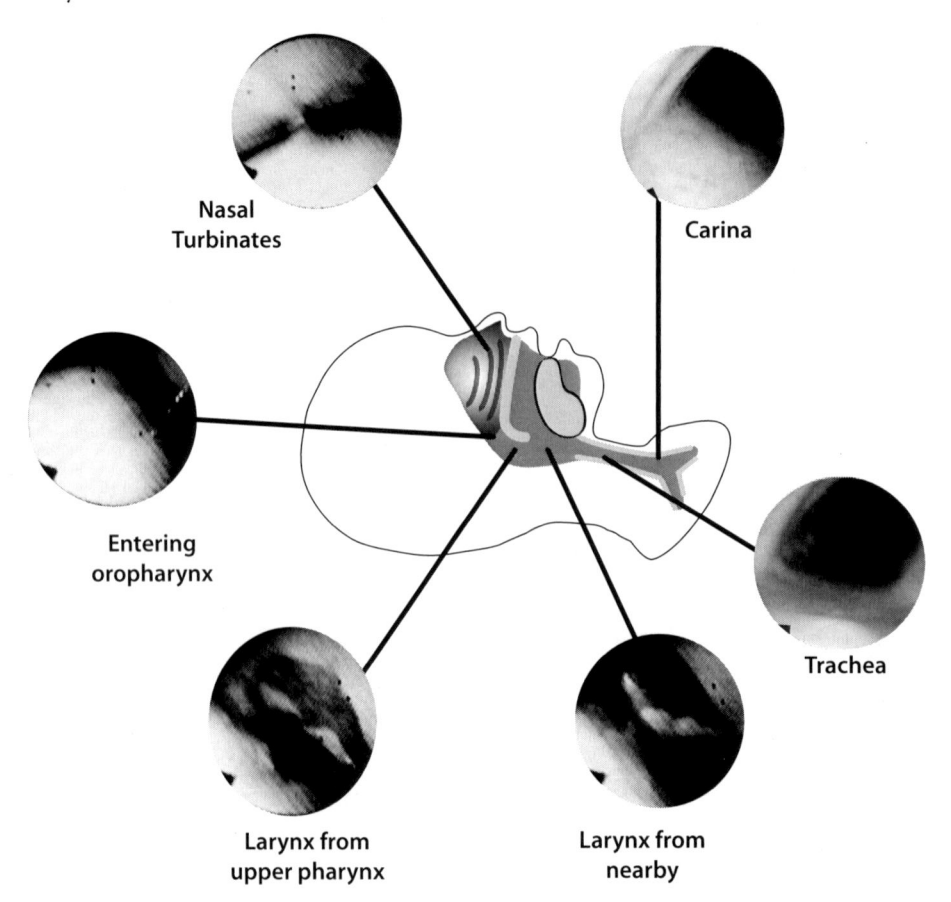

Fig. 18-4. Views of the larynx and trachea seen during fiberoptic bronchoscopy.

— NOT through the scope. Introducing while looking through scope tends to place the tip lateral. Once inserted, keep your left hand on the guide or the fiber as it exits the mouth so that it doesn't drift off toward the side. You can rest your hand lightly on the chin to keep it stable. Protect the patient's eyes.

Keep the cable fairly straight between your hands. The cable is very flexible. If allowed to loop you'll lose tip control and be unable to direct its placement. Rotating the scope head with your arm and shoulder, not just your hand. Don't expect to find the larynx by just flexing the tip. And don't just push the scope forward. Note that if the ETT rotates it will pull your fiber away from the larynx.

The fiberscope is like a telescope: it only lets you see what's in front of the lens. Identify structures. (Fig. 18-4). You must locate the target in the center of your field. Use tip deflection and tip rotation to aim. Both are controlled at the body of the scope, not the tip. Ensure your guide is aimed well. Make certain the tip isn't in the tube when you flex it or the threads may break. Make sure the cable exits the tube tip, not the Murphy eye.

Work in small increments. Rotate the entire scope to bring it into the flexion plane. Flex the tip to center the target (larynx). Advance the scope slowly a small amount. Repeat. Rotate, flex, advance. Small and slow repeat cycles will allow faster intubation than trying to rapidly correct.

The laryngeal target will be moving. As the patient inhales the larynx will move up and down. It moves a lot if the patient swallows. Freeze your action for the few seconds it takes until the larynx stops moving and drops back into view. Then repeat the rotate, flex, advance cycle again. If you "chase" the larynx as it moves you will make the intubation more prolonged.

Pass the lens through the vocal cords. However, return the tip to neutral position before you advance it down the trachea. The image blurs during the passage through the vocal cords. A clear image of the tracheal rings appears on the other side and you'll see the carina if you advance far enough (Fig. 18-4, Mov. 18-1, KF. 18-1abc, KF. 18-1 def). Hold the instrument steady and slide the tube down the cable using it as a guide. If the tube won't pass, rotate it gently to allow the tip to slide off the anterior commissure.

Remove the cable, attach your 15 mm adapter and oxygen source, and ventilate. Check breath sounds. Optimal position places the ETT tip mid trachea.

When you can't identify landmarks, withdraw slightly to look at the big picture. The scope may be too deep and in the esophagus. Pull the cable back until recognizable landmarks appear. When the lens is inside the tube you'll see a grey tunnel with a stripe. If your cable is twisted around and misdirected into the nasopharynx, you'll see a confusing picture of the turbinates and choanae.

If the epiglottis is floppy, have your assistant pull the tongue forward or have the patient stick the tongue out. A jaw thrust enhances visualization. Instruct the patient to take deep, panting breaths. The resulting muscle action pulls the larynx posteriorly and downward away from the tongue and opens the airway maximally. Guide the fiber tip over the tongue and under the epiglottis.

Oral fiberoptic intubation in edentulous patients can be hard. Without the teeth to give form and structure to the mouth, the oral guide tends to position itself against the back of the pharynx. The resulting position changes the angle of approach to the glottic opening and can block ETT passage. Pushing the endotracheal tube into the mouth tends to shove both guide and tube back against the wall of the pharynx. Have your assistant hold the oral guide forward in a more standard position. You may find it helpful to keep the ETT back on the cable, and first advancing only the cable into the guide and trachea.

If the cable won't pass despite a clear field of view it's often because the angle it must turn is too sharp. Pull the endotracheal tube back or otherwise reposition the guides or the patient's head and try again.

When an intubating oral airway is not available, you can use anything leading to the base of the tongue to guide you to the larynx, for example, a Macintosh blade held by an assistant. Simply follow the curve with the tip of the cable.

It's often better to start with the fiberoptic bronchoscope whenever you think you might eventually need to use it. Multiple prior attempts at blind intubation may bloody the airway and make identification of structures difficult.

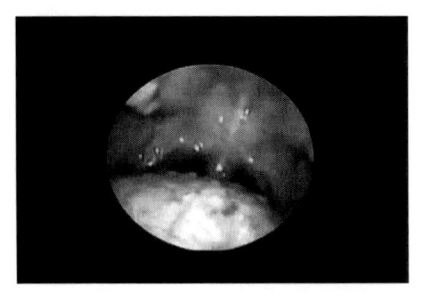

290 Anyone Can Intubate

Keyframe 18-1a. Oral fiberoptic intubation. Pass the fiberscope over the tongue.

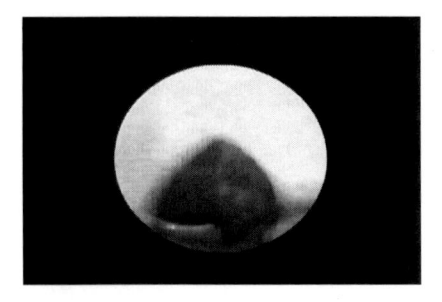

Keyframe 18-1b. Curve the fiberscope down into the supraglottic space and look for the epigottis.

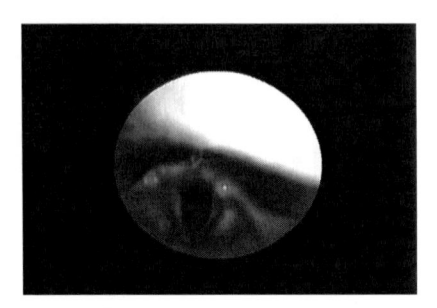

Keyframe 18-1c. Watch the larynx come into view. If the patient is breathing the larynx will be rising and falling. If the patient swallows you may lose the view. Don't chase the larynx. Wait a moment, and the view usually returns.

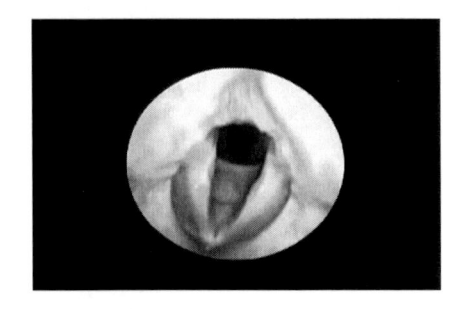

Keyframe 18-1d. As you approach the larynx, try to time your entry to when the patient is inhaling.

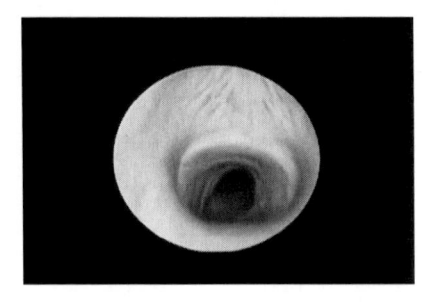

Keyframe 18-1e. Once through the vocal cords you will see tracheal rings. The rings are anterior, the muscular wall posterior.

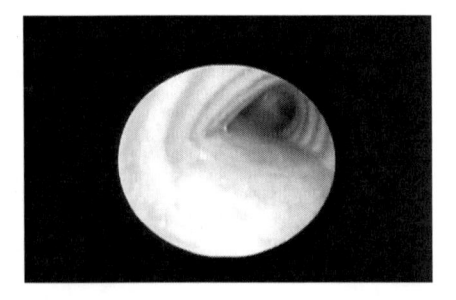

Keyframe 18-1f. The carina is in the distance down the trachea.

(Used with permission Sass Elisha, Jeremy Heiner 2012)

Insertion Technique : Nasal Route

Insert the cable into the endotracheal tube. For nasal intubations the tube may either be kept back on the cable or advanced through the nose until it just turns into the posterior pharynx. Keeping it out of the nose until the trachea is cannulated may improve maneuverability of the cable, but it risks being later unable to pass the tube through the nose if the tube is too large. Placing the tube through the nose first can be helpful, because it allows the tube to act as your guide and it verifies that the tube will fit. On the other hand, you risk nosebleed, which can profoundly interfere with the use of the fiberoptic.

Here, we'll assume that we are keeping the tube back on the fiber. Insert the tip of the fiber into the nose and identify the inferior turbinate. Advance parallel to the turbinate, stay in the middle of the channel to avoid brushing against the sensitive and capillary rich mucosa. Slowly flex the tip downward as you turn the corner into the posterior pharynx, behind the uvula. As you pass around the base of the tongue you should see the epiglottis and then the larynx.

Rotate, flex and advance your tip slowly toward the larynx, passing under the epiglottis. Aim for the anterior commissure. As you arrive above your target flex the tip slightly posteriorly which should straighten the fiber — allowing it to more easily pass between the cords and into the trachea.

Stabilize the fiber at the nose with your left hand and slide your well lubricated endotracheal tube down the fiber, into the nose. Advance it until it enters the trachea. You may need to rotate the endotracheal tube slightly if it meets resistance going between the cords. Look through the fiber again to verify that you can see tracheal rings. Withdraw the fiber and verify correct placement.

If you start the nasal fiberoptic intubation with the nasotracheal tube already through the nose and with its tip already in the posterior pharynx, make sure that its curve is aimed toward the larynx. If not, your "guide" will aim you laterally. If the nasal tube is advanced too far, it can also limit tip flexion. If you can see the larynx but are having trouble "getting there", withdraw the nasal tube slightly and check the direction of the curve. Have an assistant hold it firmly to keep if from rotating during insertion of the fiber. Movie 18-2 and keyframes 18-2 abc and 18-2 def show a fiberoptic nasal intubation

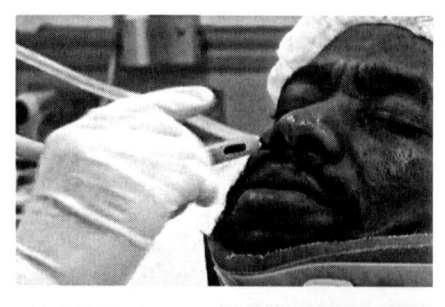

Keyframe 18-2a. In this case, the fiber is inserted first. The strategy is to enter the trachea with the fiber and then pass the tube into the nose.

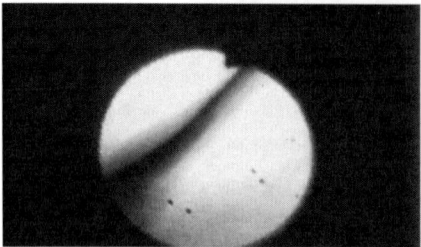

Keyframe 18-2b. View of the turbinates inside the nose.

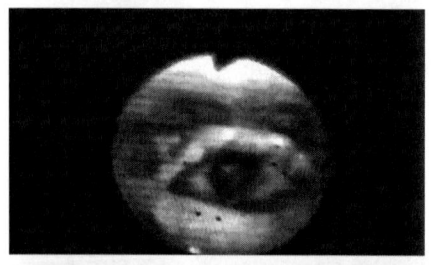

Keyframe 18-2c. When standing facing the patient, the larynx will appear upside down in your viewfinder.

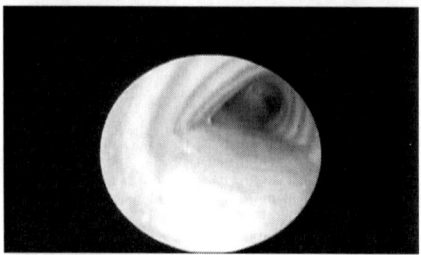

Keyframe 18-2d. View of the trachea, with the carina in the distance.

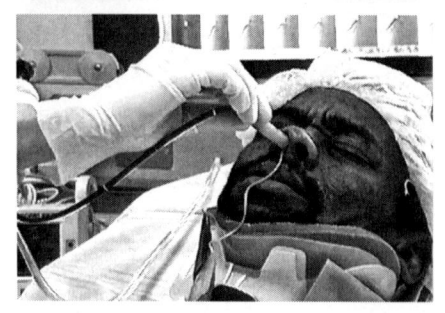

Keyframe 18-2e. Use the fiberscope as a stent to guide the tube. Be gentle passing the tube into the nose. Twist gently if it meets an obstruction. If the trachea is well numbed the patient may not feel the tube enter the trachea. Coughing and risk of neck movement is minimized.

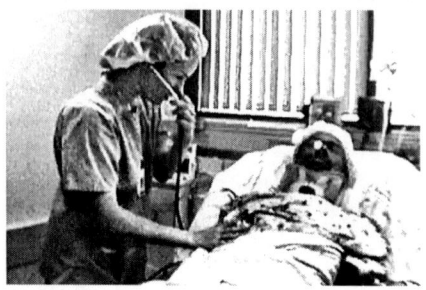

Keyframe 18-2f. Always verify placement after intubation.

Apneic Fiberoptic Intubation

Intubation with the fiberoptic can take quite a few minutes. If your patient is apneic you must use a strategy to maintain ventilation for the time it takes to intubate. Stopping the attempt to ventilate often means removing all of the instruments and then replacing them for the next attempt. Time is lost.

Specialty circuit adapters equipment with a bronchoscopy port can be used to ventilate while using the fiberoptic.

If you don't have one, you can improvise. For example, ventilate with a nasal airway plus an endotracheal tube adapter (Fig. 18-5). After placing the nasal airway, an assistant ventilates while sealing the mouth and nostril around the instrument. The intubator then performs fiberoptic bronchoscopy through the mouth or opposite nostril. This technique can be used on apneic patients and also to maintain deep anesthesia during intubation under general anesthesia — a technique very helpful with difficult intubations in children. Always have someone monitor the patient and periodically verify breathe sounds. Suction frequently.

Use of the fiberoptic bronchoscope requires practice. Emergencies are a poor time to learn the skill. If you have a fiberoptic, practice intubating the manikin. You can apply clay or other obstructions in the airway to mimic the difficult intubation. Anesthesia and surgical personnel can use it during routine intubation of patients scheduled for elective surgery. Don't wait until you need it to use it.

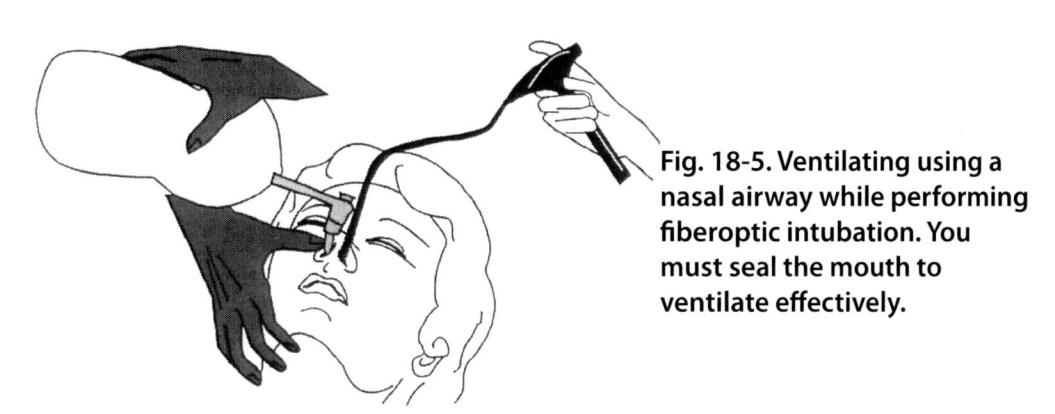

Fig. 18-5. Ventilating using a nasal airway while performing fiberoptic intubation. You must seal the mouth to ventilate effectively.

The Keyframe (KF) sequences in this chapter are taken from video clips that are available on-line, for free, from anyonecanintubate.com at:

For Chapter 18 video clips go to:
http://bit.ly/14tRnPt

All video chapter files appear on Anyone Can Intubate Portfolio at:
http://bit.ly/U7EV7f

19
COMPLICATIONS

Intubation has potential complications, many serious. Complications from intubation can occur at any time — during the intubation procedure, while the patient remains intubated, or following the extubation (Table 19-1). Review of the American Society of Anesthesiology Closed Claims Project data suggests that 33% of all deaths completely attributable to anesthesia are due to airway mismanagement, the most frequent cause of morbidity and mortality.

Complications Occurring During the Intubation

The actual intubation procedure is the time when physical trauma and hyperdynamic physiologic responses are most likely to occur. In order to protect your patient, pay close attention to your technique, as well as to your patient's responses.

Can't Intubate/Can't Ventilate

Difficult intubation, even if the intubation is ultimately successful, predisposes to injury from trauma, ischemia, hypertension, or tachycardia resulting from prolonged or multiple attempts. However, failed intubation, especially the potentially catastrophic "can't intubate/can't ventilate" scenario can be deadly.

The key to salvaging this situation is to quickly recognize the problem and *ask for help early,* even if that means you sometimes don't need help when it arrives. If you wait until O_2 sat. starts to drop before asking for help, you don't have much time to recover control. See the difficult airway algorithm in Chapter 10.

Esophageal Intubation

The incidence of esophageal intubation is unknown because the vast majority of esophageal intubations are recognized soon after intubation and corrected before injury to the patient can occur. However, if unrecognized, it can lead to ischemic brain damage, cardiac arrest, and death. Rates of pre-hospital misplaced intubation are reported to range from 0.4% to 25% with most being less than 10%. In a review of over 1600 intubations by paramedics, only 2 % were unrecognized esophageal intubations but 57% of the failures were in trauma patients.[1]

The availability of devices that measure the presence of exhaled CO_2 has greatly improved early recognition of esophageal intubation.

Aspiration

The incidence of aspiration in the emergency population varies from 1 to 20% depending on the population and situation, with pre-hospital incidence as high as 39%.[1] Aspiration can potentially cause chemical pneumonitis and acute respiratory distress syndrome (ARDS).

Fast action can often prevent aspiration if your patient vomits during intubation. Turn the patient on her side and quickly suction the pharynx. Place the bed in Trendelenburg if possible to allow emesis to pool away from the larynx. Immediately suction the endotracheal tube and verify breath sounds.

Table 19-1. Complications of Tracheal Intubation.

DURING INTUBATION

Failed intubation/Can't ventilate
    Esophageal intubation
Aspiration
Mechanical Trauma
    bleeding in the oropharynx, nose
    corneal abrasion
    pneumothorax caused or worsened
    spinal cord injury
    submucosal dissection
    trauma to teeth and soft tissue
    tube damage requiring change
Mainstem intubation
Harmful Physiologic Responses
    arrhythmia, including tachycardia
    bronchospasm
    hypertension
    hypercarbia and acidosis
    hypoxia
    laryngospasm
    CPR interrupted > 15 seconds
    myocardial ischemia
    death

WHILE INTUBATED

tube obstruction: secretions, blood.
biting tube, kinking
mainstem intubation
esophageal intubation
accidental extubation
mucosal ischemia: excessive cuff
    pressure, tube tip
higher resistance to breathing
aspiration around cuff or tube
pneumonia
sinusitis (with nasal intubation)

AFTER EXTUBATION

Acute
    laryngospasm
    vomiting and aspiration
    sore throat
    hoarseness
    laryngeal edema, subglottic edema
    postextubation croup
    postobstructive pulmonary edema
Chronic
    mucosal ulceration
    tracheitis
    tracheal stenosis
    vocal cord paralysis
    arytenoid cartilage dislocation

Minor aspiration can be asymptomatic. Aspirating as little as 0.4 ml/kg of pH 2.5 liquid can cause severe pneumonitis. Wheezing, unequal breath sounds, an acidic pH of tracheal secretions, or actual particulate matter in the endotracheal tube indicate a major aspiration. Treat major aspiration aggressively with bronchoscopy, tracheal toilet, and chest physiotherapy.

Thick particulate material can plug your endotracheal tube and be difficult to suction. You may need to consider removing and replacing a plugged tube with a clean one if ventilation is difficult. Weigh the risks of further aspiration.

If the patient aspirates upon extubation you must use your clinical judgment as to the necessity of reintubation. Extubated patients are better able to cough and deep breathe than intubated patients. On the other hand, applying positive inspiratory pressure or high concentrations of oxygen is much easier in the intubated patient. Let the patient's status be your guide.

Mechanical Trauma

Mechanical trauma is more likely to occur in the emergency situation, if positioning is suboptimal and if the patient is struggling. Prolonged or multiple intubation attempts can also predispose to edema, bleeding, and damage to teeth and soft tissue. Sore throat and hoarseness are common after any intubation.

Nasal intubations can easily cause nosebleeds. Additionally, submucosal dissections can occur if the tip of the nasotracheal tube tears the mucosa and dissects underneath it. While rare with oral intubation, reports of submucosal dissection have occurred using the GlideScope, most likely due to the intubator staring at the *monitor* during insertion of the endotracheal tube into the mouth, rather than directly observing the tip of the tube until it passes the uvula.

Protect the eyes. Corneal abrasions can easily occur as you lean over the patient and touch the face. The list of objects uncannily attracted to the eyes includes stethoscope bells, name badges, and your pocket pen protector.

Cervical spine injury is always a potential risk in the trauma patient. It can also occur in the patient with cervical disc disease, spinal stenosis or spinal cord tumor. Even the patient with severe osteoporosis can suffer cervical vertebral injury with severe neck extension. Use neck stabilization in patients at risk, but always use gentle technique when manipulating head and neck.

Pneumothorax

Failure to adjust the pop-off valve when switching from mask to tube ventilation can result in over-pressure injury and pneumothorax. Additionally, too large a tidal volume, or "stacking" breaths and failing to allow the patient to exhale completely before the next breath comes, can also cause pneumothorax.

Always suspect pneumothorax if the patient's respiratory status acutely deteriorates. Don't forget that in an over-pressure situation pneumothorax can be bilateral, creating equal but abnormal breath sounds.

Physiologic Response

Intubation, especially if prolonged, predisposes to the harmful physiologic responses (Table 19-1). Hypertension, arrhythmia, hypoxia, hypercapnia and respiratory acidosis, vomiting, and aspiration can all occur — even in patients intubated awake. Laryngospasm and bronchospasm from airway irritability or aspirated secretions can occur. The temptation to interrupt CPR for longer than 15 seconds is great. It's also easy to forget to ventilate the patient between attempts and to suction the mouth.

Complications Occurring While Intubated

Once the patient is intubated, don't stop worrying about airway protection. Being ventilated thorough an endotracheal tube places the patient at risk for a variety of complications. You should monitor the patient for physical harm from the ongoing presence of the endotracheal tube.

Bronchospasm

Wheezing commonly occurs if the endotracheal tube tip touches the carina or enters a mainstem bronchus. When you hear wheezing, check the depth of insertion and listen for equality of breath sounds, although breath sounds may be equal if the ETT tip is merely touching the carina. Try pulling the tube back slightly to see if bronchospasm improves.

Patients with irritable bronchi such as asthmatics, those with chronic obstructive pulmonary disease, and those with an acute respiratory infection can develop bronchospasm. Squirting several puffs of albuterol down the tube often breaks the bronchospasm. Spraying 1% lidocaine — for example cardiac lidocaine 3-5 ml (30-50 mg) — may improve the patient's tolerance to the tube.

If wheezing continues, consider getting a chest X-ray. Pulmonary edema and pneumothorax can cause wheezing or unequal breath sounds.

Problems From Tube Movement

Extubation, esophageal intubation, and mainstem intubation can occur at any time. Patient movement will move the endotracheal tube. If the nose points up, the tube rises in the larynx. If the nose points down, the tube descends.

A high riding endotracheal tube cuff can migrate inside the cricoid ring where it can place prolonged and potentially excessive pressure on the recurrent laryngeal nerves just under the mucosa. Recurrent laryngeal injury causes transient, and sometimes permanent vocal cord paralysis.

Because nasal intubations minimize upward and downward migration of the ETT tip with head movement, at one time nasal intubations were commonly used for long-term intubations in ICU settings. However, nasal intubations predispose to sinusitis and this practice is no longer routinely recommended.

Loose taping of the tube allows excessive movement. The point where the tape or other securing device wraps around the ETT will usually be where the ETT tends to rest. If you want the tube depth to be 21 cm at the teeth, but you place the tape wrap at 23 cm, the tube will invariably go to 23 cm deep. Therefore place the tape wrap at the depth marker you desire.

Twisting of the tube can force its tip against the mucosa and cause ulceration. Secure the tube well to minimize the risk of trauma and misplacement.

Cuff Inside the Cricoid Cartilage

Positioning the ETT cuff inside the cricoid ring risks recurrent laryngeal nerve palsy or paralysis because the nerves run within the mucosa and are vulnerable to compression in this location. Vocal cord paralysis, either permanent or transient can result.

Cuff positioning inside the cricoid ring can occur most commonly with ETTs that are secured at too shallow a depth for the patient. Having the ETT over-ride the tongue can fool you into thinking the ETT is deeper than it actually is because some of the tube inside the mouth, that you can't see, is not inside the trachea.

When using a cuffed tube in a child, be aware that the tip and cuff and move significantly with head movement. Extension of the head can place the cuff inside the cricoid ring. As in adults, positioning of the cuff inside the cricoid cartilage can injure the recurrent laryngeal nerves.

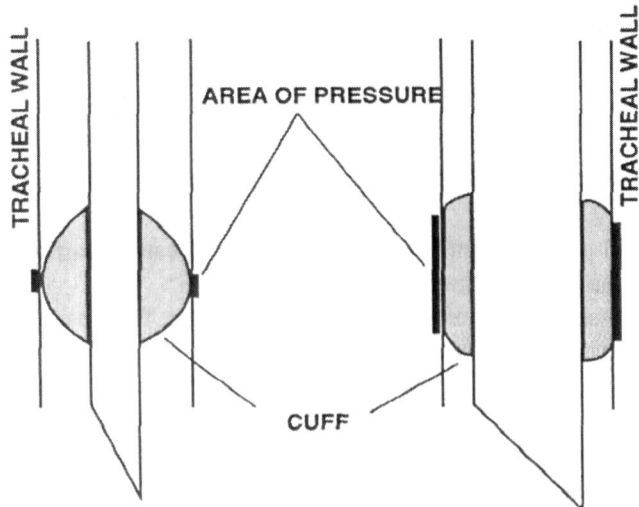

Fig. 19-1. The pressure is distributed differently on the tracheal walls depending on the size of the cuff.

Cuff Inflation Over-Pressure

Excessive inflation of the tube cuff can cause mucosal damage. Using the largest tube possible reduces the gap that the cuff must seal and therefore lowers the cuff volume and pressure needed to do so. It spreads pressure more equally over the tracheal wall. The cuff on the smaller tube becomes rounded when distended and applies point pressure to the wall (Fig. 19-1).

In addition, use of high-volume, low pressure tubes is recommended in order to more evenly distribute pressure and decrease risk of wall injury. However, even over-inflation of even high-volume, low-pressure cuffs can destroy ciliated epithelium. When this damaged area heals it can create a barrier for mucous transport and produce a chronic cough.

The tracheal wall is asymmetric: cartilaginous anteriorly and muscular posteriorly. Shifting of the ETT with under-inflation in the face of cuff asymmetry can cause the tip to be angled against the tracheal wall, causing rubbing and friction injury such as ulceration and necrosis..

Inflate cuffs to "minimal seal", the pressure just needed to seal the trachea. Normally it takes about 15-20 cm H_2O to seal the trachea enough to prevent aspiration and allows adequate tidal volumes. Cuff pressure should be below the critical 25 cm H_2O pressure when mucosal ischemia starts to occur.

When using an uncuffed tube in a child, we are looking for a leak around 20 cm H_2O. Even though there is no cuff, the sides of the tube can press too hard against the firm inside of the cricoid ring.

Endotracheal Tube Obstruction

Secretions and dried blood can plug endotracheal tubes to the extent that ventilation is impossible. Tubes can kink, sometimes inside the mouth where it may not be obvious. Obstruction can also occur if the patient bites the tube. Consider a bite block or oral airway. In all of these cases it will be difficult to ventilate the patient and pass a suction catheter down the tube.

Use of larger tubes, meticulous attention to tube positioning, and periodic cleansing of the tube will help prevent obstruction from plugging and kinking. If the tube is badly plugged you may need to exchange the ETT for a new one.

Infection

The larynx is a major barrier to infection. The endotracheal tube violates this barrier. Although sterile at the start, the endotracheal tube passes through the mouth, allowing bacteria to enter the trachea. Patients intubated for prolonged periods have poorer oral hygiene, increasing the risk.

In addition, intubated patients can't close their glottis to generate the higher pressures needed to cough. Pneumonia can occur from secretions leaking past the cuff, from impairment of coughing and poor clearance of secretions, and from drying of the mucous membranes and cilia impairing natural defenses.

Edema from minor tube trauma can cause obstruction of the sinuses and eustachian tubes, especially with nasal intubations. Edema predisposes to ear and sinus infections. Close attention to oral hygiene, careful asepsis, and frequent examination of the patient will help prevent infection as well as diagnose it early.

Complications Following Extubation

Acute and chronic problems can follow extubation. Vomiting and aspiration can always occur. Sore throat and hoarseness are also common. The most serious acute problems following extubation are laryngospasm, post-obstructive pulmonary edema, and post-extubation croup and respiratory insufficiency.

Laryngospasm

Laryngospasm is reflex spasmodic closure of the vocal cords. It can occur when the vocal cords are stimulated in a semi-conscious patient, a time when airway protective reflexes are hyperactive. An example is Stage II of an anesthetic induction or emergence. Patients suffering from head trauma or heavy sedation are also at risk. If it occurs, vocal cord closure can be so forceful that it prevents ventilation or passage of the endotracheal tube.

If laryngospasm occurs, suction the airway clear of secretions, thrust the jaw upward, and apply positive pressure ventilation administered by bag-valve-mask. Pulling the jaw forward often opens a small gap between the vocal cords. Positive pressure then forces oxygen below the cords, which "balloons" the larynx below the cords and forces the cords further apart, usually breaking the spasm.

Intravenous lidocaine 0.5-1 mg/kg sometimes helps. If the spasm doesn't break, sedative drugs and/or muscle relaxants may be needed. You don't need a full dose of muscle relaxation: about 20% the intubating dose will usually break the spasm and allow ventilation. The patient can breathe after this small dose but will be weak and need assistance until it wears off. Reassure your awake patient since such weakness may be frightening.

To prevent laryngospasm:
- ensure the pharynx is clear of secretions before extubation;
- avoid stimulating the vocal cords in a semiconscious patient;
- extubate either awake, or in a deep plane of anesthesia – not semiconscious

Post Obstructive Pulmonary Edema

Patients with post obstructive pulmonary edema (or P.O.P.E.) develop sudden, unexpected and potentially life-threatening pulmonary edema after relief of airway obstruction. P.O.P.E. Type I follows acute airway obstruction. P.O.P.E. Type II, which is much less common, develops after surgical relief of chronic upper airway obstruction, such as a tumor.

P.O.P.E. Type I occurs when forceful attempts to inhale against an obstruction create highly negative intrathoracic pressure. This negative pressure, in turn, increases venous return, decreases cardiac output and forces intravascular fluid to shift into the alveolar space. The typical P.O.P.E. patient is young, healthy, and strong.

A common case history for P.O.P.E. Type I, is the patient who goes into laryngospasm immediately following extubation, resulting in transient airway obstruction. The patient then complains of dyspnea and respiratory distress. Symptoms can be mild, ranging from unexplained, asymptomatic hypoxemia, to severe — requiring reintubation and ventilatory support. Clinical signs include blood tinged frothy sputum, tachypnea, tachycardia, rales and rhonchi. Symptoms usually begin within an hour, but have been reported as late as 6 hours later.

Treatment consists of supplemental oxygen and support. Gentle diuresis with low dose furosemide may help. Reintubation may be required plus low levels of positive end-expiratory pressure. Full and rapid recovery can be expected with appropriate management.

Post-Extubation Croup

Minor sore throats and hoarseness are common. Severe edema causes airway obstruction and can present as post-extubation croup. Post-extubation croup is caused by inflammation of the subglottic region due to mechanical irritation from the endotracheal tube. It's most common in children 1 - 4 years old. Young age predisposes to problems simply because of small airway size. One mm of circumferential edema in an average adult with a 10 mm cricoid opening reduces that opening 20%, leaving considerable reserve. The same 1 mm circumferential edema in a baby's 3 mm cricoid reduces the opening by almost 70%.

Other contributing factors include trauma during intubation, excessive tube movement, airway infection, a tight fitting tube with no leak at 25 - 40 cm H_2O, surgery in the neck region, children with previous history of croup, and a duration of intubation of more than 1 hour.

The patient, typically a child, develops a barking cough. The patient may have stridor or dyspnea. Conservative therapy consists of humidified oxygen by mask or "croup tent" or treatment with aerosolyzed racemic epinephrine, which helps to shrink the mucous membrane and resolve obstruction. The dose of racemic epinephrine is 0.25 - 0.5 ml of 2.25% solution in 5 ml saline every 1-4 hours depending on the severity. Dexamethasone, 0.15 mg/kg may help prevent further edema formation. Croup can develop as long as 1-2 hours following extubation.

Because swelling can worsen again after the epinephrine effect wears off, it's important to observe the patient for recurrence. If obstructive symptoms are severe and do not resolve with treatment then reintubation may be needed.

Every patient should be monitored in the immediate post extubation period for potential respiratory insufficiency or obstruction. Early recognition and treatment of respiratory compromise is essential.

Laryngeal and Tracheal Injury

Tracheitis, tracheal stenosis, vocal cord paralysis, arytenoid cartilage dislocation all represent chronic complications. You can minimize the risk of the problems by the use of gentle technique and care throughout the patient's intubation. Avoid allowing the cuff to over-pressurize or remain inside the cricoid ring where such pressure can injury the recurrent laryngeal nerves and mucosa.

Creating a Safe Culture of Care

While complications can occur even with perfect care, understanding the causes and routinely taking the steps to prevent them help ensure that complications remain uncommon.

An estimated 200,000 patients die each year, or 22 patients die each hour, from completely avoidable medical errors. A recent book, *Why Hospitals Should Fly* by Nance notes that although we can't prevent human error, we can minimize its effects by creating teams of mutually respectful and supportive colleagues, checking one another for the common goal of keeping our patients and ourselves safe from unnecessary harm.

- Prepare for every patient contact as though something will go wrong.
- If problems arise communicate with your team.
- Ask for help early: leave your ego at the door.
- Be flexible and think out of the box.
- Speak up if you see a problem. Don't let fear keep you silent.
- Seek emotional support if you are involved with a poor outcome.
- Learn from your mistakes.
- Share your failures so that others don't repeat them.
- Minimizing personal stress results in maximum professional function.

Personal illness, fatigue, hunger, dehydration as well as stressful personal situations at home and at work can compromise your function. Be mindful that these distractions make you prone for error and consider letting your team know if your function is potentially compromised so they can watch your back.

By being proactive, we can greatly decrease the risks of complications to those that depend on us for safe health care.

20
BOREDOM, INTERRUPTED

It has been said that "Airline travel is hours of boredom, interrupted by moments of stark terror." Procedures involving anesthesia and airway management are never exactly boring, but things can proceed very smoothly for hours, and then suddenly turn into a potential disaster in seconds.

This chapter details some of my most unexpected and difficult "moments of sheer terror." There are specific lessons from each case, but there is one overriding thing you should never forget: Fear is the mind-killer. Different generations have various expressions for this thought: "put your emotions aside" (50s), "don't lose your head" (60s), "keep your cool" (70s), and today's "stay frosty." An anonymous post on the internet, in response to the question of why more medical students don't become anesthesiologists, sums it up quite nicely:

> "When $%*# hits the fan you MUST not fall apart, you MUST think very fast, and you MUST not be wrong."

When a patient's status is deteriorating and decisions must be made quickly before all of the facts are in, you have to be able to generate likely diagnoses and formulate a plan. You must then be able to revise that plan as the patient responds for better or worse — all of this while also controlling your own emotional reaction and leading your team.

The practice of medicine is an art, based not only on knowledge, skill, and experience but also on imagination. My teachers always used to say that if you haven't seen something, it's because you haven't been practicing long enough. My goal is to spark your imagination about how to apply the information in the preceding chapters, and to teach you something about how to approach clinical problem solving.

Case 1. The Baby with Severe Bronchospasm

Ex-premies who spend the first month on a ventilator can suffer lung damage. In this case, the baby was an ex-premie, weighing 6 kg with a complicated history of bronchospasm. Once the baby was deeply anesthetized, I performed laryngoscopy with a Miller 0 blade and smoothly inserted the 3.0 endotracheal tube. However, the chest did not rise with ventilation and I could not hear breath sounds. The bag felt stiff and poorly compliant. There was no end tidal CO_2 on the capnograph. O_2 sat. dropped into the 90s: all classic signs of an esophageal intubation.

I immediately extubated, then manually ventilated using a mask and ventilation bag. Ventilation was difficult at first but insertion of an oral airway and deepening anesthesia seemed to help.

When saturation returned to 100%, I re-intubated. Once again the bag felt stiff, there were no breath sounds and no end tidal CO_2. I repeated laryngoscopy. Although the ETT was in the trachea, I still couldn't ventilate.

I extubated again, only this time I couldn't ventilate with the bag and mask. I heard a faint wheeze. The baby was in such severe bronchospasm that there wasn't enough air movement to either produce breath sounds or expire enough CO_2 for us to detect.

O$_2$ sat. fell. I grabbed an albuterol inhaler, detached the bag, and squirted several puffs through the hole in the top of the mask while holding it tightly against the baby's face. This formed an improvised aerochamber, which concentrated the albuterol. After a few breaths of albuterol, the bronchospasm started to break. Suddenly I could hear musical wheezes.

With O$_2$ sat in the upper 90s, I again intubated the baby. Wheezing worsened but after further treatment with albuterol through the ETT and deepening anesthesia, bronchospasm resolved and surgery proceeded.

Lessons learned:

As always, ventilation takes first priority.

If you know the equipment, and its relationship with anatomy and physiology, you can improvise and use equipment in a different way than intended.

When all of the signs pointed to esophageal intubation, the first choice should be to pull out the endotracheal tube, mask ventilate the patient, and repeat intubation. When the second intubation attempt also appears to be esophageal, performing laryngoscopy to verify ETT location may make sense if you had a good view of the ETT passing the cords.

When you can't ventilate through an endotracheal tube the potential reasons include:
- the tube isn't in the trachea after all.
- the tube is plugged or kinked inside the mouth
- something is preventing air from entering the patient's lungs, such as: a foreign body, mucous plug, bronchospasm, or pneumothorax.

Case 2. The Girl with Epiglottitis

The child was sitting on the bed, drooling. She was in the tripod position, leaning forward over her knees, arms and neck straight– a position that maximizes descent of the diaphragm and offers the least resistance to breathing. The child had significant stridor and complained in a hoarse, muffled voice of being unable to swallow because of sore throat. She was restless and anxious but her lungs were clear and her O$_2$ sat. was 94%. She had a fever of 102°F and a heart rate of 120.

There was no history suggestive of foreign body aspiration. There also was no history of prior upper respiratory symptoms or barking cough suggestive of croup. Because the child seemed to be ventilating adequately, we allowed her to sit in her mother's arms to avoid scaring her. We used blow by oxygen because whenever we tried to put the non-rebreather mask on her face she started to cry, which might have made her obstruction worse.

The Emergency Room physician and the Head and Neck surgeon on call suspected immediately that the girl probably had epiglottitis. As anesthesiologist I accompanied the child to the OR in the event she decompensated on the way. I had my full intubation kit with me as a precaution.

We brought the child, still sitting on her mother's lap in a wheelchair, into the OR. The girl looked exhausted and struggled slightly to breathe with each stridorous breath. Her saturation was in the low 90s and her respiratory rate about 35. With her terrified mother singing a lullaby I placed the anesthesia mask over her face and slowly increased the concentration of anesthetic mixed with O$_2$. Once asleep we placed her on the OR table and sent her Mom to the waiting room. We now quickly started an IV. There is always some risk to waiting to start the IV after induction but in this case I thought the risk of wrestling an IV into an awake child with airway obstruction was greater. Medicine is built on such judgment calls.

I slowly increased the anesthetic concentration. I wanted to keep her breathing on her own as long as possible. We did not want to risk giving a muscle relaxant. A muscle relaxant would have prevented laryngospasm. However, it could also have caused collapse of the airway muscles in the posterior pharynx that were helping to hold the airway open.

Finally the child was ready for intubation. I chose an endotracheal tube one full I.D. size smaller than normal. This 5 year old would normally take a size 5.5 uncuffed tube. In this case I had chosen a 4.5. I also had a 4 and a 3.5 ready.

I performed laryngoscopy. Where the vocal cords should have been, I saw the swollen cherry red blob that was the epiglottis. No vocal cords were visible. Where to aim? I had an assistant push on the chest while I watched and saw a bubble of air exit the glottis revealing where the opening was. With one smooth move I aimed toward the bubble and the tube entered the larynx.

Lessons learned:

When you cannot directly see an opening, there are other ways of determining where it must be. Use your mind as much as you use your hands.

Case 3. Out of Sight Déjà Vu: Endotracheal Tube Obstruction

The 30 year old woman was lying on the gurney outside the treatment room. Although she was intubated, the patient was quite cyanotic and it was obvious my colleagues were having difficulty ventilating her. Breath sounds were present and equal but the force required to squeeze the bag was impressive.

The woman had been undergoing a septoplasty, a type of nasal surgery, under sedation combined with local anesthesia when she suddenly lost consciousness. The CRNA monitoring her had intubated immediately. My partner had already treated for bronchospasm even though there was no audible wheezing.

O_2 sat. was now 65% and dropping, and worse, the patient was developing a bradycardia of 40. Acute bradycardia in the face of hypoxia is a bad sign that often means impending cardiac arrest. There was a lot of blood in her mouth — drainage from the nasal surgery that had stopped before completion.

I flashed back to a case I had managed years before. My prior patient had suffered from Acute Respiratory Distress Syndrome (ARDS) and had been on the ventilator in the ICU for about a week when she suddenly developed extremely high ventilation pressures. A chest X-ray ruled out pneumothorax. Like the present case, she was intubated but we couldn't ventilate through the ETT. After I had reintubated her, we had found her ETT was filled with hardened secretions, onion-skinned around the inner surface until barely 1 mm of open channel remained.

But this patient had just been intubated minutes before. I tried suctioning down the tube and couldn't pass a catheter. The tube didn't seem kinked.

"Take out the tube and reintubate." I suggested. My partner hesitated, as well she should have. Taking out a perfectly good endotracheal tube in a patient who you think is about to arrest is not something to be done lightly.

"Take it out. I think it's plugged."

My partner grabbed her laryngoscope and under direct vision, extubated and quickly reintubated with a new ETT. Immediately we could ventilate. O_2 sat. rose, BP and pulse normalized. She started to wake up.

The ETT we had removed was plugged with an enormous organized blood clot. Apparently our patient had been silently aspirating blood during the procedure, a combination of deep sedation plus topicalization had taken away her cough reflex. The blood clot had caused obstruction and an increasing CO_2. An acute PCO_2 above 70 is sedating and can lead to worsening hypoventilation leading to higher PCO_2.

Lessons learned:

Be lucky. We were very lucky that the initial intubation forced the clot into the endotracheal tube. While it didn't help the immediate crisis, this scenario made it easy to remove the clot during extubation. Had the clot been below and outside the tube, blocking the carina, we might never have known.

Be knowledgeable. In this case, it was very helpful that I had faced a similar situation before. Every patient you care for adds to your "data base", and provides the scientific basis for your 6th sense intuition. Listen to it, but always have plan B.

Be imaginative. This is also another instance where a failure of imagination could've led to a bad result. After all, the patient had been easily intubated, and the ETT was inspected and properly placed. It would have been easy to assume that the fault lay in something other than the airway. The problem was that the ETT had been compromised after it was inserted, out of sight but, fortunately, not out of mind.

Case 4. Can't Intubate, Can't Ventilate, What Can You Do?

We were about to induce general anesthesia in an obese woman for an emergency C-Section. The baby's heart rate was very low, so we would not have time to do any form of regional anesthesia. We prefer spinal or epidural anesthesia for C-Sections to allow the Mom to participate in the birth. Equally important, regional anesthesia is considered safer because pregnant women are at high risk of aspiration and airway management problems.

I pushed my induction medications and paralyzing drug together as a rapid sequence induction. The OR nurse held cricoid pressure for me. I did not test ventilate this "full-stomach" patient in order to minimize the risk of aspiration.

I used my MAC blade to pick up her jaw. I saw no landmarks, absolutely nothing but tongue. I quickly switched to my Miller straight blade. Still nothing. I could hear the tone on the oxygen saturation monitor behind me alarm as her saturation fell below 90%. Pregnant patients have little reserve because there are two patients sharing the same oxygen "tank": Mom and baby.

I reached for the oxygen mask, placed an oral airway, and began to ventilate. And I couldn't get any oxygen into her lungs. I couldn't intubate and I couldn't ventilate and I had two patients' lives in the balance, not one. My blood ran cold.

I called for back up but it would take many minutes for help to come up from the Main OR two floors away, time neither of my patients had. I could use transtracheal oxygenation but the obstetrical nurses had no idea where the jet ventilator was kept, or what it looked like.

The week before, the hospital had taken its first delivery of a new device called a laryngeal mask airway, or LMA. Although trained on a manikin, I had never used one before in a patient. I grabbed the LMA off the cart and slid it into the patient's mouth. With heart pounding I squeezed the bag. Her chest rose effortlessly. O_2 saturation normalized and I told the obstetricians to deliver the baby.

Both Mother and baby did fine.

Lessons learned:

"Can't intubate/can't ventilate" is a scenario all of us hope to never see and all of us must be prepared for every single time we intubate. In this case I was exceedingly lucky — and I know I was lucky — not only to have an LMA available, but that my very first time using one worked perfectly. Don't rely on luck.

That case taught me to always have plan B, as well as plan C, before I need it. I check and recheck equipment. I make sure my assistants know where the emergency supplies are kept and how to help me. I also try to have a second provider standing by if I suspect an intubation might be hard.

I practice with any new equipment on manikins and on elective patients before I need it an emergency. Because medical technology is growing at such an incredible rate, I go to seminars and manufacturer demonstrations.

Case 5. Ventilate, Intubate and Communicate

The child on the OR table in Kenya during our volunteer medical mission was about 3 years old and scheduled for cleft lip repair. Dr Y, the anesthesiologist, was still mask ventilating the patient when he called for help. During the process of getting ready to intubate the child he found he could not open the boy's mouth. Malignant Hyperthermia, a severe reaction to certain anesthetics, can present with trismus or jaw rigidity, so we were worried.

The surgeon joined us. "You won't be able to open his mouth," he said. "He had an infection when he was one and his jaw is frozen shut. I'm going to fix that before I repair the lip." He paused. "It's in his chart," he said defensively.

Dr Y. looked sheepish and replied, " I didn't read his chart. I saw that you had signed off on it and figured if there was a problem you'd have told me."

Because we were a small team with the goal of operating on 100 patients in 5 days, I had made the command decision to have our physician's assistant help with preop exams. I glanced at the chart. Sure enough, buried in the physician assistant's note about a normal healthy little boy with a cleft lip was a short comment about his frozen jaw. I had countersigned the note.

I had failed to teach the P.A. the signs of difficult intubation, so she didn't know that it was important to tell me. I had been too preoccupied to read the note in detail past the words healthy child. I hadn't personally examined all 100 children. My colleague had been too focused on getting the case started.

"What's the problem, just intubate him?" asked our surgeon, who clearly didn't realize he should have told us about the frozen jaw.

I examined the child. A locked jaw is not a common problem in the US — rapid medical care prevents it from developing. Children in the third world lack access to medical care and may have to live with such a disability for the rest of their lives. Smaller than normal peers, children with frozen jaws often have short, poorly developed mandibles. This child looked like he had Pierre Robbin, a congenital syndrome associated with a much smaller than normal jaw.

I lubricated a small nasal airway with local anesthetic ointment. Attaching the adaptor from an appropriately sized endotracheal tube, I slid it into the boy's left nostril and hooked up our anesthesia breathing circuit. The child could continue to breathe the anesthesia gas spontaneously through the nasal airway, allowing us to nasally intubate through the other nostril while he was still asleep. The surgeon did the surgery, and the child recovered.

Lessons learned:

Communicate. Never assume your teammates, no matter how talented or highly educated, know what you consider important — or that they will remember to tell you.

Never skip a safety step, regardless of how "easy" or "safe" the case seems. No intubation is easy, and all involve some risk. Commercial airline pilots will tell you that the more difficult approaches are often also the safest. In a difficult approach, everyone in the cockpit is intently focused, and distractions are not tolerated, because the crew knows the landing is not easy. In contrast, an easy landing approach invites overconfidence and distraction, which can lead to disaster.

Always have a plan B and the necessary equipment to carry it out.

Case 6. The Popping Polyp

Looking at the video of the larynx of this 30 yo patient was indeed sobering (Mov. 20-1, Fig. 20-1abcd). This 8 mm spherical polyp was popping in and out of a laryngeal opening of about the same size with each breath like a potential cork. According to the surgeon she had come to the clinic because she had been experiencing some increased shortness of breath. Having the video was a rare advantage.

My surgeon recognized that we needed to strategize together to come up with an optimal plan. He needed a smaller than average tube size to allow him to operate on the polyp. He was also worried this might be fragile tissue, easy to bleed. However he felt certain that if I anesthetized her in the normal fashion I would be able to intubate with normal laryngoscopy.

However, I worried that if I did paralyze her for induction and failed to intubate, that I might not be able to ventilate her. The polyp could plug the trachea with manual ventilation.

If I did an awake fiberoptic intubation with the patient breathing, I would be able to pass the fiber into the larynx under direct vision. Unfortunately, I would then have to pass the endotracheal tube down the fiber blindly over the fiber. In the worst case scenario, the tube could rip the polyp off its stalk and shove it down the trachea, causing bleeding and perhaps airway obstruction down at the carina.

I decided to use the GlideScope, which doesn't require as much jaw lift as conventional laryngoscopy. This would allow me to pass the tube under direct vision with the patient awake. The surgeon stood by with his tracheostomy equipment nearby just in case things did not go as expected.

After pre-treatment with glycopyrrolate to dry secretions, and some slowly titrated midazolam and fentanyl, I topicalized her oropharynx with local anesthetic spray. I then performed glossopharyngeal nerve blocks to block her gag reflex.

Using the Glidescope to visualize the larynx, and timing my forward insertion of the tube into the larynx to when the polyp was visible above the cords, I easily passed a 6.0 mm endotracheal tube.

Lessons learned:

There are many different ways to have safely intubated and anesthetized this patient. The important point was that the surgeon and I discussed the concerns and together came up with a plan. We also had plans for what we would do if we lost the airway.

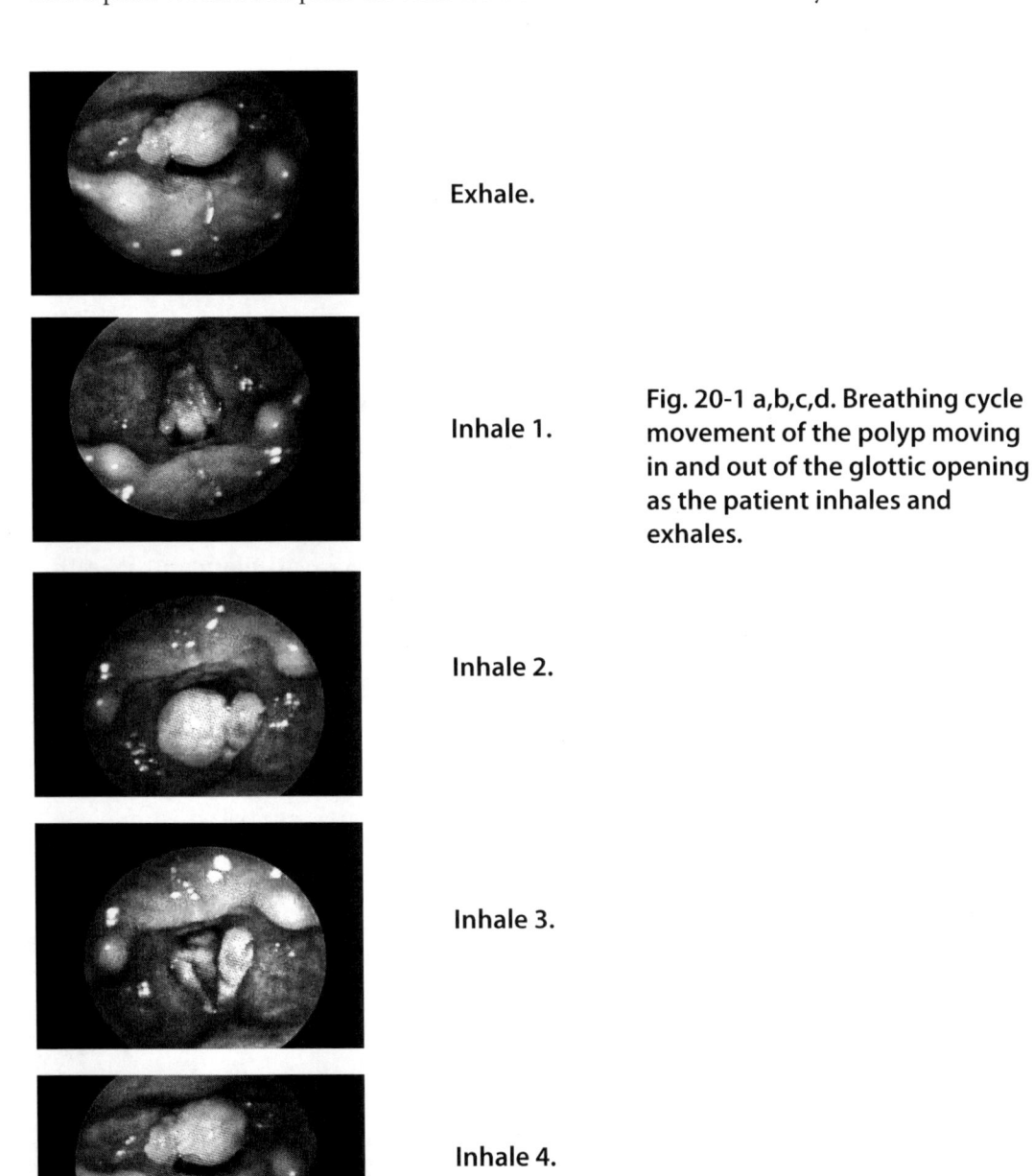

Exhale.

Inhale 1.

Fig. 20-1 a,b,c,d. Breathing cycle movement of the polyp moving in and out of the glottic opening as the patient inhales and exhales.

Inhale 2.

Inhale 3.

Inhale 4.

Case 7. Anaphylaxis Analysis

The 45-year-old woman in the Preop area suddenly developed hives after receiving antibiotics and complained that her tongue felt like it was swelling.

By the time I reached the preop area, she had a grossly swollen tongue, a uvula that looked like a small water balloon filling the back of her oropharynx, congested conjunctivae, and diffuse wheezing over both lung fields. Her voice was hoarse. This looked like classic and full-blown anaphylaxis.

We immediately administered 0.3 mg of epinephrine subcutaneously and gave 50 mg of benadryl IV while the RNs were setting up an epinephrine drip. She was also breathing 100% oxygen by non-rebreather mask. Her O_2 sats were 97% but she was quite dyspneic. Her BP was 90/40 and her pulse was 120s. I cautiously started the epinephrine drip, watching the monitor for arrythmias.

I had two choices. I could wait to see if the epi drip reversed the swelling or go ahead and try to intubate her. If I waited, I might be able to avoid an unneeded, and potentially challenging intubation. She might not tolerate any induction medications and I didn't want to use muscle relaxants on an airway that was at best questionable. On the other hand, if her swelling worsened, I might not being able to intubate her, which could prompt the need for an emergency cricothyrotomy.

At this point the patient lost consciousness and her BP fell to 60 systolic. Time to intubate. I grabbed my straight blade since I expected that her swollen tongue would make a MAC harder to use. With a great deal of difficulty and with a lot of cricoid pressure, I could barely make out the back of her arytenoids cartilages..

One of the simplest and most valuable adjuncts to intubation is the bougie. I slid a bougie into the gap between and above the arytenoids and pushed it down what I was hoping was the trachea. I could feel "clicks" as the tip of the bougie bumped over tracheal rings on the way down. Good sign.

I slid a 6.0 ETT down the bougie to the proper depth. I never saw the cords therefore I immediately checked placement. Bilateral breath sounds, equally wheezy throughout but less so than several minutes before.

Over the next few minutes the swelling seemed to stabilize, blood pressure rose to 100/60 and the patient started to wake up. We gave hydrocortisone, 5 mg/kg IV and some midazolam so that she would tolerate the endotracheal tube.

The patient remained intubated in the ICU for the next 12 hours. Once the swelling started to subside, we tried the leak test, and satisfied, pulled the endotracheal tube — with our re-intubation equipment standing by of course.

Lessons learned:

Deciding when or if to intubate during an allergic reaction can be difficult because the situation is constantly evolving and can deteriorate rapidly. You can always remove an endotracheal tube if the swelling goes down. You may not always be able to put one in. If the treatment is not improving the airway, and intubation proves impossible, emergency cricothyrotomy may need to be your next step.

Case 8. Accidental Extubation in Ludwig's Angina

The 40 yo man had Ludwig's Angina, a serious, potentially life-threatening cellulitis infection of the tissues of the floor of the mouth, often occurring in an adult with a dental infection. Ludwig's Angina has nothing to do with cardiac angina. "Angina" is a word that comes from the Greek and means strangling — in this case strangling from airway obstruction. This gentleman had swelling so bad that it was hard to tell where his chin ended and his neck began. He was a big man anyway, over 6 ft tall and 110 kg (240 lbs.).

After 5 mg of valium and 50 mcg of fentanyl (both very small doses for a man his size) and an aerosolized lidocaine/pontocaine mixture he was ready. We did not perform injected nerve blocks because of concern of injecting into infected tissue. We needed to be gentle to avoid rupturing an abscesses in the oropharynx.

The nasal fiberoptic intubation went gratifyingly easily. The patient cooperatively took deep breaths on command as I pulled his tongue outward with a gauze pad. My resident expertly intubated him in less than 2 minutes.

We taped the tube. With the airway secure and the anesthetic proceeding uneventfully I left OR 3 and went to the adjacent OR 4 to see how my other resident was doing with his case. As I walked out, the surgeons were just starting to position the patient for surgery.

It wasn't three minutes before the door burst open and an RN yelled that they needed me stat in OR 3. Upon arrival I saw my resident mask ventilating our Ludwig's Angina patient, the ETT, on the ground. The surgeon had tripped over the anesthesia breathing circuit while turning the table and pulled the tube out.

Normally we could have awakened him and redone the awake intubation, but my resident had just paralyzed him with a long acting agent. Instead, I inserted a lubricated nasal airway with an endotracheal tube adaptor into the left nostril to which we attached our breathing circuit. My resident ventilated, closing the patient's mouth with his left hand while squeezing the bag with his right.

In the meantime I inserted a new endotracheal tube into the right nostril and repeated the fiberoptic visualization. With the mouth tightly closed there was a fortuitous fold in the swollen tongue forming an open channel in the midline leading straight to the larynx. I followed it down and reintubated the patient. We retaped the tube and this time we turned the table for the surgeon, while holding the tube securely. The rest of the case was uneventful.

Lessons learned:

Watch your feet. Eveyr room is different. An inlet can be on the left in one room and on the right in another. Take note of the arrangement of equipment before you begin.

Always tape your endotracheal tubes as though your patient's life depends on it, because it does. Hold onto the tube where it exits the mouth when moving the patient. Always be ready for accidental extubation, not just with healthy patients, but also ones in poor health.

Case 9. A Flood of Blood in the Airway

The 18 year old on the transplant list had end stage cirrhosis, due to what at the time was called "non A- non B" hepatitis. She had been admitted to the ICU that day to be worked up for a stable upper GI bleed. The most likely etiology was her esophageal varices: superficial esophageal veins that have become abnormally distended due to portal hypertension in end stage liver disease. So far she had been rock stable — that was about to change.

When I reached the bedside, the patient was coughing and sputtering blood onto the bed sheets and there was blood everywhere. Her varices were bleeding profusely and she was going to drown in her own blood if we didn't intubate her now. Her blood pressure was 80/50 and her pulse was 150.

I ordered the crash cart and asked for blood to be brought from the blood bank while we were giving her a bolus of crystalloid. We kept her on her side, in trendelenburg position until the last possible moment to allow the blood to drain out of her mouth. Once ready, I administered an induction dose of ketamine and succinylcholine. Ketamine would help to maintain her blood pressure.

As the drugs took effect we laid her flat, still in steep trendelenburg. This position usually lets the blood pool up and away from the larynx allowing the intubator to see the landmarks. All I could see was a puddle of blood welling up. Sucking the blood through the yankauer catheter could not clear the mouth fast enough to keep it clear. Intubation was impossible under these conditions; something needed to be changed, quickly.

We turned her onto her left side and placed the open end of the suction tubing itself into her mouth to allow it to suction continuously. The side position allowed the blood to drain out as fast as it entered her mouth and let the tongue fall to the left, where I wanted it to go anyway. I was able to intubate her.

After resuscitation with 9 units of blood, 4 units of FFP and a 6 pack of platelets plus about 5 liters of normal saline, the bleeding slowly stopped and we stabilized her. She eventually went on to successful transplant.

Lessons learned:

Active bleeding in the airway makes intubation very challenging: airway bleeding, in both the acute trauma and postoperative settings, means that the anatomy may be altered and landmarks difficult to identify; hemodynamic instability makes choice of sedative/hypnotic agents and muscle relaxants problematic; and usually, the patient has a stomach full of blood ready to aspirate. Know how to deal with this dangerous and demanding situation.

The interventions described above will work for any liquid in the airway, including emesis. Patients in shock frequently vomit, sometimes profusely. Putting the bed in trendelburg, ensuring adequate suction and helpers, and turning the patient onto the side can all help.

Case 10. Tomorrow's Diseases Today: Post-Obstructive Pulmonary Edema

To set the scene, the year was 1983. We had Reagan and *Thriller* – but we didn't have pulse oximetry, end-tidal carbon dioxide monitoring or even automated blood pressure cuffs. Nobody imagined the syndrome now known as Post-Obstructive Pulmonary Edema.

The patient was a healthy 6'3" tall and 250 lbs, 20 year old man, all muscle and clearly in great shape. He had just had knee surgery under general anesthesia and was on the verge of waking up.

Because he was coughing on the endotracheal tube, and was such a big man the resident extubated him because he was afraid that he would injure himself while struggling. However, the resident missed the fact that the patient was in Stage 2 of anesthetic emergence, a period when the airway reflexes are hyperdynamic.

Within seconds the patient went into laryngospasm, intense spasmodic closure of the vocal cords and other laryngeal muscles. There followed several minutes of struggling to re-establish an open airway. Finally the spasm broke with the use of positive pressure and the patient awoke.

However the mood in the room quickly turned from relief to concern. The patient started to panic, claiming that he couldn't breathe. His color was poor. He was wheezing badly, with pink frothy sputum bubbling out of his mouth. He was awake enough to communicate with us but so panicked that he started to fight the team of caregivers.

We didn't know what had happened to put him into what appeared to be pulmonary edema but we knew that we needed to act quickly. We quickly administered an inhaler and IV aminophylline to try to break the bronchospasm but this didn't seem to help. He was now blue and he clearly was getting confused with the hypoxia. His blood pressure was now 260/130 and his pulse was 150.

The patient's breathing was so labored that his peripheral IVs flowed more rapidly when he took a breath and stopped flowing when he exhaled. This showed how much the pressure was changing inside his chest cavity with each breath.

We also worried that if we induced unconsciousness and paralyzed this clearly hypoxic man that we might not be able to ventilate him adequately by bag-valve-mask given the intrathoracic pressures he was clearly generating to breathe.

Therefore we topicalized his nose and did an awake nasal intubation. He literally seemed to suck the endotracheal tube into the trachea during inhalation. Once intubated we slowly sedated him and then gave muscle relaxation so that we could put him on the ventilator. About 15 cm of positive end expiratory pressure (PEEP) was needed to maintain his oxygenation. He gradually improved and he had recovered sufficiently by the next day to extubate.

Looking back, the most likely diagnosis was Post Obstructive Pulmonary Edema — a diagnosis that really wasn't known back in 1983. I had never imagined a patient who could generate intrathoracic pressure changes so great that he could alter a peripheral I.V. flow rate, and I've never seen another one since then. I hope I never will again, but I have to imagine that I might.

Lessons learned:

Beware a failure of imagination. Just because you haven't seen it before doesn't mean it won't happen. Be ready for anything, even the impossible.

The Keyframe (KF) sequences in this chapter are taken from video clips that are available on-line, for free, from anyonecanintubate.com at:

For Chapter 20 video clips go to:
http://bit.ly/UGZRQd

All video chapter files appear on Anyone Can Intubate Portfolio at:
http://bit.ly/U7EV7f

Video Clip Web URLS for Anyone Can Intubate

Video clips are an important addition to this 5th edition.
You have several options for viewing and/or downloading the chapter video clips.
If the shortened bit.ly link does not work for you, the longer, original URL is also provided.

1. A page contiaiing links to the URLs can be found at:

    http://www.anyonecanintubate.com

2. A portfolio page containing all of the video clip chapter files that are available on-line, for free can be found at:

    http://bit.ly/U7EV7f
    or
    http://vimeopro.com/user15487933/anyone-can-intubate-5th-edition-chapter-video-clips

3. For individual chapter files, you may use the following URLs. If the shortened *bit.ly* link does not work for you, the longer, original URL is also provided.

    For Chapter 1, Anatomy and Physiology, video clips go to:
    http://bit.ly/12cAQki
    http://vimeo.com/user15487933/review/57831861/e21f15bdff

    For Chapter 2, Assessment, video clips go to:
    http://bit.ly/11b8zLU
    http://vimeo.com/user15487933/review/57896822/339e962d06

    For Chapter 3, Establishing an Airway, video clips go to:
    http://bit.ly/12cVIYL
    http://vimeo.com/user15487933/review/57902045/19cab8dba3

    For Chapter 4, Direct Laryngoscopy Equipment, video clips go to:
    http://bit.ly/WDXPOg
    http://vimeo.com/user15487933/review/57915152/6a2d9555ad

    For Chapter 5, Oral Intubation of the Adult Patient, video clips go to:
    http://bit.ly/XMjIu8
    http://vimeo.com/user15487933/review/57915489/5d53a4f666

    For Chapter 6, Common Errors, video clips go to:
    http://bit.ly/W30hzE
    http://vimeo.com/user15487933/review/57915491/cf9fb74389

For Chapter 7, Verifying Placement, video clips go to:
http://bit.ly/14AtjLQ
http://vimeo.com/user15487933/review/57915490/c2237454a7

For Chapter 8, Ventilating and Intubating the Child, video clips go to:
http://bit.ly/WB5mAG
http://vimeo.com/user15487933/review/57916690/9a8533dc66

For Chapter 10, Tricks of the Trade, video clips go to:
http://bit.ly/WDE2RZ
http://vimeo.com/user15487933/review/57916691/2cf2559839

For Chapter 11, Nasal Intubation, video clips go to:
http://bit.ly/Vy6vLe
http://vimeo.com/user15487933/review/57931813/723b3887a9

For Chapter 12, Specialized Ventilating Techniques, video clips go to:
http://bit.ly/11kZOhk
http://vimeo.com/user15487933/review/57931815/b38bb9b4a5

For Chapter 15, Awake Intubation, video clips go to:
http://bit.ly/XoVRCu
http://vimeo.com/user15487933/review/57931817/54a6b639d9

For Chapter 16, Extubation, video clips go to:
http://bit.ly/WB65BS
http://vimeo.com/user15487933/review/57931816/44cd2eae20

For Chapter 17, Specialzed Intubating Techniques, video clips go to:
http://bit.ly/WVoIhZ
http://vimeo.com/user15487933/review/57933662/c2b1175e56

For Chapter 18, Fiberoptic Intubation, video clips go to:
http://bit.ly/14tRnPt
http://vimeo.com/user15487933/review/58070033/0d1d0d1043

For Chapter 20, Boredom Interrupted, video clips go to:
http://bit.ly/UGZRQd
http://vimeo.com/user15487933/review/57933660/3e20513e71

NOTES

Some of these references are available as pdf files on-line. We have provided links to these pdfs on our website anyonecanintubate.com.

Introduction

References

1. Macintosh, RR. A new laryngoscope. Lancet 1943; 1:205.

Further Reading

Doyle, DJ. A brief history of clinical airway management. Revista Mexicana de Anestesiología 2009; 32 (Supl. 1):S164-S167.

Chapter 1: Anatomy and Physiology

Further Reading

Gray, H. *Gray's Anatomy of the Human Body,* 30th Ed. Philadelphia: Lea & Febiger, 1985.

Mehta S; Myat HM. The cross-sectional shape and circumference of the human trachea. Ann. R. Coll. Surg. Engl. 1984; 66(5):356-358.

Notter; RH. *Lung Surfactants: Basic Science and Clinical Applications.* New York, N.Y: Marcel Dekker, 2000; pp. 119-120.

Shier; D.; Butler, J.; Lewis, R. Hole's *Human Anatomy & Physiology.* New York: McGraw-Hill, 2002.

Chapter 2: Assessment

References

1. West, JB. *Pulmonary Physiology – The Essentials*, 8th Ed. Philadelphia: Lippincott, Williams & Wilkins, 2008.

Further Reading

Hazinski, MF (Ed.). *PALS Provider Manual.* American Red Cross, 2002.

Chapter 3: Establishing an Airway

Further Reading

Hagberg, CA. *Handbook of Difficult Airway Management.* Philadelphia: Churchill-Livingston, 2000.

Hazinski, MF (ed.). *PALS Provider Manual.* American Red Cross, 2002.

Lopez, NR. Mechanical problems of the airway. Clin. Anes. 1968; 3:8.

Linscott, MS; Horton, WC. Management of upper airway obstruction. Otolaryngol. Clin. North Am. 1979; 12:351-373.

Roberts, K; Porter, K. How do you size a nasopharyngeal airway? Resuscitation 2003; 56(1):19-23.

Walls, RM; Murphy, MF (eds.). *Manual of Emergency Airway Management.* Philadelphia: Lippincott Williams & Wilkins, 2004.

Chapter 4: Direct Laryngoscopy Equipment

Further Reading

Jahn, A; Blitzer, A. A short history of laryngoscopy. Log. Phon. Vocol. 1996; 21:181-185.

Chapter 5: Oral Intubation of the Adult

Further Reading

Arino, JJ; Velasco, JM; Gasco, C; et al. Straight blades improve the visualization of the larynx while curved blades increase ease of intubation: a comparison of Macintosh, Miller McCoy, Belscope, and Lee-Fairview blades. Can. J. Anaesth. 2003; 50:501-506.

Hagberg, CA. *Handbook of Difficult Airway Management*. Philadelphia: Churchill-Livingston, 2000.

Walls, RM; Murphy, MF (eds.). *Manual of Emergency Airway Management*. Philadelphia: Lippincott Williams & Wilkins, 2004.

Chapter 6: Common Errors and How to Avoid Them

References

1. Srikantha, LR; Kunselman, AR; Schuler, G; DesHarnais, S. Laryngoscopy and Tracheal Intubation in the Head-Elevated Position in Obese Patients: A Randomized, Controlled, Equivalence Trial. Anesth. Analg. 2008; 107:1912-1918.

Chapter 7: Tests for Tube Placement

Further Reading

Pollard, BJ; James, B: Accidental intubation of the esophagus. Anaes. Intern. Care 1980; 8:183.

Chapter 8: Ventilating and Intubating the Child - done

References

1. Ogden, CL; Carroll, MD; Curtin, LR; McDowell, MA; Tabak, CJ; Flegal, KM. JAMA. 2006; 295(13):1549-55. Prevalence of overweight and obesity in the United States, 1999-2004.

2. Litman, RS; Weissend, EE; Shibata, D, et al. Developmental changes of laryngeal dimensions in unparalyzed, sedated children. Anesthesiology 2003; 98:41–45.

3. Weiss, M; Gerber, AC. Editorial: Cuffed tracheal tubes in children – things have changed. Pediatric Anesthesia 2006; 16:1005–1007.

4. Khine, HH; Corddry, DH; Kettrick, RG; et al. Comparison of cuffed and uncuffed endotracheal tubes in young children during general anesthesia. Anesthesiology 1997; 86:627–631.

5. Deakers, TW. Reynolds, G; Stretton, M. et al., Cuffed endotracheal tubes in pediatric intensive care. J. Pediatr. 1994; 125:57–62.

6. Newth, CJL; Rachman, B; Patel, N.; et al. The use of cuffed versus uncuffed endotracheal tubes in pediatric intensive care. J. Pediatr. 2004; 144:333–337.

7. Tse, JC; Rimm, EB; Hussain, A. Predicting difficult endotracheal intubation in surgical patients scheduled for general anesthesia: a prospective blind study. Anesh. Analg. 1995; 81:254-258.

Further Reading

King, BR; Baker, MD; Braitman, LE; Seidl-Friedman, J; Schreiner, MS. Endotracheal tube selection in children: a comparison of four methods. Ann. Emerg. Med. 1993; 22(3):530-534.

Gerber, AC. Cuffed tubes for infants and children in anaesthesia and intensive care: Why we should change to cuffed tubes in paediatric airway management (review). Journal of Paediatric Respirology and Critical Care, 2008; 4(4):3-9.

Motoyama, EK. Endotracheal intubation. In: Motoyama, EK; Davis, PJ (eds.). *Smith's anesthesia for infants and children*, 7th Ed. St Louis, MO: CV Mosby, Pages 335-337, 1996.

Weiss, M; Knirsch, W; et.al., Tracheal tube-tip displacement in children during head-neck movement--a radiological assessment. Br. J. Anaesth. 2006; 96(4):486-491.

Chapter 9: Pre-Intubation Evaluation

References

1. Crosby, ET; Cooper, RM; Douglas, MJ; et al. The unanticipated difficult airway with recommendations for management. Can. J. Anaes. 1998; 45:757-776.

2. Morton, T; Brady, S; Clancy, M. Difficult airway in accident and emergency departments. Anaes. 2000; 55:485-488.

3. American Society of Anesthesiologists. Practice guidelines for the management of the difficult airway: a report by the American Society of Anesthesiologists Task Force on Management of the Difficult Airway. Anesthesiology 1993; 78:597-602; see also: Practice Guidelines for Management of the Difficult Airway: An Updated Report by the American Society of Anesthesiologists Task Force on Management of the Difficult Airway. Anesthesiology 2003; 98:1269–1277.

4. Rose, DK; Cohen, MM. The airway: problems and predictions in 18,500 patients. Can. J. Anaesth. 1994; 41:372–383.

5. Mallampati, SR; Gatt, SP; Gugino, LD; et al. A clinical sign to predict difficult tracheal intubation: a prospective study. Can. Anaesth. Soc. J. 1985; 32:429-434.

6. Samsoon, GLT; Young, JRB. Difficult tracheal intubation: a retrospective study. Anaes. 1987; 42:487-490.

7. Ezri, T; Medalion, B; Weisenberg, M; Szmuk, P; Warters, RD; Charuzi, I. Increased body mass index is not a predictor of difficult laryngoscopy. Can. J. Anaesth. 2002; 50:179–183.

8. Tse, JC; Rimm, EB; and Hussain, A. Predicting difficult endotracheal intubation in surgical patients scheduled for general anesthesia: A prospective blind study, Anesth. Analg. 1995; 81:254.

9. Dimov, V. Tension Pneumothorax. http://clinicalcases.blogspot.com/2004/02/tension-pneumothorax.html.

10. Hiremath, AS; Hillman, DR; James, AL; et.al. Relationship between difficult tracheal intubation and obstructive sleep apnoea. Br. J. Anaesth. 1998; 80:606–611.

Further Reading

Kheterpal, S; Han, R; Tremper, KK; et al. Incidence and predictors of difficult and impossible mask ventilation. Anesthesiology 2006; 105:885–891.

Langeron, O; Masso, E; Huraux, C; Guggiari, M; Bianchi, A; Coriat, P; Riou, B. Prediction of difficult mask ventilation. Anesthesiology 2000; 92(5):1229-1236.

Chapter 10: Tricks of the Trade

References

1. Collins, JS; Lemmens, HJ; Brodsky, JB; et al. Laryngoscopy and morbid obesity: a comparison of the "sniff" and "ramped" positions. Obesity Surgery 2004;14:1171-1175.

2. Kristensen, MS. Airway management and morbid obesity (review). European Journal of Anaesthesiology 2010; 27(11):923-927.

3. Munnur, U; de Boisblanc, B; Suresh, MS. Airway problems in pregnancy. Crit. Care Med. 2005; 33(10)(Suppl.):S259-S268.

4. Reisner, LS; Benumof, JL; Cooper, SD. The difficult airway: risk, prophylaxis and management. Pages 590-620 In: Chestnut, DH (ed.) *Obstetric Anesthesia: Principles and Practice*. St. Louis: Mosby, 1999.

5. Cormack, RS. Diffcult tracheal intubation in obstetrics. Anaes. 1984; 39:1105-1111.

6. Dennehy, KC; Pian-Smith, MC: Airway Management of the Parturient. Int. Anesthesiol. Clin. 2000; 38:147-159.

7. Nolan, JP; Wilson, ME: Endotracheal intubation in patients with potential cervical spine injuries: An indication for the gum elastic-bougie. Anes. 1993; 49:630-633.

8. Sutera, PT; Gordon, GJ: Digitally assisted tracheal intubation in a neonate with Pierre Robin syndrome. Anesthesiology 1993; 78:983-985.

Further Reading

Benumof, JL. Management of the difficult intubation, with special emphasis on awake adult intubation. Anes 1991; 75:1087-1110.

Benumof, JL. Obstructive sleep apnea in the adult obese patient: implications for airway management. J Clin Anesth. 2001;13:144–156.

Benumof, JL. ASA difficult airway algorithm: New thoughts and considerations. Pages 31-48 In: *Handbook of Difficult Airway Management*, 1st Ed. Hagberg, CA (Ed.). Philadelphia, PA: Churchill Livingstone, 2000.

Brechner, VL. Unusual problems in airway management: I. Flexion, extension mobility of the cervical vertebrae. Anesth. Analg. 1968; 47:362.

Block, C; Brechner, VL. Unusual problems in airway management: II. The influence of the temporomandibular joint, the mandible, and associated structures in endotracheal intubation. Anesth. Analg. 1971; 50:114.

Brodsky, JB; Lemmens HJ, Brock-Utne JG; Vierra M; Saidman LJ: Morbid obesity and tracheal intubation. Anesth Analg. 2002; 94:732–736.

Caplan, RA; Benumof, JL; Berry, FA; et al. Practice guidelines for management of the difficult airway. A report by the American Society of Anesthesiologists Task Force on management of the difficult airway. Anes. 1993; 78:597-602.

Davies, OD. Re-anesthetizing cases of tonsillectomy and adenoidectomy because of persistent postoperative hemorrhage. Br. J. Anaes. 1964; 36:244.

Ovassapian, A; Glassenberg, R; Randel, GI; Klock, A; Mesnick, PS; Klafta, JM. The unexpected difficult airway and lingual tonsil hyperplasia: a case series and a review of the literature. Anesthesiology 2002; 97:124–132.

Srikantha, LR; Allen, RK; Schuler, HG; DesHarnais, S. Laryngoscopy and Tracheal Intubation in the Head-Elevated Position in Obese Patients: A Randomized, Controlled, Equivalence Trial. Anesth. Analg. 2008; 107:1912-1918.

Chapter 11: Nasal Intubation

Further Reading

Chung, YT; Sun, MS; Wu, HS. Blind nasal intubation is facilitated by neutral head position and endotracheal tube cuff inflation in spontaneously breathing patients. Can. J. Anesth. 2003; 50(5):511-513.

Click, M. Airway another way: blind nasotracheal intubation. JEMS. Feb 1996:58-63.

Pederson, B. Blind nasotracheal intubation: A review and a new guided technique. Acta. Anaesth. Scandinav. 1971; 15:107.

Chapter 12: Special Ventilating Techniques

References

1. Yancey, W; Wears, R; Kamajian, G; Derovanesian, J. Unrecognized tracheal intubation: a complication of the esophageal obturator airway. Ann. Emerg. Med. 1980; (9):18-20.
2. Scholl, DG; Tsai, SH. Esophageal perforation following use of esophageal obturator airway. Radiology. 1977; (122):315-316.
3. Bryson TK, Benumof JL, Ward CF. The esophageal obturator airway: a clinical comparison to ventilation with a mask and oropharyngeal airway. Chest. 1978; 74:537-539.
4. Smith, JP; et al. The esophageal obturator airway: a review. JAMA 1983; 250(8):1081-1085.
5. Hankins, DG; Carruthers, N; Frascone, RJ; et al. Complication rates for the esophageal obturator airway and the endotracheal tube in the prehospital setting. Prehospital and Disaster Medicine 1993; 8:117-120.

Further Reading

LMA (Laryngeal Mask Airway)

Parmet, JL; Colonna-Romano, P; Horrow, JC; Miller, F; Gonzales, J; Rosenberg, H. The laryngeal mask airway reliably provides rescue ventilation in cases of unanticipated difficult tracheal intubation along with difficult mask ventilation. Anesth. Analg. 1998; 87(3):661-665.

Brimacombe, J; Berry, A: Insertion of the laryngeal mask airway - a prospective study of four techniques. Anaesth. Intensi. Care 1993; 21(1):89-92.

Pennant, JH; Walker, MB: Comparison of the endotracheal tube and laryngeal mask in airway management by paramedical personnel. Anesth. Analg. 1992; 74:531-534.

Combitube™

Wissler, RN: The esophageal-tracheal Combitube. Anesthesiology Review 1993; 20(4):147-152.

Blostein, PA; Kestner, AJ; Hoak, S. Failed rapid sequence induction in trauma patients: esophageal Combitube is a useful adjunct. J. Trauma 1998; 44 (3):534-537.

Davis, DP; Valentine, C; Ochs, M; Vilke, GM; Hoyt, DB. The Combitube as a salvage airway device for paramedic rapid sequence intubation. Ann. Emerg. Med. 2003; 42(5):697-704.

Cricothyrotomy

Peep Talving, P; DuBose, J; Inaba, K; Demetriades, D. Conversion of Emergent Cricothyrotomy to Tracheotomy in Trauma Patients (review). Arch. Surg. 2010; 145 (1):87-91.

Macdonald, JC; Homer, CN. Emergency battlefield cricothyrotomy. CMAJ. 2008; 178(9):1133–1135.

Chapter 13: Airway Management of Trauma

References

1. Hastings, RH; Marks, JD: Airway Management for Trauma Patients with Potential Cervical Spine Injuries. Anesth. Analg. 1991; 73:471-482.
2. Podolsky, S; Baraff, L; et al. Efficacy of Cervical Spine Immobilization Methods. J. Trauma 1983; 23:461-465.
3. Meschino, A; et al. The Safety of Awake Tracheal Intubation in Cervical Spine Injury. Can. J. Anaesth. 1992; 39:114117.
4. Hall, CEJl Shutt, LE. Nasotracheal intubation for head and neck surgery. Anaesthesia 2003; 58:249–256.
5. Sloan, EP; Zalenski, RJ: Smith, RF; Sheaff, CM; et al. Toxicology screening in urban trauma patients: drug prevalence and its relationship to trauma severity and management. Journal of Trauma. 1989; 29:1647-1653.
6. Donen SC, Merigan KS, Hedges JR, et al: A comparison of blind nasotracheal and succinylcholine assistant intubation in the poisoned patient. Ann. Emerg. Med. 1987; 16:75—77.
7. Grande C.M., Barton C.R., Stene J.K. Appropriate Techniques for Airway Management of Emergency Patients with Suspected Spinal Cord Injury. Anesth. Analg. 1988; 67:714-715.
8. Suderman, VS; Crosby, ET; Lui, A. Elective Oral Tracheal Intubation in Cervical Spine Injured Adults. Can. J. Anaesth. 1991; 38:785-789.
9. Majernick TG, Bierniek R, Houston JB, et al. Cervical Spine Movement During Orotracheal Intubation. Ann. Emerg. Med. 1986; 15:417-420.
10. Grande CM, Stene JK, Bernhard WN: Airway Management: Considerations in the Trauma Patient. Crit. Care Clin. 1990; 6(1): 37-59.
11. Wright, SW; Robinson, GG; Wright, MB. Cervical Spine Injuries in Blunt Trauma Patients Requiring Emergent Endotracheal Intubation. Am J Emerg. Med. 1992; 10:104-109.
12. Ollerton, JE; Parr, MJA; Harrison; Hanrahan, B; Sugrue, M. Potential cervical spine injury and difficult airway management for emergency intubation of trauma adults in the emergency

department—a systematic review. Emerg. Med. J. 2006; 23:3–11.

13. C Y Yang, CY; Huang, CC; Chiu, HF; Chiu, JF; Lan, SJ; Ko, YC. Effects of occupational dust exposure on the respiratory health of Portland cement workers. J. Toxicol. Environ. Health, 1996; 49(6):581-588.

14. Van Zundaert, A; Kuczkowski, K; Tinssen, F; Weber, E: Direct laryngoscopy and endotracheal intubation in the prone position following traumatic thoracic injury. J. Anesth 2008; 22:170-172.

15. Britt, LD; Trunkey, DD; Feliciano, DV (eds). *Acute Care Surgery: Principles and Practice,* 1st Ed. New York: Springer, 2007.

16. Bohn, D; Armstrong, D; Becker, L; Humphreys, R: Cervical Spine Injuries in Children. J. Trauma 1990; 30:463-469.

17. Fesmire, F; Luten, R. The Pediatric Cervical Spine: Developmental Anatomy and clinical Aspects. Emerg. Med. 1989; 7:133-142.

Further Reading

Walls, RM; Murphy, MF (eds.). *Manual of Emergency Airway Management*. Philadelphia: Lippincott Williams & Wilkins, 2004.

Alam, M; Moynagh, M; Lawlor, C. Cement burns: the Dublin National Burns Unit experience. J. Burns Wounds 2007; 7:33-38.

Kramer, DC; Grass, G. Challenges facing the anesthesiologist in the emergency department. Curr. Opin. Anaesthesiol. 2003; 16(4):409-416.

Walz, JM: Zayaruzny, M; Heard, SO. Airway Management in Critical Illness. CHEST 2007; 131(2):608-620.

American College of Surgeon's Committee on Trauma. *Advanced Trauma Life Support Course, Instructor Manual.* Chicago: American College of Surgeons l984:157-160.

Søreide, E; Grande, CM. Prehospital trauma care. Informa. Health Care, 2001; 486-497.

Chapter 14: Rapid Sequence Induction

Further Reading

Gajapathy, M; Giuffrida, JG; Stahl, W; et al. Hemodynamic changes in critically ill patients during induction of anesthesia. Int. Surg. 1983; 68:101-105.

Reynolds, SF; Heffner, J: Airway management of the critically ill patient: Rapid-sequence intubation. Chest 2005; 127:1397–1412.

Yamamoto, LG; Gregory, KY; Britten, AG: Rapid sequence anesthesia induction for emergency intubation. Ped. Emerg. Care : 1990; 6:200-213.

Chapter 15: Awake Intubation

References

1. Benumof, JL. Management of the difficult adult airway, with special emphasis on awake tracheal intubation. Anes. 1990; 72:1087-1110.

2. Rosenblatt, W. Awake Intubation Made Easy! ASA Refresher Courses Chapter 14, 2009; 37(1):167-174.

3. Riker, RR; Shehabi, Y; Bokesch, PM; Ceraso, D; Wisemandle, W; Koura, F; Whitten, P; Margolis, BD; Byrne, DW; Ely, EW; Rocha, MG. Dexmedetomidine vs Midazolam for Sedation of Critically Ill Patients: A Randomized Trial. JAMA 2009; 301(5):489–499.

4. Paris, A; Tonner, PH. Dexmedetomidine in anaesthesia. Current Opinion in Anaesthesiology 2005; 18(4):412–418.

5. Ramsay, MA; Savege TM; Simpson BR; Goodwin R. Controlled sedation with alphaxolone-alphadalone. BMJ 1974; 2:656-659.

Further Reading

Durbin, Jr, CG. Sedation of the agitated, critically ill patient without an artificial airway. Crit. Care Clin. 1995:11(4):913-936.

Gaskill, JR; Gillies, DR: Local anesthesia for peroral endoscopy. Arch. Otolaryng. 1966; 84:654-665.

Kramer, DC; Grass, G. Challenges facing the anesthesiologist in the emergency department. Curr. Opin. Anaesthesiol. 2003:16(4):409-416.

Meschino, A; et al. The Safety of Awake Tracheal Intubation in Cervical Spine Injury. Can. J. Anaesth. 1992; 39:114117.

Chapter 16: Extubating and Exchanging Endotracheal Tubes

Further Reading

Abdy, S. An audit of airway problems in the recovery room. Anaesthesia 1999; 54(9):372-375.

Benumof, JL: Additional safety measures when changing endotracheal tubes. Anes. 1991; 75:921-922.

Benumof, JL: Management of the difficult adult airway. Anes. 1991; 75:1087-1110.

Caplan, RA; Benumof, JL; Berry, FA: Practice guidelines for management of the difficult airway. A report by the Americal Society of Anesthesiologists Task Force on management of the difficult airway. Anes. 1993; 78:597-602.

Koga, K; Asai, T; Vaughan, RS; Latto, IP. Respiratory complications associated with tracheal extubation. Timing of tracheal extubation and use of the laryngeal mask during emergence from anaesthesia. Anaesthesia 1998; 53(6):540-544..

Kulkarni, AP; Agarwal, V. Extubation failure in intensive care unit: Predictors and management. Indian J. Crit. Care Med. 2008; 12:1-9.

Miller, KA; Harkin, CP; Bailey, PL: Postoperative tracheal intubation. Anesth. Analg. 1995; 80:149-172.

Chapter 17: Specialized Intubation Techniques

References

1. Cooper, RM. Complications associated with the use of the GlideScope videolaryngoscope. Can. J. Anesth. 2007; 54(1):54-57.

Further Reading

Davis, L; Cook-Sather, SD; Schreiner, MS. Lighted Stylet Tracheal Intubation: A Review. Anesth. Analg. 2000; 90:745-756.

Dogra, S; Falconer, R; Latto, IP. Successful difficult intubation. Tracheal tube placement over a gum-elastic bougie. Anes. 1990; 45:774-776.

Ellis, DG; Jakymec, A; Kaplan RM; Stewart RD; Freeman JA; Bleyaert A; Berkebile PE. Guided orotracheal intubation in the operating room using a lighted stylet: a comparison with direct laryngoscopic technique. Anesthesiology. 1986; 64(6):823-826.

Ferson, DZ; Rosenblatt, WH; Johansen, MJ; Osborn, I; Ovassapian, A. Use of the intubating LMA-Fastrach in 254 patients with difficult- to-manage airways. Anesthesiology. 2001; 95(5):1175-1181.

Guggenberger, H; Lenz, G: Training in Retrograde Intubation. Correspondence. Anes 1988; 69:292.

Liem, EB; Bjoraker, DG; Gravenstein, D. New Options for Airway Management: The Intubating Fibreoptic Stylets (review). Br J Anaesth. 2003; 91(3):408-418.

Liu, EH; Goy, RW; Chen, FG. The LMA CTrach, a new laryngeal mask airway for endotracheal intubation under vision: evaluation in 100 patients. Br. J. Anaesth. 2006;96:396–400.

Nolan, JP; Wilson ME: Endotracheal intubation in patients with potential cervical spine injuries: An indication for the gum elastic-bougie. Anes. 1993; 49:630-633.

Patil, V; Stehling, L; Zauder, H. Fiberoptic Endoscopy in Anesthesia. Chicago-London: Year Book Medical Publishers.

Chapter 18: Flexible Fiberoptic Bronchoscopy

Further Reading

Hagberg, CA. *Handbook of Difficult Airway Management*. Philadelphia: Churchill-Livingston, 2000.

Popat, M. *Practical Fibreoptic Intubation*. Oxford: Butterworth-Heinemann, 2001.

Walls, RM; Murphy, MF (eds.). *Manual of Emergency Airway Management*. Philadelphia: Lippincott Williams & Wilkins, 2004.

Chapter 19: Complications

Further Reading

Byrum, LJ; Pierce, AK: Pulmonary aspiration of gastric contents. Am. Rev. Respir. Dis. 1976; 114:1129.

Harley, HR: Laryngotracheal obstruction complicating tracheostomy or endotracheal intubation with assisted respiration. A Critical Review. Thorax 1971; 26:493-533.

Mehta, S; Myat, HM. The cross-sectional shape and circumference of the human trachea. Ann. R. Coll. Surg. Engl. 1984; 66(5):356-358.

Nance, JJ. Why Hospitals Should Fly: The Ultimate Flight Plan to Patient Safety and Quality Care. Second River Healthcare Press, 2008.

Stauffer, J; Silvestri, R. Complications of endotracheal intubation and tracheostomy. Am. J. Med. 1982; 27:417-434.

Vandam, LD: Vomiting of gastric contents during the operative period. N. Eng. J. Med. 1965; 273:1206.

Van Kooy, MA; Gargiulo, R.F.: Postobstructive pulmonary edema. Am. Fam. Physician. 2000; 62(2):401-404.

Chapter 20: Boredom, Interrupted

Further Reading

Schwartz, DE; Matthay, MA; Cohen, NH. Death and other complications of emergency airway management in critically ill adults: a prospective investigation of 297 tracheal intubations. Anesthesiology 1995; 82:367–376.

Tarle, DA; Chandler JE; Good JT; et.al. Emergency room intubation — Complications and survival. Chest 1979; 75:541.

Divitia, JV; Bhowmick, K. Complications of endotracheal intubation and other airway management. Indian J. Anaesth. 2005; 49(4):308-318.

Index

A

Acid-base balance   34–36
Airway Obstruction
  diagnosis of   , 57–58, 68, 138–142, 31–33
  mechanics of   29–32
  snoring   31–32
  treatment of   68–75, 140–142, 175–176
Alveolar Gas Equation   38–39
Alveoli   19, 50
Anatomy
  larynx   10–20, 150, 152
  lungs   18–22
  nasal   185–186
  pediatric airway vs adult   , 140–142, 21
  trachea   18, 251
Arytenoid cartilage   11
Aspiration   157, 294–296
A.V.P.U. Scale   56

B

BAAM   195–196
Bougie   179–180
Breathing
  control of   33–40
  mechanics of   60–62
  respiratory distress   55
  respiratory failure   55, 64
  respiratory rate   64
  sounds of   59
  work of   60–62, 66
Burn Victims   231

C

Cervical Spine Protection   222–226
Combitube   209–212
Complications   199–200, 294–299
Cricoid Cartilage   11, 135, 152
Cricoid Pressure   , 121–122, 177–179, 111–113
Cricothyroidotomy   211–213
Croup   156–157, 300
Cyanosis   61–62, 219

D

Dead Space. *See* Ventilation
Diaphragm   46
Difficult Intubation Algorithm   181–183
Digital
  digital   180

E

Endotracheal Tube   148–151
  checking   91–92
  cuffed or uncuffed   148–150
  cuff leak   132
  depth of insertion   103, 153
Endotracheal Tube Exchanger   267
EndotrolTM Tube   195
Entrapment   228–229
Epiglottis   11, 135, 152
Epiglottitis   154
Esophageal Intubation   128–130, 153, 294
Esophageal Obturator Airway   201–203
Esophageal-Tracheal Combitube. *See* Combitube
Etomidate   238
Extubation
  Criteria   261–262
  Technique   262

F

Fiberoptic Bronchoscopy   283–291
Functional Residual Capacity   46–48

G

GlideScope   270–273
Glossopharyngeal Nerve Block   251, 253

H

Head Injury   232
Hemoglobin   43–46
Hering–Breuer reflex   34
Hyperventilation   34–38
Hypoventilation   34, 37–38, 61, 62, 195
Hypoxia   39, 61, 62, 139–140
Hypoxic pulmonary vasoconstriction   53

I

Intubation
  awake   247–259
  difficult   154–157, 168–183, 191–194. *See also* Airway Obstruction
    algorithm   181–183
  head position   97–100
  indications   65–67
  mainstem   132, 153
  nasotracheal   184–198. *See* Airway Obstruction
  obese patient   120, 171–172
  oral technique   100–108, 122–124, 222–226
  pediatric   147–149, 150–153
  straight vs. curved blades   107–109

J

Jet Ventilation   211–213

K

Ketamine   239

L

Laryngeal Mask Airway   201–208
  LMA Assisted Intubation   275–276
Laryngeal Trauma   233
Laryngoscope
  assembly   88–89
  Macintosh curved blade   147, 170
  Miller straight blade   147
Laryngospasm   16, 32, 137–138, 296, 15, 299
Larynx
  anatomy   10–14
  laryngeal movement   13–17
  photographs   118, 122
Light Wand   268–270
LMA Fastrach   275–279
Lungs   18–22
  tidal volume   47
  volumes & capacities   45–49

M

Malignant Hyperthermia   243–244
Midazolam   240
Muscle Relaxant   227, 242–246

N

Nasal Airway   72–73, 144
  ventilation with   74, 199–200
Nosebleed   200

O

Obese   165
Obesity   165
Obstruction, airway. *See* Airway Obstruction
Oral Airway   74–76, 142
Oxygenation   24
  oxygen saturation   39–41, 61, 62
  supply and demand   27

P

pH of blood   24, 33
Pneumothorax   27–28, 60, 132, 165, 296–297
Post Obstructive Pulmonary Edema   300–301
Propofol   239–240

R

Rapid Sequence Induction   236–246
Recurrent Laryngeal Nerve
  injury   14, 17, 131
Reversal Agents   245–246

S

Safety   234–235, 301
Sedation   226, 238–242, 256–260
Shunt   48–49
Snoring. *See* Airway Obstruction
Stress   235
Stridor   32
Stylet   92–93, 125–126
Succinylcholine   242–243
Superior Laryngeal Nerve Block   255–256

T

Thyroid cartilage   11
Tidal Volume   47
Transtracheal Nerve Block   251

V

Vecuronium   244
Ventilation
  and dead space   49–51
  and perfusion match   48–53
  causes of difficult   85–86
  definition   24
  in edentulous patients   87
  in obese patients   85
  physiology of manual   47–49
  technique   78, 80–86, 145–146
Ventilation/Perfusion Mismatch. *See* Ventilation
Vocal Cords   13–15, 152, 166
  paralysis   131, 301
V/Q Mismatch. *See* Ventilation

ABOUT THE AUTHOR

Christine E. Whitten, M.D., is a practicing anesthesiologist at the Kaiser Permanente Medical Center in San Diego, California, where she was Chief of Anesthesia and Director of Perioperative Services for 10 years. Dr. Whitten also served as the Southern California Permanente Regional Coordinator of Pain Management for 10 years, and was involved in the national development and implementation of the multidisciplinary Chronic Pain Management Programs for Kaiser Permanente.

Dr. Whitten received her medical degree from Johns Hopkins Medical School in 1979. After her anesthesiology residency at the U.S. Naval Hospital in Portsmouth, Virginia, she completed fellowships in regional anesthesia and intensive care. Following training she was on the teaching staff, Director of Regional Anesthesia, and Co-Director of the Chronic Pain Clinic at the U.S. Naval Hospital in San Diego from 1983-1986. She left the Navy with the rank of Commander and joined the staff at Kaiser Permanente San Diego in 1986.

Chris Whitten examines an impatient patient during a volunteer medical mission to Vietnam.

In addition to Anyone Can Intubate, Dr. Whitten's publications include:

- Whitten, CE. Anesthesia for the Developing Countries of the World. in: A Different Kind of Diplomacy: A Source book for International Volunteers. Plastic Surgery Research Foundation, San Diego, California, 1987.

- Whitten, CE. Experiences in Third World Anesthesia: Peacetime Training for Operational Deployment. Military Medicine 1988; 153(12):629-632.

- Whitten CE. Anesthesia in Distant Places: Prevention of Anesthesia Mishaps. Seminars in Anesthesia 1993; 12(3):154-164.

- Whitten, CE; Evans, CM; Cristobal. K. Pain Management Doesn't Have to be a Pain: Working and Communicating Effectively with Patients who have Chronic Pain. The Permanente Journal 2005; 9(2):41-48.

- Whitten, CE; Cristobal. K. Chronic Pain is a Chronic Condition, Not Just a Symptom. The Permanente Journal 2005; 9(3):43-51.

- Whitten, CE: Donovan, M; Cristobal, K. Treating Chronic Pain: New Knowledge, More Choices. The Permanente Journal 2005; 9(4):9-18.

She has also filmed and produced a series of educational videos demonstrating various techniques of intubation and airway management.

Dr. Whitten is a frequent volunteer for Operation Smile, a worldwide health care mission to provide free surgery to children of less-developed countries. She has participated in surgical teams, and also instructed anesthesia providers, during trips to Mexico, Vietnam, Honduras, Kenya, Nicaragua, the Philippines, Thailand and Colombia.

Made in United States
North Haven, CT
27 August 2025